Baseball and the
House of David

ALSO BY OR EDITED BY P.J. DRAGSETH
AND FROM McFARLAND

*Gib Bodet, Major League Scout:
Twelve Thousand Baseball Games
and Six Million Miles* (by Gib Bodet,
as told to P.J. Dragseth, 2014)

*The 1957 San Francisco Seals:
End of an Era in the Pacific Coast League* (2013)

*Major League Baseball Scouts:
A Biographical Dictionary* (2011)

*Eye for Talent: Interviews with
Veteran Baseball Scouts* (edited, 2010)

Baseball and the House of David

The Legendary Barnstorming Teams, 1915–1956

P.J. Dragseth

Foreword by Brian Ziebart

McFarland & Company, Inc., Publishers
Jefferson, North Carolina

This book has undergone peer review.

PJ Dragseth died January 7, 2020, having completed the manuscript for this book after several years of research and writing. The publisher gratefully acknowledges the efforts of her husband, Richard Dragseth, and Israelite House of David archivist Brian Ziebart, whose late-stage assistance made publication possible.

Library of Congress Cataloguing-in-Publication Data

Names: Dragseth, P. J., author. | Ziebart, Brian, other.
Title: Baseball and the House of David : the legendary barnstorming teams, 1915-1956 / P.J. Dragseth, Brian Ziebart.
Description: Jefferson, North Carolina : McFarland & Company, Inc., Publishers, 2021. | Includes bibliographical references and index.
Identifiers: LCCN 2020025390 | ISBN 9781476670119 (paperback : acid free paper) ∞
ISBN 9781476639222 (ebook)
Subjects: LCSH: Baseball—United States—History—20th century. | Jewish baseball players—United States—History—20th century. | House of David (Religious society)—History.
Classification: LCC GV863.A1 D73 2021 | DDC 796.3570973—dc23
LC record available at https://lccn.loc.gov/2020025390

British Library cataloguing data are available
ISBN (print) 978-1-4766-7011-9
ISBN (ebook) 978-1-4766-3922-2

© 2021 Dragseth Family Trust,
Richard Dragseth, trustee. All rights reserved

No part of this book may be reproduced or transmitted in any form or by any means, electronic or mechanical, including photocopying or recording, or by any information storage and retrieval system, without permission in writing from the publisher.

Front cover: The 1922 House of David team
(Brian Ziebart, House of David Commune Files)

Printed in the United States of America

*McFarland & Company, Inc., Publishers
Box 611, Jefferson, North Carolina 28640
www.mcfarlandpub.com*

To the members of the House of David
and City of David baseball clubs
and the Negro teams they played:
thanks for your valuable
contributions to the game.

Table of Contents

Acknowledgments ix
Foreword by Brian Ziebart 1
Preface 2
Introduction 6

1. Commune History 13
2. Play Ball! The Legend Begins 39
3. The Twenties: The Bearded Beauties Roared on the Diamond 57
4. The Thirties: Baseball During the Depression 89
5. The Forties and Fifties: Two Abbreviated Decades End an Era 117
6. Memorable Players 133

Epilogue 162
Appendix 165
Chapter Notes 185
Bibliography 207
Index 215

Acknowledgments

Many people assist in a variety of ways during the process of researching and writing a non-fiction historical book. To those who contributed their own expertise, I extend my sincere appreciation and gratitude.

My usual thanks to longtime baseball scout and patient friend George Genovese, who asked me to write about House of David baseball. Sadly, he passed away before the project was completed. Throughout my writing experiences, he was always there to share his stories, answer questions and put me in touch with others along the way. I miss him.

Most sincere thanks to Mel Atwell in Pasadena, California, whose elder brother Dick Atwell played with both the House of David and the City of David teams in the early '30s. Mel shared his sentimental collection filled with memories, newspaper articles, letters, and photographs from and about the House of David. Their son Brian also donated a photo of his "Uncle Dick."

Of course photographs which allow us a more "up close and personal" look at the life and times of these teams and the players are essential. Unfortunately, many players in team pictures are not individually identified. However, they provide a look at the various teams and uniforms over the years. Furthermore, they are important to readers who may remember that Grandpa played for the team in one year or another and may recognize him in a photo or two.

The majority of photographs were donated by the following: the House of David Commune Files, by historian/archivist Brian Ziebart and Ronald Taylor, historian/archivist of Mary's City of David Commune Files; Jill Rauh, reference and government documents librarian at the Benton Harbor Public Library, House of David Room; Ms. Claudette Scrafford of the National Baseball Hall of Fame Museum Archives, who donated copies of their House of David files, news clips and photos; and Mel Atwell. Additional photos were purchased from Mark Tillson—special collections coordinator of the Hamilton College Digital Archives Photo Collections; John Horne—rights and reproductions coordinator, National Baseball Hall of Fame; co-authors Joel Hawkins/Terry Bartolino, and Larry Lester of NoirTech Research, Inc. Thank you all.

Thanks to "computer gurus" Randy James, who has been with me for many years through many writing projects, and Valerie Brown. The contributions of both are sincerely appreciated.

Thanks also to Debbie Boyersmith, granddaughter of commune member Earl Boyersmith, who briefly appeared on the baseball team, ran the trains in their amusement park, and worked in the machine shop. Today Debbie volunteers with a preservationist group involved in restoring the baseball park and original amusement park buildings. Thanks for your help and best wishes to you in your newest endeavors.

Ronald Taylor, trustee/historian/archivist from the Israelite House of David Reorganized by Mary Purnell, was the first person I interviewed. The information and photos he shared got me on my way, and he was always available to answer questions.

Words cannot express my deep appreciation and gratitude to Brian Ziebart. Near the end of my research, I hit the jackpot when Brian answered the phone the day I called the Israelite House of David office in Benton Harbor, asking to purchase photographs. We had a lengthy discussion about the commune itself, the baseball team, and the players.

He expressed his pleasure that the book was being written and requested to be my proofreader and fact-checker. He worked tirelessly as we checked and double-checked relevant facts. He invested more hours than I can count. Brian, because of your efforts and generosity with many facets of this project, this is a better book noteworthy of those whose stories are told in it. Thanks so much.

And, as usual, a special thank you to my husband Rich, who always takes my writing journeys with me.

With sadness, I share that my beloved wife, P.J. Dragseth, passed on in January 2020. I want to express my sincere gratitude to everyone who shared and suported her passion for the sport of baseball, eclipsed only by her love for the people in her life. A special thank you to Brian Ziebart, whose continued support to me was invaluable to get the final draft to publication. I also want to extend my heartfelt appreciation to everyone who shared our incredible journey over the years and to P.J.'s loyal fans. While P.J. will always be missed, I hope her last book continues to inspire the excitement she felt hearing the sound of a bat cracking a home run!

Richard Dragseth

If you would like to learn more about P.J. Dragseth or have a memorial tribute you would like to share, visit baseballwise.com. A virtual ballpark for friends, colleagues, and fans to share memories of a life well-lived!

P.J. and Rich Dragseth in 2018.

Foreword
by Brian Ziebart

Back in 2007, I was spending an afternoon with my friend Lloyd Dalager, who was the last living House of David colony member to play on their baseball team. We spent many hours discussing the colony and especially the baseball team. Though Lloyd only played one year on the traveling team, his career with the House of David team spanned decades. Lloyd loved baseball as much as I did, and being 94 [at that time], he lived through and remembered many great moments from our nation's pastime.

As we spoke about the House of David players, I thought that a book dedicated to the team's history was needed. I started saving whatever information I could find about the colony teams, franchise teams, and even the "outlaw" teams. My friendship with Lloyd for the next four years provided me with some great stories. I promised him that "someday" I would make sure the story was told.

Fast-forward ten years and "someday" still hadn't come. One late summer day, I received a phone call in the Israelite House of David office. On the other line was PJ Dragseth, who was inquiring about obtaining some photos of the teams and players for a book she was writing about the House of David baseball teams. We spoke for almost two hours about the research she had done over the previous five years. We swapped stories and anecdotes about the teams. I volunteered to share the colony's archive photos and any other information I had accumulated over the last ten years. After the call, I realized that "someday" had arrived.

In the following months, I had the pleasure of reading the books she had written about baseball, and enjoyed each one. We exchanged many emails and calls about the House of David baseball story. Her love of the great sport of baseball started her on a quest to write a book about a fascinating part of its history. The call was a blessing. This great story was finally going to be written. My dream conjured up all those years ago while talking to Lloyd was coming true. But a better blessing was that I gained a friend. Thank you, PJ!

Here's to Andy, to Tuck, to Ol' Doc, to Cookie, to Horace, to Barney, to Francis, to Eggs, to Tommie, to Dutch, to Zeke, to Hip, to Red, to Mud, to Tex, to Mooney and especially to Lloyd. Your story is told.

Brian Ziebart is a trustee, historian, and archivist for the Israelite House of David Commune in Benton Harbor, Michigan.

Preface

As a card-carrying member of the "hooked on baseball before age ten" club, I had heard about the House of David baseball team even in my youth, but for most of my life I knew nothing about them. Then, decades after I first heard about them, longtime baseball scout and friend George Genovese told me stories about the days when his older brothers played with the team and he was a sometime batboy. He asked why I had not written about them or the era in which they played. I could not answer his question but assured him my curiosity was aroused … and this journey began.

The purpose of this book is to enlighten readers about one of the most unique periods on the baseball history timeline: the barnstorming era. It was a colorful time when semipro and amateur teams traveled to varied locations to face each other in exhibitions when, in most cases, neither team was considered the "home team." It gave hundreds of talented players the opportunity to play the game and permitted fans everywhere to see them.

To achieve this goal, I focused on the House of David from Benton Harbor, Michigan, a team from a religious commune that played from 1914 to 1956 and became a national curiosity. Called unique because of their hirsute appearance, they played their own style of fast baseball and became one of the winningest and most popular teams of the era on their way to becoming a barnstorming legend.

The book is organized by decade, and some of the chapters are necessarily longer than others. The primary source of information was the daily press coverage and magazine articles about the team, as well as events within the commune itself that did not involve baseball. Over time, media attention waned, particularly during World War II, followed by the appearance of Jackie Robinson and the end of the color barrier.

Though barnstorming is best known for its popularity during the Great Depression, it was not a product of it. Instead the concept was born when the game itself was a fledgling sport over 40 years before the establishment of the House of David commune. It was a time when the all-white Brooklyn Excelsiors, known as the game's first barnstorming team, toured upper New York State on a two-week jaunt while the game competed with cricket for recognition as the national pastime in the early 1860s. According to baseball historians, Jim Creighton of the Excelsiors was the game's first star. With the passage of time, the barnstorming Negro teams produced numerous memorable stars like Josh Gibson, Judy Johnson, Satchel Paige, John Donaldson, and so many others.

Because no baseball team plays in a vacuum, I have included additional material about events during that era that directly or indirectly impacted the House of David.

Some of these include the creation and dissolution of various Negro Leagues; the teams and players they faced over the years, the likes of J. L. Wilkinson's Kansas City Monarchs and Gus Greenlee's Pittsburgh Crawfords, among others; and such events as the *Denver Post* Tournament and others that came to the fore. Much of this is accented by humor and colorful stories that appeared in newspapers and magazines during their travels.

This book begins with a brief history of the House of David Commune that was founded by Benjamin Purnell in Fostoria, Ohio, in 1902. Events during the initial 14-month experiment forced a move to Benton Harbor in 1903, where it flourished until internal strife caused its permanent fracture over 20 years later. Attention is paid to the religious foundation and lifestyle of the commune and the significant economic contributions it made in Michigan and surrounding regions that are still felt today.

In the beginning, team manager Francis Thorpe and his young ballplayers were all colony members. Baseball was initially played as recreation for the release of pent-up energy among celibate young men. However, thanks to the patience and teaching of Thorpe, the young athletes quickly improved enough to compete locally, where success was almost immediate. In just their second year of play, they won the Berrien County Championship and never looked back.

In 1915, they spread their wings and joined the barnstorming ranks with other semipro teams who had no leagues or official schedules other than games set up by team promoters as they toured. Because of their unique long-hair and bearded appearance, required by their faith, the team was an automatic curiosity. That, coupled with the pepper games they are credited with inventing plus the fast-paced style of baseball they played, made them one of the most sought-after attractions of the era.

The House of David team gained importance as a cog in the barnstorming machine that kept interest in baseball alive in rural America during the upheaval of the Depression, long before major league baseball expanded west of the Mississippi. Their lifestyle was not easy as they donned their woolen House of David uniforms and frequently played two games in different towns and sometimes three in the same day. These towns were usually separated by long rides on dirt roads and games were played on weedy fields littered with potholes during their 25,000-mile, 200-game seasons in the United States, Canada and Mexico.

Almost from its inception, the House of David commune itself was consumed by in-fighting, dissension, and continuous legal problems brought on by its leaders. After the death of founder Benjamin Purnell in 1927, things were somewhat resolved but never repaired. His widow, Mary Purnell, founded a second commune essentially across the street. The Israelite House of David as Reorganized by Mary Purnell was officially incorporated in 1930. Both factions fielded baseball teams that were winners in every sense of the word. The press either did not make the effort or was unable to distinguish between the two teams and wrote about both of them as the House of David, which created confusion regarding rosters, games, and histories.

Because some of their competition was barnstorming Negro teams, they inadvertently played a small role in ending the so-called Gentlemen's Agreement that created the hated color barrier that barred Negroes and other non-white players from organized professional baseball.

They were among a variety of players and teams of the period who happened to be in the right place at the right time, particularly in 1934, when they won what has often been referred to as the most important semipro invitational of them all, the *Denver Post*

Tournament. It was the first year this all-white invitational event invited a Negro team, the famed Kansas City Monarchs, to participate. In the era when barnstorming baseball was king, Negro pitcher Satchel Paige and his catcher, Cy Perkins, were "rented" to the House of David from their team, the Pittsburgh Crawfords, owned by Gus Greenlee.

For financial reasons during the depth of the Great Depression, they frequently traveled with the team called the greatest Negro team of them all, the Kansas City Monarchs, for a few weeks in the summer. The Davids played exhibition games with them as well as local teams at a time when such racial interaction was looked upon with skepticism or worse. Lloyd Dalagar, House of David catcher and utility player, 1927–1936, essentially spoke for all the players when he recalled in an interview with Adam Langer, "We didn't care what color they were. To us they were just gifted athletes who weren't allowed to play in the big leagues."[1]

In addition to the high quality of baseball and fierce competition between the two clubs, they offered the new attraction of night baseball five years before lights appeared in the major leagues, thanks to the foresight of Monarchs owners J. L. Wilkinson and Thomas Baird. The club owned a portable lighting system which was frequently rented to House of David teams along with a traveling crew to install and remove them before and after games.

Because of their early success, one House of David traveling baseball team evolved into three in order to meet all commitments: the Western Travelers, the Central Traveling team, and the Eastern Traveling team. Thus, by the early '20s there were not enough players from within the commune to fill out three rosters. This necessitated the hiring of "outsiders," as they were called, who were not required to join the commune, follow the faith, or grow long locks. But they were required to grow beards. In 1919 they experimented with an all-girl baseball team composed exclusively of commune members. Although they won the championship, their title was later voided when it was discovered that some of the women's brothers disguised themselves as females and played on the team. It was the only year of the team's existence.

Thanks to the efforts of such promoters over the years as Ray Doan, Dutch Witte, and others who saw to it the teams received the best advance press coverage by way of handbills and popular broadsides (standing wooden billboards of the day frequently made at the House of David print shops) carried and displayed from town to town. That, coupled with newspaper articles, created high anticipation to see the House of David play.

Recordkeeping per se was not the microscopic pitch-by-pitch or inning-by-inning stats and analyses we expect today. Daily statistics were not kept for the barnstormers, and the confusion about rosters is apparent. Instead, knowledge of semipro teams consisted of limited information coupled with erratic recordkeeping that often included misspelled names of players.

Research into the history of the House of David commune has been difficult. For one thing, founders Benjamin and Mary Purnell resisted talking about themselves or their lives before their arrival in Benton Harbor. According to scholar Robert Fogarty in his 1981 book, *The Righteous Remnant: The House of David*, after the schism that split the commune into two factions, there was a suspicion of the motives of the press and others from the outside world whom they perceived as hostile. As a result, personal diaries and manuscripts have remained closed for decades.

Although my writing has always included voluminous personal interviews with players and other actors on this stage, this time the passage of time has severely reduced the list to a handful of former players. Among them were outfielder Joe Palladino and catcher Joe "Red" Petrongolo, close friends now in their nineties, who played on a 1948 squad as teens fresh out of high school and shared scant memories. A few years ago, Mr. Palladino donated his House of David jersey to the Baseball Hall of Fame Museum in Cooperstown.

In addition, one MA thesis and some Ph.D. dissertations, old newspaper accounts, and previous work by other baseball historians have aided in putting together the commune history. The 1999 book by Clare Adkin, Jr., *Brother Benjamin: A History of the House of David*, which presented commune history and personal interviews with over 200 commune members, was a golden resource.

Introduction

The greatest milestone for professional baseball occurred when Jackie Robinson was signed by Branch Rickey to play for the Brooklyn Dodgers organization. It defied the tenets of the so-called Gentlemen's Agreement which had barred all non-white players from the professional game for six decades. Over time, that event morphed into legend practically giving "Mr. Rickey," as everyone called him, credit for single-handedly breaking baseball's infamous color line. Actually, according to historian William Donn Rogosin, Rickey and Robinson "were merely the actors who ratified the inevitable."[1]

By the time the House of David of Benton Harbor, Berrien County, Michigan, joined the barnstorming ranks in 1915, the foundations of the world which they entered were in place. The story of the barnstorming era began nearly a hundred years prior to the signing of Jackie Robinson: before the Civil War, before the Reconstruction Era and the horrors of Jim Crow, and long before the colorful House of David teams entered the fray. History demands we take a closer look at the times from which barnstorming evolved and eventually provided a secure foundation for the baseball world which the House of David teams entered.

Within ten years following the Civil War, the unwritten Gentlemen's Agreement among major league owners codified the separation of the races in baseball. In essence it could also be noted as the beginning of large-scale barnstorming as we remember it today, as that was the only avenue available to African American and other non-white athletes who were determined to play the game. Over time, barnstorming baseball became popular in every town and hamlet across the country as the most affordable form of family entertainment and community pride.[2]

Although baseball didn't reach beyond the New York City region before 1857 as the Civil War approached,[3] what has been called the earliest known newspaper account of an organized team of young men playing organized baseball with some regularity was found in the *New York National Advocate* on April 25, 1823. Rudiments of it can be traced as far back as 1825, when what has been noted as the earliest evidence of a challenge to play a game called "bass-ball," one of several spellings at the time, appeared in a New York newspaper in July 1825,[4] that read as follows:

> The undersigned [names listed, but not included here] challenge an equal number of persons in any town in the County of Delaware to meet them at any time at the house of Edward B. Chace, in said town to play the game of base-ball for the sum of one dollar per game. If no town can be found that can produce the required number, they will have no objection to play against any selection that can be made from the several towns in the county.[5]

Interviews given by former slaves when they were old men revealed a version of baseball (rounders or town ball) had been played on plantations years before the Civil War. Records of this were kept mostly in private journals, diaries, and letters by those who lived it.[6] The first amateur ball game between two black teams reported in a newspaper took place in October 1855. The one-sentence article said, "The St. John's team was leading the Union Clubs, 10–2 after two innings when the game was rained out."[7] Thus, the legacy of baseball among black teams was born and growing. It was destined to be highlighted not only by their determination to play the game but also by a willingness to endure hardship, discrimination, and privation along their journey.

Early documentation of their games varies. According to one account, in a November 1859 recorded game between two all-black teams, the Henson Base Ball Club of Jamaica, Queens, defeated the Weeksville Unknowns from Brooklyn, 54–43.[8] Another says the first documented baseball game occurred on September 28, 1860, also in Brooklyn, when Weeksville defeated the Colored Union Club, 11–0.[9] And there are volumes of others.

During this time, all baseball was considered amateur though it was common knowledge that certain players were allegedly "paid under the table."[10] In order to "promote the standardization of playing rules, to regulate interclub competition, and to encourage the growth of baseball,"[11] the National Association of Base Ball Players (NABBP) had been formed in New York in late 1857, and activated in January 1858. Called "national," the association was actually forged by four of New York's oldest clubs: the Knickerbockers, the Eagles, the Empires, and the Gothams. By the Civil War, its membership had grown to over 60 members.[12] By the end of the war, the NABBP included over 100 teams from cities throughout the country. It grew to more than 300 by 1867.[13]

Never very stable, the association underwent regular changes in its constitution and qualifications for membership throughout its brief, 13-year existence.[14] During that period, the first known black barnstorming club, the Washington Mutuals, played a series of games in upstate New York against Lockport, Niagara Falls, Buffalo, Rochester, Utica, Canajoharie, and Troy.[15] Additional African American teams simultaneously made names for themselves: the Albany Bachelors, Chicago Uniques, Camden Blue Skies, Detroit Rialtos, Washington Mutuals, and Baltimore Hannibals, among others.[16]

Meanwhile the concept of barnstorming among so-called structured teams "officially" began in 1860 when the game was still a fledgling sport. It was a time when cricket, recorded in the United States as early as 1837,[17] was emerging as the popular sport of choice after the University of Pennsylvania established an official cricket club in 1842,[18] followed by Harvard and other universities.[19]

During those years, amateur baseball and cricket were in a tug-of-war to become the national pastime. The first barnstorming team, the Brooklyn Excelsiors, an all-white club formed in 1854, was one of the top teams in New York State.[20] By April 1860, plans were in the works for what they termed a "Grand Excursion," an experimental 12-day train trip through the hinterlands[21] for the purpose of publicizing baseball and attracting spectators to see it for themselves. This very first barnstorming tour surpassed all expectations.[22] From July 2 to July 11, they faced the best local team from each of six areas and handily defeated them all: Albany Champion (24–6); Troy Victory (13–7);

Buffalo Niagara, called the Falls of Niagara (50–19); Rochester Flour City (21–1); Rochester Live Oak (27–9); and Newberg Hudson River (59–14).[23]

Game three, played against the Falls of Niagara on Thursday, July 5, received the most notoriety. Each team's twirler went the distance as hitters saw a total of 598 pitches, 354 from Niagara's Franklin Sidway and 244 by visiting Jim Creighton. The Excelsiors crossed the plate two dozen times in the fifth inning on their way to their 50–19 victory.[24] Perhaps this was the beginning of barnstorming baseball's reputation as "wild and wooly."

In addition to being "a landmark event in the development of baseball ... and adding greatly to the advancement of the game everyplace they played,"[25] this experiment allowed the Excelsiors to showcase their own talented players, especially premier young pitcher Jim Creighton. He was an established cricket star who chose baseball and immediately initiated an aggressive style of pitching at a time when the plate was 45 feet distant. That, combined with his amazing hitting, earned him the spotlight as baseball's first bona fide star.[26]

He pitched 32 games in his entire career, including the game's first shutout on November 8, 1860. He is said to have changed pitching forever when he challenged all batsmen rather than feeding them pitches of their choice, as had been the custom. Everywhere he played, he was rated one of a kind.[27] Creighton was the stuff legends are made of, which was just what baseball needed at the time.

Though his star was bright, it was also brief, as he suffered an untimely baseball-related death at the age of 21, which became the foundation of his legend.

Brooklyn Excelsiors, 1860, as they began their Grand Excursion, considered the beginning of barnstorming baseball. Pitcher Jim Creighton, third from left, was dubbed "baseball's first star" (National Baseball Hall of Fame).

In the seventh inning of a game against the Union team of Morrisania, New York, he took a fierce swing for a home run. As he crossed the plate, he told a teammate he had heard a snap and thought he had broken the buckle of his belt. However, further examination revealed that his belt was fine. Shortly thereafter, he experienced extreme pain and was transported to his father's house in Brooklyn, where he died four days later.

The cause of death was identified as a ruptured bladder or an inguinal hernia, depending on the source. Because of his star status as a cricketer, controversy immediately arose as to whether a prior injury he received in a cricket match with the St. George club against the Willow club a few days earlier or the vicious home run swing was the actual cause of his death.[28]

Baseball did not want responsibility for his death, fearing it would leave a blemish on the newly energized sport. As a result, the "baseball or cricket" debate continued for years afterward.[29] John Thorn and other baseball historians refer to Creighton as the game's first hero who deserves to be in the Hall of Fame for the way he redefined pitching and changed how the game was played.[30]

"During the Civil War baseball was played everywhere by soldiers, both blue and gray. It was a time when the country was divided philosophically but there are reports of Union prisoners and Confederate guards playing baseball games."[31] Following the war, interest in baseball literally exploded nationwide,[32] and its popularity among Negroes skyrocketed.[33] Two well-known all-black teams, the Washington Mutuals and the Alert Baseball Club of Washington, D.C., toured upstate New York, but this was not yet called barnstorming.[34] Charles R. Douglass, son of abolitionist Frederick Douglass, played on both teams.[35]

However, by 1867 the wheels of change had already been turning. That year, the well-known, all-black Philadelphia Pythians had developed into the most popular and respected African American team in Philadelphia, the city with the largest burgeoning Negro population in the Northeast.[36] The Pythians, known as a club of gentlemen players, was led by social activist Octavius Valentine Catto, a well-educated young scholar who "exemplified the quest for the self-determination among African-Americans in the post Civil War Era."[37] When the Pythians applied for membership in the Pennsylvania Association of Amateur Base Ball Players (PAABBP) in October 1867, they were denied. Two months later, their application for membership in the National Association of Base Ball Players (NABBP) was also spurned.[38]

Baseball explained it as a desire to avoid the potential political ramifications and possible social problems that could arise by mixing the races on the diamond.[39] However, historians suggest it was a reflection of the country's new post-war racial attitudes. It was the only time in baseball history (1867–1871) that there was a *written* resolution (not a code, law or rule) excluding non-white players. All organized baseball participated in the tacit understanding (never officially written into any bylaws) among all owners not to sign contracts with non-white players. This became known as the Gentlemen's Agreement.[40]

At the same time, the first professional club appeared on the scene when future Hall of Famer Harry Wright, the first openly paid player for the New York Knickerbockers in the early 1860s, organized a group of financial backers and assembled a group of premier paid-to-play players for the Cincinnati Red Stockings Base Ball Club.[41] The team had ten paid players described as "an unaffordable luxury" that spawned a lot of controversy.⁴² In their first game on June 1, 1869, they defeated the Mansfield Independents by the score of 48–14.

More professional teams appeared in short order, resulting in the collapse of the NABBP as teams jumped to the newly established National Association of Professional Base Ball Players (NAPBBP), also known as the National Association, formed in 1871. Like its predecessor, this alliance was not up to the task of regulating or operating professional baseball. Instead it was an unstructured confederation that underwent constant but ineffectual attempts at reform until it was disbanded in 1876,⁴³ when Charles Hulbert, assisted by Harry Wright, Albert Spalding, and Lewis Meacham, formed the National League.⁴⁴

Meanwhile, without leagues, many black teams played white teams when white owners scheduled black-white exhibitions; it was considered good for business. Those games always attracted multitudes of curious fans who flocked to games, eager to see the skills of black players.⁴⁵ Baseball may have been segregated, but the teams still found ways to play each other.⁴⁶ For example, in 1869 what has been called the first game ever between all black and all-white teams on record saw the Pythians defeat the City Items, a team composed of newspapermen, by the score of 27–17 in a raucous battle.⁴⁷

During the Reconstruction Era, African American baseball teams were organized earlier in the North than in the South, followed by the East and Mid-Atlantic states. The game became a popular form of entertainment and community pride everywhere. Black players formed hundreds of barnstorming teams.

One of them, the Argyle Athletics, later known as the Original Cuban Giants (1885–1914), was founded by Frank P. Thompson, headwaiter at the luxurious 350-room Argyle Hotel, a Victorian vacation spot on Long Island, and was the first professional (paid) black team.⁴⁸ His plan was to hire top-quality players who could build a fan base of their own and make African American competition a lucrative business in a Jim Crow world. The team was the first black team to gain national renown due to its playing ability. Not only did they successfully barnstorm throughout the northern states, where they frequently encountered difficulty recruiting opponents because they were so good, but they also held their own against such white major league clubs as the New York Metropolitans, Philadelphia Athletics, St. Louis Browns, and others.⁴⁹

In 1887, the first league of black players, the National Colored Base Ball League, organized in Babylon, New York, appeared on the scene.⁵⁰ Each participating team paid a $100 admission fee. In addition to the reorganized Philadelphia Pythians, the league included the Baltimore Lord Baltimores, Boston Resolutes, Louisville Falls City, New York Gothams, D. C. Capital Citys, Pittsburgh Keystones, and Cincinnati Browns.⁵¹ Although black versus white baseball games became more common and quite popular throughout the country as time passed, that's not to say there were no tensions or incidents involving racial discrimination.

Quite the contrary. For example, on July 15, 1887, a bold headline in the *New York Herald* read: "The Color Line," resulting from an incident and subsequent hullabaloo in the International League following an exhibition scheduled between the Newark Little Giants and the Chicago White Stockings, managed by future Hall of Famer Cap Anson, often dubbed "the greatest player-manager of the 19th Century."⁵² But he was also a well-known bigot. It was a chance to make extra money for the two teams who both drew abundant and diverse crowds.

But when Anson saw that the Little Giants had two Negro players on their roster, he threatened to forfeit the game rather than permit his team to go on the diamond against a team with a black battery: pitcher George Stovey and catcher Moses Fleetwood Walker.[53] He later reluctantly changed his tune when informed that forfeiture of the game also meant forfeiture of their salaries.[54]

One of the most publicized incidents occurred in 1887, in the American Association, dubbed the Beer and Whiskey League because it allowed the sale of alcoholic drinks at games.[55] During its ten-year existence, 1882–1891, the league had a major league classification, and the St. Louis Browns club had won the league championship four consecutive seasons, 1885–1888.[56]

In early September, the Browns were slated by team owner/president Chris Von der Ahe to play a post-season exhibition game with the Cuban Giants, a crack black team based in New Jersey. The game was expected to attract a minimum of 15,000 fans and make extra money for both teams. However, the night before the game, a mutiny occurred when a letter was presented to Von der Ahe signed by the entire Browns team with the exception of Captain Charles Comiskey, who was absent due to a broken thumb, saying they refused to play a black team.[57] An angry Von der Ahe held a private meeting with his team, asking them to reconsider. When they refused, he released them all on the spot, which forced him to cancel the game despite a threatened $700 lawsuit.[58]

By the early 1900s, Negro baseball had come into its own, and by the end of World War I it was firmly established as the most popular entertainment among the black populace. On the national scene, multiple barnstorming circuits, some quite lucrative, flourished in rural as well as urban areas across the country, where the arrival of teams was always exciting and much anticipated.[59]

It was also an era of novelty teams. One of them was put together by former pitcher and baseball innovator James L. Wilkinson, "Wilkie," who would later become the only white co-owner of an all-black team, the famed Kansas City Monarchs. He enlisted the best female ballplayers he could find, including Mae Arbaugh, who played first base under the name Carrie Nation to attract fans, though she had no connection to the social activist.[60] The team was one of numerous squads named "Bloomer Girls" because they wore loose-fitting trousers designed by Amelia Jenks Bloomer, a woman's activist who fought for less restrictive clothing for women. They played quality baseball and held their own against women's as well as men's teams. Though they never played each other, their barnstorming exploits saw them successfully challenge local teams across the country.[61]

In addition, Wilkinson developed a colorful team of players with diverse ethnic backgrounds called the All-Nations team. It was the first team to barnstorm coast to coast in their own Pullman car, Loretta.[62] On June 12, 1912, the *Duluth News Tribune* colorfully described some of the players as follows: "A Chinaman whose physique tallies with the size of a Spalding bat; an Indian who acquired his 'stick talent' by swinging a tomahawk in the Custer massacre; a Turk who doesn't smoke cigarettes; a Mexican revolutionist; a Cuban insurgent; a smoke hurler who averages 15 'S.O.s' per game; a straw hat cleaner from Greece; a Japanese; [and] an American."[63]

The team included many outstanding players throughout its existence. Baseball scholars agree that the most notable was pitcher John Donaldson, described as "the greatest colored twirler in the world," who won 80 of his 85 starts in 1915.[64] He later joined Wilkinson's Kansas City Monarchs when that team began in 1920.[65]

With barnstorming semiprofessional baseball established and thriving by 1915, the table was set for the arrival of the House of David "Bearded Beauties." Though relegated to the status of a colorful footnote in the history of the game, the teams from the House of David and the City of David earned a place among the most revered and famous barnstorming teams of the era.

1

Commune History

In 1906 the following essay appeared in "A Twentieth Century History of Berrien County, Michigan."

> A peculiar colony of people called the House of David under the lead of Benjamin and Mary Purnell was established a few years ago [1903] east of the city of Benton Harbor. The corporate name of the association is Benjamin and Mary Purnell, the Israelite House of David, the Church of the New Eve, the Body of Christ.
>
> Large tracts of land have been purchased and large and commodious buildings erected. The colony already numbers several hundred, and has been constantly increasing. The people of the colony share everything in common. It is claimed that it is a religious and communistic association based on the general principle of each member contributing all possessions, labor, and earnings in a common stock in which all members share alike.
>
> It is claimed that Benjamin and Mary jointly constitute the seventh angel or messenger recorded in Revelations as delivering the final message on earth; that the members of this association are the elect people and that they will finally number one hundred and forty thousand.
>
> These people now own about one thousand acres of land and they have devoted their attention largely to the culture of fruit as well as grain, having a dozen orchards on their lands. They also have various trades represented in their establishments.
>
> They have already erected a cannery and drying house, a carpenter shop, a coach factory, a tailor shop, and a steam laundry. They have sent into the market in one day over one thousand bushels of peaches. They have three brass bands and two orchestras, and have already established a zoological garden containing a large number of birds and animals from Africa and South America.
>
> The buildings are lighted with electricity by an electric plant owned and operated by the association.
>
> The people have a reputation of being thrifty farmers and keep their grounds attractive. The future of this association may be looked upon with some curiosity and interest, as this is the first purely communistic organization established in Berrien County.[1]

Religious communes, common in the United States during and after the Civil War, played a significant role in the life of Benjamin Franklin Purnell, founder of the Israelite House of David at the turn of the 20th Century. His commune, listed as the third-oldest continuing American religious community, was formed after the establishment of The United Society of Shakers at Sabbathday Lake in Maine, followed by the Hutterite communities in Montana.[2] It was populated by Millennialists, a religion that preached the coming end of the world and offered what was called a last chance for salvation to 144,000 chosen people who did not believe in death of the body and joined a movement known as the Ingathering.[3]

On May 3, 1903, the commune, " The Israelite House of David, Church of the New Eve, Body of Christ" was formally incorporated as a "religious ecclesiastical organization" in Benton Harbor.[4] The name "Israelite House of David" was selected because Jesus Christ was in the lineage of David (Luke 1:27).[5]

Without digging too deeply into the complexities of the religion, it was not a local phenomenon. Its long history can be traced back to Joanna Southcott, a domestic born in 1750 in Devonshire, England, at a time when women were denied religious expression on the pulpit. Hence, she became one of many self-proclaimed prophets who founded religions of their own. She had revelations that she was the first of Seven Messengers, also called "seven angels," each to be sent by God in succession to head a church to save the world before the establishment of the millennial kingdom. Southcott was a prolific writer who for the next 60 years authored six volumes titled *The Strange Effects of Faith* in an effort to bring her ideas to the attention of the Church of England. During her lifetime, the movement gathered upward of 100–150,000 followers, including British nobles and bishops of the Church of England.[6]

Following her death in 1814, a series of the six subsequent messengers she predicted took their turns at the helm, each changing the religion in his own way: Richard Brothers, George Turner, William Shaw, John Wroe, James Jezreel, and Michael Mills in Detroit, whom Benjamin Purnell discounted as a fraud, declaring himself the Seventh Messenger in Mills' place.[7]

The most influential of all the messengers in terms of the establishment of the House of David was a 24-year-old soldier, James Jezreel, born James Roland White. While on a troop ship to India, White wrote *The Flying Roll*, explaining the theological foundations of his faith, which was rooted in the Judeo-Christian tradition. It was rejected by the Trustees of the Christian Israelites.[8] Though he never rewrote it, around 1879 Jezreel wrote the first of his trilogy called *Extracts from the Flying Roll*, sermons about the Lost Tribes of Israel. They were later sold door to door. In 1882, he traveled the globe gathering converts, especially in America where it is said that at the height of his success, membership in America transcended the numbers in England.[9] By the time the Israelite theology reached Western Michigan, it had been studied and written about in several theological sources.[10]

The founders and head of the Israelite House of David commune in the United States were Benjamin Purnell and his wife, Mary, who rarely spoke about their origins. Benjamin was born in a log cabin in Lewis County in the Kentucky hill country in 1861, one of 12 children. Census records described his parents, Madison and Sarah Purnell, as illiterate farmers[11]; Mary, one of nine children, was born in Virginia during the Civil War before her pacifist father moved the family to a farm at the Smokey Fork of Tygarts Creek, Carter County, in rural Kentucky.[12]

After Benjamin's mother died when he was six years old, he was sent to live with his older brother, Madison, and his wife, Elizabeth, farmers who lived near Dalesburg in Fleming County, Kentucky. It was an environment populated primarily by Southern Baptists and Southern Methodists who espoused fundamentalist doctrines in an era of itinerant preachers who conducted fervent revival meetings and attracted thousands to tent meetings. Whether true or not, for the remainder of his adult life Benjamin told everyone he was aware of his religious callings at a very young age, saying he taught himself to read from the New Testament and preached to trees when people were not available.[13] Sources agree that the rest of his education was informal at best, in keeping with the rural traditions of the period.[14]

Purnell wrote that he was raised in The Disciples of Christ Church under the direction of Alexander Campbell, whose followers were known as Campbellites (pronounced "Camelites"), who had relocated from the nearby state of New York into Northeastern Kentucky 30 years prior to his birth.[15]

By the time he turned 16, Purnell left home to make his way in the world. He soon met and married 19-year-old Angeline Brown in Greenup County, Kentucky. Despite his professing to have been recognized as a child evangelist, the *Buffalo Times* (May 27, 1927) reported that at his 1927 trial, a bitter Angeline said, "he had not gotten religion during our years together ... he was shiftless and liked to lay [*sic*] around in the sun and eat and sleep ... and had no more religion than a possum." She remembered him driving a huckster wagon in Greenup when he did work.[16] After just two years, when their infant daughter, Sarah, was six months old, he left them. She said he was shiftless and no good, as she denied all of his claims that he maintained infrequent contact over the years.[17]

From there he drifted, never able to hold a job for long until he met 17-year-old Mary Stollard, the daughter of a pacifist farmer from Carter County in Western Kentucky. The couple married in August 1880, in Aberdeen, Ohio, and started married life living with her parents.[18] There is a consensus among sources that "Mary was his lifelong companion and her intelligence, sense and cunning promoted his prophetic career considerably."[19]

Details of both marriages remain vague. In the court proceedings two decades later, Purnell testified that he had tried to file a bill of divorcement from his first wife shortly before his second marriage, but "eighteen or nineteen" lawyers told him Kentucky law at that time did not require divorces if one of the partners were age 16 or under when the marriage took place.[20] Mary Purnell later testified that records of her marriage to Benjamin in front of a justice of the peace were lost in March 1913, when the Ohio and other rivers flooded in one of the most devastating statewide disasters in Ohio history.[21] Some

Benjamin and Mary Purnell at Benton Harbor Commune, circa 1910. Benjamin always wore what became his trademark white suit for special events (Mark Tillson, Hamilton College Digital Archive Photo Collection).

scholars even suggested that both marriages may have been common law, an issue that was never addressed at his trial in 1927.

During the early years of their marriage, the Purnells were migrant laborers. After the birth of their two children, son Samuel Coy and daughter Hettie, they settled in Richmond, Indiana, in 1887, where Benjamin worked briefly in a broom-making factory. During this time, he arduously devoured Jezreel's writings and became an ardent follower. The pair became members of Jezreel's Sixth Church, and Benjamin began writing his first major work *The Star of Bethlehem: The Living Roll of Life*.[22]

Although exact details about their affiliation with Jezreel himself are vague, it is thought he assigned the pair to the Detroit commune, where the largest group of Southcottians was based under the leadership of Michael Keyfor Mills, "Prince Michael," the self-anointed Seventh Messenger of the faith.[23]

When friction broke out at the Detroit commune, Purnell, always the opportunist, fanned the flames of discontent until the circumstances seemed right to him. He then broke from Mills, saying, "Michael didn't have any faith," and proclaimed himself the Seventh Messenger on March 12, 1895.[24] However, the flock in Detroit found him untrustworthy and essentially expelled the pair shortly thereafter.[25]

They spent the majority of their time as itinerant ministers assigned the mission of recruiting converts. Their faith and zeal remained undaunted during what became a seven-year sojourn throughout the Midwest (1895–1902), while he wrote, honed his oratory skills, and became very good at rousing audience zeal at camp meetings. He was usually broke and regularly solicited the charity of strangers during that period. Years later, commune members recalled that Benjamin had discussed those years as a period of hard times with many sacrifices, while Mary recalled the experience as the happiest time of their lives.[26]

Now using his self-ordained new title of Seventh Messenger, the Purnells went to the outskirts of Fostoria, Ohio, in 1902 with the intention of setting down roots for their own commune where they could preach their Millennialist philosophy. They were taken in and supported by wealthy farmers Dan and Clara Pelton, who later described them as a destitute pair pushing a cart filled with junk when they arrived.[27]

Unable to attract a desired flock of converts there, they decided to move closer to the population center of Fostoria, where they were taken in by truck gardeners Cora and Silas Mooney, recent converts to the Israelite faith. Despite his hard work, converts were still slow in coming[28] During that time, he continued working on *The Star of Bethlehem: the Living Roll of Life*, and later had it distributed with other pamphlets throughout the region to attract attention to his message and his commune. After their arrival in Benton Harbor, he produced an eight-page monthly newspaper called "The Shiloh Messenger of Wisdom," filled with his messages and articles plus some items from members of the commune. Copies of these issues are still distributed today.[29]

Benjamin and Mary Purnell had two children, Coy Samuel or Samuel Coy Purnell depending on the source, and a daughter Heather, called Hettie. Accounts of Coy's life vary. One says he was dressed like a dandy and preached with his parents at age nine during their travels before he ran away at age 12 to become a bugler in a Kentucky regiment, and later was a mining prospector.[30] Another says that father and son, Coy and Benjamin, had been estranged for years because Coy had rejected Benjamin's religious teachings by marrying outside the faith and leaving the commune in his early 20s. Coy later explained his actions in a letter to the local newspaper in defense of his father's commune, saying he had never accepted his parents' religious teachings or the rigid lifestyle at the House of David because, "I can not walk the straight and narrow path they walk."[31]

In the last years of his life, he returned to the commune, but he and Benjamin were never able to reconcile their differences, and Benjamin refused to visit his son on his deathbed. Coy died in 1924 from pneumonia caused by "a lingering disease" which historians described in the *Cincinnati Enquirer* and other newspapers as alcoholism.[32] He was buried according to House of David tradition, in a white shroud at Crystal Springs where other commune members were buried. Although his ex-wife and children were among the few mourners at his service, Benjamin did not appear at the event. Mary remained true to her faith and did not attend.[33]

Through tragedy, Hettie may have played a pivotal but more likely a coincidental role that hastened in the foundation of the House of David in Benton Harbor. On February 16, 1903, the 16-year-old was killed on her first day on the job at Peter & Fox Magazine Cane Factory that manufactured munitions, when an unexplained explosion and fire destroyed her building. Papers like the *Bismarck Tribune* reported that all employees in the building were killed, while the *Indianapolis Journal* and others said eight were killed and four others were injured.[34]

The townspeople were irate and confused when Benjamin and Mary followed the tenets of their faith that the true believers would never die and that death of the body was punishment for sin. They followed the biblical teachings of Matthew (8:22) to "let the dead bury the dead."[35] Most of the citizens of Fostoria, non-commune members who did not understand this faith and were already concerned about having "a strange religious sect in their midst," gave Hettie a small service of their own, which her parents did not attend. The Purnells left Fostoria within a month.[36]

Though tales about the Purnells being run on the Fostoria make for good stories, they may be off the mark. On the same day of Hettie's death, the Purnells received a letter from Louis Baushke advising them that they were ready for Benjamin and Mary to come to Benton Harbor. This shows that plans were already in place for the Purnells to make their way to Benton Harbor and reestablish the colony there.[37] The city of Fostoria is still considered the birthplace of the Israelite House of David.[38]

Because the Fostoria congregation was always small and failed to grow due to Purnell's inability to attract converts, scholars speculate that he had been searching for a place to relocate before Hettie's death. He had been in touch with the wealthy and influential Baushke family in Benton Harbor, who informed them there was a large group of Jezreelites in Grand Rapids near Benton Harbor who were eager to accept them. They then donated much of the land where the commune was established.[39]

When the Purnells announced that they and five members of the Fostoria congregation were ready to make the move to Benton Harbor, Albert Baushke sent them $500 to pay the train fare. On St. Patrick's Day, March 17, 1903, they arrived in Benton Harbor with followers Joseph Fowler, Silas and Cora Mooney, Charles E. Norris, and Johnnie Schneider.[40] They had a variety of reasons for deciding to relocate in rural Benton Harbor in southwestern Michigan, but two seem the most likely. Not only was that community one of the fastest growing and best agricultural areas in the region, but it was also close to Grand Rapids, the hub for the dissemination of Jezreelite literature.[41]

The Baushke family remained their most prominent contacts and ardent supporters in Benton Harbor. There were the four influential Baushke brothers, who, in addition to being wealthy, were successful, and listed by fellow Israelites as among the first merchants in Benton Harbor before and after the village was incorporated. They owned and operated the Louis Baushke and Bro. Wagon Shop. Over the years, they owned and operated a large carriage house, a successful blacksmith shop, and a wagon factory, and were involved in numerous other ventures.[42]

In 1894, two of the four brothers, Albert and Louis, with William Worth built one of the first gasoline powered horseless carriages in the United States, which was introduced on November 26, 1895. Albert did the iron work and Louis did the woodwork. Later dubbed "the 1895 Benton Harbor Motorcycle," the five-passenger "autymobile," powered by a 7.5 horsepower gasoline engine, is said to have reached speeds up to 20 miles per hour. It has been displayed at the Antique Auto Club of America Museum in Hershey, Pennsylvania, since 1995, and is considered the oldest "still running" car in the country.[43]

Records say the original commune was a ten-acre site which included good farmland and garden areas, and a population that was steadily increasing. In 1903 membership included 22 members of the Baushke family.[44] Their site included good farmland and garden areas to enable them to produce their own food for the steadily increasing population. All the while, Purnell continued to buy land in preparation for anticipated future growth of the commune, and members rolled up their sleeves and worked at assigned tasks as they busily created the necessary buildings. The first major structure, the Ark, was completed in 1903 to accommodate the immediate need for parishioner housing, Purnell's printing shop, and his business office.[45]

The first decade was a time of frenzied excitement, primarily on the two fronts of actually building the commune itself and attracting converts. While the Bethlehem House was under construction in 1904, Benjamin and Mary left for Melbourne, Australia, in November, where they evangelized within the church of John Wroe, the fifth messenger of the church. When they returned in early February 1905, they were accompanied by 85 new members, including most of the leadership of the Wroe church. This largest single bevy to join essentially doubled the population.[46]

This group immediately became the focus of newspaper articles and public attention. It was composed of such educated and accomplished members as greenhouse horticulturists, architect William "Billy" Wright from Australia, and others who were immediately assigned the responsibility of building additional member housing, plus members of the Joseph Hannaford family, who created top quality musical instruments in Australia and later for colony members as well as tourists who came later. One of the Hannaford sons, Ezra, better known as "Cookie," formed Cookie Hannaford's Original House of David Orchestra that successfully toured the country for many years.[47] In 1906, Purnell sent two commune members as envoys to Australia. They brought back 17 more converts.[48] Between 1905 and 1915, it was not unusual for groups of 10 or 15 to join at one time.[49]

The third building, the Jerusalem House, was completed in 1906 and connected to Bethlehem House by a triple archway inscribed "The House of David 1906." The archway was symbolic of the joining of the Fifth and Sixth Churches of Israel to form the Seventh, the Israelite House of David.[50]

Once Shiloh House was completed in August 1908, it became the new Colony

Headquarters: business offices on the first floor with Mary Purnell as business manager, and residences for members on the upper floors. It was one of the places where the Purnells resided at different times, living in separate rooms like the parishioners. Mary remained in the same room until she left the commune in 1930.[51] In 1972, the 100-room Shiloh Mansion was added to the National Registry of Historic Places.[52]

In 1921, further expansion included another work by William "Billy" Wright, the Diamond House, built as living quarters for members. So named because it was built of hematite stone composition that glistened in the sunlight, it was acknowledged as the best example of Israelite architecture. On September 29, 1986, it was heavily damaged by a lightning fire,[53] and was later repaired.

In the beginning, the commune attracted new members faster than they anticipated. Thus, the August 8, 1908, edition of *Shiloh's Messenger of Wisdom* newsletter (still published today)[54] included a notice requiring potential new members to avoid arriving randomly. It read in part, "It is absolutely necessary that each case be given due consideration and applicant [sic] wait for the call to come home, as there must be order in the Lord's house." This was included in every publication for 15 years. However, despite of these warnings, converts kept coming. By 1907, the population had reached 385.[55]

Life in the commune was rigid. New members who had been screened and accepted were required to sign a contract of compliance known as the Articles of Faith and Membership before being accepted into the ranks.[56] It required forfeiture of all personal property assets, with all earnings to be held in trust for the House of David, and they were henceforth prohibited from acquiring any personal property. Additional essential requirements included complete abstinence from alcohol, tobacco, and sex—both inside marriage and out.[57]

They followed a vegetarian diet regimen because they were pacifists in pursuit of the pure holiness of God and did not believe in killing any of God's creatures; men did not shave beards or cut their hair. In accordance with their non–Sabbatarian practices, they had no specific day called Sabbath and no building designated as "church," as they were encouraged to worship privately any place—any day of the week. There were modest dress codes for men, and women were encouraged to wear colors rather than black, which was a symbol of death, since they did not believe in death of the body. They practiced communal living, with separate quarters for men and women, for husbands and wives, and boys and girls.[58] A notable practice at the House of David, for which Mary was given most of the credit, was that women were supported in leadership roles and encouraged to vote on all matters within the commune years before the 19th Amendment was approved in August 1920.[59]

Similarities between the Adventist tenets of the Shakers and Benjamin's commune in Benton Harbor were noted by historians, despite the fact that it has never been confirmed that Purnell had any knowledge of or contact with them.[60]

Music quickly became part of daily life and an integral part of their worship. By 1910, all-men and all-women bands and choirs performed regularly at the commune and were sent on tours, appearing on vaudeville stages all over the country during the fall and winter months. It didn't take long for their "music industry" to become a major factor in their financial success. On their West Coast Tour in 1921, John Philip Sousa was reportedly a guest conductor when they appeared in San Francisco.[61] The entertainment they offered was always available at the Outdoor Theatre built within the commune.

Scholars have divided the followers of the Purnells into three groups: a small number of believers who joined in the earliest days at Benton Harbor, the converts who arrived from Australia in 1905, and native-born Americans, most of whom joined between 1905 and 1917. Between 1903 and 1907, the population of the commune grew to over 300, which included 60 new arrivals from London[62] plus the George Wheeler family, who reportedly walked over 1,000 miles from their home in Arkansas, pushing a cart packed with all their worldly belongings to join the Ingathering. They preached the colony's message along the way, and upon their eagerly anticipated arrival they were welcomed with much pomp and circumstance.[63]

Throughout this first decade, things were bustling around Benton Harbor. From the beginning, the commune was always financially independent and self-sufficient thanks to the combined efforts of Benjamin's business acumen and Mary's efficient running of the business offices. Baseball had not yet arrived on the scene.

Ben Purnell was known for fine, stylish clothing. In his traditional white flannel suit, white hat, boots, and fine jewelry, he mounted his white steed and daily rode from work place to work place, supervising activities. However, the faithful said he posed like that for post cards and other publicity but never rode the horse around the region.[64]

From the start, numbers of curious onlookers wanted to see what was what with the new religious group in their midst. Remembering the pressure from distrusting onlookers at Fostoria, Purnell wanted to protect the privacy of the living quarters of the Benton Harbor members. In 1908, a money-making proposition presented a workable solution. He hired a local landscape architect, Peter Muller, who designed and

The commune celebrated the long-awaited arrival of the Wheeler family—standing in front of their wagon, circa 1907. The family walked to Benton Harbor all the way from Arkansas to join the commune (courtesy Brian Ziebart, House of David Commune archives).

built the Eden Springs Amusement Park away from the living quarters.[65] It was on a 30-acre parcel purchased from the Eastmans adjacent to Eastman Springs, a successful, Victorian-like spa with hotels and gardens that shipped its healing waters as far as Chicago and Milwaukee.[66]

Eden Springs Amusement Park is remembered as the most lucrative and successful business endeavor Purnell ever made. It soon became one of the most popular pre–Disneyland-type tourist attractions in southwest Michigan. It included numerous nature paths for walkers and hikers, a movie theater, a zoo that included monkeys, lions, an aviary, and other animals brought over by Australian converts, an ice cream parlor where they invented the first sugar cones, plus as many as 25 mineral springs where they bottled and sold the different flavored waters.[67]

Across the street from the House of David administrative offices was the depot for the steam-operated, so-called "pygmy railroad" that gave tours throughout the complex. There were two different groups of trains, the original eight and later three larger ones in 1948 to replace the old ones. These Cagney American steam engines, miniature versions of the famed New York Central Railroad engine #999, popular features in amusement parks shortly after the Civil War, were used at the House of David Park.[68] Over the years, it has been rumored, debated, and reported but disproved that another one had been purchased by Walt Disney for $100 in the early 1950s.[69]

In the early '20s, when Judge H. T. Dewhirst[70] arrived from California, he was surprised to find that a version of a new popular sport, bowling, had already arrived in Benton Harbor. The commune soon invented the automatic bowling pin setter, called the "Uncle Sam's Bowling Machine," which they later manufactured and sold.[71]

Earlier, in 1909, a major addition to the money-making ability of the commune

Early visitors to Eden Springs Amusement Park, circa 1910 (courtesy Brian Ziebart, House of David Commune archives).

occurred when 14-year-old Henry Kirkham arrived from Sydney, Australia, and soon became the official House of David photographer. In that capacity, he took thousands of pictures of the baseball teams and individual players, the bands, and the compound in general. He printed them on postcards that were prominently displayed and sold everywhere the team played, in addition to being available to tourists who visited the commune. It was a satisfying and profitable arrangement. Today the postcards are recognized as among the last remaining sources for pictures of the House of David.[72]

From the beginning, the commune built large greenhouses and took great care to plant more and more diversified orchards as they acquired more land. Benjamin also assigned some of his select "ministers" to communities as far East as New York and surrounding areas to spread the religious message of the House of David in hopes of expanding membership.

By 1907, there were problems when the local populace became suspicious about all the land Purnell was acquiring and said it was too much tax-exempt property for the needs of a religious corporation. Following a legal back and forth, the matter was settled when the House of David agreed to forfeit their listing as a religious corporation and was reorganized as a voluntary religious organization, which changed their tax status.[73]

Ron Taylor, archivist of the City of David, recalled that throughout their existence, harvest time was a big event in which everybody participated.[74] The farms were large, with many workers doing a diverse assortment of essential tasks, but no matter what their assigned jobs were or where they worked, they all got involved in the harvest.

Since people normally worked on different farms in different locations, harvest time was like a reunion. Every day, cooking crews prepared big Thanksgiving-type meals

One of the most popular postcards printed at the commune features (from left to right) Walter Faust, Francis Thorpe and David Harrison (courtesy Brian Ziebart, House of David Commune archives).

Ladies picking apples at the huge Rocky Farm Orchard were a big draw at the annual harvest festivities (courtesy Ronald Taylor, City of David Commune Files).

which were very popular and enjoyed by all. Every year, their production increased. In 1943, they packed and shipped 40,000 bushels of apples, and at one time their food processing plant was the largest in the world.[75]

During the busy building frenzy, circa 1910, at Purnell's request a baseball Park with a seating capacity of 3,500 was built by Floyd Fitzsimmons for his own baseball club, the local semipro Speed Boys. It was understood that the House of David could use the field to teach the game to its young players, then play local teams there when the Speed Boys were out of town.[76] It was unique for a barnstorming baseball team to have its own home ballpark.

At that time, Francis Thorpe began teaching baseball to the young men. They played local teams to hone skills. In 1915, they entered the barnstorming world and became Berrien County Champions in 1916. They were on the road throughout times of turmoil within the commune, which minimized the impact upon them. Baseball at the House of David and the teams will be discussed in later chapters.

In 1912, Purnell, a religious entrepreneur who never resisted a business opportunity, seized one that presented itself on High Island, five miles long and 30 miles west of the Port of Charlevoix, one of the nine islands in the Beaver Archipelago located in Northern Lake Michigan.[77]

It was described as the most beautiful of the islands, well timbered, with good soil,[78] and a paradise in the summer months. Purnell purchased the timber rights plus a defunct logging operation and old sawmill that had been there since the late-19th century and converted it into another profitable enterprise for the commune. At one point it was the largest portable sawmill in the United States.[79] In addition to good fishing, it was cultivated as good farmland, primarily noted for its potatoes.[80] The *Wisconsin State Journal* colorfully described life on the island as follows: "No money, no doctors, no crimes, no telephones, no profanity, no haircuts, no bald heads, no razors, no neckties, no tobacco, no prohibition, no meat, no grocery bills."[81]

At its peak, the High Island population approximated 200–250 people who lived on the east side of the island and maintained a relatively self-sustaining existence into the early 1920s.[82] For the first few years, supplies from Benton Harbor arrived regularly by steamboat, the *Rosa Belle*, that brought sugar and miscellaneous items that could not be raised or made on the island, then returned to Benton Harbor with products from lumbering and farming.[83] Their timber cutting and truck farming business supplied lumber for numerous buildings in the main commune as well as the town of Benton Harbor and surrounding communities.[84]

P. Hendricks, captain of the Fitzsimmons Speed Boys, circa 1910 (courtesy Brian Ziebart, House of David Commune archives).

Former commune member Ramon Nelson fondly recalled memories of his youth on High Island. He and his family (parents Elisha and Hattie, brother Otto, and sister Mary Ellen) were transferred from one of the farms at Benton Harbor to High Island, where they lived from 1920 to 1927. Although he left and went to Mary's City of David after the schism and then left the commune altogether in the mid-1930s, he remained supportive.[85]

Like the lifestyle in Benton Harbor, days were spent doing assigned jobs. The men operated the dairy farm, tended to the chickens and horses, plowed-planted-harvested all crops, and ran the blacksmith shop in addition to going into the woods to fell timber and haul logs on horse-drawn carts to the sawmill. The women did the cooking, canning, and clothes-making out of colored cloth, obeying the rule against wearing black.

Before spending the day in the one-room schoolhouse under the tutelage of hired teacher and non-colony member Lucille Gillespie, children aged 6–16 completed their assigned chores that included chopping and distributing firewood and other duties in the communal living houses. Their classroom curriculum included such studies as English language usage, spelling, geography, arithmetic, and hygiene. All the children, boys and girls, studied and played together. Just like in Benton Harbor, the older students added hands-on learning to their regimen as they worked with the blacksmiths, bakers, and horticulturists in the greenhouses, equipment repairmen, seamstresses, kitchen cooks, and others as they learned the occupations necessary for the continued operation of the group. Depending on the season, free time was spent reading, ice skating and ice games, bobsledding, swimming, hiking, and Purnell's favorite: baseball.[86]

Due to the celibacy oath, a second generation was not anticipated, but the commune worked with the children who arrived with original members. All in all, however, writers indicate that both the Benton Harbor and High Island members were not particularly attentive to children. In 1912, the Michigan State Superintendent authorized the two branches of the commune the right to operate their own schools, which offered as much as an eighth grade education for those who wanted it. They used space in the Ark Building as classrooms in Benton Harbor and built a one-room schoolhouse at High Island. Students from there and throughout the commune went to Lansing, the state capital, to take a state test to get a certificate of completion if they passed.[87]

By the early 1920s, the House of David was winning the respect and admiration of the business community and the general population of Benton Harbor as a whole. However, by this time internal conflict of one sort or another had already become a perpetual and disruptive part of life within the commune.

During the early period of growth within the commune, disillusioned members became dissatisfied and wanted to leave the commune, and the faith, as early as 1906. They complained that they had submitted all their worldly goods and lived at a subsistence level while self-anointed "King Benjamin and Queen Mary" lived lavishly by comparison.[88] They wanted Benjamin to refund their donations, sometimes amounting to thousands of dollars, plus remit their back salaries.[89] Benjamin denied later requests, saying such remittance was not the policy of the House of David, and there was no contingency for this situation in the Articles of Faith and Membership all new members signed.[90] During this period, there were also charges of immorality against Benjamin for taking advantage of young girls and women sexually in the name of religion.[91]

The longest single conflict lasted from April 1917, through May 1922. Though Purnell was not found guilty of any wrong-doing, the court ordered him to remit the sum of $24,190.55 to the John Hansel family in return for property they donated to the community. On appeal, the court upheld that judgment. All countersuits and appeals that were launched by the colony were denied.[92] At that point, additional families who had left the commune were labeled "scorpions" by Purnell, accused him of accepting property under false pretenses and breach of promise regarding their pay.[93] Legal problems persisted at a never-ending pace.

Concomitantly, the residents on High Island struggled with the slow decline of business. Things came to a head after the *Rosa Belle*, their supply ship, mysteriously sank in Lake Michigan while bringing supplies to the island. Visits from another supply boat became sporadic, then stopped.[94] After months of investigation into the fate of the *Rosa Belle* and its 11-man crew yielded no results, the commune announced, "no boat will be operated this year, and it is through with High Island for all time."[95] At that point, a majority of the residents migrated back to Benton Harbor, while those who stayed remained self-sufficient by selling timber, crops, and additional fruits of their labor on the mainland.

The beginning of the end for Benjamin Purnell came in 1923. After years of complaints by minor women and their mothers, accusations of indecent conduct escalated into morals charges when some women and 13 young girls came forth and accused Purnell of seducing them in the name of religious faith. A subpoena was issued by the court for him to appear and face those charges, but it could not be served because nobody was able to locate him. Hence, a warrant was issued for his arrest, and he was listed as a fugitive.[96] Purnell went into hiding for three years, during which time several newspapers offered rewards for his arrest, the largest being $1,000 by the *Detroit Free Press*, while it continued writing scathing articles against him and the commune.[97]

On November 17, 1926, bold headlines in the *News-Palladium* and papers across the country read: "Benjamin Purnell Under Arrest; Seized at Midnight at Colony." Although the accompanying article said the police broke down the doors at colony headquarters (Shiloh) with axes to get him, he was actually found at the Diamond House Annex in a peaceful action.[98]

After hiding for three years, he was finally arrested on November 16 after a former colony member, Bessie Daniels Woodworth, who had left the commune in 1925,[99] told the police he had been hiding at the commune the entire time, protected by loyal followers.[100] All were surprised to find "a vastly changed man shrunken with illness" hiding in his bed in his second-story bedroom, where he had apparently been from the beginning.[101] He was taken to jail but was soon released on bonds totaling $120,000, put up by local businessmen.[102]

In 1927, Purnell faced numerous charges, the most salient as follows: having illicit sex with women and minor girls as a religious rite; defrauding his followers; teaching his followers to perjure themselves in order to protect him; and teaching followers to obstruct justice by hiding him.[103]

There was a sensational trial in southwest Michigan in 1927 that was essentially reported in newspapers throughout the United States. Because Purnell was ill and frail, he was only required to appear in court on days when he testified.

> Purnell was brought to the court house in an ambulance; three body guards carried him in on a stretcher; and the witness chair was removed while Benjamin Purnell reclined on his cot as he testified. He looked weak. He wore a cap pulled down over his long gray hair. Although he admitted being a bigamist, he made a sweeping denial of the charges preferred against him, one at a time, saying, "No," or "I never did." Purnell's voice was so weak the stenographer asked him to speak up for the benefit of the court.[104]

In the end, after a trial that lasted from May 17 through August 17, 1927, with a delayed verdict that was not rendered until November 10 of that year, none of the charges of sexual misconduct were proved, but Purnell was convicted of religious fraud.[105]

As a result, the court banished Benjamin and Mary Purnell from the commune, ordering them to sever all ties with it, and the colony was to be placed in receivership until a new leader could be selected.[106] On December 16, 1927, Benjamin died from complications related to diabetes and tuberculosis.[107] Members of the commune, believing in Purnell's teachings that the faithful can not die, kept his body in state at Diamond House, awaiting the promised resurrection. Michigan law required embalming of the dead within 72 hours, and that was done; then his body was returned to Diamond House for all to view.[108]

Thanks to the persistent efforts of Mary over the following two-year period, the fraud conviction was overturned by the Michigan State Supreme Court. On June 3, 1929, headlines in the *Herald-Palladium* read: "Supreme Court Rules in Favor of House of David. Colony Scores Sweeping Victory Before High Tribunal. Receivership Lifted. Davidites Left to Carry On Colony Affairs as They May Elect."[109]

However, due to intense in-fighting over commune leadership, their troubles were not over. Judge H. T. Dewhirst from Redlands, California, a former businessman and elected civil court judge who joined the commune with his family in June 1920, had immediately gained Benjamin's confidence. He was soon appointed to the powerful position of Secretary of the House of David, where he always functioned as Benjamin's right-hand man. This forced Francis Thorpe, who held that position since 1908, to step aside begrudgingly. Following Benjamin's death, Dewhirst challenged Mary's authority as well as her ability to follow in her husband's footsteps as commune leader.[110]

The essence of the matter involved more than control of the commune which, according to some scholars, was taken by Dewhirst when he re-wrote by-laws after Purnell's death and stripped Mary of the financial control she had been given at the commune's founding.[111] Perhaps more important were policy discrepancies which impacted the entire future of the commune and the direction it took going forward.

Historian Ron Taylor, whose loyalty has been to Mary's City of David since his arrival there in 1974, summed it up as follows: "Benjamin had no successor when he died. Mary was the legal heir because the properties were entrusted to her and Benjamin as a single unit. Because of that she became sole trustee." However, sustained legal back and forth between Mary and Dewhirst was difficult for everyone. Hence, to put an end to it, Mary Purnell and Judge Dewhirst finally agreed to dissolve the commune and divide assets.[112]

The terms of the division of assets have always puzzled historians. It was decided that the Dewhirst faction would remain at the original House of David site and receive $60,000 cash. In the property settlement, they retained ownership of several farming properties and were awarded High Island, though by that time the island's ventures were virtually non-existent. Today the uninhabited island, considered one of the most beautiful in the state, is owned by the State of Michigan and managed by the Michigan Department of Natural Resources.[113]

Financial interests and holdings of the House of David were estimated, though never verified, at as much as $10 million. Mary kept all the money that was in her name and Benjamin's name alone, separate from the House of David funds. In addition, she received the House of David Hotel (still under construction), the commune's largest farming project (the 400-acre Rocky Farms near Berrien Springs), several other farm projects,[114] and the right to use the name "The Israelite House of David as Re-organized by Mary Purnell."[115]

She divested herself of all holdings in the House of David, relinquished her leadership role, and left. Mary and 217 followers, approximately half the population at that time, purchased property across the street about a half-mile away and established the Israelite House of David as Reorganized by Mary Purnell, which was officially incorporated in March 1930. It was later commonly known as Mary's City of David, or just City of David.[116] Members of this group initially lived in tar-paper shacks and tents while, for the second time, they rolled up their sleeves, built residences, and created an attractive new community in just seven years.[117]

The two communes existed two blocks apart, and members of each, though staunchly loyal to the faith, were different. Members of Mary's faction were primarily people from the largest farms and the last returnees from High Island. There was an immediate excitement as they began building their new commune. The Dewhirst faction consisted primarily of business people and office personnel. Ironically, they coexisted peacefully though they didn't interact with each other as families or friends for many years.[118] Throughout its existence, the commune was conducive to the fulfillment of personal potential, an atmosphere that continued after the schism.[119]

Mary's City of David catered to a large Jewish clientele, saying the Christian House of David and City of David considered Jews as cousins who were always welcome, and it became an attractive and welcoming place for Jewish vacationers. By 1938, it had grown to include a motel with Mary's Vegetarian Restaurant and Bakery; a vacation complex of log cabins and Paradise Park Cottages; and a synagogue for Jewish resort guests.[120] In addition, thanks to funds raised by Jewish doctors from Chicago, they built and operated the King David Hospital and Clinic, known as the only kosher hospital in the country which, without explanation, closed after only 18 months in operation.[121]

Under Dewhirst's leadership, the House of David also continued to expand. He constantly reminded the media, "no other institution has done so much to put Benton Harbor on the map as the House of David." Other sources described the commune as "the biggest industry in the area,"[122] with continued operations of Eden Springs Park, an amphitheater, a beer garden opened after the repeal of prohibition, and a new motel called the Grande Vista Motor Court, considered years ahead of its time, which included gas stations on both sides of the road. In 1933, they built the largest greenhouse in southern Michigan,[123] and the House of David Cold Storage was reportedly the largest open-air fruit and vegetable market in the world.[124] They also owned and operated the Oldsmobile-House of David Motor Sales, where they sold Oldsmobiles, Cadillacs, Chryslers, and LaSalles.[125]

Things had gone so well that Judge Dewhirst threw his hat in the ring in the 1936 Congressional election.[126] He ran as a Republican in the Fourth Congressional District in Michigan. Despite the support he had due to his business acumen, he was unsuccessful. Clare E. Hoffman, with an 8,000-vote lead,[127] handily won the seat in the November 3, 1936, election.[128]

It's often written that the intelligence, inventiveness, work ethic, and devout religious commitment of the commune, in addition to the national prominence gained by the baseball teams, put Benton Harbor and Berrien County on the map. Their prosperity survived the impact of World War II, when several members were conscripted into the military as conscientious objectors, and continued into the mid–1950s. But the writing was on the wall: the inability to sustain a viable membership by recruiting new members plus the departure of grown children and others who, it is said left the colony but not the faith, and the anticipated toll of celibacy, natural attrition occurred as members passed away.

Attendant deterioration occurred throughout as there were fewer and fewer members to run businesses and maintain the properties. According to material presented by

Dr. J. Gordon Melton of the Institute for the Study of American Religion, membership in the House of David was recorded as 350 in 1935, 150 in 1955,[129] and by 1966 the numbers were reduced to fewer than 100 aging members.[130]

Mary's Hotel and the House of David's Eden Springs Park both closed their doors in 1975. Mary's Jewish resort in the City of David was closed to the public in 1976. The community as a whole, still self-sustaining with rental properties and limited agriculture, went into seclusion for many years until 1997. Since that time, Mary's City of David has become a living-history site with Ronald Taylor offering summer tours.[131]

At a meeting of the Saugatuck-Douglas Historical Society in 1992, former Benton Harbor Library historian Florence Rachuig, whose grandfather arrived with his four children as an original member of the House of David in 1903, recounted spending several years collecting and cataloguing Israelite literature and records in which she repeatedly referred to "the infamous Ben Purnell." She said, "From 1903 to about 1907, the City of Benton Harbor treated the House of David members as weird strange people and some of them were downright antagonistic towards having them there. Slowly that changed and the townspeople grew to respect and protect them."[132]

House of David and City of David Communes

Throughout the years, the commune continually built housing, offices, businesses, and the famed Eden Springs Amusement Park.

Entrance to the House of David Commune, 1926. This bridge connects the Jerusalem House (left) and the Bethlehem House (right) (courtesy Brian Ziebart, House of David Commune archives).

Shiloh House, completed in 1908, built to house the commune's administrative offices on the first floor and provide member housing on the upper floors. In 1972 it was added to the National Register of Historic Places (courtesy Brian Ziebart, House of David Commune archives).

The House of David Zoo, one of the commune's first attractions, initially housed a variety of animals brought with new members from Australia in 1905 (courtesy Brian Ziebart, House of David Commune archives).

1. Commune History 31

Entrance to the House of David Amusement Park (courtesy Brian Ziebart, House of David Commune archives).

House of David Restaurant and guest residences (courtesy Brian Ziebart, House of David Commune archives).

Early photograph of the House of David Ice Cream Parlor, always a favorite gathering place at the commune. Benjamin Purnell is in the foreground in his white suit; Mary Purnell is next to him (courtesy Brian Ziebart, House of David Commune archives).

The miniature railway was one of the most popular attractions at the amusement park. Note the "official" Railroad Crossing sign and the sign on a tree directing visitors to another popular spot, the midget auto speedway (courtesy Brian Ziebart, House of David Commune archives).

Embarking at the miniature railway depot passengers could ride the train to many locations throughout the amusement park (courtesy Brian Ziebart, House of David Commune archives).

One of a variety of concession stands in the amusement park which always featured homemade "goodies" and other items (courtesy Brian Ziebart, House of David Commune archives).

The cars used at the midget auto speedway were built at the commune machine shop (courtesy Brian Ziebart, House of David Commune archives).

Earl Boyersmith (center) in an area of the House of David Machine Shop (courtesy Brian Ziebart, House of David Commune archives).

The bowling alley using the pin-setting device they invented called "Uncle Sam's Bowling Machine." Signs in rear read as follows: "Bowling Alleys Are Manufactured and Sold by the House of David" (courtesy Brian Ziebart, House of David Commune archives).

Mary's Shiloh at City of David, with members out front circa, 1932–34 (courtesy Ron Taylor, City of David Files).

Free parking for all visitors (courtesy Brian Ziebart, House of David Commune archives).

Bethany House in the 1930s where George Anderson, John Tucker and Doc Tally lived (courtesy Ron Taylor, City of David Files).

Mary Purnell after Benjamin's death during the era when she successfully saved the commune from going into receivership (courtesy Ron Taylor, City of David Files).

Synagogue built at Mary's commune for Jewish guests in 1938 (courtesy Ron Taylor, City of David Commune Files).

Mary's City of David Bakery (courtesy Ron Taylor, City of David Commune Files).

Mary's City of David Vegetarian Cafe, a popular attraction throughout Benton Harbor and beyond (Ron Taylor, City of David Commune Files).

2

Play Ball!
The Legend Begins

Benjamin Purnell was a fierce advocate of healthy exercise like hiking and bicycling but favored baseball, which he called "a very scientific sport."[1] He especially encouraged learning the game as a way for the young, celibate men to work off excess energy.

Despite the fact that he was the consummate opportunist, always seeking financial means to support the commune, at this time sending out barnstorming teams was an afterthought. However, by the time the House of David squad entered their ranks, barnstorming teams were dominated by talented Negro clubs who found it their only available avenue to play the game. Through them, barnstorming had become popular in every city, town and hamlet across the country, and they would offer substantial challenging competition for the men of the House of David.[2]

The first decade in Benton Harbor was a busy construction period when the major buildings of the commune were erected. Concomitantly Purnell hired Floyd Fitzsimmons, owner of the Speed Boys, a local semipro team, to build a 3,500-seat ballpark for his team at Eden Springs in 1910.[3] It was understood that the park could be used by Purnell's team when the Speed Boys were on the road. By the mid–1920s, the park was also rented out to other successful semipro teams in the area.[4]

Fitzsimmons was also the manager of boxer Jack Dempsey, who won the World Heavyweight Championship in 1919, then defended his title in Benton Harbor in 1920 at the new open-air arena.[5] Decades later, at age 95, the last surviving member of the House of David baseball team, catcher Lloyd Dalager, recalled the open-air arena that had become a magnet for various activities and celebrations in the area. He said that when he was seven years old, he used to climb onto the roof of the commune barn to watch the people arrive.[6]

When Purnell saw the skill level of the young team and realized baseball could be another money-making proposition for the commune, he put forces dedicated to the development of a competitive baseball team in motion. He wanted a barnstorming team sent out with the twofold goal of spreading their religious message to recruit new members and earning money for the coffers of the commune.

Purnell was in charge of all job assignments in the commune. In that capacity, he appointed colony secretary Francis Thorpe to the twofold job of mentoring the young men into players and developing them into a good competitive team. The challenge was a big one. But with the help of commune players Jesse Lee Tally and his two brothers, Barlow and Swaney,[7] Thorpe turned out to be more successful than even Purnell

One of the earliest ballgames by Thorpe's new team at House of David Park, circa 1915 (courtesy Brian Ziebart, House of David Commune archives).

could have imagined. He had excellent rapport with the young players, many of whom were from Australia and Germany and had never seen a baseball game before. From the beginning, they enjoyed learning the rules of the game and took it seriously as they became fundamentally sound. They mastered offensive and defensive skills: effective hitting, base running, sliding, stealing, and bunting. All of this converted into wins on the diamond.[8]

Prior to 1910, their baseball was considered a loosely played version of rounders, and seen as after-school recreation only. But once the ballpark was completed, they were permitted to use it for their training and eventually played well enough to work out with the Speed Boys. Soon they faced and defeated some of the best factory teams in the region before they tested the waters against teams in the broader Michigan region in weekend games. By 1912, they played against and defeated some of the best local factory-sponsored teams in western Michigan,[9] which caught the interest of the local community.

From 1912 through 1914, their games had been more or less pick-up games in the western Michigan region, which allowed them to continue to develop their skills. Gradually, as word of mouth aroused interest in the youthful team, more and more fans attended their games, and they charged admission.[10]

In 1969, 72-year-old Howard Olson, who began his career in baseball before becoming a well-known St. Joseph entertainer and silent film actor who often played opposite Charlie Chaplin, found a 50-year-old photo of a House of David team of 1923–1924 (vintage based on their uniforms) in one of his scrapbooks.[11] Olson was a promising young pitcher who had made quite a name for himself with the Speed Boys, the St. Joseph Locals, and the Saginaw Ducks in the Southern Michigan Association, 1913–1914.

Players ready to play an exhibition game: the United States Cavalry team, front right, House of David players grouped behind them (courtesy Brian Ziebart, House of David Commune archives).

However, during a tryout with the White Sox in June 1915, he injured his pitching arm. In his attempt at a comeback on the day before Labor Day, 1916, the last game he ever pitched was a 2–1 loss against the House of David, which he called a very good team. He especially remembered how the David players ran the bases so fast that their caps flew off and their long locks flew behind.[12]

Even before they officially barnstormed outside southwest Michigan, the House of David squad was considered a unique team, primarily because they represented a religious commune. Many were too young to have much of a beard at that time. One scorching Sunday afternoon in July, the grandstand was packed for a doubleheader involving two different opponents, a common practice at that time. The House of David handily defeated the "traditional" opponent, the Onward Athletic Club of Chicago, 9–3, in game one, which was scheduled for seven innings. In the nine-inning second game, they faced their most unique challenger to date: the United States Cavalry Troop D, a mounted unit that arrived on horseback. That game was called after seven innings with the score tied "because the players were fatigued."[13]

Later that month, the Waites "Come and See" brought a large entourage of fans with them to face the young Davids at Eden Springs Park. After an exciting afternoon of baseball in which regular pitcher Jesse Lee Tally was absent and was replaced by Frank Wyland, it was the first time the home team was unable to hit opposing pitching. They were handed a 7–2 defeat, their first of the year against local teams.[14]

August saw a demonstration of just how far the skills of the young commune players had come. It began when they hosted the Chicago All Stars at Eden Springs Park for a highly publicized game which turned out to be a pitching duel that kept members of the large crowd on the edge of their seats. Led by the best hitting to date by young Richard Marcum and Frank Hornbeck, the game wasn't decided until the bottom of the

Game day at House of David Park draws another sell-out crowd (courtesy Brian Ziebart, House of David Commune archives).

ninth inning. When the dust settled, House of David was on top, 3–1, in what has been described as one of the best games played on the Eden Springs diamond.[15]

The House of David team began to test its competitiveness among existing barnstorming teams in hopes of attracting larger crowds. One unique method was a June 4, 1914, game advertised as "Free! Free! Free! House of David team to play Chicago Onward Athletics, June 7."[16] Perhaps it was their way of testing the waters with the more established semipro teams, as Benton Harbor fans saw a lot of semipro baseball which often included appearances by Cy Young following his retirement in 1911.[17] In mid–August, after the House of David defeated Berrien Springs at the Young People's Picnic, the press announced that "the House of David team wishes to tender their thanks for the courteous treatment and hearty cheers given them."[18] They were anxious to represent the commune and Benton Harbor in the world of barnstorming baseball.

In 1915, Francis Thorpe, who would adroitly manage the House of David and later Mary's City of David teams for a combined 17 years, 1912–1930, presented the first *uniformed* House of David team. Always sporting a fluid roster, this group consisted of 14 players, only five of whom would play in future seasons: Ezra "Cookie" Hannaford, Paul Mooney, Frank Wyland, Jesse Lee Tally, and Swaney Tally.[19] Considering the circumstances, they played well together as they began establishing themselves as a money-making proposition.[20] From that point on, they stretched their wings and played in small towns farther and farther from Benton Harbor.[21]

As the House of David team expanded its playing territory, tournaments among barnstorming teams entered the scene, with teams from Kansas, Oklahoma, Utah, New Mexico, Nebraska, Montana, and Colorado participating.[22] The *Denver Post* Tournament, DPT, first played in 1915, the only ones in which the commune clubs participated

First known photograph of the House of David team in their new uniforms, 1915. Standing L-R, Frank Hornbeck, Horace Hannaford, unidentified, Swaney Tally, Manager Francis Thorpe, Paul Mooney, Jesse Lee Tally, Frank Wyland, Monroe Wulff. Sitting L-R, Ruben Jaft, Ezra Hannaford, Richard Marcum, unidentified, Barlow Tally. Benjamin Purnell standing to left in street clothes (courtesy Brian Ziebart, House of David Commune archives).

(1932, 1934) has been described by many sources as one of the necessary precursors to the integration of major league baseball.[23]

Initially, it was an annual invitational tournament organized and played by white semi-professional teams outside the perimeters and restrictions of organized baseball, with significant prize money offered to the top three teams. It grew in size and prominence until it reached its pinnacle in 1934. That year it invited the first black team, the highly respected Kansas City Monarchs, to participate in hopes of appealing to larger crowds. This attracted national attention as the first major competition of the 20th century in the United States to bring black and white teams together in something other than exhibition games.[24]

The tournament was the creation of two employees in the circulation department of the popular *Denver Post* newspaper,[25] Jabe Cassidy and Frank Newhouse, both respected umpires in the region. Cassidy later became West Coast circulation director for Hearst Publishing. Newhouse, on the other hand, remained in Colorado and wore many hats as a paragon on the sports scene for more than 30 years that included time as a bird dog scout for major league baseball.[26] The owners of the *Denver Post*, Fredrick Gilmer Bonfils and Harry Heye Tammen, known as "Bon and Tam," supported the project as one of many events their paper sponsored over the years.[27]

The early success of the DPT resulted in expansion far beyond that boundary. With an average of two games daily, the annual competition generally lasted up to ten days, then longer as more teams participated. The loss of two games resulted in a team's elimination. A required "guarantee of appearance" deposit of either $100 or $200 (depending on the source) was returned to each team upon elimination. Because the number of participating teams from year to year was not written in stone, the first-second-third place money varied accordingly.[28]

Practically from the get-go, the norm was for teams to fortify their rosters with additional players, including former major leaguers, who added to gate receipts while helping their teams win. Therefore, each letter of invitation included a list of guidelines and protocol concerning player eligibility. The rules, which remained essentially unchanged for the life of the event, were as follows:

1. players in organized or outlaw ball on or after July 4 of the season involved are barred from participation;
2. organized or outlaw baseball teams that have a schedule with two or more games a week are also barred;
3. any team playing an illegal player will result in automatic forfeiture of games ... but ... one pitcher who has played organized or outlaw ball will be allowed on each team entered if he has not played after July 31;
4. five men can be added to each ten-man team but only two can be from Class A level or higher, and they must stay as part of the battery only;
5. players from Class B or under can remain on the extras list and may perform at any position. All tournaments will be managed by the participating teams while the *Denver Post* newspaper will act as sponsor for the event.[29]

"Play Ball!" was shouted for the first *Denver Post* Tournament game in September 1915, in Broadway Park, built in 1893 as the home of the Denver Bears in the new Western League. By prearranged agreement, the tournaments would be played while the Bears were on scheduled road trips.[30]

Throughout its existence, each of the annual DPT tournaments had a personality of its own, beginning with the 1915 event, when the team from the Colorado farming town of Brush won first place money, $400.[31] For the price of a 15-cent bleacher seat or a 10-cent spot in the grandstand, fans saw Brush's future major league pitcher Rolla "Lefty" Mapel garner 27 strikeouts in a 12-inning, 8–2 victory over the Lithias from Pueblo, the last-place finishers. It was a record that was never broken.[32] For that effort, he was given an engraved gold baseball.[33] Mapel went on to appear in four games with the St. Louis Browns in 1919, accruing a record of 0–3,[34] then pitched for different tourney entrants over the years before managing the Sedalia Athletics in the early '30s.[35]

During that 1915 season, a military team presented itself to face the locals in a game of baseball in Benton Harbor. It was quite a spectacle as 60 mounted soldiers of Division A, Fifth Cavalry were well received as they rode through Benton Harbor to the local fairgrounds, where they encamped for two days. After a reportedly exciting game (no score available), they continued on travels of their own.[36]

The House of David approached the 1916 season with confidence as they continued learning the game and how to work together as a team. And the face of the roster was changing. In addition to five players returning from the 1915 squad, Jesse Lee Tally, Swaney Tally, Cookie Hannaford, Frank Wyland and Paul Mooney, commune members Glenn Klum, Barlow Tally, Horace Hannaford, Frank Hornbeck, Austin "Tex" Williams, and Jerry Hansel became part of the squad. They would soon be recognizable and popular within the ranks of barnstorming baseball.

During 1916, the Benton Harbor crew discovered just how good they were as they took on their most grueling schedule to date, playing weekend games with some of the best teams in the region. They were up to the task as they won the Berrien County Championship[37] after facing such teams as the Waites "Come and See," Coloma, Water-

House of David team, circa 1916 (courtesy Brian Ziebart, House of David Commune archives).

vliet, the Galien Grays (champions of the south end of the county), the Dowagiac Independents, the Vicksburg Nine, the Mishawaka Boosters, and the Glendora Grays, as well as some teams who came to Eden Springs Park from Chicago: the Chicago Onwards, Dolan's Athletics of Chicago, and the Chicago Ashlands.[38]

While two-game sets were played on Saturday and Sunday, three-game series stretched to the following Saturday. Briefly, during the season, a confusing pattern was noted when local newspapers pointed out that the club won most of the games played at Eden springs Park but seemed to be jinxed in other parks on the road.[39] In any event, they were on their way, entering a world without leagues, standings, or official schedules, only games scheduled by team promoters or set up by the teams themselves as they toured. They attracted larger and larger crowds as time passed. For three decades, they competed against some of the best semipro teams as they traveled throughout the United States, southern Canada, and northern Mexico.

From the beginning, the battery of Paul Mooney and Jerry Hansel, plus the pitching talents of Jesse Tally, steadily gained prominence. By August 1917, Mooney had won every game he pitched.[40] When they won the rubber game of the three-game set against the Galien Grays, considered "the other best team in the county," in a series described as a slugfest, Eden Springs Park became known as a hitter's paradise.[41] The two nines faced each other in late September for their final series in what the *Chicago Defender* reported as the best series of the season, when a packed house watched the Davids shine.[42]

By this time, the House of David's second team or junior team, comprised of younger players in the commune, played primarily at Eden Springs against local factory teams like the Covel Manufacturing Company. It was their version of a farm team years before Branch Rickey developed the concept. The *Fort Wayne Journal-Gazette* reported on September 23, 1917, that, to the delight of the fans, before every game they gathered in full uniform and boarded one of the miniature trains that crossed through the commune and dropped them off at the ball park. It was during that time that a young pitcher, Hubert "Hip" Vaughan (given the nickname after major league pitcher James "Hippo" Vaughan), first caught the eye of the press.[43] He subsequently graduated to the traveling team and played from 1918 to 1922.[44]

After the season, Thorpe took advantage of their status as Berrien County Champions and formed an All-Star team, advertising them as "the best team of Israelite Athletes," resulting in many connections and invitations to play beyond southwest Michigan into northern Indiana, Chicago, and Wisconsin.[45]

In addition to baseball, during those formative years the players conducted brief prayer meetings before their games to explain their faith, which they hoped would be an effective recruitment tool.[46] Years later, popular infielder George Anderson recalled, "When we were first starting out we used to talk about religion before the games, but later we didn't do that. People didn't care to hear about it. They wanted to see us play."[47]

Cookie Hannaford and his first wife Violet on their wedding day. Sadly, she took ill with the Spanish Flu and died a couple of years later (courtesy Brian Ziebart, House of David Commune archives).

Unlike today, common methods of player recruitment of that era were long lists in the want ad sections of newspapers throughout the country, soliciting players and playing dates: "Feeney's Owls, a newly organized semipro team is open to book games with first class teams in Indiana"[48]; "The Gasoline Supply Company would like to book games with first class semi-professional teams desiring games."[49]

As time went by, similar ads which included listings of future appearances of teams in varied locations became the convenient way to let fans know when teams were coming to their areas and inform those who wanted to play to come try out.[50] Finally a new publication in Brooklyn, *The Citizen Daily*, featured a regular column, "Players seeking positions-Clubs seeking players," that worked well in the Northeast.[51]

Once, when the House of David needed to hire non-commune members, the team managers wrote personal letters inviting players of special interest they had seen to join

Players boarding the miniature railroad train on their way to the ball park. They did this for years to the delight of the fans (courtesy Brian Ziebart, House of David Commune archives).

the team. This effort was enhanced by hired booking such as Eddie Phalen, Ray Doan, and others who also had the responsibility of scheduling and promoting games.

On January 20, 1917, when many ballplayers nationwide were serving in the military, an interesting if not surprising player-recruitment article appeared in the *Oakland Tribune*, which more or less addressed semipro baseball as a threat to organized professional baseball: "Semipro clubs are gathering the cream of the talent. Minor league baseball as represented by Class B, C and D is being killed off by the increasing attention given to semipro baseball. Semipro teams pay bigger money for 4–8 games a month than Class C clubs pay players for 30 days of playing."[52]

In an attempt to present a lighter side, an entertaining article appeared in several newspapers about the barnstorming circuit giving the readers an alleged "bird's eye view" of an umpire's job at one of the House of David games in 1917. The following is a brief excerpt:

> "What sort of a day did you have yesterday?" asked an acquaintance of the umpire. (No umpire has a friend.)
>
> "Rotten," said the umpire. "I'm good and sore, I am. I'm hired to go up to Benton Harbor and umpire a game between a fast semipro team from Chi and the team from Benton Harbor. When I gets there and they ain't no one on the field except the team from Chi, but the grand stands is all filled up. When I seen it I nearly took a Brodie. It was filled up with a brass band of dames wearin' pants and a lot of guys with long hair and whiskers they could of run for president with. They looked like a lot of hair restorer ads.
>
> So after a while the Benton Harbor team comes on the field, and believe me, if I hadda been hittin' the old red eye I would of sworn off right there. I thought they had rung me in to umpire a game with the bloomer girls because that Benton Harbor team looked like the Seven Southerland Sisters. They had hair down their backs like a bunch of poets. Then I seen they wasn't dames because some of 'em was wearin' a full set of whiskers.
>
> So I says to myself, 'I am goin' to have a cinch with this bunch because if they make a kick on any of my decisions I am goin' to pull a handful of their foliage out.'
>
> But when I seen 'em practicin' I changed my mind. They was there forty different ways. They

sure could handle that old pill. But it was all wrong. A guy with a full set of bushes and hair like a poet ain't got no right to be a ballplayer...."[53]

Proud of winning the Berrien County Championship in 1916, the team began its 1917 season with much fanfare and a parade led by grand marshals Benjamin and Mary Purnell, followed by the House of David Brass Band. For the first game, the players rode one of the miniature trains from the amusement park through the commune to the baseball park.[54]

It's often said that one way of judging a team's caliber of play is by the quality of its opponents, and Thorpe's team eagerly proved the accuracy of that.[55] After defeating factory teams, they were invited to play everywhere around Berrien County in 1917.[56] They stepped up a notch when they joined the Inner-City Baseball Association of Chicago, a very popular consortium formed in 1887 that originally consisted of the best eight independent regional teams, mostly sponsored by local businessmen. They faced the Chicago Leland Giants, Barber Colts, Gunthers, Chicago Union Giants, Chicago All-Stars, Carnations, Marquettes Roseland Eclipse, and Rube Foster's Chicago American Giants.[57] That 30-game season ended with a 17–13 record, a winning percentage of .567.[58]

At the conclusion of the season, Thorpe wrote a heartfelt letter of appreciation to the men on his young team, acknowledging their efforts and progress:

> Beloved Brethren, I'm wishing to compliment you for the excellent progress you have made in the two years since our organization began public exhibitions. I hereby present to you a tabulated record of this season's work. The patronage we enjoyed during the fall games was more eloquent than words. Nevertheless, I have received many compliments and expressions of appreciation of you from the fans! These expressions bear out the record that all semi-pro teams have the fight of their lives against you, even though they use the highest class batteries obtainable.
>
> With best wishes for the winter season, and trusting you may all be with us with the usual "pep" I am yours for the only game worthwhile, Francis Thorpe, Mgr.[59]

During those early years, members of the pacifist colony went about their lives as storm clouds of war continued the threat of eruption in Europe, until everything changed on June 28, 1914, when headlines the world over reported the assassination of the heir to the throne of Austria-Hungary, Archduke Franz Ferdinand, and his wife while on tour in Sarajevo, Bosnia and Herzegovina. Europe plunged headlong into World War I, The Great War, that would not end until November 11, 1918. In accordance with his campaign promises, President Woodrow Wilson delivered a Message of Neutrality to Congress, explaining his efforts to keep the United States out of the conflict. But the ability to keep that promise became impossible as the situation in Europe worsened.[60]

President Wilson warily addressed a joint session of Congress, asking for a declaration of war on Germany on April 6, 1917, and six weeks later, Congress passed the first conscription law requiring all males between ages 18 and 45 to register for the draft, which impacted the House of David and its baseball team. Purnell wrote a patriotic letter to the president the following day, requesting religious exemption from the draft for commune members, explaining they were well-known pacifists and able to contribute to the war effort in numerous other capacities. His request was denied.[61]

Thus, eligible men in the House of David commune registered for the draft, and 33 (some sources say 35) were drafted, including two baseball players taken in the very first draft, Monroe Wulff and Manna Woodworth. Later, as many as two dozen men from the House of David were also drafted. Within three months of the declaration of war, construction began on Camp Custer in Battle Creek, Michigan, a recruitment center for new inductees from the Midwest.[62]

All House of David recruits were sent to Fort Custer, where things were made difficult for them.[63] The *New Philadelphia Daily Times* mockingly wrote that the conscientious objectors from the House of David would rather have their throats cut than their beards.[64] Though selected as conscientious objectors, they were not treated as such. From the get-go, they had explained that it was against their religion to fight war, or handle guns and munitions. They endured hard work, the lack of vegetarian meals, as well as constant ridicule and condemnation from those around them. But when they were assigned to the quartermaster corps with the duty of loading and unloading raw beef, they refused, again citing their religious beliefs.[65]

They were threatened with court martial and a year's imprisonment at Leavenworth for their actions. However, at the last minute, they were given the choice of prison or remaining soldiers and working on the military farm.[66] Shortly thereafter, Jesse Tally, Allen Holliday, Dick Calahan, and some others from the House of David decided to be test cases on the matter of conscientious objection. Eventually a military commission made the decision to keep all conscientious objectors together with assignments of farm labor.[67] Tally later said, "The nickname 'Doc' was bestowed upon me because I was sent to a cavalry unit to groom horses—sort of a veterinary assistant."[68]

After news of this reached Benton Harbor, things were made difficult for the entire commune and its place in the overall community. But the baseball team continued barnstorming throughout the region without any difficulties. At home, colonists were generally unpopular and collectively labeled as unpatriotic slackers. In addition, the governing council of the nearby township of Watervleit Village passed resolutions forbidding all advertisements of baseball games and any other literature from the House of David.[69]

Finally an angry Francis Thorpe responded with a front page column in the *News-Palladium* in which he succinctly explained how the commune was patriotic in other ways: they provided much food for the military from their farms; they gave benefits for the Red Cross; and the House of David Band, which he said was worth $100 a night, performed without charge wherever needed.[70] Another column titled "Letters from People" was inundated with letters stating the many ways the House of David was patriotic and had assisted in the war effort.[71]

A more-publicized and not uncommon way the commune honored the war effort was with regular free fireworks displays, always advertised as "distinctively House of David Fireworks" and always called "the biggest and best of the season."[72] Other events often began with a game, such as with the Chicago Roseland Eclipse, the Goshen Grays, and others who came to town. "Enjoy the best in baseball while your wives and children are entertained in a clean park by the famous Ladies' Band. Admission: 25c + 2c war tax; grandstand 10c + 1c war tax."[73]

At the same time, the baseball team prepared for spring training for the 1918 season. The press took notice of their long hair and bearded appearance while referring to them as "a ball team that has become the terror of semi-professional teams around Chicago and Southwest Michigan."[74] One article in the *Brooklyn Daily Eagle* reported, "The House of David Team Plays Good Ball Despite Their Camouflages."

Overseas the war effort trudged on, while at home newspapers around the country featured articles about the value of the baseballs themselves in anticipation of

The House of David Band, circa 1922. Music was always important at the commune. Every year several players took time off from baseball to tour with the 20-piece band, then return to the team. Some members included Charlie Falkenstein, Glenn Klum, Horace Hannaford, Dwight Baushke and Cookie Hannaford (courtesy Brian Ziebart, House of David Commune archives).

the approaching 1918 season. Fans were requested to return foul balls retrieved in the stands during past seasons because the government needed to use the horsehide outside as well as the rubber and yarn on the inside for the war effort. Additionally, they asked all teams to reduce the number of balls used in games for the 1918 season.[75]

Judging by early publicity for the 1918 season, the Davids eagerly anticipated the success it would bring. The newspapers wrote that the House of David nine had been much strengthened in several places to give their fans the same class and exciting performances they had seen in 1917.[76]

Two young players recruited from High Island, shortstop Walter Faust and first baseman John Tucker, were later regarded as two of the colony's best ballplayers of all time. Jewel Boone, ace pitcher for the 1919 Girls Team, a player personally discovered by Purnell, who had the men teach her how to pitch,[77] recalled:

> John Tucker and Walter Faust spent time on High Island as kids when it was a vacation spot. The baseball team went up to the island where they had a nice [playing] field and garden. Someone told the officers we had some baseball players up there and one of them was John Tucker. So the news was that Tucker had left his family there and was sent down to play baseball in the spring.
>
> Purnell went to watch Tucker play ball on what some say was his one and only trip to the island. He was pleased with what he saw. Everything was good. But when word came along that the commune needed help in the fields for harvest, one of the kids picked for the task was Tucker. When the ferry reached the mainland, he was picked up and taken by horse-drawn wagon to the farm. The baseball team was all in a dither about the whole thing because he was supposed to be practicing. They went out to the farm to get him and were told, "He's working here and we need him. You guys go play your game. We're working here."

So they went to Purnell, who went out to the farm and said, "Tucker plays ball!" So that was the end of that.[78]

Perhaps best of all was the return from Camp Custer of Jesse Tally, who reported that his pitching arm was better than last season and he looked forward to facing their first opponents, the formidable Chicago Union Giants.[79] The first game of the season was played Sunday, May 5, Decoration Day, a national holiday declared in 1868 to honor the Civil War dead. The large, enthusiastic crowd at Eden Springs Park left in disappointment as the host club suffered a 2–0 defeat. Even worse, the Davids got only two hits while committing five errors.[80] Nevertheless the future looked bright.

Not to be down long, after a few adjustments, a consistent first team roster emerged as the core traveling squad: Charley Falkenstein, Ezra "Cookie" Hannaford, Horace Hannaford, Jerry Hansel, Frank Hornbeck, Glenn Klum, Paul Mooney, Jesse Lee "Doc" Tally, Hubert "Hip" Vaughan, Art Vieritz, Austin "Tex" Williams, Frank Wyland, and Manager Francis Thorpe. According to a photo found in the House of David Museum, the 1918 roster was the last squad comprised exclusively of commune members.[81]

Young John Tucker when he was first recruited for the baseball team from High Island. His excellence at first base and his sense of humor made him a favorite for many years (courtesy Brian Ziebart, House of David Commune archives).

According to reports in both the *Chicago Defender* and the *News-Palladium*, in addition to the Chicago Union Giants, some of the other nines they played that year included Michigan City, the Goshen Grays, the Chicago Barber Colts, the South Bend Hoosier Creams, the Chicago Ivanhoe club, the Chicago Carlisle Athletic Club, the Chicago Holy Name Athletic Club, the Chicago Garnet Social and Athletic Club, the Gary White Eagles, the Indiana All-Stars, and the South Bend Silver Edge. During the period, the black teams were independent, constant road travelers without parks of their own due to lack of finances.[82] In lieu of season schedules, the barnstormers, both black and white, had fluid "catch as catch can schedules," comprised of frequent pick-up games. In addition to all this, the House of David teams were always open for visitors to challenge them at their own park in Benton Harbor.

Recordkeeping and newspaper coverage were always welcome reading in local papers, though more or less haphazard. Articles were often less than accurate regarding such salient information as teams involved, winners, losers, and infrequent box scores with players listed by last names only that were frequently misspelled. Of course things were better in some places and with some newspapers. One glaring exception was the American humorist and sports writer noted for major league coverage, Ring Lardner, who periodically mentioned the adventures of the House of David in his syndicated column, "In the Wake of the News by Ring W. Lardner," that appeared in papers from coast to coast.[83]

Lardner wrote a colorful account of a 1918 game the House of David squad lost to the Goshen Grays on July 8 at Eden Springs, noting that Ezra Hannaford was listed on the scorecard simply as "Cookie," and the way the manager gave signs to his players by "waving his ringlets in different combinations." He was especially amused by the ad on a left field fence that invited batters to "hit it and win five free baths."[84] One of his favorite topics was the progress and success of up-and-coming House of David pitcher Paul Mooney.[85]

When the Armistice was signed on November 11, 1918, ending the Great War, the nation still had many issues on the table. There was the Great Pandemic of 1918–1919—a world-wide influenza epidemic that infected 28 percent of Americans, resulting in an estimated 665,000 deaths that absorbed the attention of the medical community.[86] In addition, labor unrest, strikes, and race riots permeated the headlines as the Great Migration, urged forward by the *Chicago Defender*, continued. The Negro population moved north, seeking work in factories and escape from the Jim Crow racism that still lingered in the South. Between 1916 and 1918, many black communities and black-owned businesses emerged as nearly 500,000 people were drawn to northern urban centers. Chicago alone experienced a population increase of approximately 200,000 between 1910 and 1930.[87]

The *Chicago Defender*, an advocate for and defender of black causes, was founded in 1905 by Robert S. Abbott, who originally published the newspaper in his apartment. In 1910, he was able to hire his first employee when circulation increased from 300 copies per print run to over 500,000 by 1920. Historians consider it the first owned and operated black newspaper with national influence.[88]

The last year of the decade was an exciting one at the major league level as baseball fans nation-wide watched Kid Gleason manage Charles Comiskey's Chicago White Sox to the pennant with an 88–52 record. The other seven teams finished as follows: Cleveland (84–55), New York (80–59), Detroit (80–60), St. Louis (67–72), Boston (66–71), Washington (56–84), and last-place Philadelphia (36–104).[89] Chicago loved the team and its players and eagerly awaited what they considered a "cinch" victory in the coming World Series against Manager Pat Moran and the Cincinnati Reds that would long be remembered for the prowess of the White Sox.

Instead it's remembered in the annals of baseball history for what became known as the Black Sox Scandal, when eight White Sox players were accused of taking money from gamblers to throw the Series and were later banned from the game for life by new Commissioner of Baseball Kenesaw Mountain Landis.[90]

To this point, things at the commune concerning baseball were positive and reflected the growing success of the team as a unit as well as the development of its young players. They had a good spring training in which the overall improvement was obvious. Added to that was the promise of new uniforms which would reach them in time to make their debut in the second game of the season.

The first game, part of a two-game series against the National Veneer Products team from Mishawaka, Indiana, described as "one of the fastest teams in Northern Indiana," was scheduled for Friday, April 27, at Eden Springs Park.[91] The excitement generated was not dampened by the team's 11–8 loss in front of a large crowd on a very cold day. The second game of the series was scheduled for the following Sunday with a battery of Paul Mooney and Jerry Hansel leading the way as the team bagged a 2–1 victory.[92]

It was immediately apparent that the team had adopted a more aggressive style of play evidenced by substantially improved fielding and batting skills. In addition to base stealing, they added the art of double-steals which quickly earned them the moniker of "Speed Boys."[93] They continued to play in the Midwest against such solid teams as the Indestructors of Mishawaka, the South Bend Overlands, the Chicago Hartford Giants (billed as the "fastest traveling colored team in the world"),[94] the Gary, Indiana, White Eagles, the Stationery Independents of Kalamazoo, and the hard-playing Michigan City Dolls, who made the long-haired squad work hard for a 7–2 win. By this season, the pre-game prayer meetings were already abandoned, and historians noted the new focus of the team changed from entertaining to winning.[95]

The House of David team as a unit was an established staple in the local press, with Jesse, later dubbed "Doc," Tally and Paul Mooney emerging as the first stars, Tally for his pitching and key hitting, and Mooney, who also played left field, for his pitching acumen. When Tally was less than great, it was newsworthy, often page one news: "Tally pitched a fair game—did not seem to have his usual pep. He allowed seven hits and two walks."[96]

It seemed Mooney could do no wrong. From the end of the 1918 season, he was mentioned as one of the heroes if not *the* hero in every outing he made. In July, it was reported that "Mooney pitched very well and is improving his batting."[97] During the course of the season, he caught the eye of several major league clubs. In fact, writers began articles about their games saying "Mooney looks about as good as any pitcher in the big leagues today."[98]

When he pitched a no-hitter against the tough team from Kalamazoo in October, Chicago Cubs manager Fred Mitchell had a lot to say. He said the team had played brilliant baseball against the best semipro teams, and Mooney's pitches were comparable to those of Eddie Cicotte, known as one of the best American League pitchers of the day. It was reported that Mitchell announced he had signed Mooney for $20,000, and he was destined to go to spring training with the Cubs.[99] Some sources say the offer was $25,000.[100] However, his prediction that the young pitcher would sign was premature. Mooney declined, allegedly because the Cubs wanted him to cut his hair and shave his beard, both against his religion. It was later noted that Mooney said he "didn't want to become affiliated with professional baseball."[101]

But similar offers did pop up as he continued his career with the House of David. The following year, 1920, the New York Yankees said, "Mooney is just about in a class all by himself."[102] They offered him $30,000 to join them. Again he declined. According to the *Bristol Press*, after his final season with the House of David in 1921, Ty Cobb, the first-year manager of the Detroit Tigers (1921–1926) did everything he could to lure Mooney into his ranks, without success.[103]

Until this time, the young women in the commune played baseball for recreation within the commune and used the Eden Springs diamond when the barnstormers were on the road.[104] They tested the waters in 1919 and were sent forth as the first House of David Girls Team. They played successfully against other ladies' teams in the area, both African American and white teams. Write-ups of their first game said they were "ballplayers who show speed and class with an unusual and unexpected display of clever plays" as they defeated the Chicago Colonels Colored Ladies' team, 7–6. In addition to the slick play, a midget pitcher on an opposing club, known only as Miss Caldwell, amused the crowd with many spectacular one-handed catches as her team lost the hard-fought game.[105]

During the 1919 season, there were often ads in the local paper billing them as the second game of a doubleheader: "Morning game, 9:30, House of David men vs. Buchanan—afternoon game, 2:30, House of David Girls Team will play a ladies team."[106] As the season progressed, they faced top teams in the region such as the All-American Ladies Team from Chicago which, like all their games, attracted large crowds of curious onlookers to see baseball highlighted by the music of the House of David Ladies Band, which had become a fixture at each game.[107]

They received numerous invitations and released regular press announcements of upcoming games that always attracted large crowds as they went on to an undefeated 1919 season. However, just as with the 1919 Chicago White Sox, the House of David had a baseball scandal of its own when it was later discovered that things were not as they seemed with the Girls Team. Six or seven "ladies" on the squad were frauds. These young men with rosy cheeks instead of beards due to their youth wore the girls' uniforms of skirts and shirts. In their book, *The House of David Baseball Team*, Hawkins and Bertolino identified six of them as Dwight "Zeke" Baushke, the Jackson brothers, Luther and Arthur, Dave Harrison, Elijah Burland, and Oscar Sassman. In a 1983 interview with Clare E. Adkin, Melvin Tucker identified the boys, including himself, as shown on a picture postcard of the girls team.

House of David Ladies Band at the entrance to the commune. The men's band is on the porch in rear, circa 1910 (courtesy Brian Ziebart, House of David Commune archives).

The House of David Girls Baseball Team in 1919, the only year of its existence. With the "assist" of seven young men wearing girls' uniforms they won the 1919 championship. However, when the truth was discovered their title was taken away (courtesy Brian Ziebart, House of David Commune archives).

As things worked out, three of them went on to play with the House of David ballclubs: Oscar Sassman, 2B, played for the junior team in 1918 before he joined the traveling team in 1923; David "Egg" Harrison, 3B, started with the traveling team in 1923, and in 1927 he managed the junior team while continuing to play with the traveling team through 1929; Dwight "Zeke" Baushke played shortstop for the traveling team from 1920 to 1923.[108]

When the hoax was uncovered, the team's record was invalidated and it was divested of its championship, then dissolved after its one-year existence.[109] One colony member recalled years later, "Sometimes we boys played on the girls team and nobody knew the difference."[110] When asked why they went along with the hoax, Baushke said, "It was a chance to play."[111]

By the end of the decade, the reputation of the House of David baseball team was firmly established. They were heavily solicited and welcome visitors every place they went. From the very beginning, their bewhiskered teams were the terror of all Michigan and so colorful that it was impossible for them to fill all of their baseball and band commitments.

The lineup for the 1919 travel team, called the first team, had become stable with manager Francis Thorpe and ten players the crowds counted on seeing: Glenn Klum, CF; Austin Williams, 2B; Ezra Hannaford, 1B; Jerry Hansel, C; Frank Wyland, LF; Hip

Vaughan, C/P; Horace Hannaford, SS; Charley Falkenstein, 3B; Jesse Tally, OF & P; Paul Mooney, P.[112]

After just four years of learning the game and playing an abbreviated barnstorming schedule, the House of David nine was firmly on its way to taking its place in baseball legend.

3

The Twenties
*The Bearded Beauties
Roared on the Diamond*

The legendary "Roaring Twenties" was a decade that began with much excitement and promise in the United States. As the country celebrated the end of the Great War—the war to end all wars—it moved forward socially and economically into an era of hedonism and conspicuous consumption. It was a time of vigorous economic growth as technology in one form or another improved the standard of living for all. Sociologists agree that the most prominent factor was refined and enhanced assembly line production that began with the Model T Ford,[1] the "Tin Lizzie" (1908–1927), and then[2] expanded to refrigeration, appliances, equipment and parts, and more. New factories dotted the landscape, more in the industrialized North than the agrarian South, which created thousands of steady jobs. The need arose for a more efficient road system as the society became more mobile for work and pleasure, which also eased travel for barnstorming baseball teams.

In homes, the radio became the first mass entertainment medium of the populace; away from home, the movie industry moved from small nickelodeons into larger and sometimes grand theaters, luring families with such stars as Charlie Chaplin, Buster Keaton, Rudolph Valentino, Clara Bow, Mary Pickford, Lillian Gish and others who reach stardom in the final years of the decade, when[3] silent films evolved into "talkies."[4] On the literary front, books from American authors such as F. Scott Fitzgerald, who introduced the term "Flapper" that became identified with the "new American woman" of the era that he named "the jazz age," Ernest Hemingway, Sinclair Lewis, William Faulkner, Edna Ferber, T. S. Eliot, Pulitzer Prize-winners Willa Cather, Edith Wharton, Eugene O'Neil and others presented insights into and critiques of the new American culture.

Shortly before, Charles "Lucky Lindy" Lindbergh had completed his legendary non-stop solo flight across the Atlantic to Paris in 1927,[5] and Adolf Hitler wrote *Mein Kampf* without recognition in the United States. Both lent a peek into the future. Meanwhile the euphoric attitudes of the Roaring Twenties raged unimpeded until the stock market crashed in 1929.

The House of David team joined the world of barnstorming baseball world near the end of the Deadball Era, 1901–1919,[6] when the game was all about pitching and defense. An article at the www.historicbaseball.com website summed it up as follows: games were low-scoring because the balls were softer and more difficult to hit long distances; balls were not often replaced during games no matter how scuffed, dirty, or difficult for batters to see; and the spitball (and other "trick" pitches such as the shine ball, mud ball, greased ball, etc.) was not only alive and well,[7] but as recently as 1914 it was considered "the greatest asset of a pitcher's repertoire."[8]

However, on August 16, 1920, in the fifth inning of a game between the Yankees and the Indians, Cleveland batter Ray Chapman was hit in the head by a spitball thrown by Carl Mays[9] and died of a fractured skull within 24 hours.[10] Debates that had been ongoing about banning the pitch became more intense,[11] and the spitball was officially outlawed[12] though the law was not retroactive. Many successful major league pitchers who depended on that pitch for their bread and butter were permitted to continue using it for the duration of their careers, but it was no longer a legal pitch for newcomers to the game. The last pitcher who legally threw a spitball, Burleigh Grimes in 1934, was inducted into the Hall of Fame in 1964.[13]

During this time, a different baseball appeared on the scene. It was more tightly wound and livelier, which allowed the batted ball to travel a greater distance. Hence the Deadball Era gave way to an era of power hitting. In January 1920, it was announced that Boston owner Harry Frazee had sold Babe Ruth to the Yankees.[14] To the delight of fans everywhere, Ruth hit 54 home runs in his first season in New York. The live ball era had arrived, relegating the Deadball Era to its place in baseball history.

As the House of David squad prepared to begin the decade when they would make their mark in the barnstorming arena, organized professional baseball experienced a shock that resulted in a very significant change. After the Black Sox Scandal, the name Kenesaw Mountain Landis came to the fore following months of discussions, disagreements, and flat-out arguments among major league owners regarding the need for and

Touring cars used by the House of David teams. Regular driver Hans Dalager and player Tom Dewhirst prop themselves on the car on the left, while players David Harrison and Percy Walker pose on the right (courtesy Brian Ziebart, House of David Commune archives).

the powers of a commissioner of baseball to oversee the integrity of the game. Landis was elected and accepted the position as baseball's first Commissioner on January 12, 1921,[15] with the stipulation that he would have full and unchallenged control to rule or he would quit. The *Pittsburgh Daily Post* headline summed it up as follows: "Landis Threatens to Quit but Later Accepts Ball Dictatorship: Curtailing Power Causes Argument; Moguls Acquiesce."[16]

Barnstorming, in existence for decades before the House of David commune was founded in 1903, was the only venue available for African American baseball players. To review, shortly after the Civil War, 1867, what has been called the first public baseball game played between two all-black teams saw the visiting Philadelphia Excelsiors defeat the Brooklyn Uniques, 42–37.[17] Over the next 20 years, 200 all-black independent teams appeared nationwide despite Jim Crow laws and related traumas of racism. From that time forward, African American players made multiple attempts to establish leagues of their own but generally failed due to weak leadership, poor financing, and the lack of home parks.[18]

But there were notable exceptions which resulted as Negro baseball history being permanently intertwined with that of the House of David as they provided exciting exhibitions over the years. The Negro National League (NNL) (1920–1931; 1933–1949) was the first of a small number of successful barnstorming leagues that played the highest level of black baseball in America at that time. Founded by visionary Andrew "Rube" Foster, considered among the best pitchers of his race and later known as "the father of Negro organized baseball,"[19] the NNL was comprised of eight teams from the Midwest: Chicago Giants, Cuban Stars, Dayton Marcos, Detroit Stars, Indianapolis ABCs, St. Louis Giants, Kansas City Monarchs, and Foster's own team, the Chicago American Giants.[20] Foster served as president and commissioner.[21]

The league played its first game on May 2, 1920. In late December, Q. J. Gilmore, sport scribe of the *Kansas City Sun,* looked back on that season and noted that the league had garnered over 700,000 paid admissions in its first year and surmised, "Baseball used to be a barroom game but it is now a social function."[22] Unfortunately, Foster's health failed due to an accident in an Indiana hotel in 1925. This, coupled with his workaholic habits, resulted in his death in 1930.[23] The impact of losing Foster plus early pressures of the Depression were considered the main factors in the collapse of the NNL in 1931.[24]

Two years after the league was established, many thought the cost of traveling from the East for games was simply too expensive.[25] That's when Ed Bolden, owner of the Hilldale Daisies out of Philadelphia, often dubbed "the Czar of Negro Baseball,"[26] took the reins and formed the Eastern Colored League, ECL (1923–1928), and populated the six-team league by raiding the rosters of NNL teams.[27]

The Negro Southern League (NSL, 1920–1936), founded by Thomas K. Wilson, owner of the Nashville Elite Giants,[28] functioned as a kind of "feeder system" for the Negro National League. It included teams representing the largest cities in the South: the New Orleans Ads, Nashville White Sox, Birmingham Black Barons, Knoxville Giants, Montgomery Grey Sox, and Pensacola. However, it was always considered a minor circuit due to instability, as over 80 teams played in the league throughout its lifetime.[29]

The Second Negro National League (1933–1948) was put together by a former bootlegger and shrewd businessman, Gus Greenlee, also known as "Big Red" because of his reddish-brown hair.[30] His goal was to make his team, the Pittsburgh Crawfords, the most powerful baseball team in America.[31] Although his motives were purely financial, one of Greenlee's most memorable acts was to "loan" (some sources say "rent") the great Satchel Paige and his catcher, Bill "Cy" Perkins, to the House of David for the 1934 *Denver Post* Tournament.[32]

Other leagues that appeared as the years passed included the American Negro League, East-West League, League of Colored Baseball Clubs, and West Coast Negro Baseball League.[33] Teams from different Negro Leagues always provided challenging and popular competition for the House of David teams throughout their existence.

Just as barnstorming was essential to the survival of Negro League teams,[34] so it was with the Benton Harbor squads, although their experiences were always very different. Years later, many Negro players discussed the fun they had despite it being a rough life: shoddy travel conditions, living out of suitcases, banned from eating or using restroom facilities in all-white establishments, sleeping on buses or infrequently in barns when they were permitted. Rare showers were always a treat. One Kansas City Monarchs player, Dink Mothel [sometimes spelled Mothell], said the thing he remembered most about those days was being hungry.[35] Roy "Bubba" Johnson, whom J. L. Wilkinson invited to join the Monarchs in 1920 after he played on Wilkinson's All-Nations club in 1919, left baseball after the 1922 season despite his affection for "Wilkie" and good pay because of poor travel conditions and racial prejudice he experienced. He said, "People yell and clap for you while you're playing, but afterward you can't even get a sandwich."[36]

J. L. Wilkinson had made a concerted effort to spare his team from being on the receiving end of such discrimination, as he worked with Harry Peebles of the Semi-Pro Baseball Association to gradually establish a "circuit of friendly communities" where the players could eat, sleep overnight with Negro families, and have improved travel conditions as they toured.[37]

Meanwhile, as the Roaring Twenties captivated the rest of nation with new, relaxed societal values, elements of the culture of the Jazz Age and its flappers, as named by writer F. Scott Fitzgerald, were only felt in a minor way within the commune.[38] Instead its energy was more focused on other matters: dissatisfied commune members sued for back pay and the return of their property they said was gained fraudulently. In addition, morals charges appeared against Purnell dating as far back as 1910, when he was first accused of violating young girls and women. Things came to a head in 1923, when he was officially charged and went into hiding for three years to avoid arrest. The baseball team played through it all, and the public, for the most part, was essentially unaware of it.[39]

Their routine had been established from the beginning. At the start of each annual trek, the players literally squeezed themselves, their personal belongings, cooking utensils, and baseball gear into vehicles with "House of David" painted on the sides and hit the road. They initially traveled in two Twin Six Packards and a Cadillac Eight, all seven-passenger vehicles.[40] Later they changed to a Packard and two Studebakers until they eventually used their own bus with "House of David Baseball" boldly painted on the side.[41] The commune could afford this comfortable mode of travel, which not only gave them the freedom to avoid the restrictions of rigid train schedules, but also gave them the ability to insert additional games whenever possible.

Just as was done by barnstorming Negro teams, they frequently parked alongside the road, removed the seats from the cars, prepared meals, and sat together in groups called "broom handles" while they ate and discussed plans and strategies for upcoming games.[42]

In a 1996 interview when he was aged 87, outfielder Tom Dewhirst recalled, "In those days there were very few paved roads. Often a player would have to get out of a car to open a gate in a cattle fence for the caravan to continue." Many times the roads were muddy and players had to push the vehicles, which sometimes made them late for appearances, but the crowds always waited for them. Upon arriving at their destinations, usually dirty and hungry, they quickly donned their uniforms and played baseball.[43] There were no make-up games in barnstorming baseball, and a missed game amounted to a missed paycheck.

The fans on the road quickly learned the names of regulars on the traveling roster, either from press announcements of upcoming appearances or from seeing them in action. Though always fluid, the lineup was still composed predominantly of commune members: pitchers Jesse "Doc" Tally (team captain) and Paul Mooney, Ezra "Cookie" Hannaford at first base, Zeke Baushke at second base, 19-year-old Charlie Falkenstein at third base, 16-year-old Walter Faust at shortstop in his first year with the squad and the only player without some semblance of a beard, outfielders Horace Hannaford,

Tom Dewhirst, 1930. He began with the junior team and joined the travelers' team at age 19. He became a power hitter who led them in home runs from 1919 through 1933 with a season average of 38. The fans flocked to games to see him. He was also well known for his good sportsmanship (courtesy Brian Ziebart, House of David Commune archives).

Glenn Klum, and Artie Vieritz, and a catcher named McCarthy. First baseman Cookie Hannaford later recalled, "Success on the field did not come easily the first year and we lost nearly half our games. From the start, Doc Tally and shortstop Walter Faust were considered by most to be as good as any minor league player in organized ball but the rest of us weren't so great."[44]

Right from the beginning, they perfected the skills taught by Thorpe and presented a style of play that was all their own. They worked hard and mastered the double steal, the strategic bunt for hits, and the pop-up or bent-leg slide which ended with the runner upright and ready to take another base if the ball was misplayed. These strategies were not only aggressive, flashy and entertaining but were considered new for the time.

Their first taste of fame, as a team and individually, was accompanied by their growing understanding of the required work ethic, responsibility, and endurance of press scrutiny required for success. Throughout their existence they launched each season in the deep South with a seven- to ten-day spring training, generally in Mineral Wells, Texas, or Hot Springs, Arkansas, before they worked their way north as far as New Hampshire as the weather grew warmer.[45]

At the same time the team accepted more and more invitations, their schedule became more and more hectic. It was not uncommon for barnstorming teams to play two games in two different towns in one day, then load up right after the final out and head out to drive all night to the site of the next day's competition. In April, after being soundly defeated, 12–6, in Hyattsville, Maryland, in a morning game, they hurriedly left for an afternoon game "a couple of towns over."[46] This schedule eventually became more the norm than the exception. It was a difficult and stressful lifestyle that most players thoroughly enjoyed.

July 1920 was a particularly fast-paced month. On their way to New York, they participated in 12 games and found themselves on the short end of the score in six. One of those, with Heinie Zimmerman's Bronx Giants, was a hard-fought battle viewed by their largest crowd to date, more than 6,000. Despite their best effort, the game got away from the Davids in the 12th inning. The following day's coverage of the game in the sports page of the *Brooklyn Daily Eagle* was headlined, "House of David Odd, but Oh My How Those Whiskered and Long Haired Persons Can Play Ball."[47]

That same month, a substantial article in the Sunday edition of the *Boston Post* featured large photos of Paul Mooney and Cookie Hannaford, describing Mooney as a prized, long-haired "slabster" who was almost in a class by himself, and Cookie Hannaford as "a player with plenty of ginger, snap, and pepper," adding that they were considered comparable to the best semipro players in the country.[48]

Later that same week, the Benton Harbor crew was saluted in an issue of the Mid-Week Pictorial in the *New York Times*. Despite their photo erroneously identifying substitute pitcher Hip Vaughn as Mooney, who was unable to play that game, the feature was a colorful tribute to the entire team.[49] They were scheduled to leave the New York region after a handful of games, but in response to the demand of a large fan base in the region, they remained over two months and pocketed over $23,000.[50]

Shortly after watching a game between the House of David and the New York Yankees, owners Colonel Rupert and Colonel Huston praised the general talent of the squad but took special notice of pitcher Paul Mooney and first baseman Cookie Hannaford, both with the team since 1917. They invited them to join the Yankees and "play with Babe Ruth,"[51] offering both what were considered astounding salaries.[52] At the time, Ruth was in the middle of one of his best-remembered seasons in New York following the long-disputed trade from Boston. The Babe was on his way to swatting 54 homeruns and logging a .376 batting average.[53]

The accolades for the two baseballers continued to appear in papers across the country, describing Mooney as looking as good as any major league pitcher with his speed, control, and hitting. They added that Hannaford was a wiz on first base who got all throws no matter now high or low they were. In response, Hannaford reported, "We have a new pitcher with our club, Hip Vaughan, who promises to outclass Mooney and we look for him to do wonders for us this season."[54] Additional sportswriters said Mooney "had a baffling 'floater' that rivaled that of Eddie Cicotte when that gent had his heart in the game."[55]

Mooney refused the Yankees, explaining, "I play the game merely for the pleasure of being in the suit," but when newspapers got word of this, they speculated that the turn-down from both players was because their religion prohibited cutting their hair as required by major league rules.[56] According to the *Bristol Press*, Ty Cobb, then player-manager of the Detroit Tigers (1921–1926) was also enamored with Mooney, but unable to sign him.[57]

This early in their barnstorming history, there was no doubt the House of David players were crowd-pleasers who put on a good show. Twice in July, over 10,000 patrons turned out in Brooklyn to see them face one of the leading Negro teams in the country, the Atlantic Bacharach Giants. They first faced each other at Ebbets Field in Brooklyn, where articles about that game agreed that the Giants' speed on the base paths earned their victory. Later, at Shibe Park in Philadelphia, a crowd of 22,000 watched them lose, 4–2.[58]

A few weeks afterward, they responded to constant public demand and appeared for a return engagement with the Bacharach Giants.[59] The large crowd showed up for the event on a cold, rainy afternoon and restlessly endured a weather delay until an umpire came out and asked them if they wanted the game to be played at all. He was met with a resounding, "PLAY BALL!" But the game was soon called when the field began flooding.[60]

First baseman Cookie Hannaford began playing baseball at the commune in 1914 and went with the traveling team 1917–1927. In 1922 he turned down offers from the New York Yankees to remain with the Davids (courtesy Brian Ziebart, House of David Commune archives).

One week later, the Benton Harbor squad faced the Bacharach Giants in front of 2,000 curious fans who expressed disappointment that the team got only one hit while making three errors. The press said the Michigan team "appeared tame and never had a chance."[61]

Generally, though not always, comments in the press were the same no matter the outcome of their games: "They fielded some of the most exciting baseball players in America."[62] Announcing an upcoming game with the Bethlehem Steel Leaguers, the *Harrisburg Telegraph* described them as "the most unique, exciting, and popular barnstorming team on the circuit that has been drawing crowds larger than big league games in Philadelphia and other cities where they have appeared."[63] Unfortunately for the boys from Michigan, two days later the same paper reported that they were no match for Bethlehem, blaming poor running and a lack of hitting for their 8–3 loss.[64]

The *Evening Report* had announced the upcoming game with the Davids, billing them as "the greatest thing for Lebanon since baseball was inaugurated." Interest in seeing the bearded squad in action was so keen that over 3,000 fans paid double gate admission to see them. However, after the locals trounced them, the same paper described the game as "a fiasco, a fizzle from the go-off." Disappointed fans concluded about the House of David team, "their press agent is their best asset."[65]

Another newspaper added its two cents by saying, "P. T. Barnum said the American people like to be hum-bugged once in a while, but the performance of the House of David was about as poor an exhibition of ball as was ever witnessed in these parts ... and the H. of D. will surely *not* be asked for a return engagement."[66] Unfavorable press continued when they lost in close, 3–2 game in the 12th inning to a crack Negro team, the Washington Giants, in what was reported as a contest mercifully called in the seventh inning due to rain. The Davids were called a team that showed "no baseball of exceptional worth."[67]

Game rained out! Although they played many games on wet and muddy fields over the years, this field was way too waterlogged (courtesy Atwell Family Collection).

However, after 12 contests on their tour in New York, headlines in sports sections throughout the region indicated they had regained favor with their fans.[68] By this time there was no doubt that Paul Mooney had become "a star attraction just about in a class by himself." Later in the season, over 4,000 fans crowded into Athletic Park in Scranton, Pennsylvania, anxious to see him pitch. They were not deterred when they learned he was not scheduled that day as they continuously clapped and yelled, "Send in Mooney!"[69]

By August 1920, the negative response had gradually declined. One article began by touting the team as "among the fastest in the country" whose ability may be "in their long locks." It concluded by continuing the focus on the merits of Paul Mooney, describing him as being "as great as Grover Cleveland Alexander ever expected to be or as full of wizardry as Walter Johnson ever had been."[70]

This spotlight remained on Mooney and never faded throughout his career. By the end of the season, when they were scheduled to play the Titusville Independents in Pennsylvania, the local news announced that "all stores in Titusville will close at 4 PM Friday so that clerks can see the game."[71] Over time, closing businesses during their scheduled games became commonplace.

Meanwhile, as news of the Black Sox Scandal came to the fore, threatening the legitimacy of the entire sport, the crew from Benton Harbor pushed forward, remaining oblivious to the addition of a commissioner and debates over his duties.[72] Judge Landis, known for his disapproval of off-season barnstorming tours in general, later issued an edict banning major league players from pennant-winning teams from engaging in barnstorming tours.[73] Little attention was paid to this among semipro barnstorming teams who were not covered by that umbrella. Instead, their efforts and energies remained focused on their own endeavors.

The House of David club was scheduled to play the opening game of the 1921 season at Kokomo against the all-black Hoosier Giants at Southside Park. They would face the Ethiopian Clowns the following week at the same park.[74] Unfortunately for the Davids, but a typical part of barnstorming baseball, the game against the Ethiopian Clowns was called after three innings due to a sudden rainstorm that drove the fans away. The vehicle carrying Francis Thorpe and Paul Mooney had broken down five miles from the city and was unable to get to them to the game before it was called.[75]

Through it all, their popularity continued to multiply, and the arrival of the House of David nine was eagerly anticipated everywhere. Such names as Jesse "Doc" Tally, Paul Mooney, Walter "Dutch" Faust, Dwight "Zeke" Baushke, Hubert "Hip" Vaughan, Horace Hannaford, Ezra "Cookie" Hannaford, Glenn Klum, and Arthur Vieritz were becoming household words around the circuit.

The schedule of this "quirky and cutting edge group of barnstormers"[76] was increasingly busy as they attempted to accept all invitations and challenges, requiring them to expand their travels significantly. Although they played at a high level of skill, it has been said that their pitchers frequently, and not too cleverly, doctored the baseballs by rubbing their fingers on their beards during games.[77]

By 1922, the press had picked up on their popularity, and a pattern of seeing the same article in multiple papers in advance of their appearances became commonplace. For example, an article by Norman E. Brown titled "Bearded Baseball Team Ready for Season, Develops Stars,"[78] appeared in such papers as the *News Herald*, May 2; *Hutchison News*, May 4; *Charlotte News*, May 5; *Hamilton Evening Journal*, May 12; *San Bernardino County Sun*, May 18; and the *Capital Times*, May 29.

In an earlier tour in Connecticut (1921) when they played Bridgeport, New Haven, Torrington and others, the scheduled conflicts rendered them unable to include the Bristol New Departures, much to everyone's disappointment. But in 1922, after completing a planned three-day trip to the Boston area that stretched beyond six weeks in response to public demand, they took their 65–28 record to what became the first of many annual appearances at Muzzy Field. This home of the New Departures in the manufacturing city of Bristol, Connecticut, was located in a large public park and was often written about as the perfect setting for big games because it was the largest and best-built park in the state.[79]

After their initial visit, the *Bristol Press* and the *New Departure News* both wrote about them as "the bewhiskered gentlemen from the Michigan lake shore resort who

House of David Roster, 1922. L-R. Dwight "Zeke" Baushke, 2B; Walter "Dutch" Faust, SS; David Harrison, 3B; Jesse "Doc" Tally, P-OF; Glenn Klum, INF; Art Varietz, CF; Manager Francis Thorpe; Austin "Tex" Williams, OF; Charlie Falkenstein, C; Horace Hannaford, INF; Hip Vaughn, Cookie Hannaford, Paul Mooney, P. (courtesy Brian Ziebart, House of David Commune archives).

looked like a bunch of decrepit old men though the majority of them were still in their early twenties and capable of displaying a snappy brand of baseball."[80]

In May 1922, after losing two games in Louisville, the team stopped for a second exhibition game with Evansville, Indiana, of the Class B Three-I League (Indiana-Illinois-Iowa, the oldest minor league that existed 1901–1961), where they lost once again.[81] Although it was suggested that the Benton Harbor nine later played in the Three-I League circa 1940, my research was unable to confirm this.

In August, sporting their popular moniker of "Bearded Beauties," the team embarked on its New England tour, where they drew some of the largest crowds of the season. During this time, while the Red Sox floundered in the cellar averaging 3,200 fans a game, the House of David drew 4–5,000 per game and on a few occasions attracted up to 10,000.[82]

Earlier there was a near riot at their home park in Benton Harbor when the Davids faced the Chicago Mutes. When the Davids came from behind in the late innings to win the game, Chicago fans in the stands stood up and yelled, "Frame-Up!" then chased the umpire from the park and gave him a first-class beating. Headlines about the incident read, "Riot Ends Ball Game."[83] Later that same month, after they won three games in a row before overflow crowds, newspapers reported their "utter shock" when, on July 17, Paul Mooney suffered a 2–1 loss to New Buffalo despite allowing only four hits.[84]

By the end of September, *News-Palladium* headlines said, "Israelite First Team, Flushed with Victory, Returns from Big Tour," which Thorpe called the longest and most successful tour to date. In the 110 games played, the 16-player squad earned a 72–38 record and played some of the best semipro teams of the day while traveling from Chicago to Memphis, back across Illinois to Michigan, Indiana, through Ohio to Western New York and Massachusetts, where they were headquartered in Boston. Thorpe called the entire season the most successful ever played by his young team, saying "the batting and defense were the best [he] had seen from them and pitchers Paul Mooney, Doc Tally, and Hip Vaughan were excellent."[85]

Still another element that was to become forever part of their legend was born on October 22 that year. As they completed pre-game conditioning during a brief stretch of games in Benton Harbor, Doc Tally and Dutch Faust "accidentally" added to their already unique repertoire while playing a game called High-Low, a fast-paced exercise they interlaced with comedic antics.

Thorpe immediately noted fan approval and saw it as a way to get more publicity and sell more tickets. He kept it as part of their daily routine. Later when Faust left the team, John Tucker, who always entertained the crowd with "crazy antics and trick plays at first base" during games, took Faust's place.[86] The novelty, vaudeville-type act quickly morphed into the famed pepper game, described as "a most entertaining baseball juggling act,"[87] which the House of David has always been credited with inventing.

It became one of the most famous exhibitions in barnstorming baseball. Described as a great show of baseball magic rivaling Houdini, it was a combination throwing-juggling act in which a "batter" and three "fielders" did everything but swallow the ball. In addition, they hid balls in their beards and did their impression of shadow ball as the fans tried to see the ball that wasn't there.[88] The pepper game team consisted of the same three fielders who continually perfected the antics, while the batter changed from one day to the next. From then on the pepper game, whose players changed over the years, was always highlighted and touted as "worth the price of admission."[89] Eddie Deal, longtime catcher and later manager of the home team (1929–1946), remembered

House of David traveling team, 1922 (courtesy Brian Ziebart, House of David Commune archives).

that pepper was "actually so popular that when games were rained out fans demanded to see pepper anyway. In response Lloyd Dalager, Davie Harrison and I went on the field barefoot and obliged."[90]

However, major change was in the air as five of the original and best-known colony players left the team at the end of that season to follow other pursuits: Austin "Tex" Williams (2B-OF, 1917–1921); Horace Hannaford (3B, 1917–1921); Paul Mooney (P-OF, 1917–1921); Glenn Klum (CF, 3B-P, 1917–1921)[91]; and Charlie Falkenstein (C, 1917–1921) who, despite being offered tryouts with two International League teams (Rochester and Toledo), continued his baseball career with Menasha, former Wisconsin State champions.[92]

Their departure was coupled with an increasingly hectic schedule as the House of David accepted more and more challenges from any team anywhere in the country, which necessitated the hiring of non-commune players, called "outsiders," after 1922 to fortify their rosters. Outsiders were not required to join the commune or practice the faith, but growing long locks and beards were a must. Among the first group were George "Lefty" Gilbert, Burnett Fish, Chick Buyesse, and Max Wolfe, who joined the nine in time for the David's appearance at Muzzy Field in Bristol, Connecticut.[93] The most noted was Bill Heckman, who used to drive from Detroit to Benton Harbor to pitch on Sundays before he was hired on a more permanent basis. During his ten-plus-year stint with the House of David and later the City of David, Heckman played first base and the outfield, often entertained as a clown, and was especially popular with the ladies.[94]

Colorful John Tucker demonstrating a classic pepper game stunt (Ron Taylor, City of David Commune Files).

Despite attempting to limit the number of outsiders, the addition of former major and minor leaguers became a necessary norm for the rest of their existence.[95] John Pickett, pitching ace for Cheyenne, later explained that semipro teams, including the House of David, had many excellent players. Using himself as an example, he said that after he graduated from the University of Nebraska in 1922, he had a tryout with the Chicago White Sox, who decided to send him down to the AA American Association for seasoning. Instead, he started his own law practice and played semipro ball on the side.[96]

The 1923 season was greeted with great anticipation. As usual, though aware of the Gentlemen's Agreement, the House of David chose to ignore the racial overtones and implications in organized baseball. Instead they continued scheduling exhibitions with all-comers, most of whom were independent Negro and interracial teams.

To emphasize their point, in early April, at the House of David Park, Eden Springs Park (the names were often interchanged), they faced and defeated the Fort Wayne Giants, easily the fastest team they'd opposed since early 1922.[97] Now revered as "the Traveling All-Stars in Benton Harbor," they were scheduled to face the La Porte, Indiana All-Stars, a team which included seven former major league players. With manager Champ Jackson, the only black manager handling an all-white team at that time, they were considered hard to beat.[98]

But the Davids, determined to pick up where they left off in 1922 despite all the changes in their roster, defeated La Porte, 7–3, in a Sunday afternoon game in front of an overflow crowd. The press facetiously concluded, "With another week of practice the Israelites are expected to put up a game with a faster team."[99] On Decoration Day, now known as Memorial Day, the first team played the Fort Wayne Kips, described in the press as "a crack white team."[100] In early June, they hosted the Grand Rapids Colored Athletics for two games. The first was tight and the second was a wild one. The Davids took both.[101]

During this time, news about the accusations against Benjamin Purnell for sexually abusing numerous young women in the name of religion resulted in internal problems at the House of David commune. Word of this, both fact and rumor, was covered nationally,

Players circa mid-twenties. Front row L-R, Dutch Faust, Cookie Hannaford, David Harrison. Back row, Zeke Baushke, Leslie Bell (courtesy Brian Ziebart, House of David Commune archives).

often as front page news. There was no doubt that it was a scandal that put the existence of the entire commune in peril. When a subpoena was issued for his arrest in February 1923, Purnell failed to appear. The press continually reported he had gone into hiding and disappeared. However, House of David historian Brian Ziebart said he was told by catcher Lloyd Dalager, there at the time, that Purnell was actually protected by loyal followers as he was "hiding in plain sight" in the Diamond House Annex at the commune. In addition, he even made trips to town to see how construction on the commune's hotel was going.

He remained in hiding for three years in an attempt to avoid the scandal and consequences of his alleged illicit conduct with minor females, and other misbehaviors.[102] By mid–June 1923, Purnell's dilemma appeared everywhere in the form of a huge wanted poster issued by Roy C. Vandercook, Commissioner of Public Safety in Michigan, offering "a suitable reward" for his arrest and return to the Michigan State Police.[103]

Ironically, some reporters knew how to spin this into a positive for themselves. For instance, in anticipation of a game against the McConkeys of Wheeling, the *Coshocton Tribune* stated, "promoters of House of David games expect the recent exposure of King Ben's love nest to bring out record crowds. Plans are being made to take care of the largest crowd that ever saw a game here; it being expected that the scandal sect brethren will outdraw even a major league team."[104]

Through it all, the squad handled questions from curious observers as best as they could without letting that curiosity derail their focus. Because many of the players were outsiders, they simply feigned ignorance of the entire matter. They followed Thorpe's advice to continue playing well and meeting their long list of commitments. In addition to a heavy road agenda, they also hosted such rivals as the Illinois Boosters, South Bend Grays, Galien Grays, New Buffalo Buchanans, K.V.P. of Kalamazoo, the Jamestown Tigers (an all-black team later called the Elkhart-Jamestown Tigers), the Chicago Mont Clares, New Troy (New York), the Chicago Passenger Club, the Auto Specialties Club in neighboring St. Joseph, the National Standard (advertised as the fastest team of Niles, Michigan), South Haven, Dukescherer & Riley, South Haven, Forest Beach, and a series of weekend games against Joe Green's well-known Chicago Giants.[105]

One of their most colorful games that year came against Maggie Riley's Devil Dogs at the Polo Grounds. Riley had built quite a reputation as "The $10,000 Wonder Girl"[106] and put together a popular all-girl nine that traveled the circuit. She always had a publicity photo of herself shaking hands with a member of the opposing club everyplace her squad appeared. One with first sacker Cookie Hannaford was carried by newspapers all over the country. After the Benton Harbor Boys came out on top, 6–5, Hannaford said, "The ladies gave us a run for our money."[107]

On one of their eastern tours, in addition to playing in New York, Philadelphia, and Boston, they made many stops at all rural points in between, always attracting large crowds. They exceeded all expectations when they played a five-game series against the Brooklyn Meadowbrooks at the Polo Grounds which was attended by more than 100,000 fans.[108]

However, amid their successes they also suffered their share of blow-out defeats, some of which were embarrassingly memorable. On August 25, the *Pittsburgh Courier* said, "Davidites Swamped by Hoosier Sluggers," and recounted how the Negro National League Indianapolis ABCs held the squad to just three singles with a dozen House of David players in and out of the game as they were trounced, 14–0.[109] Later, close to the end of the season, the *News-Palladium* reported that "Francis Thorpe's 'premier pastimers' took one of the hardest beatings of their lives from Joe Green's Chicago Giants by a chilling score of 10–1. The House of David got only five hits while making three unusual errors."[110]

By September, they had worked their way to California. Manager Lon Tyre of the Santa Cruz Moose team wrote a letter to Francis Thorpe in response to a challenge for a game during the Davids' upcoming winter tour. In his lengthy and flowery reply, Tyre, the town barber, praised the quality of the team and accepted the challenge with "hearty approval." He set the date of the game for October 21, then went a step farther and offered a discount on haircuts for the players because he "noticed the House of David players were badly in need of good haircuts."[111] In addition to letters, Thorpe had placed numerous ads to let it be known his team was looking to hook up with semipro clubs for their scheduled country-wide winter tour and made stops along their journey as invitations popped up.[112]

In the first week of April 1924, Francis Thorpe announced that things would be different in the new season. Thirty men practiced at the home park, where 16 of them made the traveling team, and the rest would play as the home team. After opening the season on Easter Sunday, April 17, with a brief series at home, the travelers were scheduled to spend less time in Benton Harbor than in any prior year. On May 15, the squad departed for the six-week Atlantic Seaboard tour. After a brief return home, separate tours were scheduled for Indiana, Ohio, and Illinois.[113]

After opening weekend, headlines in the *News Palladium* read, "Thorpe, Indian Wonder, Here Tomorrow." Jim Thorpe, America's greatest athlete, was a regular player on the South Bend Singers, later called the Independents, composed of "the most expensive players ever put together in South Bend." The team also included such former major leaguers as Paul Costner (Chicago White Sox), Joe Newkirk and Bill Rossiter (Chicago Cubs), among others. The World's Greatest Athlete, a title given to Thorpe by King Gustaf of Sweden after the 1912 Olympics, was a major attraction everywhere.[114] Following the Olympics, he appeared in 289 major league games in parts of six major league seasons (1913–1915, 1917–1919) with the New York Giants, Cincinnati, and Boston before joining the South Bend squad.[115]

Thorpe had actually made what was termed his pro debut with the Rocky Mountain Railroaders in the Eastern Carolina League in 1909, where he played parts of two seasons and may have received minuscule pay before going to the Olympics.[116] He was unaware that this classified him as a professional, thus ineligible to compete. Consequently, he was later stripped of all his Olympic medals in a controversial move that remained unresolved until 1984, when the medals were returned to Thorpe's family, nearly 30 years after his death.[117]

When the House of David faced the South Bend Independents the first week of the 1924 season at House of David Park, the local paper said the Benton Harbor crew was already up to mid-season speed. It didn't let up against a squad said to have spent vast sums of money to put together the South Bend Singers nine, who had "nothing short of big league talent," including Jim Thorpe. The Bearded Beauties suffered a loss despite a stellar effort.[118]

For most of June, they had beaten the best semipro teams in the Northern states as well as representatives in Class A and B minor leagues. As an added attraction, the Davids' center fielder, Artie Vieritz, performed a comedy routine of his own before games.

Major league scouts followed them throughout their season in an effort to sign some of the stars, but it was to no avail.[119] After the team had been on the road for over a month non-stop, the *Cincinnati Enquirer* reported that the "Whiskerinos" had been on the road since April, playing an average of five games a week, and as of June 7 they had lost only two games. Later, Francis Thorpe discussed their success, explaining, "It isn't the big teams that we hate to face. They play real baseball and we can give them a real battle. It is the little hick teams from the backwoods that fool us."[120]

The House of David sent notice they would bring their best players to face the Champions at Dodsworth Lot in Ohio. To ensure maximum advance ticket sales, it was announced that for their appearance, the entire field would be enclosed in canvas, making it impossible for people without tickets to stand on the outer fringes and see the games.[121] That must not have made many friends for the squad, because there was no such effort in the future. After a roaring ten-game winning streak during June, Artie Vieritz was injured and had to leave the game when he was hit in the arm by a pitch and everyone wrongly thought his arm was paralyzed.[122]

When the New Philadelphia (Ohio) Noakers beat the Bearded Beauties, a Philadelphia newspaper described the team as "those shaveless athletes from the Michigan lakeshore." The columnist added, "our boys looked forward to seeing 'the kid' Walter Faust, who was sensational last year, and the sensational Jesse Tally who slammed 34 round trippers in 132 games in 1923. And in the first 31 games this season he already has 11." The article concluded with a bit of humor: "Because the players are vegetarians it's not likely any butchers will attend the game."[123]

In their two-month, non-stop road trip through Michigan and Ohio, the club played 55 games in 57 days, garnering a 35–20 record. Along the way they faced some of the best teams in the Midwest, including the Kelloggs, Fairbanks, Morse, Coshocton, and Wyandottes. During the long tour, an Ohio newspaper dubbed Francis Thorpe "the John McGraw of the House of David" because he always got the best out of his players.[124] More often than not, broadsides advertising their games

Over the years David Harrison wore many hats in House of David baseball. He began his career as the first batboy for the team when he was too young to play. The speedster was later playing manager for the Junior team, in addition to playing many seasons with the traveling team (courtesy Brian Ziebart, House of David Commune archives).

read, "all seats reserved," with an explanation that in case of a rainout, fans could turn back tickets for a full refund minus a small fee the management was required to give to the Davids as "rain insurance."[125]

In late August, in publicity before two games in Indiana, Pennsylvania, a local paper praised the Davids' ability to attract amazingly large crowds for semipro baseball during their Greater New York tour. It mentioned impressive examples: a Monday afternoon exhibition game at Shibe Park in Philadelphia drew 12,455 paid fans; a mid-week game at Baltimore attracted 11,422; 10, 528 enthusiastic fans watched them play a game in a rainstorm in Bronx Field; 5,920 spectators witnessed their game in Harrison, New Jersey; Bethlehem, Pennsylvania, accommodated 6,437, "and large turnouts were evident at other cities too numerous to mention."[126]

Saying their appearance was eagerly anticipated would be a blatant understatement. As had become the usual fare, they were the talk of the town on street corners, in restaurants, and everyplace baseball was discussed. People talked about and compared favorite players as well as how the Whiskered Wonders from Benton Harbor were steadily emerging as the "very best" in semi-professional baseball. Headlines on page one of the *Indiana Gazette* on the day of the first game read, "House of David Team Arrives: Unique Baseball Nine Comes to Indiana by Automobile Route and Is Ready for Today's and Friday's Games."[127]

Because their schedule was tight, it was not unusual for them to arrive literally in the nick of time for the first of the two games. Both games were exciting. The 2,500 ardent fans who attended each game loudly cheered the boys from Benton Harbor as their favorites, even in the game when the Davids received a 21–6 trouncing by the host team.[128]

Following that tour, they returned to Benton Harbor for some home games in September that are remembered as part of one of their most successful seasons since 1915. Thorpe said they drew the largest crowds of the season at every park they played in, and they had an especially successful two weeks' venture into Chicago. Thorpe said they had defeated the best semipro teams in northern Michigan, Indiana, and Iowa. They won all contests in Iowa except for the Fort Dodge club in a close 3–1 game in front of 5,000 cheering spectators. He also commented on the muddy, rocky and often impassable roads in Iowa, which required them to abandon their cars along the roadside in order to get to games on time.[129]

This hectic schedule was a norm they encouraged, expected, and continued throughout their existence. They returned to Benton Harbor for a weekend stay with plans to resume their road travels for a few weeks, followed by a return home to complete the season.[130] One Sunday afternoon, in front of an overflow crowd, the scheduled game against La Porte turned into one of the most unforgettable ever played there. Despite the Davids logging 13 hits in the "nail biter of all time,"[131] the game went into the bottom of the *nineteenth* inning tied at zero when the first and only run crossed the plate, giving the House of David the victory. Ever since that game, the local press referred to La Porte as "The La Porte Gang of 19 Inning Game" every time the two teams faced each other.[132]

The last half of the '20s was filled with a vagary of experiences on all fronts, as the baseball-playing House of David was firmly established, respected, and enjoyed, win or lose. Things began early in February 1925, when pitcher Lloyd Miller, from Indiana, who had made a name for himself on the mound, got permission from the commune to sign with manager Blake Harper of the Fort Smith Twins in the Class C Western Association. Colorfully described as one of the most picturesque figures in baseball with "locks down to his knees," he was expected to be a big drawing card.[133]

Miller had defeated teams from both the National and American Leagues in exhibition games. John McGraw had tried to sign him for the New York Giants organization at the same time, but Harper won the signing battle by not requiring him to alter his appearance.[134] He arrived in Fort Smith in April[135] and pitched three innings, long enough to earn an ERA of 12.00 and a 0–0 record. He later pitched 206 innings with the Canton Terriers in the Class B Central League in 1928, where he posted a 7–13 record and a 4.20 ERA.[136] Miller returned to the Benton Harbor nine in 1930 and helped them win ballgames.[137] By 1936, the former ace was still pitching, but a nagging sore arm limited him to a relief role, not particularly common at that time.[138]

That set of events was temporarily confused by speculation in the *Springfield, Missouri Republican* (March 31, 1925, 5), the *Altoona Pennsylvania Tribune* (April 1, 1925, 10) and papers who reported that Walter Faust had also signed a contract to play with Fort Smith, lured away from the commune by pitcher Lloyd Miller.

Conflicting information indicates that Faust actually signed a contract with the Dallas Steers in the Class C Texas Association a year later on March 4, 1926.[139] However, there are no records indicating Faust ever played with the Steers, due to alleged injury issues. There is no mention of Faust's 1927 season away from the Davids. Nor does his name appear in the box score of a game played in East Helena, Montana, in early June 1927.[140] Later in 1928, he appeared on the roster of the Akron Tyrites, an independent team in the Class B Central League, where he played 65 games, including 15 at second base and 40 at shortstop, batting .240.[141] He returned as a hired player with the House of David (1929), and later the City of David (1930–1931). After that, he played for the commune teams on and off for a brief time in which he even tried his hand at pitching.[142]

In 1925, they came up on the short end in several short series like the two-game loss one Saturday and Sunday against the Chicago Galligans, when the press indicated that despite excellent defense, the House of David had not played up to their usual standards.[143] In addition to their pepper games, a new element of non-game entertainment made its debut in Davenport, Iowa, before a contest with the Knights of Columbus at St. Ambrose College. Artie Vieritz added his own comedy act in the style of the popular comedic baseball satirist of the day, Nick Altrock.[144]

As the team lost four players to the annual vaudeville tour once again, the consensus was that the barnstormers had a very successful season which drew thousands of fans, particularly when they defeated the Sioux City Soos, 7–3, in front of a crowd larger than the one attracted when the St. Louis Browns played in Sioux City a few months earlier.[145] As usual, their yearly tour into southern Canada was exciting and well-received. When they more or less dominated the Ottawa Santa Fe nine, it was reported that the House of David was one of the fastest teams ever seen there.[146]

That year, the young home team started out on a rampage of its own. Initial predictions before their season warning all pending competitors that "the House of David boys are not to be toyed with" turned out to be more accurate than anticipated. On May 4, in its first game of the new season, the club came from behind in a ninth-inning rally to top the Baroda Independents, 11–10. They went on to defeat most teams they faced at the House of David ballpark: Fort Wayne Giants, La Porte, Notre Dame, P.M.C. of South Bend, South Bend Studebaker, Hammond Morris Athletic Club, Chicago Raphaels, and others, all played in front of large crowds. This went on as they won 19 of their first 24 games.[147]

Promoter Ray Doan, "somewhat of an outsider equivalent to Bill Veeck, developed a sophisticated marketing machine for the House of David that always drew maximum crowds."[148] An early example of this occurred when he scheduled a tour of the western states that included trips throughout southern Minnesota, Nebraska, and stops in his home state of Iowa: Muscatine, Davenport, Cedar Rapids, and Dubuque. He sent notices to those places and others along the way, enticing managers interested in scheduling games with his squad to contact him in Muscatine.[149] This exceeded expectations. Local newspapers everywhere contained articles extending invitations to the Davids to schedule games with local teams of all ages while in their area. All were accepted.[150]

As late as two weeks before the season, manager Francis Thorpe also focused on scheduling games for the fourth consecutive season almost totally on the road. By that time, the team itself was considered one of its own best advertisements. News about team activity always preceded them, and it became a given that games not scheduled in advance would be plugged in along the way as time permitted.[151] Because of their prolonged travels away from Benton Harbor, the trend of fans to travel to see them also became common, as occurred in August 1925, when 30 fans from Greene, Iowa, made the slow drive to Charles City, about 30 miles away, to watch them tackle and whip the Charles City Collegians, 5–3, in front of the largest crowd of the year in Greene.[152]

As usual, in mid–May the team was reinforced by the return of several of their band members who had been a big hit on the vaudeville circuit during their 25-week tour. Cookie Hannaford, leader of the House of David Band, his brother Horace, Dwight Baushke, and Wesley Schneider changed uniforms and settled right back into baseball.[153]

Though nothing new, players always got a kick out of colorful newspaper articles like the one that greeted them when they arrived in Emporia, Kansas: "Every man with a beard was looked upon with curiosity this morning on Commercial Street. Emporians were speculating as to which ones were the House of David baseball players who are in town today. When they play Emporia it will be the game of the season, the highlight the fans have been awaiting."[154] The press started adding more clever twists when covering the games, such as "Carrying the added weight in the shape of a bumper crop of whiskers, the House of David team, long famed for its elaborate hirsute adornment, was trimmed by the Kay-Bees in a Chicago League game at White City."[155] Another said, "The House of David Ball Club Probably Wins Lots of Games by a Whisker."[156]

In July, the Whiskered Wonders faced the professional Moline Plowboys of the Class D Mississippi Valley League in front of a scant crowd. It was a hard-fought contest where the only "star" of the game was flashy defense from both teams and the final score was almost mentioned as an after thought. In contrast, near the end of the season the *Sedalia Democrat* reported that despite losing to the New York Yankees 5–1 at the Polo Grounds in front of over 20,000 fans, the House of David road team was having a most successful year, winning 137 of 149 games played. The article noted the attention given to their hirsute appearance "almost overlooks the fact that these players are powerfully built and finely conditioned athletes."[157]

Also during their 1925 travels, there was an auto accident in North Dakota. Their longtime driver, Hans Dalager, nicknamed Barney after racecar speedster Barney Oldfield—"last to leave and first to arrive," was driving too fast and drove another vehicle off the road, killing the driver and totaling one of the House of David's Packards. Some players received minor injuries. Judge Dewhirst, who later became the head of the Original House of David after Purnell's death in 1927, immediately jumped in with both feet to squelch the commune's responsibility with an out-of-court settlement that avoided legal action and bad publicity. From that point forward, the incident was kept under wraps until 1928, when the future of the commune itself and its baseball teams were on the line.[158]

The 1926 season was unique as they played what is on record as the longest barnstorming trip ever undertaken by a baseball team. In mid–February, business manager Ray Doan announced that the team would leave on March 15 for its normal spring training trip through the South, where they were scheduled to play a series of exhibition games with major league teams training in Georgia and Florida.[159] From there they encountered many of the fastest amateur, semipro, and professional teams in the Midwest and the West.[160]

As part of their westward tour to California, they played almost daily while driving every night for the next day's game for nearly three months. During a nine-day jaunt in Montana, they played in Sidney (Monday), Wibaux (Tuesday), Miles City (Wednesday), Billings (Thursday), Livingston (Saturday), Lewistown (Sunday), Great Falls for two games (Monday and Tuesday), and Havre (Wednesday), for a total of 779 miles in that one week. (Distances determined by a Montana road map, 1996 Gousha Road Atlas.)[161]

Amid all that excitement, a different kind of coverage of the team emerged in Hughes' "Brief Bites of Sports Gossip" column. While announcing an upcoming appearance of the barnstormers in Manitowoc, Wisconsin, he wrote, "The House of David baseball team which comes here was rumored to have been a fizzle this year, especially when they took a blistering defeat from the Galesburg squad. However, rumor has it that particular HOD team was a crowd of imposters playing on the strength of the House of David reputation."[162]

Tales of such imposter teams as the Spring Valley (Illinois) House of David and the Colored House of David, to name just two, became more prevalent. It seemed like a direct ratio: the more successful they were and the more prosperous they became, the more imposter teams appeared on the scene. Not only were the officials back at the commune in Benton Harbor outraged, but the players themselves were furious at fraudulent teams who were trading on their success with inferior players, losing games and tarnishing their reputation, which jeopardized future invitations.[163] Throughout their existence, this was a constant menace.

In 1926, while American competition swimmer Gertrude Ederle prepared to be the first woman to swim the English Channel in the first week in August, the Davids, described as "bewhiskered barberless pill smackers," readied for an appearance against the undefeated Anchor Hocking Glass Team before heading north for their annual trek into Canada.[164]

The *Winnipeg Tribune* announced the upcoming arrival of the boys from Benton Harbor for two games at Wesley Park as a "real treat" for baseball fans in the region, highlighted by the game between the Benton Harbor crew and the local all-stars. "The House of David is respected as one of the best baseball attractions in the country, not because of their long hair but because they play a good brand of competitive baseball." The team, aged 18–30 with the exception of older catcher Bert "Beans" Johnson, always received individual accolades and compliments for favorites. With Paul Mooney gone, infielder Walter "Dutch" Faust assumed his popularity along with Doc Tally, both written about as players who could go to the big leagues at any time.[165]

They played a two-game weekend set at Wesley Park against the Winnipeg All-Stars. With the score knotted, 2–2, Friday's game was called due to darkness, which was not an uncommon occurrence in those days.[166] They faced off on Saturday in front of "the largest crowd assembled on the local lot for many years." Smith, House of David pitcher, "with a reddish-tinged beard that he didn't allow to get in his way," gave up only four hits, while third baseman Harrison and shortstop Faust gracefully fielded grounders and threw 18 runners out at first.[167]

Their success on the diamond continued with their early trip to the West Coast, while things in Benton Harbor developed in a different way. The page one headlines of the *News Palladium* on November 17, 1926, read, "EXTRA! Benjamin Purnell Under Arrest; Seized at Midnight at Colony: State Police Break Down Doors with Axes to Get King." Everyone was stunned that he had become a broken-down and frail old man with a long white beard.[168] He had been sought since February 23, 1923, and had been hiding within the commune under the protection of selected colony members.[169] Though he was initially jailed, several hours later, after legal entanglements and discussions, Judge Dewhirst, Francis Thorpe, and Mary Purnell arranged to get him out on $50,000 bail, primarily due to his debilitated condition.[170] None of the commune members involved were arrested or prosecuted.

While members of the commune and the state of Michigan awaited the upcoming trial of Purnell, elsewhere the '20s continued to roar on a happier note as populations on both sides of the Atlantic Ocean were mesmerized by news of the flight of Charles Lindbergh in the Spirit of St. Louis, May 20–22, 1927. All the while, the Whiskerinos from the House of David continued playing sparkling baseball on the road.

During their Canadian tour in mid–August, they played a three-game series against Gilkerson's Colored Giants of Chicago at Wesley Park in Winnipeg, a team they had faced in several prior exhibitions in different venues over the years. The series drew intense publicity as some kind of "show down" as they were considered evenly matched on paper, and this set was to determine "once and for all" which team was the best.[171] The House of David took the first game, 4–3, in front of 5,000 fans who agreed they had seen a snappy game played in one hour and ten minutes.[172] Six thousand onlookers witnessed game two, which began as a pitcher's duel but ended in volcanic eruptions from both nines before the game ended in a 5–5 tie. The final game saw the Giants defeat the Benton Harbor crew, 9–4, in a slugfest in front of 5,000-plus spectators.[173] By this time fewer than a handful of colony members remained on the club.[174]

Court proceedings against Purnell began May 16, 1927, coinciding with the Canadian tour. No matter what part of the allegations he faced, the procedure was the same. Purnell was so frail that he was brought to court on a stretcher in an ambulance and permitted to testify reclined on a cot with a commune nurse nearby.[175] His voice was almost unintelligible, it was so weak, and the court stenographer frequently asked him to speak up. His testimony proceeded at a maximum of 15-minute intervals followed by 10-minute recesses, allowing him to rest. His entire testimony consisted of his answering "No," or "I never did," to every question.[176] Since his discovery at the commune and throughout his testimony at his trial, he insisted, "This is a frame-up. I didn't do any of those things."[177] By December, before things were allegedly close to being resolved, headlines read "King Benjamin Purnell, Famous Cult Leader, Dead."[178] But the matter was far from concluded. Little did they realize this would be the first stage of a three-year ordeal that was the beginning of the end of the commune and the baseball teams as they were known at that time.

Meanwhile the barnstorming tour and 1927 schedule continued as usual. The team was accorded public approval and acclaim based on their prowess on the diamond separate from opinions about events within the commune. They were simultaneously amused by advance publicity as they moved from town to town, such as the article that appeared in Ty Cobb's column in *The Sporting News* saying, "the players sport beards several feet long!"[179]

They had spent April, May and part of June wending their way through the West in California, Oregon and Washington, where they were welcomed with the usual fanfare. After playing several teams in the Los Angeles area, they moved into the Central Valley to face the Modesto Reds at Davis Park, where the local paper reported the "Benton Harbor baseball busters" were humbled, 4–1, thanks to the pitching of Freddie Connell, who fanned 13 Davids while he held them to one run scored in the final inning.[180] In anticipation of their arrival in Woodland, California, the manager of the Woodland Northern California League sought and got permission from the manager of the Woodland-Sacramento Valley League to bring in reinforcement players to face the Whiskered Wonders. Though treated as a unique event, it was not.

To justify the request which had become commonplace, the local newspaper sang the praises of the entire team, though misspelling many names. It read as follows:

> In Walter Faust, this vicinity will see the world's greatest shortstop; Lloyd Miller, one of the greatest right-handers outside organized baseball; left-fielder Beckman [sic—Heckman] is a real big league hitter who batted .423 in 1926; centerfielder A. B. Hip has one of the greatest arms in baseball; Bell, in right field, is a natural hitter able to break up a game at any time; Jay Sharrock, a real spit-baller for four seasons in the Class D Michigan State League (1912–1915 where he earned a 48–43 record) now playing first base and [outfielder Tom Dewhirst] has been called the Babe Ruth of the club,

"Home Run Tommie Dewhirst—The Babe Ruth of House of David." This photograph was often used by the press when the spotlight was on him (courtesy Brian Ziebart, House of David Commune archives).

hit 48 homers in 140 games and logged a .386 batting average for the club in 1926; and they had two of the greatest catchers out of the majors, Falk and Swanson.[181]

When they moved into southern Oregon, the press reported the fans were "hopped up" over an upcoming game against the Klamath Falls Pelicans at Fair Grounds Field. They described the team as one of the best in the country, and lumber companies and other businesses closed for the day to permit everyone to see the Davids in action and decide for themselves.[182] The game, played on a muddy field on a very cold day, was said to be one of the best ever seen there. Pelican Pitcher Hal Chase (no relation to the infamous "Prince Hal" Chase of the same era) threw a "zig-zag, floating double curving spit ball that was too much for the House of David to fathom," as the Michigan team lost by a 2–1 score.[183]

In May, they played the Bend Elks in Oregon the day after defeating Hood River in a 12–0 blowout. The *Bend Bulletin* announced with pride that the House of David team that brought a record of 51 wins with just six losses thus far in the season was defeated by the Elks, 6–3.[184] By the time they reached Bend, their arrival had been advertised for several days. The game, seen by the largest crowd ever assembled at the Bend Park, was not disappointing. Headlines the next morning said it all: "Bend Elks Beat House of David Team in Best Ball Game of Season." On this road trip, as with many, nationally known tenor Soldier Caruso, who sang on behalf of disabled soldiers, traveled with them, performing at the end of the second inning.[185]

Following a winning tour in Washington, they headed east. As had become the fashion throughout the circuit, games with the Davids were scheduled at least an hour early to allow time for the fifth-inning pepper exhibition and return to complete the games before darkness set in. Most local businesses closed up shop in order to attend the event. The advance publicity for that particular game added a unique note: "The management requests that fans please refrain from treating the House of David players to hot dogs when they hit homeruns."[186]

Ed Hamman, a young pitcher who began pitching for $5 a day as a high school senior in Oakland, Indiana, was later noticed by a representative of the House of David. Hamman was doing ball-handling tricks while warming up before a game with the Wheeling Stogies in the Class C Middle Atlantic League. He was offered a contract by the Davids for $200/month, far better than the money he had been paid in the minor league.[187]

Knowing he would have to give up his dream of eventually playing major league baseball, he grew a beard and joined the House of David in 1926 and entertained with them for two seasons[188] without donning their woolen baseball uniform. Instead he appeared as a white-faced clown in a costume of his own design and built a reputation presenting his own brand of baseball chicanery.[189] This white player who spent most of his career with American Negro League baseball teams, was also a featured performer with the Harlem Globetrotters, and later general manager and part owner of the Indianapolis Clowns baseball team with the great promoter Syd Pollack, 1933–1973.[190]

Always full of stories, one Hamman was particularly fond of telling was about a harrowing adventure he had one night when he appeared with the House of David in Boston. Thanks to a rainout, the players had a rare night off. Hamman and a couple of teammates took a walk through the Boston Common at a time when men with beards were feared as Bolsheviks. The police were summoned. Although Francis Thorpe appeared in court and explained, newspaper headlines everywhere read, "House of David Players Arrested as Bolsheviks!"[191]

Despite events within the commune that included Purnell's death, baseball went on as usual. March 11 marked the first day of the 1928 season, which has often been described as the beginning of a nine-year span, 1928–1936, that was the height of their popularity and excellence, highlighted by their winning the first place purse at the 1934 *Denver Post* Tournament.[192]

An expected though unwelcome outcome of the popularity and financial success of the club was an even greater myriad of imposter teams. When the *Decatur Herald* reported on April 23, that Bloomington in the Class B Three-I League had defeated the Davids, 13–2, an angry Judge Dewhirst took action in the form of a stern letter to the editor: "You are notified officially that neither manager nor any of the players of that so-called House of David ball team are in any manner connected with the House of David. The said team is a fraud."

His letter went on to outline the schedule of the authentic team, explaining that following spring training in Hot Springs, Arkansas, they would go to southwest Texas and other western states on the way to California, Oregon, and Washington for May and June. He concluded, "Therefore any team now playing in Illinois is defrauding the public." Dated April 26, 1928, the letter was signed, House of David, H.T. Dewhirst, Secretary.[193]

Unfortunately the situation didn't improve until an incident in 1934 following a well-publicized spring training exhibition with the House of David facing the New York Yankees. As a gag, Babe Ruth adorned a false beard as he played right field.

Judge Dewhirst fumed and filed suit against the promoter of that fake team. He actually received a verdict in the case, or at least a partial verdict as far as he was concerned. Federal Judge John M. Woolsey enjoined that promoter from using the House

A staged photograph for pre-game publicity during their Western tour (courtesy Brian Ziebart, House of David Commune archives).

of David name but refused to intervene in the matter of beards, saying, "the law allows anyone to purposely imitate another's facial shrubbery."[194] Doc Tally responded to this with an angry letter of his own.

On April 12, 1928, the House of David was one of the first barnstorming teams to play at newly built Warren Park, home of the Bisbee Miners in Arizona, in the newly-formed, four-team Class D Arizona State League. In an exciting back-and-forth game, the Davids defeated the Miners, 11–9.[195] While both the home team and the barnstorming team from Benton Harbor embarked on a busy season, the issue of an imposter team once again appeared. According to the *Pittsburgh Press*, on June 15, 1928, former House of David promoter in 1924, Lou Murphy, had sent his team, fraudulently named the House of David, on the road. When Thorpe learned of this, he wrote letters to newspapers explaining that Murphy was firmly advised to cease and desist, explaining that his "real" House of David team had never been out without manager Thorpe being with them personally. Henceforth Murphy, who headquartered a team in Spring Valley, Illinois, said he annually paid a $1,000 fee to use the House of David name, then followed this with want ads seeking better pitchers with more experience plus a good shortstop for his team.[196] This dilemma continued throughout the existence of the House of David squad, without resolution.

Meanwhile, the Benton Harbor crew received one of their warmest welcomes and highest praise when they arrived in Bismarck, North Dakota, near the end of June. Baseball was extremely popular in the region, and many of the teams were strong competitors. The area as a whole was known for its history of racial tolerance and sported several Negro and interracial teams, with the Bismarck Churchills perhaps the most well-known. After the Bearded Beauties defeated the Bismarck Grays, the local paper explained it away in an article titled, "Four Bismarck Errors Donate Game to Daves: Blackmore, Pederson, & Hip Play Well for Bearded Aggregation." The article included positive comments about both competitors. High praise was showered on Bismarck's pitcher, Joe Day, described as "a big Indian hurler who whipped Bismarck a short time ago when pitching for the All-Nations team," and the House of David received accolades as "the best ballclub that has played in Bismarck this year."[197]

The main pitching staff of the 1928 House of David team logged a combined record of 60–32 against such impressive foes as Milwaukee of the American Association, the Dallas Steers of the Texas League, and such other barnstorming teams as the Fresno Tigers, Gilkerson Union Giants, and Spencer Cubs. Individual records for the HOD hurlers were as follows: LHP (?) Jebo, 7–4; Page Neve, 18–8; George "Lefty" Gilbert, 13–12; Joe "Windy" Radloff, 19–8; Doc Tally, relegated to the outfield due to his powerful bat, 3–0.[198]

Something we would never see today was not unusual during the barnstorming era. Near the end of the season, August, as part of an exhibition in Canada, the bearded nine played three games against Gilkerson's Colored Giants of Chicago on the same day, each game in front of a different large crowd. The Davidites won the morning game, 7–3, and the afternoon game, 6–4, before losing the twilight game, 3–1. The Israelites used just three pitchers, Neve, Jebo, and Radloff, in the three games described as "snappy and fast paced," lasting an hour and a half apiece.[199] Their rivalry, well established, would see them face each other again that summer and many more times over the years.

In his annual end of season report, Francis Thorpe stated that although the House of David made money, 1928 fell short of prior seasons because at any one time, there were as many as three bogus teams out there playing a lesser brand of baseball that impinged on their uniqueness and success at the gates. However, additional information about the season appeared in the Benton Harbor *News Palladium* on January 1, 1929, titled "Baseball Has Bumper Year in Berrien [County]: House of David Wins Title in Semi-Pro Race." According to popular and respected sports columnist Jim Enright, baseball in Berrien County had a better following in 1928 than ever before in its history. All 15 teams from the region that competed did well financially in front of more than 100,000 spectators who attended semipro and amateur baseball games during that summer.[200]

The House of David nine in particular drew heavily as the team won the championships of Berrien County and Southwest Michigan. Along the way, players posed for what became the last team picture before the colony split into two factions: Percy Walker, Bert "Beans" Johnson (a catcher who also functioned as Walker's right-hand man), "Long" John Tucker, George "Andy" Anderson, David "Eggs" Harrison, Walter "Dutch" Faust, Tom Dewhirst, Bob Dewhirst, Miles Crow, Al Stemm, Mason "Mac" Perry, and Frank Wyland.[201]

After Purnell's death (December 16, 1927), prolonged litigation ensued over the state's attempt to put the commune into receivership while finances and other tangles were worked out. Friction and strife prevailed. In addition to the continuing tensions between Judge Dewhirst and Francis Thorpe that had long festered under the surface, conflict between followers of Benjamin Purnell and those loyal to Mary Purnell escalated, which culminated in the permanent and irreparable division of the commune,[202] which also saw a division among the players.[203]

Life went on as preparations for the 1929 season began. Judge Dewhirst retained control of what he called the Original House of David, including the baseball team. His son, outfielder Tom Dewhirst, infielder David Harrison, and driver-baggage man Hans Dalager remained, while those considered the best players of the day as well as the heart and soul of the club—Doc Tally, George Anderson, and John Tucker [Tuck]—walked away with their families to follow Mary. They immediately became the core of her Israelite City of David baseball team. Francis Thorpe, manager since the team was conceived, took over the City of David squad while supporting and guiding her throughout all facets of running her new commune.[204]

In February 1929, it was announced that both communes planned to field good barnstorming teams that season. Judge Dewhirst and the board appointed pitcher Percy Walker, who remained with the original squad, as team manager and gave him the expeditious task of filling out the roster.[205] Walker, an adept, bespectacled pitcher who now worked in a relief role, was praised as a good manager who knew how to handle players. He quickly fortified the club by adding pitcher Albert "Lefty" Tolles from Michigan State University to an already strong 16-man roster.

He also wanted Walter Faust to return and travel with them, which depended on his status with the Dallas Steers. Faust had written to them requesting early retirement from his contract, but received no answer.[206] Walker then wrote directly to Commissioner Kenesaw Mountain Landis, asking to have Faust released from his professional baseball obligations to return to the colony team. After first angrily banning Faust from professional baseball and saying he would never again be allowed to play in any league, Landis slowly yielded and permitted him to join the 1929 roster. It was a move many Israelites considered "divine intervention."[207]

Judge Dewhirst's Original House of David baseball team in preparation for the 1929 season, the first after the commune fractured. Front, L-R: 1B Ernie Selby, P Jack Crow, 2B Clay "Mud" Williams, SS Sidney Smith who drowned in Lake Michigan in 1938. Back L-R: 3B Davie Harrison, OF Bob Dewhirst, Manager Percy Walker, OF Tom Dewhirst, P/OF Frank Wyland (courtesy Brian Ziebart, House of David Commune archives).

Additionally, commune member Wesley Schneider was selected to manage the Home Team, where he had played in 1920.[208] That squad, composed of the youngest players, essentially functioned as their player development program, their farm club, years before Branch Rickey formalized the concept.[209] Actually, according to the *News-Palladium* (July 3, 1929), the 48-year-old Schneider had the job of running the team on paper, with such duties as hiring outside players to complete his roster as soon as the travelers left and keeping track of expenses, while "Beans" Johnson, regular catcher on the home team, 1925–1928, was in charge of all field activities.[210]

Behind the scenes, Dewhirst continued to work tirelessly to prevent Mary Purnell from having a team and "taking a share of the profits."[211] The first week in March, he flexed his muscles by posting a resolution at the Registrar of Deeds Office in what he called an attempt to protect the commune against liability and protect the general public from deception. In it he emphasized that the only authorized traveling team legally representing the House of David was managed by Percy Walker, with promoter Ray Doan. In addition, he labeled Mary's House of David squad, managed by Francis Thorpe, as an outlaw team, and warned baseball managers not to book any traveling teams using the name unless contracts were signed by Walker and Doan.[212]

Ignoring Dewhirst's threats, later in the month Francis Thorpe and his City of David team left Benton Harbor for an unannounced Southern tour on his way to spring training, while Walker was still in the process of assembling his roster. Shortly thereafter, Walker departed with a 16-man squad in three cars for an abbreviated two-week spring training in Hot Springs, Arkansas, followed by ten pre-season games set up by

Doan, who announced that their tentative schedule included a tour of middle western states on the Western side of the Mississippi River, then possibly as far north as southern Canada.[213]

That was the end of an era for Benton Harbor baseball. Commune members would never again be in the majority on House of David or City of David teams, now forced to rely almost exclusively on hired players to fill their rosters. Additionally, it was the first time in history that the House of David would have rival teams barnstorming the country.[214] Later there were a few "All House of David Days" when the two teams faced each other.

Since the press inadvertently referred to both traveling teams as "House of David," things were difficult for historians as well as fans reading sports pages along the way. However, there were two or three ways to tell the teams apart: (1) all games played at Eden Springs were the Dewhirst teams when they were not on the road; (2) Thorpe's City of David squad played all games on the road, as Mary's City of David had no home park, though they sometimes played at the Benton Harbor Airport in later years; (3) though box scores were more often omitted than included in news releases about games, those that did appear with more than just a line score mentioned manager or player names (last names only, frequently misspelled) that helped readers identify teams.

During that time, the country was hypnotized with daily reports about Chicago's 1929 St. Valentine's Day Massacre and the ensuing investigation, with the focus on Al Capone and other mobsters of the day. Actually, Capone was no stranger to Berrien County. Though it's said he owned homes throughout the region, on his frequent visits he generally stayed at the Whitcomb Hotel in St. Joseph or the Hotel Vincent in Benton Harbor, while he enjoyed the local golf courses and the amenities at Eden Springs Park.[215]

Earl Boyersmith, commune member from 1921–1936, backup player in 1931, was a driver for the Central States team and ran the trains at the commune in the off-seasons. He said he found Capone the most unforgettable of the hoards of visitors to Eden Springs Park. He remembered Capone and some "of his buddies boarding the train at the main entrance at the South Depot, rode through the park and got off at the North Depot. It was in the afternoon and they had their automobiles parked along the cottages right by the ballpark, between the South entrance and the depot. They had Pierce-Arrows, Cadillacs, Packards ... all bulletproof. Sometimes we tried to start a conversation with his men but they weren't too eager to talk."[216]

The commune's baseball teams went about their regular business of adjusting to the change as each club prepared for the 1929 season. After a two-week spring training in Hot Springs, Arkansas, Walker's group headed for the Pacific Coast with a scheduled stop to face the Joplin Miners in the Class C Western Association.[217] His new team included only three commune members: 19-year-old team captain Tom Dewhirst, son of Judge Dewhirst, already known as "The Bearded Bambino," played left field; David "Eggs" Harrison, last season's home team captain, manned third base; and utility player Hans Dalager. Hired players included outfielders Bill "Snake" Siddle (RF), A.B. Hipp (1B), Merle Drager (1B), Bill Heckman (1B), H. V. "Van" Atherton (2B), Dutch Faust (SS), with Eddie Deal behind the dish. The pepper game trio of Hip Vaughan, Dutch Faust, and Lloyd Miller (back from his stint in organized baseball) topped the package.[218]

It's generally agreed that Percy Walker made one of the best decisions of his new managerial career when he hired catcher Eddie Deal, who had played in the

Earl Boyersmith, a popular member of the commune who played baseball briefly, ran the trains and could always be found in the machine shop (courtesy Brian Ziebart, House of David Commune archives).

Three-I League and other leagues in professional ball before becoming the longest tenured non-commune player in House of David history.[219] Deal, described as a responsible, happy-go-lucky guy, was catcher and team captain from 1929 to 1935, then player-manager of the team from 1936 to 1940, when he retired from playing and became the full-time manager through 1942. Off and on during that time, the Iowa native received major league offers, but he preferred to remain with his bearded teammates.[220]

The rigorous barnstorming schedules continued throughout the 1929 season, while welcoming host towns were often oblivious as to which team they faced: the House of David or the City of David. In mid–May, the *Angola Herald* announced upcoming games against the Logan Squares and the South Bend Colored Giants, followed by a contest with the local Angola Colts. Their new manager, Jock Somerlott, former Washington Senators player, 1910–11, stated he would "trot his spring Colts out to give the Whiskers the wind," even if they had won 12 straight games coming in. But the home crowd was disappointed when the Colts went down, 14–3.[221]

On June 1, the *Winnipeg Tribune* announced that the House of David would play a three-game set against the local All-Stars as part of their Canadian tour.[222] In addition to such regulars as Dutch Faust, Tommy Dewhirst, and David Harrison, the Benton Harbor team, always a great attraction at Wesley Park, had added Winnipeg favorite Bill "Snake" Siddle, who had played junior, intermediate, and senior baseball there from

Catcher Eddie Deal had the longest playing career of any hired player for the Davids, 1929–1942. He was playing manager on the Central States Davids' team when they joined the professional Michiana League and proceeded to win the championship in 1940. Deal always said the secret to his longevity on the diamond was smiling and being happy (courtesy Brian Ziebart, House of David Commune archives).

1912 to 1916.[223] On June 7, the *Tribune* reported, "The House of David Ball Team Trims All Stars: Bearded Boys Have Picnic at Expense of Local Team and Wins 12–4."[224] The final game on Saturday, which the visitors lost, 8–7, as bespectacled pitcher Lefty Tolles was battered hard, was described by a single headline: "Local All-Stars Beat House of David Team: Winnipeg Boys Once More Too Much for Bearded Ball Players at Wesley Park." Throughout the contests Siddle, a well-remembered fan favorite, received a warm reception.[225]

Thorpe's City of David squad simultaneously played a busy schedule of its own. By the end of June, they had toured the Eastern regions of Pennsylvania, New York, the New England States, and New Jersey, in front of large crowds at every stop.[226] Their exhibition, described as "a novelty side show and good baseball for a cricket field," was played in front of one of the largest crowds attracted in recent years by the Altoona Works nine. The *Altoona Mirror* warned that "although the team looks ancient and vulnerable, their play is plenty fast and furious, with Tally, Anderson and Tucker leading the way. Few teams can boast wins over the House of David."[227] The game, a nail-biter start to finish, saw them nosed out, 6–5, a game they reported as the squad's sixth loss in 47 games. John Tucker was praised as the main attraction of the event for his hitting and fancy fielding at first base plus the style he brought to the pepper game.[228]

During their tenure in the barnstorming circuit, the House of David encountered young players who would later make names for themselves as major league stars and even go on to the Hall of Fame. In June 1929, one of them was 18-year-old Hank Greenberg, when he played with the Bay Parkway team in Pittsfield, Massachusetts.[229] On a Sunday afternoon double tilt with many scouts in attendance, including Paul Krichell, who signed Lou Gehrig and others of that ilk, Greenberg hit two home runs in the first game and one more in the second as the Davids lost both ends.[230]

July was busy for the Home team, dominated by new faces with catcher Beans Johnson at the helm: Sol Price (RF), Al Stemm (3B), Chief Coughlin (1B), Pinky King (LF), Bobby O'Signac (SS), Clay "Mud" Williams (2B), Tom Dewhirst (CF), Frank Whiting (P).[231] After they hosted the Oak Park, Illinois, squad called "the Oak Parkers" to start things off, they got disappointing reviews in the local *News Palladium*: "Despite the fact they won, 10–5, the locals displayed some terrible baseball and at some times looked like a green high school team."

Dewhirst's "Original" House of David concluded the month with a few stops in Oregon. They won two games in southern Oregon (Klamath Falls), then proceeded north to Bend for an afternoon game in front of what was reported as the largest crowd in the history of O'Donnell Field.[232] From there they travelled west to face the Salem Senators at Olinger Field. Outfielder Tommy Dewhirst had become quite an attraction at age 19, when he was dubbed the "Babe Ruth of Benton Harbor."

Before that match-up, the Whiskerinos strengthened the team with the addition of minor league pitcher Bob Fitzke, who had played with Cleveland in the American League.[233] He temporarily left minor league baseball, grew a beard to join the team, then returned to the Class B New York Penn League in 1931 before he ended his career with five seasons in the then–AA Pacific Coast League.[234] Unfortunately for the House of David, the battery of Fitzke and Deal led the team to a 9–3 loss.[235]

During that era, they also played against teams considered every bit as unique as they were. Popular all-brother teams appeared on the barnstorming circuit and proved to be formidable competition. One was the Acerra Brothers from Long Branch, New Jersey, who played 13 years and are recognized as the longest-playing brothers team in the history of the game.[236] Another, the Deike Brothers, was reputed to be "the best brothers baseball team in the history of Texas."[237] Still another was the Fredrickson Brothers team from Minnesota, extremely popular in the late '20s, composed of a dozen brothers who worked on their father's 220-acre farm and played amateur baseball within a 30-mile radius of home whenever possible. Their style of playing raucous baseball with a reckless abandon often resulted in bench-clearing brawls.[238]

After drawing huge crowds at the Polo Grounds (25,000), Detroit (20,000), and Philadelphia (20,000), the House of David pepper team of A.B. Hipp, Lloyd Miller, and Dutch Faust entertained with a shadow ball exhibition in Butte, Montana, at the Houana, where they were always warmly welcomed as "the greatest novelty baseball club in the world today."[239] The Michigan squad edged John Donaldson's Cuban Giants, who had traveled earlier in the season as the Colored House of David. Their game was played during rain showers in what turned out to be one of their prettiest exhibitions of baseball, loaded with thrills with their bats and in the field.[240] In early September, Dewhirst's boys from Benton Harbor again faced the Cuban Giants, this time in Bismarck, North Dakota, in a game the press advertised as a "black-white clash."[241]

They wound up the weeks of the decade in their usual fashion. Things were especially exciting in Benton Harbor in mid–August in preparation of the anticipated visit by Charles Comiskey's Chicago White Sox on August 28. Promoter Floyd Fitzsimmons sponsored the last visit of a major league team to Eden Springs when the Chicago Whales of the Federal League had come to town over ten years earlier. Arrangements were made for additional seating for the largest crowd ever expected at their home park There was great anticipation to see the many major league headliners expected to appear.[242]

Among them were rookie first baseman Art Shires—later branded "The Great Shires"—pitcher Ed Walsh, son of the spitball pitcher (1904–1917), future Hall of Famers Big Ed Walsh and Ted Lyons (1923–1946), catcher Moe Berg, a Princeton graduate who later became a successful spy during World War II, third baseman Willie Kamm, and infielder-outfielder Johnny Kerr.[243] The event was such a success that Art Shires returned with an all-star team of his own at the conclusion of the major league season.[244]

During that period, scouts from more organizations followed the team, sometimes game by game. One of them, well-known St. Louis scout Jack Ryan, caught up with the squad in Spokane, Washington, and signed three players for tryouts with the Cardinals: outfielder Frank Hall, and pitchers Albert "Lefty" Tolles, and E. McCall, saying the pitchers were the best prospects he'd seen that year. However, when the Cardinals offered Tolles a minor league contract, he refused, explaining that the salary was too low.[245]

As the decade wound down, baseball in Benton Harbor had survived many irrevocable changes. As usual, the popularity of the team that gotten them invitations to play all over the map as they become an exciting element in the baseball world and the American culture as a whole.

When the decade began, there was one traveling team populated solely by members of the commune, with the purpose of spreading the religious word and earning income for the commune. When it ended, there were two communes, each with its own traveling nine, plus a home team more or less functioning as a farm team providing players for the Dewhirst faction that was based almost entirely in Benton Harbor. Their overall success had changed their outlook from one of spreading their religious ideals to one of winning ballgames. Although the faces in their woolen uniforms were in constant flux for the remainder of their existence, their caliber of play and appeal that emerged in the '20s survived in dazzling style.

4

The Thirties
Baseball During the Depression

Whereas the '20s was a noisy, free-wheeling and exciting decade, the '30s were a more serious and thoughtful period as the nation adjusted to the shock of the stock market crash and a myriad of events, both good and bad, that filled the headlines from coast to coast.

The "Star Spangled Banner," which had been sung at ballparks for years, was officially named our National Anthem in 1931[1]; a horrified public followed the chilling developments of the "Crime of the Century," the kidnapping and death of aviator Charles Lindbergh's young son and the subsequent circus-like "Trial of the Century" that permeated headlines on a daily basis[2]; the 21st Amendment repealed Prohibition[3]; Al Capone was sentenced to 11 years in Alcatraz for tax evasion[4]; the hard-hit auto industry changed body styles and added comforts in more affordable models to boost sagging sales as the "Big Three" (GM, Ford, and Chrysler) emerged on the scene.[5]

The Civilian Conservation Corps (CCC), created in 1933, followed by the Works Progress Administration (WPA) in 1935, had measured success,[6] and construction of Hoover Dam (then called Boulder Dam) was completed.[7]

It was a time when thousands called "Okies" fled homes lost to the Oklahoma dustbowl, bank repossessions, and related problems, and headed west, seeking a better life[8]; the Empire State Building was completed[9]; Amelia Earhart became the first woman to fly solo across the Atlantic[10]; notorious Bonnie and Clyde met their demise in Louisiana[11]; Orson Welles' "War of the Worlds" Halloween radio broadcast in 1938 caused nationwide panic[12]; Wylie Post and Will Rogers died in a plane crash in Alaska[13]; and more expositions and county fairs appeared than during any other decade in history.[14] The song "Brother, Can You Spare a Dime?," reflecting the hopelessness of millions, became a lasting theme of the era. In 1933, Adolf Hitler became Chancellor of Germany.[15]

The Davids had played through the 1929 season as favorites of fans everywhere, though most spectators were unaware that there were now two teams which were both called the House of David. Both communes fielded some of the best athletes of America's rowdiest era, especially as Francis Thorpe went forward and brought Mary's nine to the highest peak of success in semipro baseball annals.[16]

As the new decade began, both communes fielded colorful athletes on their squads. Francis Thorpe led Mary's Israelite House of David nine to unexpected highs.[17] Many have ranked that club as equal to any Class A team during the '30s, "and vastly superior to any semipro team in the entire land, with few exceptions."[18]

Records show that all-black and all-white teams faced each other in 438 games during the Depression, with black teams winning 309 games and white teams 129. To prepare for games, black teams warmed up in pantomime, a fast-moving exhibition they called Shadow Ball which caught on immediately with the fans.[19]

Baseball in the Great Plains began in 1922 with the founding of the Colored Western League, where all-white teams frequently faced all-black teams. However, the league, composed of nine teams from Oklahoma City, Tulsa, Omaha, St. Joseph, Coffeeville, Topeka, Independence, Kansas City (Kansas), and Wichita, collapsed after just one year. In 1925, the black Wichita Monrovians played against and bested the all-white Ku Klux Klan Number 6 squad, 10–8, in a game without incident. By the early '30s, a racially integrated league appeared in North Dakota that included players from varied Negro Leagues. Greater racial tolerance in the Great Plains is attributed to the fact that African Americans were a small minority in the total population and were thus no threat to the social order.[20]

Baseball in Canada, which actually began on a small scale in 1926, became an established part of the House of David's travels in the '30s. In 1926, the squad had tested the waters in southwestern Canada. Because there was no semipro baseball, the only home teams were local all-stars assembled for the event. The Benton Harbor nine became instant crowd pleasers in Winnipeg, Manitoba, where intense pregame publicity attracted large turnouts at Wesley Park, as in early August when they drew over 3,500 fans for a two-game set.[21] Both games were thrilling, but when game one ended in a 5–5 tie, the press excused the House of David as "being tired after their long drive from Brandon."[22]

For the most part, they faced other barnstorming teams from the States, such as annual contests with Gilkerson's Colored Giants from Chicago.[23] Sometimes they were known to play each other in a three-game "series" all in one day: the first at 10:20 in the morning, the second at 2:00 in the afternoon, and the final at 8:00 in the evening.[24] Numerous other times they faced three different clubs in the same day.[25] By the '30s, regular stops in the House of David travels included exhibitions in Alberta, Manitoba, Saskatchewan, Ontario, and Quebec, and sometimes the Western Travelers made it all the way to British Columbia.

During the same time period in the early '30s, there were two communities known as Laredo: the original, Laredo, Texas, and Nuevo Laredo, across the border in Mexico. Prior to 1930, baseball in Mexico, called "borderland baseball," consisted of games among teams of the Monterrey–San Antonio border region. However, in 1930, after learning of the financial success barnstorming brought the House of David, manager Erasmo Flores wanted to take his La Junta club on a tour in the United States.

He asked House of David promoter Harold "Dutch" Witte to put together a barnstorming schedule they called "The Good Will Tour," which was a three-month trip that took them all the way to North Dakota. They played 83 games in the U.S. and logged a record of 62–18 with three ties. The La Junta club later became part of the evolving Mexican League in the 1940s.[26] Throughout the decade, annual appearances of the House of David in Mexico were celebrated events.[27]

A major change that gradually impacted the entire game was night baseball. The Israelite House of David played in the first night game ever under electric lights at Riverside Park in Independence, Kansas, on April 17, 1930,[28] five years before the first major

City of David squad in Puebla, Mexico, November 6, 1934. The team was always warmly received there (John Horne, National Baseball Hall of Fame Files).

Baseball under the portable lights at House of David Park (Brian Ziebart, House of David Files).

league night game was played in Crosley Field in Cincinnati on May 24, 1935, after President Roosevelt flipped the switch in Washington, D.C.29

Earliest coverage of House of David activities in 1931 focused on basketball. The January 8, 1931, *Illinois Dispatch* reported on a contest between the House of David cagers and a ladies team from Chicago, the Taylor Trunks. This championship squad was noted as one that always played to win. In what was described as an "exceptionally rough game," John Tucker was knocked to the floor on a jump ball and had to be revived by a doctor before the game resumed. The Davids lost 11–9.

By September 1931, when the House of David was on a roll with a 34-game winning streak, the team made an appearance at Sportsman's Park in Alton, Illinois. They took their own portable lighting system with them to face the Standard Oil club in the first night exhibition there. It was a circus atmosphere as 2,000 fans filled the seats inside the park, with an equal number crowded on the hilltop above the outfield wall. However, they were more interested in the ins and outs of the lighting system than the game. A pepper game demonstration was presented after the second inning before the baseball game continued, and later was moved to the fifth inning. At the end of nine innings, the boys from Benton Harbor were victorious, 6–0.30

Even as lights became more common, it remained nothing short of an event when they took their lighting system on the road. A fleet of two trucks with "The House of David Night Baseball" written on the sides carried the lighting equipment that consisted of six towers around 30 feet tall, a 100,000-watt generator operated by a 250-horsepower marine engine, and light bulbs that yielded 1,500 watts each.31 Because the system yielded better light when it was totally dark, games usually started at 8:30 p.m. or later. After the game, the team, lighting crew, and lighting system left for the next day's destination.32

Frequently overlooked, however, is the historical account of what was recorded as the first game played under lights that occurred on September 2, 1880, a year after Thomas Edison invented the incandescent lamp. Two prominent department stores fielded teams in a face-off on the back lawn of the

In a basketball game against the Chicago Taylor Trunks, a hard-playing ladies' team that often defeated the Davids, John Tucker was knocked to the floor on a jump ball and was unconscious for a few minutes before he returned to play (courtesy Brian Ziebart, House of David Commune archives).

Sea Foam House at Nantasket Bay on the ocean side of Hull, Massachusetts.[33] Three hundred curious onlookers witnessed the game that played second fiddle to the experimental test of the elaborate lighting display staged by Boston Northern Electric Lighting Company.[34]

Their lighting system was comprised of three large towers, each erected with platforms on top housing 12 electric lamps connected to three electric generators that produced a combined 30,000 candle power.[35] The next day, the press described the game, replete with errors due to poor lighting, as one played "with scarcely the precision as by daylight."[36] Records showed that at least eight more night games were sporadically played in the 19th Century with the explicit purpose of using the novelty to increase attendance. Night baseball was not played regularly until the 1930s.[37]

Manager Percy Walker got his 1930 squad off to an exciting start, winning nine of their first 12 games, including one against the Falcon Independents, managed by future Hall of Fame pitcher Stanley Coveleski, a 14-year major league veteran with Washington and Cleveland, known as one of the best spitball hurlers of the era.[38]

While on a visit to his former home in San Bernardino, California, Judge Dewhirst gave a newspaper interview that was circulated in many publications, expressing his concern that fans would attach undue importance to the fact that the House of David was no longer one entity.[39] His worries were superfluous. In 1930, he sent three "Original" House of David teams on the road, hired a steady flow of players from outside the commune to fill the rosters, and had a successful year.

Baseball salaries were cut during the Depression years, the number of barnstorming teams decreased, and subsequent barnstorming tours were reduced. However, throughout it all the Bearded Beauties, billed as the most popular team for their appearance, style of play, and their pepper game, continued facing the best semipro teams in the country.[40]

The squad from Michigan was especially in demand to face

Percy Walker was an asset when he pitched for the House of David club. Following the commune split when Francis Thorpe and many players walked with Mary Purnell to the City of David, Judge Dewhirst named Walker manager of the Original House of David team (courtesy Brian Ziebart, House of David Commune archives).

challenges from teams in the eight-county Leatherstocking area of New York. One of them was the ethnically mixed Brooklyn Bushwicks team owned and managed by Max Rosner that included many players who went to the major leagues and some who went as far as the Hall of Fame. The colorful Bushwicks played exhibition games against all barnstorming semipro clubs and, like the House of David, held their own against minor league teams that included such future major league players as Dazzy Vance and Waite Hoyt.[41] Rosner was especially proud that his gumption was often compared to that of Bill Veeck, whom he greatly admired because, he explained, "Veeck never quit."[42]

The "Wicks" quickly emerged as one of the most skilled and respected semipro teams in the New York Metropolitan area. Their exciting brand of baseball regularly filled their home field, Dexter Park, to capacity. They frequently attracted more fans than the major league Brooklyn Superbas (now the Dodgers) when both squads played in the city at the same time.[43] Owner Max Rosner, who managed the club for 31 years,[44] is considered a pioneer of night baseball at Dexter Park.[45]

Meanwhile, the press remained salted with enticing advertisements of upcoming games, the likes of "Don't Miss the Most Unique Baseball Team in the Whole World,"[46] and "The House of David, the Most Novel Baseball Exhibition in the History of Bridgewater, New Jersey."[47]

Baseball for the House of David and others of their ilk was played regardless of weather conditions, that is, unless the fields were not playable, usually due to water or mud hazards. In June a game was scheduled between the Oshkosh Indians and the touring House of David, who brought their lights for the night game. Though it was raining the day before the game, all plans were set in motion to play anyway because the Indians needed the revenue.[48] The teams took the field before a few hundred brave fans as the exhibition went forward despite muddy conditions on the field. The Davids took a 4–0 victory in a game hard-fought by both teams.[49]

One of the highlights of the season occurred on August 26, when the House of David hosted the National League New York Giants in front of 4,000 fans. Outstanding 19-year-old shortstop Sid Smith, the star for the

Pitcher Clifford "Count" Clay, City of David, 1937–41 (courtesy Brian Ziebart, House of David Commune archives).

home team, got the only hit in their 6–1 defeat.[50] Another followed in September, when former major league catcher Bill Killefer, then manager of the St. Louis Browns, faced the Berrien County All-Stars. The hometown roster was headed by manager-first baseman John Tucker from Francis Thorpe's City of David, Chief Coughlin at third, Sid Smith at shortstop, outfielder Tom Dewhirst, pitcher Al Stemm, and alternate David "Egg" Harrison.[51]

In 1931, the great pitching star of the 1926 World Series, Grover Cleveland Alexander, who had 373 wins[52] behind him and the Hall of Fame in his future (1938), was hired by Ray Doan as player-manager, expected to pitch for an inning or two in daily games. Ol' Pete lived by different rules from the others. His contract said he was not required to grow a beard, and he was given two bits a day for a shave.[53] He was paid $1,000 per month plus expenses for himself and his wife, the former Aimee Arrant, who took care of him, guarded his sobriety, and drove him everywhere on the road in their personal car.[54]

Despite Alexander's well-known problems with alcohol and the commune's past objection to imbibing, most of the players were outsiders by this time and quickly embraced him, as did all opponents who were eager to see the great hurler. In May they faced the Bushwicks for a doubleheader at their Dexter Park, where 8,000 spectators enjoyed an exhilarating afternoon in which each team took away one victory. On a return visit to Dexter Park in early October, the *Brooklyn Daily Eagle* said the Bushwicks "mowed down the House of David twice."[55]

Lou Murphy's House of David team, circa 1930 (courtesy Brian Ziebart, House of David Commune archives).

As each of the two games reached the final innings, the crowd patiently waited for the ball to be handed to Alexander, not realizing that the team they were seeing was actually Lou Murphy's House of David squad. When he failed to appear, they thought he had remained in the dugout without so much as a nod to them. The sportswriters more or less ignored that and, without explanation, they focused on the beards of the House of David players, mentioning that first baseman Jimmy Woods and center fielder Howard Shadowen "had the thickest growths in yesterday's games."[56]

As publicity for their future game in Ogden in August, the local newspaper reprinted some of the colorful comments and descriptions about the Bearded Beauties that had appeared around the country. One described the team as "unique, odd, novel, strange 'n' everything, besides they can play ball." Another said, "A novelty side show and good baseball all under one tent." Still another added, "Unlike most novelties, the novelty is only an extra measure. They can play real ball."[57] That year, 17-year-old Eddie Popowski was seen playing on a Sayreville, New Jersey, town team and was signed by the House of David, where he remained through the 1936 season.[58]

The Milwaukee Red Sox, a minor league affiliate in the Wisconsin State League, invited the House of David to bring its lighting system to face them in a night game at Borchert Field. Before the game, they were guests for lunch at the Milwaukee home of pitcher Harry Laufer that was prepared by his mother. Events like this were common as they traveled to hometowns of players. According to the *Montana Standard* (August 5, 1934), Laufer gave some pitching tips to Babe Didrikson when she was with the House of David.

Red Sox manager Eddie Stampf borrowed Brewers pitcher Claude "Bubber" Jonnard, later a longtime baseball scout, whose hardball was known to be especially effective at night. However, when Jonnard was unable to pitch that night, manager Stampf went with Ralph Blatz. As a result, the Bearded Beauties had an exciting day in front of 8,000 fans who watched them win the game, 9–4. *Kansas City Star* reporter Ernie Mele said he had previously seen one of their night games in Kansas City, and the ball could be seen "as well as it is during day games."

Apparently two of Stampf's players, Art Shires and Walter Christenson, each guaranteed $25 to play, later complained that they

Outfielder Bill Jacobs, 1934 (courtesy Brian Ziebart, House of David Commune archives).

deserved more because of the large attendance. Stampf forcibly explained that they would have gotten their pay if nobody turned up, and that's all they were entitled to get. It was reported that incidents of that sort were more typical of the era than fans realized.[59]

Though some feared a decline in the fan base due to the Depression, the barnstorming schedule remained exciting in the early years. Therefore, advance publicity for all games, including the *Denver Post* Tournament (DPT), gained a more important status. Promoters from all teams sent advance men a day or two ahead of scheduled games to spark local interest and generate ticket sales. Of course the newspapers were used whenever possible, such as an article that appeared in August 1931, that read: "The Original House of David team is the outstanding road team in America. During the past five weeks in competition with leading clubs of the west coast and Pacific Northwest House of David athletes romped home with every contest played."[60]

By that time, Frank Newhouse and Jabe Cassidy had passed the torch of DPT supervision and management to legendary *Denver Post* editor Otto Floto, who died in 1930 after a brief tenure[61] and was succeeded by Charles Lyman "Poss" Parsons, a sportswriter with the paper since 1923.[62] He had an outstanding sports career as a nine-letter athlete at the University of Iowa before serving in World War I, where he was wounded twice in France and received two Purple Hearts.[63] During Parsons' reign, the history of the House of David and the *Denver Post* tournament became somewhat intertwined in the fabric that helped destroy the color line.

Parsons saw his responsibility as continuing the success and popularity of the DPT, and he proved to be an invaluable asset who would play a big part in changing the face of play in all of baseball. Early on, he recognized that a major shortcoming of the entire tournament was the omission of racial minorities, and he knew that the color line created by the 1887 Gentlemen's

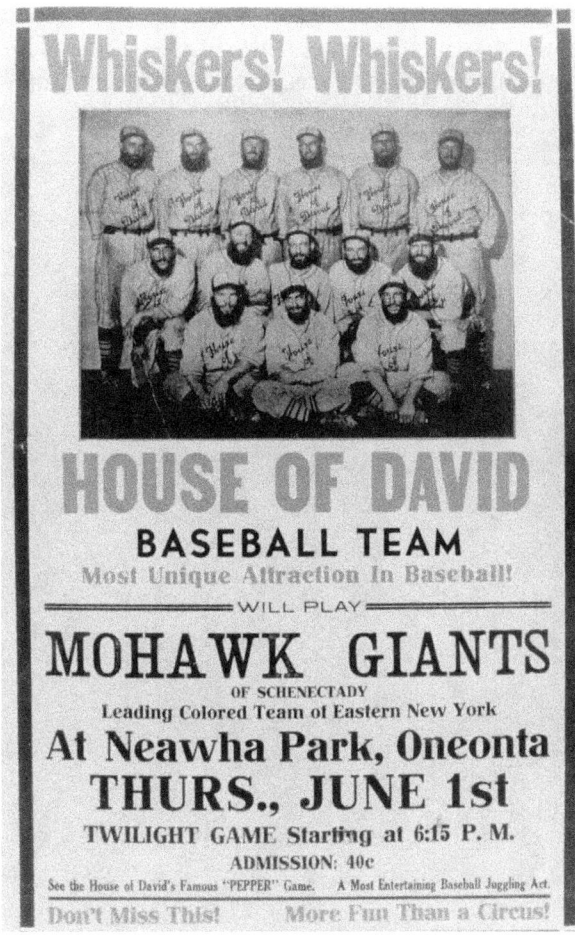

A sample of the advertisements and broadsides used by barnstorming teams throughout their travels. This one from Lou Murphy's House of David team in 1933 bears Lou's signature promise: "Whiskers! Whiskers!" (National Baseball Hall of Fame Files).

Agreement, still enforced by organized baseball, did not apply to the DPT.[64] That year, the returning Sioux City Stockyards club roster included center fielder Jake "Congo" Collins, the first African American player allowed in the tournament,[65] in his first of two appearances. "He proved to be a stellar addition as he helped lead his team to a third place finish."[66]

Meanwhile, back in Denver, after the number of teams fell to 11 in 1930 because small businesses dropped the expense of team sponsorship in order to survive, Parsons worried that number could drop further in 1931. But he came through once again when he invited the first "traveling" team: the all-white American Canadian Clowns, with its roster of players from the northwestern United States and Canada, to join 18 other entrants.

It was considered a stroke of genius on Parsons' part, even though the Clowns finished out of the money in fourth place. This, coupled with the tourney's first games under permanent lights that had been installed at Merchants Park for the Western League Denver Bears two days after the end of the 1930 season,[67] produced results even better than he anticipated. Over 51,000 in attendance broke all prior records, and a new high purse of $13,000 was shared by the three top teams.[68]

City of David team at the 1932 *Denver Post* Tournament. Seated L-R: Ray Powell, John Tucker, George Anderson, tournament mascot Tessie, Francis Thorpe, Doc Tally, William Lawrence, Pee Wee Bass. Standing, L-R: Emery Savage, Flip Fleming, Rolla Mapel, Dick Atwell, Tom McAfferty, Page Neve, Lefty Gilbert, Chuck Noel. The team finished seventh in a field of 20 (courtesy Atwell Family Collection).

4. The Thirties

As a result of the acceptance and success of the traveling Clowns in 1931, Parsons decided to continue the trend in 1932. He invited what he referred to as "the premier traveling team of the era," the House of David (actually Mary's City of David), managed by Francis Thorpe, for its first of only two appearances at the *Denver Post* Tournament, 1932 and 1934.[69]

In February 1932, a news bulletin from the Chicago Cubs' training camp at Catalina Island reported that when Grover Cleveland Alexander concluded his tenure as an aide for Cubs manager Rogers Hornsby, he would return for his second year as player-manager for the House of David Eastern Travelers.[70] With Alexander at the helm, his Eastern Travelers won 20 consecutive games, including five against such minor league clubs as Rochester (International League), Hartford (Eastern League), Binghamton and Hazleton (New York Penn League), and Chattanooga (Southern League). Afterward the streak was written about as "the greatest record any traveling team has ever had."[71]

Win, lose or draw, interests in all things about the House of David players and accounts of their travels littered the press like locations on road maps.[72] In June, the House of David faced off against the Erie Sailors in the Lake Erie area. The well-publicized game attracted the largest crowd in many years for a game in the region, as they went to see two mound greats: Erie Sailors hurler Charley "Chief" Bender and House of David pitcher Grover Cleveland Alexander. Although they were in the majors at the same time, they had never faced each other. Bender pitched three innings to Alexander's two, and the Sailors defeated the Bearded Beauties, 5–4, thanks to a ninth-inning come-back

(L-R) Old baseball friends, pitcher Doc Tally, Grover Cleveland Alexander, and unidentified player, circa 1933 (courtesy Brian Ziebart, House of David Commune archives).

rally.[73] Later, the two future Hall of Famers would also add the title "Manager, House of David," to their resumes.

On June 29, a unique notice appeared on page 14 of the *Chicago Tribune* regarding the July 4, three-day celebration at Benton Harbor when the Whiskerinos would host two games with Joe Green's Chicago Giants. It was one of the first times news regarding the House of David was sandwiched in among other events rather than headlined. The list mentioned other activities such as a "music festival, open air dancing, miniature trains, baseball, hotel, cabins, restaurants, aviary and zoo, bowling, two bands, two daily vaudeville acts, free parking." It continued with "Take a Goodrich Boat—Chicago to Benton Harbor. Boats leave Chicago daily—10:00 a.m. Boats leave Benton Harbor daily—4:30 p.m."[74] During that season, the baseball scene in Benton Harbor changed. Tom Dewhirst's Home Team answered far more out-of-town invitations than usual and traveled through Michigan, Wisconsin, Illinois, Indiana, Ohio, and Iowa.[75]

Thorpe's squad approached the 1932 DPT in mid–August heavily favored to win.[76] At the halfway point of the competition, they were one of four undefeated teams when things fell apart. They lost their first game to the Sioux City nine in front of the largest crowd to date in tournament history, and were quickly dealt their second defeat, this time by the Phillips 66 team from Texas, resulting in their elimination with a disappointing third-place finish. Veteran pitcher Rolla Mapel took the loss for the "embarrassed Michigan club."[77] Colorful first baseman John Tucker was voted most popular player of the event.[78]

Afterward, the Benton Harbor fans were elated to learn that Tom Dewhirst's Central States nine and Alexander's squad had scheduled a rare game against each other at Eden Springs Park in Benton Harbor. Alexander's squad had just returned from what was called an "invasion of the Midwestern cities" where they won more than half their battles. It would be just his second scheduled appearance to pitch at Eden Springs Park.[79]

The 1933 season was one with different changes and challenges for the House of David. Before it began, Ray Doan signed future Hall of Fame pitcher Charles Albert "Chief" Bender as manager of the Eastern Traveling team, moving Alexander to head the Western squad. Bender, whose mother was half–Chippewa Indian, had pitched 459 major league games over 16 years (1903–1925), including three complete games in the 1911 World Series.[80] Like Alexander, he was not required to grow a beard or long hair and was paid 35 cents a day, the cost of a shave.[81] His contract stipulated that he pitch at least one inning per game, but he usually scheduled himself for eighth or ninth inning appearances and hoped for rain.[82] Always called "Chief," which he felt was a racial slur, he signed all autographs "Charley Bender."[83]

Unfortunately his tenure there did not go as planned. During one exciting game, he was seriously injured when a teammate's bat flew out of his hand and into the dugout hitting Bender squarely on the knee and shattering his knee cap. Bender was relegated to bed rest during his two-month recovery. To add insult to injury, despite a signed contract for the entire season, the House of David refused to pay his medical bills or his salary for that period. He sued the commune for $700 in lost wages at $350 per month before severing all ties with them.[84]

There were other difficulties in 1933. In April, before the start of the season and Bender's injury, Francis Thorpe and Ray Doan signed a mutual contract by which Thorpe would not take his City of David squad on the road for the entire season in exchange for a payment of $1,000 to be made in four installments of $250. In addition, Thorpe gave him rights to three players, Tally, Tucker, and Anderson, as long as the payments were made. Then Doc Tally and John Tucker were moved to the Western Travelers, managed by Alexander, and George Anderson to Bender's Eastern Travelers. Not to be cheated, after the season ended a dissatisfied and angry Thorpe sued Doan on the basis of non-payment of this contract.[85]

On a more positive note, a new pitching attraction, 19-year-old southpaw Jackie Mitchell, was loaned to the House of David for the season by the Chattanooga Lookouts of the Class A Southern Association.

Remembered as one of the first female pitchers in semipro or professional baseball, she traveled with the team with her mother as chaperone.[86] Repeated publicity said she had struck out both Babe Ruth and Lou Gehrig on seven pitches[87] in an exhibition at Engle Stadium, home of the Chattanooga Lookouts, on April 2, 1931, when she was just 17 years old.[88]

Always busy, in 1933 Doan opened the Ray Doan Baseball School, also known as Ray Doan's All-Star Baseball Academy, in Hot Springs, Arkansas, which later changed locations a few times. The first four-week session was attended by 66 young players.[89] During the depth of the Depression, he attracted an average of 400 students.[90] Over the years, Doan maintained an impressive staff of instructors, most of whom were future members of the Hall of Fame: Grover Cleveland Alexander (1933–35), Rogers Hornsby (1933–38), Burleigh Grimes (1934–36), Dizzy Dean (1934–37), Schoolboy Rowe (1936–37), Tris Speaker (1936), Red Faber (1938), and Cy Young (1938).[91] In 1940, Babe Ruth joined the staff as an instructor at Doan's school in Palatka, Florida.[92]

The season began with the traveling teams setting attendance records once again. They attracted 15,000 in St. Louis against the Cardinals, and 20,000 in Chicago, as they became known as "the greatest novelty baseball attraction."[93] At the end of the season in September, they faced and defeated the St. Louis Cardinals, 8–6, in front of 10,000 cheering fans at Sportsman's Park. Jackie Mitchell started the game and pitched with her usual poise, giving up a single which was soon voided by a slick double play. When she batted in the first inning, she was out on a pop fly to Leo Durocher.[94]

Alexander's nine had successful outings most times out of the gate during the season, the most notable when they defeated a star-studded St. Louis Cardinals club that included Ducky Medwick, Leo Durocher, and Rogers Hornsby. During that period, they were credited with teaching the famed Gas House Gang the pepper game.[95]

During this time, Parsons and his staff hoped the success of the 1932 *Denver Post* Tournament would serve as a magnet for the upcoming 1933 event. However, as fate would have it, the impact of the Depression permeated Denver for the first time, almost four years behind the rest of the country. Thousands who lost their jobs in the hardest-hit industries—agriculture, mining, and tourism—applied for relief. Extra money for baseball all but dried up.[96] Nevertheless, Parsons went all-out and invited the largest turnout in the life of the event to date: 22 teams from eight states with 17 former major league players scattered among those rosters.[97] However, though more teams required more games and more trips through the turnstiles, attendance dropped to 46,000, with the lowest purse since 1929: $9,882.[98] It was even described as "lackluster due to the absence of entertaining teams and great storylines that had previously pulled fans to the invitational."[99]

After the 1932 minor league season, the Denver Bears pulled out of the Western

League and disbanded, leaving the DPT as the only recreational outlet and baseball showcase in the region.[100] Despite the lure of baseball under the lights combined with the attraction of more former big league names than in the past and the curiosity about the first team sponsored by the Democratic political party, known as the Kansas City Rabbits, the 1933 event was never described as better than "underwhelming."[101] The tournament was in trouble.[102]

By the time the 1934 season began, Alexander and Mildred "Babe" Didrikson were already signed. Didrikson, considered the greatest female athlete of her generation after her performance in the 1932 Olympics, announced she would barnstorm with the House of David for the 1934 season. With Alexander managing the Eastern team, she would perform as the main attraction, making $1,000 a month while most of the other players made $200–$300.[103]

Prior to donning their uniform, she enrolled in Ray Doan's baseball school in Hot Springs on March 4 and received pitching lessons from instructor Burleigh Grimes before she joined the squad. Photos taken of her training appeared in newspapers across the country and became successful publicity packages. Although she contributed to the team on the field and at the box office, she did not travel with them. Thus she missed out on a lot of the camaraderie and fun they shared, which she explained as her aversion to traveling with the players in their sweaty wool uniforms when there was no time or place to change after games.[104]

The much-anticipated first game of the season of the Eastern Travelers was in Chicago against the Logan Squares, with Didrikson on the mound in front of over 4,000 spectators. In two innings, she gave up two runs, walked one batter, struck out another, and hit a ground ball single in her second trip to the plate. Everything she did gained applause from all in attendance as the Bearded Beauties claimed a 12–3 victory.[105]

After a week to ten-day spring training session at Eden Springs Park, Judge Dewhirst predicted a successful season and turned over all general managing chores and details to the former booking agent for the team, Ray Doan, who planned to travel with the Western nine to handle affairs at the gate and on the playing field. In addition to Alexander's appointment as Eastern Travelers manager, he appointed Tommy Dewhirst, one of the sons of Judge Dewhirst, manager of the traveling Central States club. The Western travelers carried the lighting system. Each team received new uniforms.[106] Perhaps 1934, with its kaleidoscope of events, was the most significant season for the House of David in terms of its contribution to the future of the game, primarily due to their role in the *Denver Post* Tournament.

But other events preceded the DPT. The matter of lawsuits continued when, on January 20, Judge Dewhirst sued Louis Murphy for $2,500, the first of many suits pursued all over the country, in an attempt to get him to stop using the House of David name for his own baseball and basketball teams. All litigants named in the suits had been warned numerous times over the past five years. Though Murphy had no commune members on his team, they did grow beards and put House of David logos on their uniforms and merchandise they sold. Finally New York Judge John M. Woolsey ruled that the use of the name by Murphy and others was unauthorized and unfair, although he did permit teams to grow their hair and beards as they wished.[107]

Through it all, baseball was played as the team and the fans were not concerned. The House of David was on fire, especially when they played the Pampa Road Runners the first week in June as part of the Pre-Centennial Pioneer Roundup sponsored by the

Pampa Junior Chamber of Commerce. Doing well in Texas had always been their forte, and that day was no exception.

When the dust settled after nine innings, the Davids were on top of a 32–21 score. Of their 34 hits, one outsider, Dick Atwell, had smashed three home runs, one a grand slam, and added two singles to the mix. Longtime commune member Dick Wykoff also got five hits, including one home run. The combined 53 tallies that crossed the plate that day beat a major league record for most runs scored in a game, established August 25, 1922, when Chicago defeated Philadelphia, 26–23, in a contest talked about for years.[108]

At this time, a new phenomenon appeared on the scene.[109] Thanks to Doan, often dubbed the "first and last word in profitable barnstorming" and a self-proclaimed father of donkey baseball,[110] Alexander's club added it to their repertoire and began traveling with a batch of Missouri mules.[111] The normal routine became the following: five minutes after the regularly scheduled contest, which included the usual fifth inning interruption for their pepper game, they brought the mules on the field for a two-inning donkey game, to the delight of the fans.[112] Alexander was featured in numerous newspaper sketches riding one of the donkeys.[113]

All the while, Parsons pondered possibilities for a new gimmick for the 1934 *Denver Post* Tournament. Oliver "The Ghost" Marcelle, considered by many as the greatest third baseman in Negro Leagues history as well as somewhat of a character in his own right,[114] had recently retired from his 14-year playing career[115] and moved to the Five Points Negro community in Denver.[116]

Marcelle knew Parsons as one of the best-known sports figures in the Rocky Mountain area and persuaded him to invite the prestigious all-black Kansas City Monarchs, the longest-running franchise in the history of the Negro Leagues. It was[117] considered by the press as the best and most popular black semipro team of the era and called "one of the best ball clubs in America regardless of race" by the *Pittsburgh Courier*.[118] Newspapers across the country picked up the story, calling it "the most significant announcement in a decade insofar as Negro baseball was concerned."[119]

When Parsons announced he had invited the House of David, led by manager Grover Cleveland Alexander, his "gimmick" was complete. The Mon-

Grover Cleveland Alexander with "his donkey" in one of many donkey ballgames (courtesy Noir Tech Research, Inc).

1934 Kansas City Monarchs. Top row L-R: Willie Foster, George Giles, T. J. Young, Norman "Turkey" Stearns, Chet Brewer, Sam Crawford, Johnson Donaldson, Charley Beverly, Andy Cooper. Bottom row L-R: Frank Duncan, Jr., Wilbur "Bullet" Rogan, Dink Mothell, Sam Bankhead, Frank Duncan III, Newt Allen, Newt Joseph, Eddie Dwight (courtesy Noir Tech Research, Inc.).

archs and Davids had toured together for roughly 40 games at the end of previous seasons, traveling coast to coast in Canada, always attracting large crowds and press coverage.[120] The travels of the two teams have been described as "the Monarchs' partnership with a money-making machine called the House of David."[121]

It functioned like a well-oiled system whereby the Monarchs played through an area first, defeating all comers, followed by the Michigan crew a few days later, who repeated the process. Then the two barnstorming teams returned together to those towns and put on "championship" exhibition games against each other.[122] Buck O'Neil recalled, "They [House of David] always had a good baseball club, and it was a payday for our bosses because we were on salary. It was quite an experience, but a lot of travel because you played a different place every day."[123]

Marcelle correctly saw this as a way to create greater interest to increase gate receipts.[124] However, there was one potential snafu. The Monarchs had severed ties with the Negro Leagues in 1930, but continued as an independent team. In that capacity they played winning baseball in 18 states as well as Canada and Mexico, frequently before large, racially mixed crowds.[125] Because they had successfully battled numerous white teams during the first years of the Depression and were widely considered a "big league attraction" in the Midwest, their eligibility to compete in the DPT with semipro status was questioned. When the dust settled, their lack of affiliation with Organized Baseball, coupled with their classification as a semipro team by the white press, cleared the air and rendered them eligible to compete.[126]

Beyond the excitement of the addition of the Monarchs, the only Negro team with white ownership, J. L. Wilkinson and Thomas Baird, pregame publicity and predictions appeared in newspapers across the country. Perhaps sportswriter Chester Washington in his "Sez Ches" column for the *Pittsburgh Courier* summed it up best with high praise for "the *Denver Post* editors' broadness of mind" and again declared the invitation of the Monarchs as "the most significant announcement in a decade by Negro baseball."[127]

The names of the 18 teams who accepted invitations to the competition were announced on July 31,[128] but the 1933 winners, Denver M&O Cigars, broke tradition and were noticeably absent though some of their players appeared on rosters of other teams.[129] Predictions that the Monarchs and the House of David would be the two featured attractions in the quest for the first prize of $7,500 proved to be accurate.[130] Throughout the 1934 games, the *Denver Post* Tournament attracted national attention as the "first major competition of the twentieth century in the United States to bring professional black and white teams together in something other than exhibition games."[131]

According to the press, the last series on the road before the tourney saw the Monarchs and House of David face off in a four- or five-game exhibition series. They were accustomed to playing each other and knew the opposing players well. Each game was viewed by a minimum crowd of 3,500 who saw the Monarchs win every contest.[132]

The pitching of Kansas City ace Chet Brewer and Ol' Pete Alexander, plus fast fielding and timely hitting displayed by both teams, was seen as a sample of what was to come in the DPT. Fans were not disappointed as they watched throughout the tournament while "each day the number of contenders winnowed by two teams" in accordance with the established elimination rule.[133]

From its inception, these two squads drew the largest crowds and greatest press attention throughout the August tourney. The Monarchs brought a power lineup to the competition: first baseman George Giles, second baseman Sam Bankhead, shortstop Newt Allen, third baseman Newt Joseph, and outfielders Eddie Dwight and two future Hall of Famers, Norman "Turkey" Stearnes and Bullet Rogan. Pitchers included Chet Brewer, Sam Crawford, and Rube Foster's half-brother, Willie, who also went to the Hall of Fame.[134] Another big name on that roster was legendary John Donaldson, then a pinch-runner at age 43, but remembered by Parsons and other sportswriters as one of the greatest pitchers in baseball during his prime.

Pitcher Norman "Turkey" Stearnes was given the nickname because his arms flapped like a turkey as he rounded the bases. Although he had appeared in exhibition games in Denver with the exciting Negro League team, the St. Louis Stars, he was not permitted to play in the DPT until 1934. He played 18 seasons in the Negro Leagues and was inducted into the Baseball Hall of Fame in 2000,[135] along with John "Bid" McPhee, regarded by most as one of the best second baseman in the 19th century. McPhee played his entire major league career in Cincinnati before becoming one of baseball's first scouts.[136]

The "Jesus Boys," a name given to the team by Satchel Paige that first became popular among the Negro squads,[137] had manager Grover Cleveland Alexander of the House of David Eastern Traveling Team at the helm. Their roster for this highly publicized competition included Warren "Lefty" Weirman, P; Moon Mullen, 2B; Albert "Lefty" Tolles, P-LF; Mel Ingram, CF; Buster Blakeney, SS; Spike Hunter, P; Dewey Hill, C; Lloyd Miller, P, and reserves Billy Joseph, John Cross, Art Murphy, Elmore E. Ambrose, and Carl Holland.[138]

In addition, the House of David booking agent for the traveling team, Ray Doan, bolstered his pitching staff by making a deal with Gus Greenlee, owner of the Pittsburgh Crawfords, to add Satchel Paige and his catcher, Cy Perkins, for the tournament.[139] This has been suggested as having a twofold purpose: in addition to helping the Davids win the tourney, it also made the statement that the commune that did not include Negro members was not prejudiced.[140]

The Monarchs and pitcher Chet Brewer quickly showed their prowess against their first opponent, the Greenlee Advertisers, who fortified their lineup with the addition of pitcher Tom "Pistol Pete" Albright, a Denver sandlot legend who had played with the Negro Denver White Elephants. Despite the lopsided 12–1 victory, the two hurlers put on quite a show as Brewer struck out 19 and Albright 15.[141]

The Monarchs continued their winning ways in their ensuing two games against less talented teams. They took game two from the Denver Athletic Club, 4–3, followed by a ten-inning affair in which they garnered a 5–4 win against Schneider Jewelry of Kansas City.[142]

In contrast, things seemed easier for the bearded club. In their first outing, Spike Hunter pitched a strong game as they handed the Denver Italian Bakery a 16–0 drubbing, with Paige making his first appearance in the final inning.[143] The next day it was reported in the *Kansas City Call* that "it is a most unusual thing in baseball circles to see a Negro pitcher hurling for a white team in an effort to cop the prize money of $5,000."[144]

Game two, when they faced the Eason, Oklahoma, Oilers, was later called "the finest game ever played in Denver by the House of David."[145] All 4,034 fans cheered in amazement as Satchel Paige struck out 14 with a fastball described as "spitting fire" while his teammates batted their way to a 6–1 victory.[146]

In addition to his reputation of relishing frequent mound appearances, Paige was known for naming his pitches.[147] In his second start in three nights, he faced the undefeated Humble Oilers from Texas, and he once again amazed a crowd that had grown to 6,314. He dominated the Oilers, striking out 17 as he handed them a 4–0 shutout. Like a magnet, for the rest of the tournament he attracted the full attention of sportswriters and fans alike.

The Monarchs and House of David, the only two undefeated teams left in the competition, faced each other in a Friday night game in their fourth round of play.[148] Anticipation was rampant. One *Denver Post* writer described the pending game as one where "the greatest Negro pitcher in the world is to face the greatest Negro club."[149]

The Merchants Park staff made arrangements for the field to handle an overflow crowd up to 4,000 beyond the venue's 8,000 capacity. Their expectations were exceeded as a record 11,120 fans saw the game inside the park.[150] The gates to the entrance of the park were closed half an hour before game time, thus an additional crowd of several thousand was turned away "The highlight of the tournament," as the game was remembered, was a nail-biter as Paige and Brewer faced off. With the game locked in at one run apiece in the eighth inning, the Michigan crew scored the tie-breaker to win the game, 2–1, handing the Monarchs their first defeat.[151]

During the final days of the tourney, there was a dust-up when Alexander caught

Paige warming up from his knees as he whipped the ball to his catcher. Alexander expressed his disapproval of the behavior, they argued loudly, then patched things up.[152]

Both teams faced challenges in their fifth game. Willie Foster pitched the Monarchs to a 5–4 defeat of the Eason Oilers. The House of David had a tougher task against United Fuel of Denver. They sent pitcher Warren Wierman, who had pitched for the Class A Chattanooga Lookouts in 1928, to face Elam Vangilder, who had won 19 games for the St. Louis Browns in 1922. The Denverites led, 13–8, in the bottom of the ninth when the Davids waged a six-run rally to take the game, 14–13, to the delight of the raucous crowd. It was no surprise that both teams had won their semifinal games.[153] The newspapers called this one the "wildest game in the tournament."[154]

The excitement level was high concerning the August 13 championship game between the Monarchs, with one defeat under their belts, and the undefeated House of David. To everyone's surprise, Alexander took the team full circle and pitched Spike Hunter, the foundation of his pitching squad, in order to save Paige in case the Davids should lose and need to play one more game. The press said "Hunter's fast one had a baffling hop on it" throughout the game, and he stopped the lone scoring threat of the Monarchs in the third inning when, with runners on, he struck out three batters on nine pitches.[155] The game ended quietly with the Davids winning by the score of 2–1,[156] and it was later called "the game of games, a standout of standouts, a Titanic struggle."[157] After Alexander led his team to the *Denver Post* Championship,[158] for several weeks headlines everywhere called that tournament the greatest in its history.[159]

When all was said and done, Chester Washington of the *Pittsburgh Courier* summed up the competition in one poignant sentence: "When Satchel Paige twirled for the House of David, the Monarchs and all competing ballclubs began having fifty-seven varieties of headaches."[160] Headlines on page one of The *Denver Post* emphasized once again "1934 Post Tourney Greatest in History."[161] It has long been the consensus of scholars that the 1934 DPT was the most significant contribution to the game of baseball made by the House of David team.

Newspapers reported that the 70,000 paid admissions smashed all previous tournament attendance records.[162] Though the total net gate receipts remain unknown due to the custom of the owners and promoters to take as much as 50 to 60 percent to cover their expenses,[163] the money was considered breathtaking for less than two weeks' work during the Depression. The Davids walked away with an estimated $5,800–$6,458.75 first place money, and the Monarchs pocketed approximately $4,844 for second.[164]

Historians agree about what was accomplished in Denver during 13 days in August 1934: "Despite many other integrated tournaments that got good press attention, the DPT brought black baseball to mainstream America."[165] According to columnist Al Warden of the *Ogden Standard*, "The $2,500 Satchel Paige is said to have received for his abbreviated appearance in the DPT is more than double the salary Pacific Coast League pitchers get for a full 25-week season of work."[166]

It's been written by one Satchel Paige biographer, Larry Tye, that Satchel's stint with the House of David in the 1934 DPT was the first time white reporters "caught a prolonged look at black baseball's best kept secret."[167]

When all was said and done in Denver, the House of David, without missing a beat, boarded their vehicles with their first prize money from the DPT safe in their bat bags and readied to hit the road to continue their barnstorming tour.[168]

But not everything during those weeks was good news. It was announced the day after the competition ended that federal government officers in the U.S. Postal Department had launched a probe investigating a threatening, unsigned letter from Benton Harbor to Davids pitcher Spike Hunter, saying that "for his own good he should lay [sic] down and throw the final game to the Monarchs." Hunter ignored it and pitched a powerful game. That case was never solved.[169]

A few weeks later, the rules committee issued a clarification, saying that beginning in 1935, no more mixed-race teams could participate in the DPT, and only one black team would be invited each year. In May 1935, the *Chicago Defender* reported another rule change, stating "no colored pitcher will be allowed to pitch on a white mixed team," as an edict everyone thought was aimed directly at Satchel Paige. Thus, when the House of David contacted Greenlee seeking Paige's services for 1935, tournament powers that be said the only way he could appear was to pitch for a Negro team.[170]

Shortly after the tourney, Washington Senators owner Calvin Griffith invited pitcher Allen "Bullet Ben" Benson to a workout with his team at Griffith Stadium. Benson was then signed as part of Griffith's efforts to lift the Senators out of the doldrums of their last-place finishes year after year. Unfortunately for the 29-year-old MLB rookie, the experience was a disaster.[171] Benson appeared in only two games and pitched 9⅔ innings, before he was released with a 12.10 ERA.[172]

By mid–September 1934, the House of David had made their way to Pampa, Texas, where they were not surprised to find additional bleachers had been constructed to accommodate anticipated overflow crowds when pregame publicity said the Davids, the

Pitcher Allen Benson grooming his beard in the Washington Senators clubhouse before his first appearance with the team (courtesy Brian Ziebart, House of David Commune archives).

squad that had defeated them 32–21 in the spring, was coming off of their win of the *Denver Post* Tournament.[173]

Before the team arrived, the *Pampa Daily News* presented a quarter-page article about the House of David roster, with brief backgrounds of each player.

> This team consists of 1B Long John Tucker, considered one of the greatest first basemen of his day, team manager and member of the pepper game trio; 2B "Hub" Hanson who played with Des Moines in the Western League in 1933 and had been scouted by many big league teams; 3B George Anderson, versatile player who was also one of the pepper game threesome; SS Dick Atwell, former Western League player who was briefly with the Pacific Coast League S.F. Seals and led the Davids with 26 homers in 1933; LF Roy Hutson, formerly in the Southern Association where he batted .370, and has batted .300 in the Texas League; RF Dick Wykoff, formerly with the Cincinnati Reds, later Columbus, and hit .382 with the House of David in 1933; CF Frank Clift, formerly with Oklahoma City and Omaha in the Western League and led the *Denver Post* Tournament in homers in 1933; C Flip Fleming, formerly with Milwaukee in American Association for several years where he caught an average of 150 games in each of those years; and Jesse "Doc" Tally, with the David team since its inception and had pitched over 400 games, had his best all-around year in 1933, and a member of the pepper trio.[174] At that time many of these players were well-known to barnstorming baseball fans everywhere.

They defeated the Pampa nine in both night games. Again shortstop Dick Atwell, who had become a favorite ever since he "posted the longest homer in a four-game series against the Monarchs in Winnipeg,"[175] received raves from the local press, this time primarily for his defense, which was described as "sensational as he roamed far and wide to pick up impossible chances and make perfect pegs." Al Nusser commanded things from the mound through six innings, when he injured his ankle sliding into third base. He refused to leave the game and pitched in the seventh before Speisman relieved him. Atwell's two-run homer over the left field fence was the difference in the score.[176]

On a visit to Mason, Iowa, on the way to their season-ending series in Omaha in late October, a tired Alexander gave an interview in the lobby of the Hotel Hanford in which he discussed the 1934 season. He called baseball a tramp's life, as he recounted the grueling schedule.[177] He had played on both the Eastern team—entirely east of the Mississippi River in New York and Eastern areas—and Western team, so that he and Babe Didrikson, who signed with the team on March 1, 1934, could switch teams throughout the summer to permit fans everywhere to see each of them in action.[178]

The DPT championship and the addition of Olympian Babe Didrikson were considered the highlights of that season.[179] Records indicate they accrued a record of 142 wins against 50 losses.[180]

During the last week of September, things lightened up when the Auto Specialties team from nearby St. Joseph issued a telegram with what became an annual invitation for a one-game event to be played for a 31-gallon barrel of beer.[181] The "official" reply was as follows: "Advise that we will play his team for an exhibition game Sunday, October 7, at House of David baseball park for a 31 gallon barrel of beer. Stop. Losers pay for beer. Stop. Tell Waldo he can use Warnicke if he wants to. Signed, House of David Baseball Club, Bob Dewhirst, Secretary."[182]

While all eyes in Benton Harbor were focused on the adventures of their own traveling teams, another tournament event appeared on the scene: the National Baseball Congress (NBC). Up to that point, all tournaments were regional, when Raymond "Hap" Dumont, called Baseball's Barnum, successfully launched the first national event, the National Baseball Congress (NBC) in Wichita, Kansas. It began as the "Kansas State

Semi-Pro Championships" in 1931, but soon became greater than even Dumont possibly imagined.[183]

Dumont initially hired well-known baseball men and future Hall of Famers Ty Cobb, George Sisler, Tris Speaker, and Fred Clarke as tournament advisors in an attempt to align the NBC with organized baseball. In its initial stages, the tournament was so successful that after its wooden baseball park burned to the ground in 1933, Dumont sought and got financing from the city of Wichita to build a 10,000-seat,[184] $125,000 baseball stadium called Lawrence Stadium, later renamed Lawrence-Dumont Stadium.[185]

It was Dumont's dream to "outdo the Denver Post Tournament in size and sizzle" by creating more interest in non-professional baseball. Because he counted on town loyalties to maximize attendance, he wanted nothing to do with barnstorming teams like the House of David, the Kansas City Monarchs, and other noted travelers.[186] The NBC grew into the most successful and longest lasting of all the tourneys. It continues today, credited with producing over 800 professional players.[187]

The 1935 season began on a high note for Mary's City of David club. John Tucker had taken the helm in 1934 when Mary requested that Thorpe step away from baseball to take on responsibilities as her right-hand man in her commune.

But Thorpe never took his eyes off their baseball situation.[188] Accordingly, when they left for spring training in Laredo, Texas, Thorpe, in his 20th year of House of David supervision of one kind or another, accompanied them to assist with player selection for the season.[189]

During that time, they faced and defeated a handful of major league clubs before heading to Chicago to play several games with strong independent teams. The *News Palladium* reported that their 1934 season was especially successful: noting that the team went 142-41 with 5 ties.[190] Austrian-born Jack Quinn, a former major league spitball pitcher for 23 seasons (1909–1933), was appointed manager of the House of David Eastern team, and Alexander was moved to manage the Western nine.[191] In an attempt to avoid confusion among the fans as to which House of David team would appear in their town, the press labeled them as the team that won the DPT in 1934.[192]

They started 1935 on a tear! Headlines across the country said, "Bearded Boys Have Won 33 of 37 Games: 4 Losses Are to ML Clubs."[193]

Doan's Western Travelers headed for a series in Denver on their

Heavy-hitting Bill Marlott, shortstop, City of David 1934–1938 (courtesy Brian Ziebart, House of David Commune archives).

way to the West Coast for the bulk of their season. As expected, they drew large crowds at all stops, especially when it was learned that Dutch Faust would join the squad.[194] A couple of weeks later, colorful pitcher Elmer Dean, the peanut-vending brother of Dizzy and Paul Dean, dubbed "Goober" by the fans but who preferred the self-titled "Elmer the Great," was with the team briefly after attending Ray Doan's baseball school. Never seen as a baseball talent, he did win a couple of games, but he was signed as someone whose playful antics would draw curious crowds.[195]

At the same time, Quinn's team headed East with a powerful and intimidating squad. It was written that "without question his infield was the best ever put out by the House of David: 1b Bosse, 2B Moon Mullen, SS Chozen, 3B Anderson, and utility player Walter Faust, who doubled as driver of the team bus."[196]

The semipro team in Bismarck, North Dakota, owned by Chrysler salesman Neil Churchill was considered one of the best teams in the region. The independent, interracial club was well stocked with such Negro Leagues stars as pitchers Satchel

Elmer "Goober" Dean (left) and Ray Doan, 1935. A bit of a character, Dean told all who would listen that he taught his brothers Dizzy and Daffy to pitch and that he was better than both of them (courtesy Brian Ziebart, House of David Commune archives).

Paige and Hilton Smith (both inducted into the Hall of Fame), and Ted "Double Duty" Radcliffe. Paige said they were the greatest team he ever played with. Initially called the Bismarcks before the name was changed to the Churchills in 1935, they won the NBC Tournament in Wichita that year, then were barred from it when the rules were revised, excluding interracial teams. The team regularly played in North Dakota and Manitoba, Canada.[197]

Knowing Babe Ruth's contract with the Yankees would expire at the end of the 1934 season, in April Ray Doan announced he had cabled Ruth and offered him $35,000 to join them in 1935. Ruth declined.[198] The following June, Tom Baird disclosed that he had extended another suggestion to Ruth, offering him $20,000 to play the remainder of the 1935 barnstorming season with the Whiskerinos after his major league career ended, explaining that he wouldn't have to grow a beard. Still no luck, although just for fun Ruth did appear for a popular photo of himself in a faux House of David beard.[199]

At the end of May, Tom Dewhirst's Central States team, with mostly new faces, played in front of 7–8,000 excited fans who were jammed into every corner of Gleason Field in Gary, Indiana. In what had become a common venue for the House of David, they played a local All-Star team assembled specifically to face them. In a common strategy in their games, the Davids scored multiple runs in the first inning to grab a lead, then defended it for the remaining innings, as they did in Gary, to win by a 5–1 score.[200]

A few weeks later, Alexander's nine was facing the Bismarck Churchills in North Dakota. The tight game on Memorial Day was in the eighth inning when tempers flared after an exciting play on the bases went against the House of David. Though the umpire loudly called their runner out at the plate, they disagreed and charged him, bringing the fans to their feet. According to the *Mandan Pioneer*, "a riot ensued" among fans in the stands. Police were needed to curtail the conflict. Nobody was hurt, no blows were struck, but everyone was shocked

Grover Cleveland Alexander, aka "Ol' Pete," made brief appearances on the mound for both teams he owned and managed after leaving the Benton Harbor teams (courtesy Brian Ziebart, House of David Commune archives).

to see the Davids players "lose their Christian cool." When the fracas ended, Bismarck pitcher Satchel Paige returned to the mound for the ninth inning and sealed his 8–7 victory.[201]

The last week in September 1935, the House of David began a barnstorming tour to five states in Old Mexico, including their annual series with La Junta, which always attracted crowds of 6,000 or more. They played in Mexico City from October 18 through November 5.[202]

When the season ended, Grover Cleveland Alexander left the House of David and moved on to manage two different teams in his final appearances in the *Denver Post* Tournament: the McVittie's House of David (no connection to the Benton Harbor teams) in 1936 and McVittie's Restaurant in 1937.[203]

He then formed and managed a team of his own called House of Alex in 1938, before he was inducted into the Hall of Fame that year.[204] For that endeavor, he partnered with sports promoter Buster Connors of Springfield, Illinois. However, their semipro bearded barnstorming team, composed of former semipro and minor league players, only lasted two seasons.[205] They traveled primarily in the northeastern United States and Canada. Though Alexander owned the team, covered as the Whiskered Wizards by the Canadian press, he rarely travelled with them, but was presented in "grand fashion" when he did.[206] They were frequently called "an imposter House of David team" because they wore beards.[207]

Pitcher Don Hendrickson, who later played two major league seasons with the Boston Braves in the mid-'40s, remembered the generosity of the House of David during the few years he played with them. He remembered the winter of 1935–1936, when he was one of 14 House of David players who went on a 21-week tour to the Philippines. He said he was guaranteed $85 a week pitching, "but we used to average about $95 because we received a percentage of the receipts. My highest pay check was $171 for one week's tour."[208]

The 1936 Summer Olympics in Berlin made headlines two months before the first competition. It was the first time the lighted torch was relayed by footmen across Europe from Olympia, Greece, to the site of the games.[209] Though what happened during the games themselves had nothing to do with House of David baseball directly at that time, it was more impactful to baseball and the hated color line than any event before it. Adolf Hitler, intending to use the games as a Third Reich propaganda vehicle, was thwarted when African American track star Jesse Owens won four gold medals for the United States.[210]

The press had already picked up the gauntlet and espoused the end of race discrimination in organized baseball. Columnist Jimmy Powers of the *New York Daily News* wrote that since blacks could compete in the Olympics in basketball and boxing, not to mention the 1936 successes of Jesse Owens in Germany, blacks could certainly play major league baseball.[211] Even the Communist newspaper, the *Daily Worker*, regularly pushed for integration.[212]

Meanwhile, the House of David completed its usual 25,000+ miles on the road as they faced the "usual" opposition all over the United States. Young catcher Lloyd Dalager, son of former pitcher and team bus driver Hans Dalager, remembered the season as a hectic and exciting one. "We went to Chicago, through Michigan, and into Canada all the way to Montreal, then came down through Niagara Falls and through New York to New York City. Playing against the New York Black Yankees we suffered a rare lopsided defeat. I don't remember the score, but they whipped us pretty bad. They were the best team we ever played."[213]

After spring training in Texas, Mary's City of David team, with an impressive and well-known lineup of players well-noted by the press, made its way to Emporia, Kansas. In addition to regulars 3B George Anderson, 1B John Tucker, and P Pee Wee Bass, the roster included players with what was termed "professional league" experience: 3B Hub Hanson, Des Moines; LF Sam Sclaing, Texas League; SS Dick Atwell, Pacific Coast League; RF Roy Hutson, Texas League; and C Bill Steinecke, who had appeared in four games with the Pittsburgh Pirates in 1931.[214] They are said to have played 212 games that year, the most since their inception, and compiled one of the best records in their history: 160 wins, 52 defeats. After traveling over 30,000 miles via bus in the U.S., Mexico and Canada, they took a month-long trip to Hawaii, where they played 13 games and won 11.[215]

However, during this period interest in baseball had temporarily waned. Attendance was down at all levels as the Depression deepened. Some sportswriters attributed it to a growing interest in football, while others said fewer and fewer towns could afford to field barnstorming or other teams. They added that the House of David teams began to decline in talent as a larger number of young players were signed by organized minor leagues, from Class C to Class AA level.

Columnist Joe Williams wrote, "An old ballplayer can't drop any lower than the House of Davids. [*sic*] This is an absolute zero in the profession. The whole setup is pretty smelly, the prostitution of the name, the burlesque comedians' whiskers and the grubby existence." He added, "Lou Murphy's House of David team isn't much of a draw in Sebring, Florida." Murphy agreed, adding, "We ain't been drawing peanuts and I'm already a thousand smackers in the red." To top that off, "over the hill major league players can no longer afford to play for a hundred dollars a week and board."[216]

In mid–December, the *Muscatine Journal and News-Tribune* included the following on its page of economic and legal notices that permanently changed things in the baseball world at Benton Harbor. It read: "Notice is hereby given that the House of David Baseball Clubs,

Pitcher Clifford "Count" Clay, City of David, 1937–1941 (courtesy Brian Ziebart, House of David Commune archives).

a corporation, created and existing under the laws of Iowa, has been dissolved, and its business and affairs wound up and terminated. Dated this 19th day of December 1936."[217] Although 1936 was the last year the Original House of David sent out a traveling team, they continued to play locally on weekends for a few more years.

In 1936, one of the most popular players on Lou Murphy's House of David squad was a small and speedy outfielder with a sparkling personality named Frank "Chick" Genovese, from Staten Island, New York. Near the end of the season, in which it is said he played every game, Boston scout Jack Egan signed him to appear in Boston at the end of their barnstorming season.[218] Genovese went on to play 12 minor league seasons, 1937–1949, many in the American Association with the AAA Louisville Colonels, followed by seven more as a minor league manager. According to his younger brother George, himself a longtime scout, "As a player he was all Boston all the way, and once played 282 consecutive games in center field without an error."[219]

Genovese managed in the New York Giants organization when Willie Mays made his pro baseball debut on the Class B Trenton squad in 1950. George recalled that Chick was Mays' manager there and taught him the famous basket catch. Chick later became a very successful scout who brought such players as Juan Marichal, the Alou brothers, Orlando Cepeda, Jose Pagan, and others from Latin America to the United States in the decade after Jackie Robinson was signed.[220]

Mary's City of David team kept right on barnstorming and added new names to the roster for 1937. On August 23, the *Ironwood Daily Globe* reported, "the House of David put on one of the finest shows the local fans have seen in many moons as they showed themselves as one of the most entertaining teams on the road."

Mary's nine and Lou Murphy's nine continued their travels in 1938. In one of the numerous articles that accompanied every appearance, Murphy colorfully discussed his best players of the day in an attempt to attract fans who may not have seen them yet. Such was the case with husky pitcher Charles "Moose" Swaney, a 50-year-old pitcher with over ten minor league seasons under his belt who had been with his House of David team since 1931,[221] and Shorty Schaudt, a 5'4" outfielder who sported a bushy red beard that made him look even shorter.[222]

In response to a request from sportswriter Paul Nickleson for more stories about the famous beards, Murphy obliged: "When the season ended last year, one player whose beard itched him beat it right from the diamond to his room where he shaved for the first time in months. Later he came downstairs and asked for his paycheck. Actually, I didn't know him again. It took him ten minutes to convince me he wasn't a fake trying to swindle me out of some dough."[223]

Early in 1938, ominous news surfaced again. It began, "House of David's famous ball club on the way out," and read, "The bearded House of David baseball team heads for oblivion. Voluntary articles of dissolution were on file in Berrien Circuit Court, signed by Francis Thorpe, Frank Baushke and Job Couch, directors." No reason was given. It was hoped that the dissolution would be followed by reorganization, perhaps under a different name, but owner Mary Purnell made no comment.[224]

For a while, there was talk about activities that indirectly involved the House of David but had nothing to do with baseball games. On April 23, 1939, Jean Lamar was convicted of killing House of David ballplayer Buford Armstrong at a tourist camp in Odessa, Texas. She claimed to have shot him in self-defense when he attempted to attack her.[225] It was later learned that prior to that, she had tried to kill two police officers with a car in Clinton, New Jersey. She was sentenced to seven years in a woman's reformatory, escaped after a few months, but was caught again in San Francisco.[226]

By May, the team had completed a successful barnstorming tour called an "invasion" throughout the South. They added shortstop Joe Mulet, described by longtime scout Paul Krichell, who had signed Lou Gehrig, as more than a priceless shortstop. He was also one of the greatest clowns in the game.[227] When the House of David played in Escanaba, Michigan, later that month, they announced that Miss Helen Stevens, called "The Missouri Cannonball," a double gold medal winner in the 1936 Olympics, was traveling with them, giving sprinting and other exhibitions before games.[228]

Shortly thereafter, the club began a tour of exhibitions with the Kansas City Monarchs across southern Canada. Large photos of the Tally-Tucker-Anderson "razzle-dazzle" pepper game trio appeared in Canadian newspapers before each appearance. When the two squads returned to the States, they continued their partnership.[229]

In the late '30s, some writers prematurely agreed that the popularity of barnstorming declined because the best talent was scooped up by professional minor league teams and replaced by "over the hill" major leaguers until even they left, saying they could no longer afford to play for $100 or less per week plus board.[230] It was reported that when they played weaker clubs, the Bearded Beauties kept the fans in stitches with antics they never used against tougher competition.[231]

As barnstorming baseball and the United States survived the Great Depression, things in Europe deteriorated. Despite British Prime Minister Neville Chamberlain's 1938 promise of "peace in our time," on September 1, 1939, Adolf Hitler marched into Poland.

The Pepper Game masters. L-R: George Anderson, John Tucker, Doc Tally (Atwell Family Collection).

5

The Forties and Fifties
Two Abbreviated Decades End an Era

For the Benton Harbor teams, the '40s was a decade interrupted, abbreviated, scarred by the sacrifices of war, and accented by changes during the post-war years. Both the City of David and the House of David teams approached the decade unsure of how things would go, as Europe endured Hitler on the march, but eager to start the 1940 season. Although the United States supported the European Allies with materials and financial assistance by means of the Lend-Lease Act,[1] it did not officially put troops into the fray until after the attack on Pearl Harbor on December 7, 1941. Just as in World War I, the patriotic juices in Benton Harbor flowed as men were being drafted, and the commune returned to the practice of holding patriotic Sunday concerts free to all.[2]

Though fractured by World War II, the decade of the '40s was a busy time for the teams: Judge Dewhirst's House of David rarely played on the road; Mary's City of David played exclusively on the road; and the Home Team, a branch of the Original House of David managed by catcher Eddie Deal, started the decade on a completely new venture.

Deal initiated the new decade by leading his team in the Benton Harbor region until he took a leap and introduced a big and somewhat unexpected change. For the first time, the Home Team would play in an organized league. On May 22, 1940, Deal informed the press that after thorough investigation that looked at the possibilities from all sides, he decided the team would join the Michiana League, which played primarily on weekends. The league consisted of seven other strong teams from Michigan and Indiana: the South Bend Conservative Lifes, Mishawaka Dodgers, Mishawaka Ball Bands, and Niles Standards, all of Michigan, plus the Elkhart Conns, La Porte Boosters, and La Porte Islemen-Dairys, from Indiana. The League offered good competition for the Davids. Except for Niles and LaPorte, all games, including some doubleheaders, were scheduled to be played on Sundays at Eden Springs Park.[3]

It was the first and only time a House of David squad participated in organized league play. The change was a good one. They started out like gangbusters, winning their first three games, all on the road, on their way to the league championship.[4] Without bragging, catcher Lloyd Dalager proudly remembered a particular game against Niles in late July when he led the Bearded Beauties to a 10–1 win when he collected four singles and a double.[5] As things go in baseball, the following day they played the tough Holland Flying Dutchmen in Benton Harbor and were limited to just two hits in a 10–0 thumping.[6] The last week in October, a celebratory banquet was held at the La Salle Hotel in

South Bend, where the House of David was proclaimed the official champion of the Michiana Loop.[7] All of their players were awarded gold baseball charms to honor their accomplishment.

It was a particularly good season for those representing any of the Benton Harbor teams, but especially for Johnny Pavlick and Big Harvey Pallas of the Home Team, who were acclaimed as the two finest pitchers in the circuit.[8] In addition to a no-hitter against the Elkhart Conns, Pavlick made a reputation for tossing shutouts[9] when he appeared with the squad through 1945.[10] Pallas had played two seasons with the Winnipeg Maroons in the Class D Northern League[11] before he joined the Bearded Beauties in Benton Harbor, and he made a name for himself with them.

In 1940, the team enjoyed its usual busy season while traveling over 25,000 miles. As in previous seasons, one of the highlights was touring with the "Satchel Paige All Stars," a tag given to the Kansas City Monarchs[12] as a way of reminding fans that Satchel Paige would appear with the team. Managed by Newt "Pep" Joseph, their reputation as one of the fastest and best-balanced baseball clubs they had in years preceded them.[13]

Battery mates pitcher Jack Crow (L) and catcher Eddie Deal, 1940 (courtesy Brian Ziebart, House of David Commune archives).

The two clubs faced each other in five series as they barnstormed through Canada and the Pacific Northwest. In anticipation of their visit, a North Dakota paper said the House of David was an outstanding traveling baseball attraction who had played most of the leading semipro teams in the country, "white and colored," and several minor league clubs, concluding that the Whiskerinos team was "a large factor in building up baseball interest in many parts of the country."[14]

When they appeared in Bend, Oregon, the first week in August, it was the Monarchs' very first appearance there. Due to more news about imposter teams, a frustrated John Tucker told the press, "*This* is the only House of David team direct from Benton Harbor."[15] A few days later, when they appeared in Salem, Satchel Paige took the mound and the Bearded Beauties came out on top, 8–7, in a nip and tuck game.

They headed to Reno, Nevada, where they were involved in a slugfest with the

5. The Forties and Fifties 119

This rare photograph was taken in 1935 when the HOD lost 6–1 against the Flying Dutchmen in their annual Tulip Time game in Holland, Michigan. The umpire was former major league star Harry Heilman (courtesy Brian Ziebart, House of David Commune archives).

Monarchs. It is said they handed the Monarchs one of the worst lickings the Negro champions ever received.[16]

The following week, in a game in Ogden, Utah, the Monarchs returned the favor in front of over 4,000 spectators as they trounced the Whiskerinos, 12–1. In his column "Touching All Bases," Matt B. Wyse noted, "the Monarchs and Davids packed 'em in everywhere. The fans demonstrated their love of good baseball regardless of which team won."[17]

In addition to the series with the Monarchs, they met all other bookings. In July they played the Western International League Spokane Indians and were defeated in an exciting game in front of approximately 7,200 fans.[18] By August, only three members of the City of David team who had walked from the House of David team when Mary left remained: George Anderson in his 12th year, John Tucker in his 17th, and Doc Tally in his 27th.[19] Before they faced the Eugene Athletics in Civic Stadium, they fortified the club with the addition of Clarence "Fats" Heatherly (2B) from the Western League, Chet Smith (SS) from the Pacific Coast and Western International Leagues, and LHP Mike Schroeder from the Western and East Texas Leagues.[20]

In early September, after they met and defeated the South Havana La Palomas in Bend, it was announced that the City of David nine would soon end the summer's tour. One of their final appearances in Benton Harbor was a bad day. After getting shut out, 9–0, in the afternoon by Kalamazoo, they took a second beating that night when Taylor Edgell's Legionnaires squad blasted a dozen hits off commune pitcher Dick Wykoff in an 8–4 romp.[21] Nevertheless, the season ended on a high note: they had played 154 games with a record of 113 wins, 32 losses, and nine ties. George Anderson had played in every game.[22]

In contrast, friction, gossip and internal strife marred the season for Lou Murphy's team, now managed by Ham Olive, who had played for the 1934 squad. In their first 35-plus games, they were described as a squad in "fine shape," as they cut a wide swath through the South along the southern coast of Florida.[23] However, it was somewhat of an irony, as they played some of their best baseball but did not draw the usual crowds, which caused serious financial pressures, not to mention frustrated players. The resultant internal friction was reported everywhere.[24]

Continual requests for back pay of $90 a month were ignored by Olive. When they threatened to sue for non-payment, he retaliated by impounding their uniforms.[25] Feeling they had no other option, they broke into his car to retrieve them, when they were arrested, charged with larceny, and taken to jail, but quickly released on $25 bail each.[26]

Headlines about Murphy's squad often erroneously identified them as Mary's House of David traveling team. Some of them read, "House of David Team Split; Many Plan to Shave Beards"[27] and "The House of David Is Disbanded."[28] The July 26 edition of the *Pennsylvania News-Herald* reported that the Davids "contemplated [their] first shave in several years as they considered an extensive road tour reorganized as the 'smooth shaven albeit aged Orphans.'"[29] However, after a week of cancelled games and no income, an agreement was reached whereby the unshaved squad continued the season.[30]

At the beginning of the 1941 season, because Judge Dewhirst was concerned that many unimpeded imposter teams used the House of David name while falling short of their talent and threatened their reputation. He toyed with the idea of sending out a new version of the Original House of David barnstorming squad, saying it was "for old times' sake." The team had not barnstormed since the end of 1936, but had confined its play to weekend games in the Benton Harbor region. However, when reminded that Mary's team was never far afield, he reconsidered and maintained the status quo.[31]

Articles about the City of David appeared in newspapers around the country in July 1941, as the nation continued the climb out of the Depression. They expressed the indebtedness of minor league towns and cities to the teams and barnstorming baseball in general

Edwin Stegall and Howard Shadowen stand behind Vincent Battle and Whitey Pierce before the game on June 9, 1940 (courtesy Brian Ziebart, House of David Commune archives).

for keeping the game alive during the lean years. "They have been a large factor in building up baseball interest in many parts of the country."[32]

As with the entire country, everything changed after Pearl Harbor. The war effort took center stage in all walks of life, including sports. On January 15, 1942, Commissioner Kenesaw Mountain Landis wrote a letter to President Roosevelt asking if baseball should be cancelled for the duration. The response quickly became known as Roosevelt's famous Green Light Letter. One excerpt from it read, "I feel it would be best for the country to keep baseball going. Individual players who are of active military or naval age should go, without question, into the services. Even if the actual quality of the teams is lowered by the greater use of older players, this will not dampen the popularity of the sport."[33]

In 1942, the Michigan State League was suspended for the duration of the war, and numerous semipro teams were dismantled as many players were drafted. But baseball in Benton Harbor continued at all levels.[34]

In 1943, in order to keep interest in the game alive while many primary stars were in the service,[35] Phillip K. Wrigley, with an assist from Branch Rickey, established the colorful and popular All American Girls Professional Baseball League, later the subject of the movie *A League of Their Own*. The league, initially four teams, soon expanded to the following eight: Grand Rapids Chicks, Muskegon Lassies, Racine Belles, Kenosha Comets, South Bend Blue Cox, Fort Wayne Daisies, Peoria Red Wings, and Rockford Peaches. Though many thought the league was a lark, it provided quality baseball for a dozen years through 1954.[36] From its inception in 1943 through the war years, 176,000 to 1 million fans, depending on the source, passed through the turnstiles of their games.[37]

Another group that appeared on the scene and often toured with the Davids was the Harlem Globetrotters baseball team, created by promoter Abe Saperstein of Harlem Globetrotters basketball fame. Called an aggregation of the finest Negro baseball players in the country, they took to the road in 1944, seeking the "fame and fortune" of their namesakes.[38] They were initially managed by the legendary pitcher/catcher Theodore Roosevelt "Double Duty" Radcliffe, who would live to age 101. He was one of the last survivors of the Negro Leagues during the era of the Gentlemen's Agreement.[39]

In step with "standard" barnstorming circumstances, all teams sported fluid rosters. In the Trotters' case, players names had to be plucked by historians from articles about their games which rarely included box scores, and then were limited to last names only. When they faced the Davids in Ogden, Utah, in August 1945, their roster was listed as follows: "Lefty" Gulley—P, from the Cleveland Buckeyes; Joe Spencer—2B, and Budd "Lefty" Treherne—1B, from Birmingham Black Barons; Henry McCall—OF, from Chicago American Giants; and four players from the Cincinnati Clowns—Bill Ortiz—SS; Bruce Wright—3B; Johnny Ray—OF (also with Monarchs); and Collins Jones—OF; and four other unnamed players completed the lineup.[40] During the first season of their ten-year existence, the Trotters were described as a dazzling group of athletes that developed into one of the nation's strongest Negro baseball teams.[41]

It seemed as though sports writers had run out of clever things to say about the contests between the Benton Harbor nine and the Monarchs when one colorfully promoted the arrival of the duo in Perris Hill, California, as follows: "They have sent fans into hysterics in every municipality and jerk water stop on the House of David itinerary." James Thomas "Cool Papa" Bell, former Negro Leagues outfielder inducted into the

Baseball Hall of Fame in 1974, ended his stellar career as player/manager of the Monarchs, 1948–1950.[42] By the time his squad faced the House of David in Salt Lake City in July 1949, both teams were described as the nation's two best barnstorming teams.[43]

During those years, House of David baseball was impacted in a variety of ways. Sports editor Jack Carberry announced that the annual *Denver Post* Tournament competitions were postponed for the duration due to gas rationing, the loss of players to the military, and other war-related problems.[44] In addition, the Ethiopian Clowns from Florida, frequent opponents, decided to restrict play to the Negro Leagues. Because many noted players were absent due to the draft or were working in defense plants and other war-related jobs, good semipro clubs such as the Buford Bona-Allens from Georgia, who had won the DPT in 1940 and placed second in 1941,[45] disbanded completely.

In several cities where professional minor leagues were abandoned, service and semipro teams filled the gap.[46] The Michigan State League, which included the St. Joseph Auto Specialties club from across the St. Joseph River, was suspended in 1942 for the same reason. However, fans in Benton Harbor and surrounding regions clamored for baseball. In an effort to satisfy that desire and maintain a degree of interest in the game, Benton Harbor players Louis Buck, George Anderson, Doc Tally, and John Tucker attempted to organize a new semipro team with Tucker as manager.[47]

But before plans for this had gelled, Buck and Anderson were drafted and inducted as non-combatants. The *Daily Telegram* and other papers wrote that the fate of their beards and long hair "was now in the army's hands." When asked if he would allow himself to get his hair cut and a shave if the army asked, Anderson smiled and replied, "Well, it will depend on how loud we're asked," explaining that he had never had a shave or a haircut in his life.[48]

Tucker carried on without them and announced that the team would play one or two games a week. He hoped to have a roster assembled and start drills for the new squad by mid–May.[49] Due to the threat of losing young players to the draft, Tucker wanted only older, experienced veterans for the club.[50] The team was a box office success that attracted 15,000 fans, earning $5,000 at home and

Lloyd Dalager during World War II when he played with the St. Joseph Auto Specialties team while the House of David took time off from playing due to the war (courtesy Brian Ziebart, House of David Commune archives).

an additional $1,000 on the road.[51] At the same time, the Y.M.C.A. attempted to organize a league but it fell apart and disappeared due to lack of interest.[52] Tucker remained a member of the commune while managing the Auto Specialties team from St. Joseph.[53]

By 1945, at the request of local sports promoters, the City of David was reorganized with Doc Tally at the helm.[54] A team of players too young to grow beards, referred to as "the short bearded Davidites," but talented enough on the field to call themselves the City of David, played a rigorous schedule that represented the commune well. They covered 24,000 miles from as far east as Montreal, as far west as Seattle, and down the West Coast to Los Angeles before they headed eastward via Nevada, Arizona, New Mexico, Oklahoma, Kansas, Missouri, and Illinois. They also toured six Southern states: Kentucky, North and South Carolina, Georgia, Alabama, and Tennessee.[55]

Another portion of their schedule included tours with the Harlem Globetrotters that were arranged by Abe Saperstein. In mid–August, their two-game series at Moana Park in Reno received advance publication predicting that would be one of the biggest attractions to hit that area in many years.[56] Before the second game, Olympic Gold Medalist Jesse Owens, often a fellow traveler with the Trotters, ran a 200-yard race against a horse named Flash, ridden by Gladys Gaines. When he lost, he blamed a sprained ankle.[57] As with all of their clashes, the games were seen as good baseball accented by shenanigans from both squads. The Trotters took both games of the set, bringing their record to 32 wins in 38 games played to date.[58]

By the end of World War II, as countries around the globe picked up the pieces and adapted to the changes it created, the baseball community was on the precipice of long-overdue changes of its own.

Barnstorming continued. It was common knowledge that Branch Rickey, who had moved from the St. Louis Cardinals to become president-general manager of the Brooklyn Dodgers in 1942, had for years viewed Negro players as an untapped well of "black gold" on two fronts. As players, their skill level was equal to or better than the best major leaguers, plus previous successes of the Negro Leagues and independent Negro teams proved they could attract a huge new fan base for organized baseball. Rickey felt the time had come for what was deemed the most profound transformation in baseball history: integration.[59]

As far back as a February 1933 Baseball Writers Association Dinner honoring John McGraw, respected sportswriter Heywood Broun expressed his advocacy for ending the color ban. Though considered a bold stand at the time, he had the support of many influential leaders in the game: John Heydler, president of the National League; players Frankie Frisch, Lou Gehrig, and Herb Pennock, among others; sports editor Jimmy Powers of the *New York Daily News* and other heavyweight sports writers; and, of course, Branch Rickey, then general manager of the St. Louis Cardinals. The "Sez Ches" column in the *Pittsburgh Courier* said this was the most significant sports news in many months. He agreed with Powers that one thing baseball could do to revive interest in the game—depression or no depression—was to end the color ban.[60]

Following the success of runner Jesse Owens in the 1936 Olympics in Berlin, the honorable service of over a million Negroes in the military in World War II, and the success of Negroes in other sports, not to mention the talents demonstrated in the Negro Leagues, were among the most salient reasons for ending the color line.

In addition, *The Sporting News* and prominent sports writers of the day like Shirley Povich of the *Washington Post* were on board. After watching Negro clubs train in

Florida, Povich wrote, "There's a couple million of dollars' worth of baseball talent on the loose, ready for the big leagues, yet unsigned by any major league."[61] By 1940, even the communist magazine *Friday* and the communist *Daily Worker* newspaper, both published in New York, urged integration, albeit for reasons of their own.[62]

But baseball owners and leaders faced a dilemma: agreeing to integration would be an admission that the unwritten law called the color line actually existed in the first place. Hence they explained it away, saying almost one-third of the players in organized baseball were Southern and would not play with or against Negroes; white players and Negro players were forbidden by law to play together in some states; integrated teams could not travel together due to accommodation problems; and the fear of riots in the stands over controversial plays on the field. They rationalized it all with the same old "logic" that Negro players did not play well enough to make it in major league baseball.[63]

However, Branch Rickey had a plan that would shake things up once and for all. Apparently without much thought of the impact of his moves on the future of barnstorming baseball, things were set in motion when it was announced in 1944 that he, Gus Greenlee, and some others were in the process of forming the United States League (USL), a new Negro League scheduled to begin play in 1945.

Rickey called a press conference to announce his intention to start a team called the Brooklyn Brown Dodgers, to be one of the six teams involved with hopes that the league might eventually join organized baseball.[64] He said the USL was to be a professionally run business in which contracts would be standardized, schedules would be uniform, and ownership would be held to a high standard.[65] He added that the Brooklyn Brown Dodgers would use Ebbets Field as their home field when the National League club was on the road, which would be good for business for both clubs.[66]

This so-called maneuver gave Rickey the necessary cover to operate under a veil of secrecy as he sent out four of his main scouts (George Sisler, Wid Matthews, Tom Greenwade, and Clyde Sukeforth) who operated independently and unaware of each other's activities. They were allegedly seeking players for the Brooklyn Brown Dodgers when they were in fact seeking a Jackie Robinson–type player.[67]

Secrecy was the essence of Rickey's style throughout the process that even developed the code name "The Young Man from the West," when discussing Robinson with others in the organization evaluating his talent.[68] Although each scout found his share of talented players, Clyde Sukeforth found Jackie Robinson, the player Rickey felt was "the right man for the job." After the signing, everyone in the game plus sports writers were surprised by Rickey's actions, and backlash from many players was anticipated.[69]

Immediately controversy brewed over whether Rickey had "snatched" Robinson from the Kansas City Monarchs, who claimed Robinson had the customary verbal contract to return for his second season in Kansas City in 1946, according to Janet Bruce in her book, *The Kansas City Monarchs, Champions of Black Baseball*,[70] and other historians. Monarchs owners J. L. Wilkinson and Tom Baird said they understood Rickey's motive, but they and other Negro team owners objected to his clandestine methods.

In addition, they felt he failed to offer the Monarchs compensation for their loss. At one point, co-owner Baird threatened to lodge a protest with Commissioner Happy Chandler, but did not follow through.[71] Actually Robinson had explained to Mr. Rickey, as everyone called him, "No sir, we don't have contracts."[72] In 1946, Robinson joined Brooklyn's AAA club in Montreal before joining the major league squad in April 1947.

When Wilkinson retired in 1948, he sold the Monarchs to Tom Baird who, as late as 1952, kept the team barnstorming while still disagreeing with those who felt integration would mark the end of barnstorming as well as Negro teams. Every Opening Day continued to be a "party" with parades, jazz music, or other entertaining events that Baird said made the major leagues look like a sideshow.[73] Eventually such operating expenses as travel, lodging, food, and player salaries became exorbitant, even though they sold eight players to major league clubs, and in 1955 Baird sold the franchise to Ted Rasberry, owner of the Detroit Stars, a Negro American League team.[74]

In 1955, when only Detroit, Memphis, Birmingham, and Kansas City were left in the Negro American League, Rasberry hired Satchel Paige to travel with the team for $250 per game plus ten percent of the gate, only to realize that even Satchel's appeal was "finally fading."[75] The Monarchs, the longest-running team in the history of Negro Leagues (1920–1965), held on until 1965, when they disbanded.[76]

While all of that was going on, the Davids prepared to carry on for the first season after the war. Manager George Anderson returned to Benton Harbor in 1946, without his beard and flowing locks that were cut off in the military. After the wartime years in which they lost many players to the service, they regrouped and resumed a hectic barnstorming schedule.[77] After spring workouts at Mount Pleasant, Texas, and the beginnings of a new beard, Anderson's nine, comprised almost entirely of new faces, was ready to go.[78]

By the end of April, they were in true House of David form, hoping fans would be eager to see them play, regardless of the outcome. Initially that outcome had mixed results. Sportswriter Harry Gilstrap wrote in his April 25 column that the "largest crowd in history of Gold Sox Field in Amarillo saw the 1946 Sockers traumatize the House of David 17–5 in the final series game before the season opener." Ticket prices were 75 cents for grandstand and 50 cents for the bleachers.[79]

In June 1946, as they readied to play the Helena Boosters of the Tri-City League in Montana, pregame publicity announced that the House of David team had played 1,051 games over six seasons and traveled over 165,000 miles prior to Pearl Harbor, posting a record of 776 wins, 270 losses, and five ties as they frequently played two or three games per day in order to fill their booking dates.[80]

Three days later, they made their first appearance in five years at Hollidaysburg, Pennsylvania, for the first night game there in years,[81] before making their annual stop in Council Bluffs, Iowa.[82] The season progressed in the usual fashion as they played their way across the country. By August, they were on the West Coast. After dropping a 13–12 game in Visalia, California, at night, the Bearded Beauties drove 350 miles south and faced the San Bernardino Outlaws, a hard-playing squad they had faced numerous times over the years.

For that task, their lineup was fortified with additional talent: C. "Pop" Griffin, formerly with the Texas and Southern Association; Red Edwards, West Texas-New Mexico League; and Earl Crappe, who had no league experience but was highly touted as a real find. An August edition of the *San Bernardino County Sun* described them as "a classy team" comprised mostly of former major or minor league players: Dick Wykoff, Cincinnati Reds minor leagues; Lee Gardner, Evangeline and Texas League; Mike Boettcher, Mid-Atlantic and Western League; George Reichelt, Michigan State League; Lew Hummel, International League; and Dick Hummel, Michigan State League and Piedmont League.[83]

In mid–September, the *News Palladium* reported that the Israelites had played to more than 100,000 fans in the U.S., Canada and Mexico before they returned to the Michigan area with a successful 1946 season under their belts.[84] Concomitantly Jackie Robinson had a successful season with the Dodgers' AAA affiliate in Canada, the Montreal Royals. He led the International League in hitting, and his .985 fielding percentage made him the best-fielding second baseman in the league.[85] The spotlight focused on him as he arrived in Brooklyn for the 1947 National League season.

A few weeks later, Bill Veeck, owner of the Cleveland Indians, signed Larry Doby as the first Negro player to join the American League.[86] A great national interest in both Jackie Robinson and Larry Doby signaled the beginning of major league baseball's acceptance of integration as the anticipated impact on future directions of the game filled the sports pages. At the same time, interest in and coverage of the exploits of the House of David and barnstorming in general began to decline.

On July 7, 1948, the American League Cleveland Indians purchased Satchel Paige from the Kansas City Monarchs.[87] The very next day, he made his debut in Municipal Stadium when he entered in relief of Bob Lemon in the fifth inning of a game against the St. Louis Browns.[88] Buck O'Neil said he was thrilled the color line was broken, but it was a bittersweet experience for black baseball because "it killed our business."[89] When Paige was signed, he gave numerous interviews in which he evaluated his own abilities: "I ain't as fast as I used to be but I'm a better pitcher. I used to over-power 'em; now I out-cute 'em."[90]

Doc Tally, always one of Paige's biggest boosters, reminisced about earlier times saying, "Satchel Paige is the greatest pitcher of all time. What he'd do to hitters in the clutch wasn't funny. I know. I was considered a fair country hitter when I was young, and when Paige bore down he'd have me breaking my back swinging. In his hey-day when we played with and mostly against him, he often hurled only as efficiently as he had to. Ah, he was a pitcher, that Satchel."[91]

In 1948, for the first time, Lou Murphy had difficulty recruiting enough good players for his team, which was then managed by Andy Hershock.[92] Two teammates on that club who have remained close friends over the years, outfielder Joe Palladino and catcher Joe Petrongolo, discussed their memories about the way things were for them.[93]

According to Palladino,

> We were both from Philadelphia and played baseball for our South Philadelphia High School team. A scout for the St. Louis Cardinals named Andy Hershock saw us and talked to us separately to see if we would be interested in playing for the House of David, and of course we said "Yes." Actually, we were seventeen playing semipro ball on weekends during our senior year and high school ball during the week, so we were seen by other scouts, too. The only one I can remember was Jocko Collins.

Petrongolo added,

> We had completed the requirements for graduation but since the House of David season had already started, we didn't stay for commencement because we had to catch up with them in Albany. It was a lot of hard traveling on one bus for the whole team and all the gear. We played in the Northeastern United States and Canada. Being young and naïve I thought we would get to see some of Canada like tourists, you know, but the schedule was so hectic we only saw ball fields, hotel rooms, and the inside of the bus.
>
> We went away in June and didn't get home until September. We were still teenagers playing ball with guys 28 or so, and some of them had played minor league ball. I remember that, but I can't recall their names any more. We were only with the team until the end of the 1948 season. I do remember we were paid somewhere between $25 and $40 a game if the fans showed up, which

House of David team, 1948 (John Horne, National Baseball Hall of Fame Files).

they always did, plus two dollars meal money. But if there was rain and we couldn't play, we didn't get paid.

Petrongolo was the more serious ball player of the pair. He explained,

The House of David sent a letter home for me to go to Wilkes-Barre and tryout for a minor league club for the following season. I was lucky and caught on with the Detroit Tigers Class D team in Thomasville, Georgia in 1949. But things didn't go that well. In 1950 I caught 101 games with the Muskogee Reds. I remember we played the Joplin Miners, Mickey Mantle's rookie team when he was 18 years old playing shortstop. I played under the name Red Coleman that year because I didn't want to jeopardize my college eligibility. Lots of guys did that in those days.

They both agreed that playing for the House of David was an experience they wouldn't have missed, even if they couldn't grow beards and they weren't there long enough to grow long locks.[94] Actually records suggest they were unaware they were with Lou Murphy's House of David, which was connected to the commune in name only as a franchise team.

Years later, Joe Palladino and members of his family traveled to Cooperstown, where he donated his House of David uniform jersey, a signed team ball, his journal with scores of games from that summer, and other personal memorabilia to the Baseball Hall of Fame. Jim Gates, librarian at the Baseball Hall of Fame and Museum, discussed the significance of this in *Memories and Dreams*, the official magazine of the Hall of Fame, in which he praised the donation for adding an "important piece to the museum collection."[95]

The more or less up and down 1949 season for the Davids was highlighted by a long tour with the Harlem Globetrotters in June, where the two squads were praised as "the best examples of traveling baseball clubs of long standing." After they drew only 809 fans to a game in Illinois, a frustrated Doc Tally said in an interview, "It would be wise for the House of David the team to head for northern Iowa, Minnesota, and the Dakotas because we're sure not drawing in the Midwest."[96] By mid–August, it seemed their rigorous schedule was catching up with them. In Pottstown, Pennsylvania, the press

Joe Palladino donated his jersey and other artifacts from his 1948 season to the National Baseball Hall of Fame in Cooperstown (John Horne, National Baseball Hall of Fame Files).

described them as "a tired-looking travel-torn House of David club that played a ragged contest watched by 1,000 as they defeated the locals but had a helluva time doing it."[97]

In addition to the loss of good barnstorming competition and the arrival of Jackie Robinson ending the color line, changes closer to home also impacted the future of House of David baseball. The *Denver Post* Tournament had played its final competition in 1947,[98] and Benjamin Purnell's successor as head of the commune, Judge H. T. Dewhirst died.[99]

As the decade drew to a close, the writing was on the wall regarding the precarious future of barnstorming baseball. The Original House of David continued to host some games at home and sometimes returned to the road on weekends, while the Israelite House of David was always on the road. Despite reports that the popularity of barnstorming was in decline as teams played before smaller crowds than in prior seasons, reports indicated that the Bearded Beauties had a total attendance of 645,000 paid admissions for the past three seasons (1946, 1947, 1948).[100]

And things got worse as the decade of the '50s dawned. It was just 25 days old when the headline on page one of the *News Palladium* read, "Doc Tally Is Dead." News of the sudden death of this fan favorite at age 53, as he prepared for the new season, sent waves of shock and sadness throughout the barnstorming world.[101] One of the oldest baseball players in point of service in the United States, Tally had assisted Francis Thorpe in the formation of the original team in 1913, then moved to Mary's Israelite House of David when the colony fractured after the 1928 season.[102] He had played or managed every year since the team's inception, with time out for military service in World War I.[103]

In August 1951, when the Davids made their first-ever tour to Alaska to play seven games in Fairbanks and Anchorage in the Midnight Sun League, local press coverage said there was rampant anticipation of their visit. Large crowds that attended every game were not disappointed. However, change was in the wind for them along the way when they hit a rough patch in the state of Washington. Pasco columnist Jack Hewins summed up the situation in one sentence: "There was a time when the House of David was a scourge on northwest baseball diamonds, but now everybody beats the beards."[104] In addition, fans were frequently disappointed in the steady stream of new faces on the squad when they expected to see the same familiar players they had enjoyed over the years.[105]

Their 1953 baseball season had started at a new spring training site in Pittsburgh, Texas. From there the squad played its way into California and spent the bulk of the season attracting large crowds on the West Coast. When the *Albany Democrat-Herald* announced an upcoming exhibition between the Davids and the Cuban Monarchs in Albany, it offered high praise to the Benton Harbor crew: "We believe this organization has done more for the good interests of baseball than every other travelling team." They added that no traveling team but the Israelites could honestly boast a winning percentage of [at least] .738 every season for 30 years.[106]

The end of the season marked the end of the Purnell era at the commune "officially" when Mary Purnell died in mid–August at age 93.[107] Additional news came that put the continuation of barnstorming baseball in peril. Rumors began to appear regarding the proposed expansion of major league baseball, always east of the Mississippi, to the West Coast by the end of the decade. That area had always been a large, successful part of the annual schedule of the House of David. Two struggling teams, the Brooklyn Dodgers and New York Giants, thought to be the subjects of the "westward invasion," would move simultaneously once such logistics as ballparks, review of travel costs for cross-country series with other ML teams, and other issues were resolved.

While the politics involved in the process were being discussed, haggled, and argued in private meetings closely monitored by the media, barnstorming continued. Finally the announcement was made in 1957 that essentially sucked the air and fan interest out of following barnstorming teams on the west coast: the New York Giants would become the San Francisco Giants, and the Brooklyn Dodgers would become the Los Angeles Dodgers in time for the 1958 season.

Although conditions around them were in flux, the City of David remained one of the most widely traveled teams in the business as they continued to cooperate with organized baseball. They never hired players on the ineligible list and never knowingly played against teams who did. As usual, scouts arrived wherever the nine appeared and often harvested young players from them.[108] They were described as the oldest independent club in the nation, whose popularity had never waned as "they had played to more than 745,000 paying customers in the past four seasons."[109] The curiosity about their lifestyle on the road was regularly written about: "Every day a different town, strange faces and new wisecracks are their daily diet, and they love it."[110]

At home and on the road, members of the team continued having interesting experiences to write home about. One of those letters was written to a friend by promoter Dutch Witte about Marv Rotblatt, a small, 5'4" pitcher on the squad. A few years earlier, after a night game in which he did not pitch, he and a friend walked to town, looking for a place to eat, when they were stopped by a policeman for being out after the 10 p.m. curfew in place for youngsters under 16. Rotblatt explained he was over 21 and a member of the City of David baseball team but had not been there long enough to grow long hair or a beard yet. George Anderson and Jesse Tally interceded, and their long locks "were the convincer." Later Rotblatt played parts of three seasons with the Chicago White Sox.[111]

The team was involved, though indirectly, in the first night game ever at Wrigley Field the end of the month, when the portable lighting system they rented from the Kansas City Monarchs was used to celebrate Goose Tatum Night in honor of the famed basketball star.[112]

As the decade progressed, advertisements of their appearances included mention of pitcher Frank "Bobo" Nickerson, one of the characters of the game, who would entertain by demonstrating one of the newer acts of the day, whereby a player catches baseballs dropped from helicopters.[113] In 1954, the House of David squad sent Nickerson to the mound to face Satchel Paige, then a member of the Harlem Globetrotters. Both were considered good pitchers past their prime who relied on clowning and silly antics to hold the interest of the fans.[114]

In October 1954, Bobo Nickerson was at it again as he put on a memorable stunt that kept fans talking for a long time. He caught a ball dropped from a helicopter 650 feet in the air as a follow-up to his successful 350-foot catch on Memorial Day in 1953, which broke the previous record held by two Cincinnati players. He said he hoped to find a sponsor for his planned "1,000 footer" in 1955. For his efforts, he was rewarded with a membership card to the "Catching-Balls-From-High-Places-Club." He appeared with the team on and off until it disbanded after the 1956 season.[115]

The squad had maintained a busy schedule in 1955. On their western swing, they had games against top semipro clubs and every team in the Class A Northwest League after touring in Arkansas, Mississippi, Louisiana, Texas, Oklahoma, Kansas, Nebraska, Missouri, Illinois, Wisconsin, Minnesota, and North Dakota from May 10 through July 26.[116] They also played three games in Canada: two games in Port Arthur, Ontario, and one in Winnipeg, Manitoba.[117]

As they readied to face the Humboldt Crabs in a two-game

Bobo Nickerson performing "in uniform" with the Davids in 1955 (courtesy Brian Ziebart, House of David Commune archives).

series in Eureka, California, in the first week of August 1955, the *Eureka Times Standard* presented an exaggerated announcement of the upcoming competition in a successful attempt to increase ticket sales. The article said the City of David was a formidable team filled with former major league players, none of whom actually played at that level. Twenty players were on that list: pitcher Homer Garner, Western League and Eastern League; Bill Lovello, Big Horn Loop, Florida State League; John Bodine, curveballer from Covington, Indiana; Edward Logan, All-Service selection from Sill, Oklahoma; LHP Bill Timko; James Keenan, Florida State League; Chuck Liska, "sidearm chucker"; LHP John Silver, protégée of Jimmie Foxx; and John Cheznok, Cotton States League.

The outfield was patrolled by Bill Stoey, Western Michigan College; Bob Self, Pony League, Mountain States League, Western Association; Frank Crosetti, Florida State League; and Ben Owens, Florida State League, Big Horn Loop, South Atlantic League. Infielders included Don Gursuch of the Virgil Trucks School; Frank Cerillo, SS, Brooklyn Dodgers system; Rocky Carlini, 3B, Class A experience; Bill Kimball, 1B, Provincial, Florida State Leagues; Ted Bus, seven-year manager, Middleboro in Mountain States League; and Chet Plazaj, C, Korean All-Star team, St. Louis Cardinals system.

After Jackie Robinson and Larry Doby proved Negro players were more than qualified to compete at the major league level, interest and focus of fans turned to organized professional baseball.

Obviously the City of David and the Kansas City Monarchs, the two most renowned clubs on the road, were impacted differently by integration. For the Monarchs, the fan base and player pool was noticeably shrinking. They had difficulty recruiting players as major league scouts signed them into organized baseball. The attitude of young black players who had previously viewed playing with the Monarchs as a zenith of their careers, suddenly sought opportunities to enter organized baseball. For example, when they attempted to add pitcher Bob Gibson to the squad, the future Hall of Famer refused, and he later said the Kansas City Monarchs were not the be-all and end-all for a Negro ballplayer.[118]

The Monarchs hung on as best they could though they knew they were swimming upstream. After struggling along in the Negro American League (NAL) after most teams had departed or collapsed, they suffered a $10,000 deficit in 1954.[119] By 1955, the viability of the Monarchs was questionable as operating costs continued to outweigh the income they generated. It was the same everywhere. In 1955, the NAL had dwindled to just four clubs: the Memphis Red Sox, Birmingham Barons, Detroit Stars, and Kansas City Monarchs.[120] During those final years, the City of David and Monarchs continued booking exhibition tours together, still attracting large, appreciative crowds.

As players always did, they collected available newspaper articles for the scrapbooks, and many kept journals regarding their own achievements and history of the team.[121] Portions of pitcher Dick Hummel's journal of the 1946 season can be found in the Appendix.

Clark Griffith had predicted that the days of barnstorming baseball would be numbered once Jackie Robinson was signed by the Dodgers. He was right. In 1951, the Homestead Grays and Brooklyn Bushwicks both folded their tents. Mary's City of David played a few years longer, but the inevitable awaited them as well.[122]

During their final years, the City of David nines scheduled benefit games to assist varied charities. Among them was an exhibition against the Hawaiian Cubans Negro squad, with proceeds going to the Joplin Shrine Crippled Children Program in May

1952.[123] Another was played against the Flyers of Malmstrom Air Force Base in Montana to benefit the Great Falls American Legion Baseball program.[124] In 1954, they faced Satchel Paige, then with the Globetrotters team in Tucson, Arizona, for the benefit of the Sportsmen's Fund for Community Youth. It was the first time either team played there in an exhibition, and it was described as "one of the finest baseball attractions ever carded in Tucson."[125]

The inevitable came for Mary's City of David nine in 1956 when, according to George Anderson, their schedule was reduced to 135 games.[126] The team, composed entirely of new faces except for Anderson, kept traveling and entertaining fans. "The Davids play it straight as they attempt to win every game. They're always ready to reach into their bag of tricks and pull clowning stunts deluxe to provide added laughter and entertainment."[127]

Until 2006, commune historians were uncertain about whether the House of David attempted to field a team in 1957, but that year a visitor to the museum explained that his father had played in earlier years with the House of David and he himself had played on the 1956 team with George Anderson. In the spring of 1957, when he wrote to Anderson asking to return to the club for that season, Anderson explained he would not be forming a team in 1957. Unfortunately the man's name has been lost.[128]

Major league post-season barnstorming teams hobbled their way through the '50s, but ceased to exist by the early '60s due to "a decline in profitability."[129] It was all quite simple, according to Bob Feller, who had a successful barnstorming team with Dizzy Dean and Satchel Paige: "Barnstorming declined as a result of integration of the big leagues."[130]

Although it has been argued that small rural communities held out and tried to support barnstorming teams, it didn't happen often enough to make a difference. It was especially evidenced by the major reduction in press coverage. An article in the *Asbury Park Press* of New Jersey was a prophetic eulogy for that unique era in baseball history: "After the Second World War, semipro and barnstorming baseball died a slow, pathetic, unfitting death."[131]

Though George Anderson attributed the end of the unpredictable and exciting barnstorming era to television, it was the victim of the passage of time and a disease called progress. The era is remembered as a unique segment on the baseball timeline that paralleled interesting and difficult periods in American history. The House of David, Kansas City Monarchs, plus a colorful array of other teams and players, held on as long as they could until the game slowly passed them by. But in its wake remains a legacy of exciting and talented teams, one of which sported long locks and flowing beards.

Perhaps the feelings and character of the players who populated the era are described best by long-time first baseman for the Murphy House of David, Jimmy Woods, who later became an umpire. In an angry retort to a fan attempting to console him after a loss, he countered,

> Look, chum, don't waste your tears on me. I'm in this game because I like it. We are going to new places every week and we've made trips that most men like us never even get a chance to read about. You sweat and labor eight hours a day at the same old grind. I play ball a little while each day and get paid for it. If I didn't get paid I'd do it for nothing because I like it. My only regret is that I'll soon get to be too old to be any good to the team, but that won't be for ten more years anyway.[132]

6

Memorable Players

Commune records suggest that between 60–65 commune members played on the teams over the years, some for a couple of seasons and others for longer periods of time. Sometimes dates of their careers conflicted and are reported as such. Unfortunately, except for players considered stars, biographical information on most of them is either not available or minimal at best. As usual, photographs of players are minimal as well.

Players from the Commune

Manager Francis Thorpe was born in Marshalltown, Iowa, in 1876. According to the 1900 Iowa Census and the 1910 Michigan Census, his last name was spelled "Thorp." He joined the House of David in 1904 at age 28. In high school, he was a better than average athlete, and he played football at Lombard College in Galesburg, Illinois, where one of his classmates was Carl Sandburg. When Purnell decided to create a competitive baseball team, he asked Thorpe to teach the sport to the youngsters and manage the team.

Those who knew him agreed he was an interesting individual who was well-read, well-educated, cultured and affable. According to historian Brian Ziebart, Doc Tally always called him "Franny." His first known job at the commune was as a proofreader in the print shop, until Purnell named him commune secretary, a powerful and trusted position.[1]

In addition to baseball, he was the longtime editor of the commune's monthly paper, *The New Shiloh Messenger*, which was produced at Mary's City of David after 1930, and he wrote books and poems which were all religious and philosophically themed. Perhaps the most notable was *Crown of Thorns: House of David Victory and Legal Troubles Reviewed, Benton Harbor, MI, 1929*, a 174-page publication that was widely studied.[2]

However, Thorpe is best known as the man who organized and managed successful baseball nines in Benton Harbor: the House of David, 1912–1928, and the City of David, 1929–1934. In 1934, Mary asked him to step down and appointed him secretary-treasurer of her commune, where he functioned as a business and spiritual leader the rest of his life ... with one eye peeled on the baseball teams. His health became an issue in the late '40s. In 1952, he lost a leg to diabetes, and he died from complications of the disease in 1957.[3]

Jesse Lee "Doc" Tally was a player and manager with the House of David, 1915–1929, and the City of David, 1930–1950.[4] One of the most popular and well-known Benton Harbor players of all time, Jesse, his father, and brothers Swaney and Barlow (both played ball briefly) arrived from Mississippi to join the commune in late October 1914, when he was 18 years old,[5] Almost immediately he assisted Francis Thorpe in teaching baseball to young men, then became a pivotal part of a burgeoning baseball team as one of the players on the first uniformed team named the House of David in 1915.[6] A right-handed knuckleball pitcher and left-handed-hitting outfielder, Tally belted home runs, stole bases, laid down bunts for hits, and did whatever the team needed to win. As time passed, his name and style of play became synonymous with the House of David.

In 1916, his pitching was a major factor in the team's winning the Berrien County Championship in the second year of their existence. When the team made its first appearance at Muzzy Field in Bristol, Connecticut, in 1922, the year he was reputed to have hit 22 or 29 homers depending on the source, the newspapers there dubbed him "the bewhiskered behemoth of biff."[7]

In addition, he was a very speedy base runner with one of the most peculiar slides in the game at that time: he hit the dirt first and ended up in a standing position as he hit the bag, so he could keep running if he had the opportunity.[8]

When he returned from military duty in World War I in 1919, he took the first House of David on the road for a 50-game schedule.[9] They reportedly won 35 of those games and ranked as the best semipro team in Michigan.[10] When the House of David team invented the pepper game that was played at every appearance for the remainder of their existence, Jesse Tally was a member of the original trio, along with John Tucker and Walter Faust.[11]

After the 1929 season, when internal friction and legal problems resulted in the fracture of the commune, Tally went to Mary Purnell's City of David along with Francis Thorpe, John Tucker, and George Anderson, where they played top-notch baseball until the end of their careers. Commune records indicate that Faust was no longer a member of the commune at that time but did play as a hired player for Mary's team from time to time.[12] Jesse Tally spent his entire life wearing different hats to serve the com-

Jesse Lee "Doc" Tally, "the bewhiskered behemoth of biff" (courtesy Brian Ziebart, House of David Commune archives).

mune, but his first love was always baseball. In a 1948 interview, he said he had played in over 2,000 games in the outfield and on the mound.[13] He is remembered as a jovial and well-liked teammate and first player-manager and traveling secretary of the team when they played extensively across the United States, Canada, Mexico, Hawaii before statehood, and Puerto Rico.[14]

In his later years, he explained that his well-known moniker, "Doc," was bestowed on him during World War I, when he was sent to a cavalry unit to groom horses as a "sort of assistant veterinarian."[15] Though sketchy, available records demonstrate his prowess as a player. Batting stats: 1925, .303 in 78 games; 1926, .301 in 130 games; 1932, .438 in the *Denver Post* Tournament. As a pitcher, he won 21 games in three years: 1925, 21–6; 1938, 21–2; 1939, 21–5. His best record was 28–5 in 1936.[16]

While preparing for his 36th season in 1950, Doc Tally died of a sudden heart attack at age 54.[17]

George "Andy" Anderson was a valued asset to sports in Benton Harbor. He was a friendly, likeable man who spent 28 years as player and manager of the baseball nines, plus he founded and managed the basketball squad for several years between baseball seasons. Born in Australia in 1910, he arrived at the commune with his mother and two sisters in November 1920.[18]

Almost immediately he displayed a propensity for baseball. A tall lad who appeared older than his years, he was assigned to the House of David junior squad to hone his skills before he was bumped up to the non-traveling home team. In 1927, the 17-year-old, versatile infielder who broke in as a catcher but proved himself capable at all infield positions, was added to the commune's traveling team, where he became a fixture at third base for the House of David and then the City of David teams until 1956.[19]

When the commune split into two factions after the 1928 season, Anderson followed Mary Purnell, along with Francis Thorpe and teammates Doc Tally and John Tucker, to Mary's City of David, where he played until his retirement in 1956 at age 46.[20] During the '30s, Anderson played every position as needed and was considered an excellent fundamental player both offensively and defensively. Always described as a slap hitter, he batted over .300 every season he played, which included a 1934 campaign in which he hit .345 in 170.[21]

Between seasons, Anderson was a workhorse who also helped organize the colony basketball team

George Anderson (courtesy Brian Ziebart, House of David Commune archives).

and served as player-manager for many years. The House of David cagers often toured with the famed Harlem Globetrotters throughout the United States and Europe.[22]

As late as 1952, Anderson, one of the best-known men in barnstorming baseball, was praised for still playing a "heady and active game."[23] When discussing his career with a sportswriter in the early '50s, Anderson recalled proudly, "One season we played 212 games and I played in every one."[24] In other interviews, he said he had played over a hundred games against Satchel Paige over 25 years, describing him as "the greatest pitcher ever was and I got lots of hits off him because he was a southpaw and I punched the ball over the shortstop,[25] and we became friends."[26]

In an interview about his life in baseball in 1950, he remembered once playing in Fairbanks, Alaska, one week when the mercury was 70 degrees below zero, then played the next week in Hawaii when the temperature was 90-plus. He also recalled several interesting ballparks in which they had played, particularly a few in North Dakota where the baselines were marked by plowed furrows.[27]

Prior to his retirement, Anderson said, he had travelled over a million miles with the Bearded Beauties, played in over 5,000 games, been on base over 10,000 times, and carried a .400 batting average.[28] George Anderson was the last active House of David and City of David baseball player who had been a member of the Original House of David commune.

After baseball, he became the transportation supervisor for the St. Joseph Public Schools and grew prize-winning roses.[29] In 1998, when he was 88, the City of David Museum hosted George Anderson Day, a very successful event that was broadcast on a National Public Radio program called "All Things Considered."[30]

Dwight "Zeke" Baushke was a member of the wealthy and influential Baushke family from Germany that had played a pivotal role in bringing the Purnells to Benton Harbor in 1903, when they donated property and finances for the new commune. They were the most prominent local family ever to join the House of David.[31]

Zeke, whose first love was music, began his baseball career in 1921 as one of the younger members of the Junior Team. He spent 1922–1926 with the traveling team, playing second base with Walter Faust at shortstop.

Dwight "Zeke" Baushke (courtesy Brian Ziebart, House of David Commune archives).

Known as "the Diamond Cutters" for their athleticism and agility, their feats made them extremely popular with the fans in the early '20s.[32]

Actually, he was given time away from the team to play with the House of David Traveling Band as long as he played. After the 1926 season, he left the colony and moved to Detroit to become a professional musician.[33]

Baushke is also remembered for his "contribution" to the House of David Girls Baseball Team in its only season, 1919, when they went undefeated and won the championship. However, it was soon discovered that six of the players were actually young men in disguise, and the squad was stripped of the title. When asked why he did that, Baushke answered, "We just wanted to play."[34]

Tom Dewhirst, the younger son of Judge H. T. Dewhirst, who took over control of the House of David commune at the death of Benjamin Purnell in 1927, was born in Illinois in 1909. Tommy was 11 when his family arrived at the commune in 1920. Although he endured fragile health in his early youth, he grew into a 6'2", 220-pound, power-hitting outfielder with above-average speed and a strong, accurate throwing arm.[35] He began his baseball-playing tenure roaming the outfield with the junior team, 1928–1929, before he graduated to the Central States Traveling Team.[36] and remained as playing manager through 1937.[37]

He always found time to attend sandlot games, where he scouted young players for the team.[38]

The affable player immediately attracted the eye of sports writers. In his first year with the junior team in 1928, a magazine article called him "The Bearded Babe Ruth," a moniker that stuck with him for the rest of his life.[39] In 1929, the *Joplin Globe* reported, "Outstanding Tommy Dewhirst only 19 years old, has developed into one of the greatest sluggers the House of David ever had."[40]

Dewhirst said of his home runs, "Two years I had 38 homers, two years 36, but they really took away half of them. You see, many of the parks did not have walls so when I hit one over 400 feet over everyone's head, all I'd get was a ground rules [sic] double. That never happened to Babe Ruth I betcha."

He continued to contribute to the House of David after his playing days. Initially assigned to take over the agriculture operations, he served as president of the Michigan Frozen Food Packers Association, was

Tom Dewhirst (courtesy Brian Ziebart, House of David Commune archives).

appointed by Governor George Romney to the State Agricultural Commission, was named Southwest Michigan Man of the Year in 1960, and took the reigns as secretary of the House of David commune after his brother Bob passed away.[41] He kept his hand in things until his death.

Charlie Falkenstein was born in 1902 in Germany.[42] Information about him is somewhat fragmented and conflicting. He was a member of the commune for 12 years[43] and began playing baseball as a shortstop on the 1913 House of David team that played locally in the Benton Harbor area.[44]

The House of David Baseball Team Research Project listed him as a full-time catcher with the traveling team, 1918–1921; however, further research notes a photo of the 1922 traveling team which hangs in the House of David Museum in Benton Harbor that includes him.[45] He has also been listed as one of the roster players who appeared when "one of the most unique attractions to play at Muzzy Field made their first visit to Bristol in 1922."[46] In addition, a segment of an article in the *News-Palladium* in 1975 called "50 Years Ago Today" included a comment from 1925 that said, "the ever popular Charlie Falkenstein still continues to make things interesting on the receiving end."[47]

He left the commune and married in 1923 but remained in the area and played with the team in 1925. During that period, the scrappy catcher, considered by many as one of the best that ever handled home plate chores, was offered tryouts with Rochester in the AA International League and Toledo in the AA American Association. He turned them down. Instead he signed to play with the Menasha, Wisconsin, Badgers, the team that had won the Wisconsin State Championship.[48]

Circa 1922–1925, working around his baseball schedule, he was a member of the

Charlie Falkenstein (L), Hip Vaughn (C), Doc Tally (R) (courtesy Brian Ziebart, House of David Commune archives).

House of David Traveling Band that topped vaudeville bills everywhere as they travelled as far as California.[49] It was typical for the press to include the schedules of the traveling band as part of its pregame announcements. One of them said, "The game against Decatur at home on August 2 will be Charlie Falkenstein's final game because he leaves for California [with the band] next week."[50]

In an interview reported in *Sports Illustrated* in 1970, Falkenstein recalled, "We had overflow crowds everywhere. When we played the Bacharach Giants from Atlantic City in front of 22,000 people, Connie Mack came around and shook our hands."

After baseball, Charlie was a florist and owned Buchanan Floral in Buchanan, Michigan.[51]

Walter "Dutch" Faust, a talented infielder who played second base and shortstop, was born in Pennsylvania in 1905 before his family joined the commune.[52] He had an on-again, off-again career with both the House of David and the City of David squads as well as a cup of coffee in two minor leagues. He was with the House of David from 1920 to 1926, a hired player with the City of David, 1929–31, and returned as a hired player with the House of David, 1933–35.[53]

At age 15 when he lived on High Island, working in the commune's lumber production, he was recruited to play with the House of David young junior team. By the time he was 17, he was promoted to the traveling team for their first appearance at Muzzy Field in Bristol, Connecticut, in 1922. His popularity was almost instant due to his baseball prowess, good looks, and alleged 38-inch-long hair.[54]

During pregame workouts in 1922, Dutch and Doc Tally were observed playing a game called High-Low, which caught the eye of approving fans. Francis Thorpe, noting that interest, decided to keep it up as part of their entertainment, and it soon evolved into their signature three-man pepper game.[55] Concomitantly his fame spread among fans in the barnstorming circuit in the United States and Canada, where the press called him "a shortstop who fields any kind of ball in his territory."[56]

His experience in organized pro baseball was also fragmented. In 1925, lured by pitching teammate Lloyd Miller, he signed a contract to play second base with the Fort Smith Twins in the Class C Western League,[57] where he was allowed to keep his long locks and beard.[58] He then endured an injury-plagued season with the Dallas Steers in the Class C Texas Association (no statistics available), followed by a partial season with the Akron Tyrites in the Class B Central League in 1928, where he appeared in 65 games, divided between second base and shortstop, and batted .240.[59]

The day before practice was to begin for the 1935 season, his third as a hired player at the HOD, Faust was being courted to possibly manage the Pural Oil Club in a new league that was being proposed. But nothing came of it.[60] A game scheduled in Eugene, Oregon, on June 25, 1935, listed Walter Faust on the roster as a utility player scheduled to perform the pepper game with pitcher Lloyd Miller and outfielder Lefty Tolles.[61] Though he left the colony in 1925, he remained in touch with family at the commune.

Ezra "Cookie" Hannaford was born in 1898. He and his large musical family were part of the 85-member congregation the Purnells recruited from Australia in 1905, where his father, Joseph, was a well-known maker of quality musical instruments. He was on the baseball team from 1914 and played on the traveling squad from 1917 to 1927 as he juggled a demanding schedule between his musical commitments and baseball.[62]

During those years, he was described as "one of the fastest first basemen ever seen

Cookie Hannaford (courtesy Brian Ziebart, House of David Commune archives).

in action" in 1920 by New York Yankees owners when the *Boston Post* reported that he turned down their offer of $30,000, considered a "startling salary" for the time.[63] Hannaford declined, saying he played ball for love of the game and not for money.[64] The standard press coverage of the refusals by both Cookie Hannaford and Paul Mooney was explained with simple headlines on sports pages that read, "Only Their Foliage Keeps Them in the Bushes."[65] In 1924, an Iowa newspaper labeled him "one of the classiest first sackers playing semipro ball."[66]

In addition to his acclaimed skills on the diamond, Cookie Hannaford was also well-known as a talented musician who played the Buescher True Tone Saxophone and clarinet[67]; he was a member of the Eden Springs Syncopaters, a small band that provided music for local events in 1924[68]; by 1925, he was the director of the House of David Traveling Band, plus Cookie Hannaford's House of David Orchestra.[69] In his "spare" time, he was also the director of the House of David Singing Band that presented jazz music.[70] After the 1927 season, he got a haircut and shave, left the ballclub, and moved to New York, then Los Angeles, where he enjoyed a long and successful career in music.[71]

David Harrison was born in Australia in 1904 and arrived at the commune with his family as part of the 85-member Australian contingency brought there by the Purnells in 1905. Dubbed "Egg" or "Eggs" because one of his duties as a youngster was collecting eggs from the chickens, he was a true vegetarian and followed all tenets of the religion throughout his life.[72]

Always a third baseman, he began his baseball career as the original House of David batboy before he played on the home team in 1921. Although he was an agile fielder who batted .273 in 108 games in his rookie season with the traveling team in 1925, most of the attention he received was for his 36-inch-long locks.[73]

In 1926, he appeared in 135 games and batted .314. He was the captain of the

1927 Junior Team, then became player-manager in 1928, when he led the squad to the Berrien County Championship. Harrison received frequent attention from the press, who described him as one of the most outstanding players on the club, the leading hitter, most dependable in a pinch, and "it was doubtful the commune would have won the championship without him."[74]

He continued from 1932 to 1936, playing for the Central States team in 1932 and 1933.[75] In 1934, when the Southwestern Michigan All-Stars played the Chicago Cubs All-Stars, Harrison was chosen to play on the Michigan squad along with the House of David's first baseman, Tony Zitta, and outfielder Bill Heckman, one of the first non-colony members hired. Harrison, a member of the House of David barnstorming basketball team in between baseball

A different look for Cookie Hannaford (courtesy Brian Ziebart, House of David Commune archives).

The 1928 Junior Team. David Harrison (seated) player-manager. L-R, Jimmie Crow, Hobson Nelson, Glendon "Red" Wiltbank, Billy Link, Ernie Selby, George Anderson, Lionel Everett, Jack Crow, Earl Boyersmith, Sidney Smith, Leo "Lefty" Wiltbank (courtesy Brian Ziebart, House of David Commune archives).

seasons, was habitually described as "probably one of the steadiest players in the game during his era."[76]

One source says Harrison remained at the commune into the 1970s, without mentioning what he did there[77]; another suggests he drove truck among other jobs. He died on Christmas Eve, 1982, at age 78.[78] In an interview years later, catcher Eddie Deal said Harrison had declined an offer of $65,000 to play with the Philadelphia Phillies in order to remain in the commune.[79]

Paul Mooney, whose family was among the original members of the commune in 1905, was born in Ohio in 1896.[80] He pitched and played outfield on the first formal baseball team in 1915, and by 1917 he was considered their first big star. During his entire five-year career on the traveling team, 1917–1921, he was considered their premier pitcher, always in demand by fans everywhere they played.[81]

He stood out when the young Davids defeated such first class teams as the Chicago Hartford Giants, South Bend Overlords, South Bend Colored Royal Giants, Sturgis, Michigan, and the Elkhart, Indiana, All-Stars. On October 5, 1919,[82] when he pitched a no-hit game in Kalamazoo, he caught the eye of numerous major league teams.[83] From then on, the press referred to him as "a first class twirler and there is no doubt that he would make good in fast company ... last year he pitched in 24 games and lost only six."[84]

Mooney generally allowed fewer than five hits per game throughout his career that included several two- and three-hit outings. In December 1919, Cubs manager Fred Mitchell announced he had signed "a great pitcher with long hair and beard ... whose pitching style resembled Eddie Cicotte's floating style and floating curve, and he was expected to report to tryout with the team the following spring."[85] In addition, Mitchell invited Francis Thorpe to bring his entire team to Chicago to play the Cubs the following spring.[86]

However, the "news flash" was premature, as headlines on page one of many papers later reported Mooney had turned down the $25,000 offer, "probably because he didn't care to

Paul Mooney (Joel Hawkins File).

cut off his long hair."[87] He was also courted by the New York Yankees with the same results.

In 1925, four years after an arm injury ended his career, he was acknowledged as the hurler whose great pitching carried his team to many victories.[88] Though he left the commune after baseball, he remained in the Benton Harbor region, working as a machinist. Mooney died in 1962 at age 66.

John Tucker, frequently called one of the best first basemen outside of the big leagues, with fielding skills second only to Hal Chase,[89] was born in Tyler, Texas, in 1902 and migrated to St. Joseph, Michigan, in 1915 with his family. They were assigned to work at High Island, a newly purchased lumber mill community where the baseball teams practiced before each season. When word got back to Purnell about an outstanding young player there, he made what is thought to be his only trip to the island to see Tucker. While there, he found Tucker and Walter Faust and had both reassigned to play baseball.[90]

Paul Mooney with his parents shortly after they arrived at the commune (courtesy Brian Ziebart, House of David Commune archives).

His baseball career was long and successful. Early on, when he was scouted by the White Sox, he said he never wanted to play major league baseball. After two years with the House of David home team, in 1924, when he was given the moniker "Long John Tucker" because of his height and long reach off the bag at first, he was promoted to the traveling team. After the schism at the commune, when the baseball team fractured into two teams following the 1928 season, he went with Mary Purnell and played with her City of David squad through 1941.

When the Benton Harbor teams took a hiatus during World War II, he was recruited as player/manager of the St. Joseph Auto Specialties, a job he kept through 1957. He led that club to the National Championship in 1946. For seven years, from 1961 to 1967, he managed the St. Joseph American Legion team,[91] reporting that as "one of the great joys of my career."[92]

The 1935 season was unusual. His season ended prematurely when he suffered a broken right leg on Labor Day while playing on a muddy field in Council Bluffs, Iowa. His younger brother, Cecil, called "the last rookie to come from within the commune," made a name for himself in his own right when he briefly manned first base. He later spent 1936–1937 pitching with the City of David traveling nine, where he accrued a

15–1 record. Unfortunately, Cecil became ill with cancer and died at age 26.[93] Tucker's other brother, Melvin, played briefly.[94]

Always a prankster with a powerful bat and fielding acumen, Long John Tucker was popular everywhere. His first year as player-manager, he batted .380 in 198 games. That was the year he took 12 players on a successful 205-game tour that ended in Mexico City the first week in November. Teammate Lloyd Dalager remembered a game played in Texas, April 10, 1935, when Tucker made 23 of the 27 putouts.[95]

One of Tucker's favorite stories concerns two games back-to-back in 1933 when his team played exhibition games against all eight Pacific Coast League teams, saying they defeated them all—except one. He was not surprised when Joe DiMaggio hit a game-winning triple with two men on base, giving that win to the San Francisco Seals. When his club faced the Oakland Oaks the next day, their manager, Ray Brubaker,[96] pulled him aside and said, "I'll play my regulars about five innings, then let you guys catch up." In the eighth inning, when Tucker's squad was ahead, Brubaker shouted across the diamond, "Why didn't you tell me you had a good club?"[97]

John Tucker (Ron Taylor, City of David Files).

John Tucker always said he owed his success in life by following a personal philosophy: "Go to bed the same day you get up, don't bring work home, don't live on a liquid diet, and learn to hit the curve ball."[98]

Charles Hubert "Hip" Vaughan (sometimes misspelled "Hipp" by the press) was born in 1899 in Texas and came to the House of David in November 1910, where he remained until September 1924. At that time, he and his wife left the commune but remained in the Benton Harbor area. From 1918 to 1922, he pitched and played outfield.[99] In a 1922 press interview about his own career, Cookie Hannaford told the press, "We have a new pitcher who promises to outclass Mooney: his name is Vaughan."[100] There are conflicting reports that his services were sought by major league clubs.[101]

According to the House of David 1920 Federal Census, his off-season occupation was listed as a chauffeur in 1920. The 1925 Local Directory listed him as working as a mechanic in Benton Harbor. There is no information about him after that date.[102]

Art Vieritz was born in Australia in 1899 and arrived at the House of David in 1905.[103] Though he had never played baseball in Australia, he learned the game at the commune and initially played outfield, shortstop, and second base. It didn't take long for him to establish his niche in center field.[104] Always available to be transferred from one House of David team to another as needed, in 1922 at age 17 he was one of the trio of players, with Jesse Tally and Cookie Hannaford, who joined the traveling team on its first trip to Muzzy Field in Bristol, Connecticut.[105]

Although one source lists his years of play as 1918–1922,[106] newspaper articles of the day show him on the roster in box scores of games through the mid–1920s.[107] When his arm was hit by a pitch in 1924, the press erroneously reported that he was paralyzed, which was a huge exaggeration. In addition to his exciting play, he became well-known for performing comedy sketches in the style of popular comedian of the day, Nick Altrock, before games and between innings.[108]

Before baseball, he worked as a farmer and returned to it after he retired from play. He remained in the Benton Harbor area until his death in 1970 at age 71.[109]

Horace Hannaford, older brother of Cookie, was born in Australia in 1889 or 1890, depending on the source. He initially manned third base on the traveling team until he was moved to first base after the 1927 season, when Cookie departed to pursue his musical aspirations. Ironically, the press noted that his hitting improved in the new position.[110] He was the landscape gardener at the commune before the demands of baseball and the colony band demanded that he spend all his time on the road.[111]

Following his playing days, he did not remain with the commune or in Benton Harbor. His last known whereabouts was in New York, where he was an official at LaGuardia Airport in 1947.[112]

Horace Hannaford (courtesy Brian Ziebart, House of David Commune archives).

Richard Marcum (sometimes misspelled "Markham"),[113] from Kentucky, was one of the earliest members of the commune when he arrived in 1905. At the age of 28, he played with the 1915 baseball team. Marcum was considered a very good mechanic when not playing ball. He was also known to have a recent history of mental lapses. When he went missing in 1916, an extensive search was launched by House of David personnel and law enforcement before he was found unconscious along the tracks of the Pere Marquette Railway, suffering from multiple injuries from which he did not recover. It was assumed he had been suffering from dementia[114] and was hit by a train.[115]

Monroe Wulff was born in Ohio in 1896. The arrival date of his family is uncertain, although the House of David Research Project listed him on the baseball team in 1915, and the 1920 Federal Census, Berrien County Genealogy Project lists him as age 24 and married at that time.[116]

He was one of the first members of the commune drafted into the army in 1917, but when he declared himself a conscientious objector, he was convicted of disobeying orders in a court martial hearing and served several months in Ft. Leavenworth Prison. He was released when the military Board of Inquiry found his beliefs sincere.[117]

When he mustered out, he returned to House of David and baseball. Although he was known to hit for power, his propensity to strike out kept him from being a starter. His best season at the plate was 1925, when he batted .260. In 1919 he was the catcher, but the rest of his career, 1920–1925, he played in the outfield. After baseball, he moved to the City of David, where he remained until his death in 1938 at age 42.

Monroe Wulff and his wife Elena (courtesy Brian Ziebart, House of David Commune archives).

Frank Wyland was described as "one of the most popular and probably the most colorful of all the players on the House of David roster."[118] Born in Jewell, Kansas, he came to the commune in 1906 and joined the roster of the 1915 team at age 28.[119] He began as a pitcher but his powerful bat earned him a spot in the outfield, where he played regularly from 1917 to 1919 and batted .319.[120]

He was one of several players from the traveling team who also played in the House of David Traveling Band. In addition, since he had been a professional boxer before joining the commune, he often gave sparring exhibitions there.[121] Between 1920 and 1927, he left baseball and concentrated on music, playing with the traveling band.

Frank Wyland (Joel Hawkins File).

In 1928, he returned to baseball and played on the last House of David team before the commune fractured.[122] Concomitantly, while tensions within the commune were high and the colony split, Wyland was deputized by the Berrien County Sheriff to maintain order.[123]

In 1931, he took the job of catcher with the Central States team when longtime catcher Bert "Beans" Johnson, an outsider, was released to make room for more commune players. Wyland was considered excellent at handling pitchers and directing play in the field. In addition, he assisted Tom Dewhirst in managing the team. The press said he was a good co-manager who displayed "a little ability mixed with brains."[124]

When he retired as a player, the *News-Palladium* (August 1, 1932) announced he would assume the role of umpire. He remained in the commune for the rest of his life. Although he was a skilled carpenter by trade, he also did a lot of the commune's gardening, more or less as a hobby. In 1943, he received a modicum of notoriety of a different sort for inventing what was called a "super sunflower" in his backyard.[125] After living at the commune for 40 years, he died in April 1946, at age 59.[126]

Jerry Hansel, born in 1897, arrived at the commune from Ohio with his parents and four of his nine siblings in April 1912.[127] His father was a mechanic, and Jerry was a mechanic apprentice when not playing baseball as a catcher on the House of David baseball team, from 1917 to 1919.[128] However, due to non-baseball-related issues, he and his family left the commune January 1, 1921.[129]

Bob Dewhirst, the older son of Judge H. T. Dewhirst, who ran the Original House of David after Purnell died in 1927, was born in Illinois in 1907 and came to the commune with his family in 1920 when he was 13. At age 21, he began playing base-

Top: **Frank Wyland, Berrien County Sheriff Deputy.** *Left:* **Bob Dewhirst (courtesy Brian Ziebart, House of David Commune archives).**

ball as a southpaw on the mound and first baseman with a better than average bat, from 1928 to 1936. He played primarily on the Home Team, and in 1935 he managed the Central States team when other teams were on the road.[130]

In addition to baseball, he loved music and gave numerous solo concerts in Benton Harbor and surrounding regions on his vibraharp, a unique instrument similar to a xylophone.[131] He played at games, graduations, and other community events, which he continued throughout his life. The vibraharp shown in the image at right is presently located in the Shiloh Building at the House of David.

After baseball, he was the manager of the commune's preserves department for preparation of jams and jellies.[132] When he died in 1966 at age 59, his obituary described him as "a versatile man with a kind heart."[133]

Austin "Tex" Williams was born in Texas in 1897. Tex played second base from 1916 to 1921. He left the colony in 1922 but continued to play sporadically for the team into the 1930s.[134]

Clay "Mud" Williams was born in Texas. There is no mention of any family members.[135] The second baseman-outfielder began playing on the Junior Team, 1928, then played on the Central States Traveling Team through 1935.[136]

In addition to baseball, Williams was a skilled basketball man who captained the traveling basketball team.[137] Because of his talent, the Cooksana Basketball team organizer added him to their roster for the Benton Harbor City Basketball League play-off game.[138] One of the most memorable basketball experiences in his career happened in 1931 when, in front of 5,000

Top: Bob Dewhirst. *Right:* Clay "Mud" Williams, who was also captain of the basketball team in the early thirties (courtesy Brian Ziebart, House of David Commune archives).

fans in Chicago, the bewhiskered bunch was beaten by the Taylor Trunk Girls squad, 18–9.[139] If playing against a girls' team was not enough, in a tussle for possession of the ball with a female opponent, John Tucker was knocked off his feet and rendered temporarily unconscious before he got up and completed the game.[140]

Percy Walker was born in 1893 in Pennsylvania[141] and arrived at the commune with his family circa 1917. Records about his career, though sketchy, show that he began playing in 1918 as a right-handed pitcher and outfielder who played on and off for the home team. By 1929, he had a reputation as a veteran spitball pitcher with tricky ball movement.[142]

In 1929, the first season with two teams, Judge Dewhirst selected Percy Walker as manager of the Original House of David Team, the first representing that faction of the commune after the break-up. The press described him as "a man with an abundance of baseball knowledge and athletic skills who knows how to handle players."[143] The team played excellent baseball under Walker's leadership and attracted large crowds everywhere.[144] Walker, who also continued pitching as needed, was credited with pitching five no-hit games for his squad by 1930.[145] His team, one of two from the fractured commune, was a strong one that included Clay "Mud" Williams, Dave Harrison, Tom Dewhirst, Bob Dewhirst, Frank Wyland, Al Stemm, and Bert "Beans" Johnson.[146]

Decades later, former catcher Lloyd Dalager recalled a game with the Yankees when, after Walker had struck out Babe Ruth, Ruth honored his own custom by giving Walker his bat as a memento of the occasion.[147]

Walker ran the commune restaurant while playing ball when the team played at home. Afterward he was a teacher at the commune school and ran the storeroom for the commune. In those capacities, he ordered and distributed all the items for the park and various kitchens. Percy Walker remained at the House of David until his death at age 60 in 1953.[148]

Jack Crow, born in August 1912, arrived at the commune with his parents from the Tyler, Texas, region in April 1914. The right-handed pitcher initially tagged "Little Jackie Crow" started playing baseball at age 16 in 1928, when he pitched and

Percy Walker and Jewel Boone, former pitcher on the girls' team (courtesy Brian Ziebart, House of David Commune archives).

won two games on the road before the local fans had a chance to see him. He was "officially" noticed by the press in 1929,[149] when he led the junior team at its peak with teammates Ernie Selby (1B), Sid Smith (SS), Wes Clark (C), Barney Dalager (2B), cousin Jimmy Crow (3B), Leo "Lefty" Wiltbank (CF), Joe O'Signac (RF), and Earl Boyersmith (LF). He pitched part of every game, and by the end of the season he was written about as "Iron Man Jack Crow."[150]

He received frequent headlines in the press in anticipation of each mound appearance. In 1931, he and pitcher Harold Daisy were considered an unbeatable pitching combo that manager Tom Dewhirst used together at every opportunity.[151] He pitched to catcher Clay "Mud" Williams in the opening game of the 1932 season at Eden Springs Park against the South Bend Athletics.[152]

Jack married a woman outside the commune in June 1934, and the pair left in 1938. Jack Crow died in January 1983 at age 71.[153]

Jack Crow (courtesy Brian Ziebart, House of David Commune archives).

Lloyd Dalager was born in Regina, Saskatchewan, Canada, in 1913 and came to the House of David in 1918, when he was five years old. He spent the rest of his life as a member of the commune. His father, Hans Dalager, a longtime driver for the House of David baseball team, was nicknamed "Barney" after race car speedster Barney "last to leave and first to arrive" Oldfield.

Starting at age 14, Lloyd honed his skills as a catcher-utility player with the Junior Team from 1927 to 1935. In 1936 he was promoted to the last traveling team fielded by the House of David as a rookie, when they put together a record of 144 wins, 46 loses, and five ties. George Anderson, then with the City of David club, asked Dalager to join his team, but permission was denied because his duties as the electrician for the Original House of David were too important.[154]

He said he did not have a specific favorite memory of those days, but loved all aspects of the lifestyle. "We used to play for thousands of people. We played every little town—every little place they wanted to see the Davids. Probably the best time was traveling with the team in 1936.[155] That year we traveled in a Dodge bus and did pretty good. We used to play against a team called Joe Green and his Colored Giants from Chicago. We made about two bucks a day eating money, but that was enough to get by back then," he told Brian Ziebart, who took care of him in his later years.[156]

When asked about the team's travels with the Kansas City Monarchs and playing against Negro League teams, his reply was always the same: "We didn't care what color they were. Those teams played good baseball. We got along with all of them. And we won more than we lost."[157]

In celebration of his 92nd birthday, the Chicago Cubs invited Lloyd to throw the ceremonial first pitch before a Chicago Cubs game at Wrigley Field and gave him a Cubs jersey with number 92 on the back to wear for the occasion. For weeks ahead of the event, he walked the House of David property, playing catch with different partners as practice to ensure he would make a good showing in Chicago.

On the big day, he was driven to Wrigley Field in a limo, made the pitch, and met many players. He was especially excited to speak with Ron Santo, who knew about the House of David.[158]

For many years, he ran the House of David Electric Power Plant and was an engineer who drove one of the miniature steam engines at the amusement park. He lived in Shiloh, the largest Victorian mansion in Michigan, and was serving as the president of the House of David at the time of his death. An era ended when this last surviving player from the barnstorming period died in 2012, a few weeks short of his 99th birthday.[159]

Glenn Klum was the son of one of the contractors who built many of the business houses and residences of the commune.[160] From 1917 to 1921, he played center field and third base and pitched for the House of David.[161] He was considered a sensational outfielder who covered a lot of territory, making shoestring catches.[162] Although not their star pitcher, Klum was considered a frequent help to the team, allowing few hits and pitching notable shutouts.[163] He was also a member of the House of David Traveling Band.[164]

Ernie Selby, a highly praised first baseman, was born in Oldham, England, in 1913. At age 18, he began a two-year stint with the House of David Junior Team, 1931–1932, then does not appear in commune records again until 1940,[165] when he was part of Eddie Deal's home team. They played mostly on weekends and won the Michiana League Championship.[166]

Lloyd Dalager (courtesy Brian Ziebart, House of David Commune archives).

In the interim, newspaper articles wrote of him playing on such different teams as the Twin Cities Merchants in 1935[167] and the Benton Harbors Pure-Oils in 1937.[168] In 1935, Ernie Selby Day honored him and his new bride at a local ballpark.[169] In 1944, he reappeared on a reformed team organized and managed by Doc Tally to satisfy Benton Harbor's request for a baseball team during the war years.[170]

After he retired as a player, Ernie Selby remained in Benton Harbor as a plumbing contractor[171] and coached Little League baseball for several years.[172]

Wesley Schneider was born in Indiana in 1880.[173] He arrived at the House of David in 1903 with his brother, Johnnie, who had previously traveled as a contortionist with the circus.

Information about his baseball career is limited. Wesley played baseball and toured the country with the House of David Traveling Band for many years, where he played an assortment of instruments.[174]

In 1929, he was appointed manager of the Home Team,[175] a title some described as "manager in name only." He managed paperwork while longtime catcher Bert "Beans" Johnson actually handled the team on the field.[176]

A sincere believer in the faith, in 1907 he and three others from the commune drove his first car, a 1906 Ford, to New York to "advertise" the House of David and spread the commune's message. He later explained they were lucky to get back because

Ernie Selby tagged out by young Jimmie Crow when practicing his slide into second base (courtesy Brian Ziebart, House of David Commune archives).

gasoline, sold in grocery stores at that time, was hard to find.[177]

Schneider, a skilled plumber, later dated Percy Walker's sister and remained in the commune until his death in 1958 at age 78.[178]

Oscar Sassman, born in 1902, came to the commune from St. Joseph, Missouri, with his parents in 1907. It is said that his parents worked at the farm, and after his father died in a silo accident, his step-mother operated the dairy for 59 years. However, very little is known about him. He played second base on the House of David Junior Team from 1918 to 1922, before he was promoted to the major traveling team in 1923. He is probably best remembered as one of the boys who, disguised as girls, played on the 1919 House of David Girls Team, along with Luther Jackson, Arthur Jackson, David Harrison, Elijah Burland, and Dwight "Zeke" Baushke.[179]

Wesley Schneider (Brian Ziebart, House of David Commune Files).

"Outsiders"

The four best-known outsiders are not included in this chapter, as elements of their stories are included within the text. Coincidentally, all four were pitchers who were involved with the Bearded Beauties in the early '30s. Two were future members of the Hall of Fame: Grover Cleveland Alexander, who pitched in the majors from 1911 to 1930, logging a 373–208 record with a 2.56 ERA, then 1931–1935 as pitcher-manager of the House of David; Charles "Chief" Bender spent 1903 to 1925 in the major leagues, posting a 212–127 record with a 2.46 ERA,[180] then, due to injury, spent only part of the 1933 season with the House of David.

The other two pitchers were women. Seventeen-year-old Virnett "Jackie" Mitchell was loaned to the Davids Eastern Traveling Team for the 1933 season after she allegedly struck out Babe Ruth on four pitches and Lou Gehrig on three in an exhibition game against the Yankees in 1931[181]; Mildred "Babe" Didrikson, multisport athlete who won multiple medals in the 1932 Olympics,[182] joined the Western States Traveling Team in 1934 before she went on to more triumphs as a pro golfer.[183]

Starting after 1918, by necessity the commune hired a large stable of players from the professional baseball ranks that included players from the low minor league to the major league level, who helped them fill out rosters and win ballgames.

Richard "Dick" Atwell, born in 1910, has been praised as "one of Pasadena's pioneer professional baseball players." At age 18, the power hitting shortstop-second baseman and former captain of the Pasadena High School baseball team joined the Keokuk Indians in the Class D Mississippi Valley League right after graduation in 1928.[184]

In a nutshell, his career with House of David and City of David is as follows: City of David, 1932; House of David, 1933; City of David, 1934–1937.[185] Interlaced with this was a decade of baseball playing in various places at various levels: the Des Moines Demons, Class A Western League (1929–1930); Joplin Miners, Class C Western Association; Topeka Jayhawks, back in the Western League (1931); Beatrice Blues in the Class D Nebraska State League (1932). During that time, he appeared in a total of 294 games[186] and was seen by numerous scouts.

In 1934, he received the following letter from the Charles Graham, vice president of the San Francisco Baseball Club dated February 7, 1934: Dear Sir: This is to advise you to report here on Monday, February 26th, at 10:30 a.m., at the Seals Stadium.

With that, he shaved his beard and returned a signed contract with the San Francisco Seals in the AA Pacific Coast League to attend spring training with the team.[187] Although it was reported he was doing well,[188] he was in for a disappointment. After appearing in just five games as a teammate of Joe DiMaggio the year the slugger had his 61-game hitting streak, Dick Atwell was released.[189]

Soon thereafter, City of David manager John Tucker wrote a letter inviting him to rejoin the City of David nine, praising his play and general comportment while promising he would be the highest-paid man on the team. Not yet ready to retire from the game, he accepted. Early in 1934, the slick keystone combo of shortstop Dick Atwell

Team aboard the S.S. *Malolo* on their way to Honolulu, Hawaii, after the 1936 season (City of David Commune Files).

and second baseman Hub Henson, with John Tucker at first base, completed 210 double plays and were regarded as one of the best of their era.[190] During the off-season, he returned to his Pasadena home, worked as a prop man for Republic Pictures, and played on their semipro team.[191]

In 1936, after playing 195 games, the team extended its season and sailed to Hawaii, where they played at army posts in Maui and Hilo, followed by several games in Honolulu.[192]

When they returned, Bill Essik, Yankees scout covering California who signed future Hall of Fame players Joe Gordon, Tony Lazzeri, Lefty Gomez, and Joe DiMaggio,[193] persuaded Dick Atwell to sign with Los Angeles in the Pacific Coast League, where he became part of a double play team with future scout Bobby Mattick. *Los Angeles Times* columnist Braven Dyer reported that "the second base problem is solved by the insertion of Dick Atwell."[194]

Unfortunately, tragedy struck after just two weeks when an unknown injury, finally diagnosed as a ruptured hernia, that required three surgeries to diagnose and repair sidelined him and eventually resulted in his release and the end of his baseball career.[195]

Dick Atwell then joined the Pasadena Fire Department, where he remained until his health failed and he died in 1985 at age 75. Over 20 years after his death, the *Pasadena Star News* wrote: "Prior to Jackie Robinson's arrival on the baseball scene, no San Gabriel Valley resident had a bigger impact on the game than Dick Atwell."[196]

Dick Wykoff, pitcher, born in 1903 in Osborne County, Kansas, was a 1996 inductee into the Osborne County Hall of Fame, honoring his many years in baseball. Before he joined the Bearded Beauties, he was a starting pitcher, versatile fielder, and power hitter for several minor league teams. In 1925, after he was seen by numerous scouts in the vicinity, the Cincinnati Reds purchased his contract from the Class D Salina Millers, paying the highest price ever paid for a Southwestern League player.[197]

From 1925 to 1932, he appeared with the Class A Springfield Hampdens, Class AA American Association Columbus Senators, and Class AA Western League Pueblo Braves. However, things did not go as planned. He broke his knee twice, in 1926 and 1928, which ended his major league dreams.[198]

But his baseball career was not over. After he pitched a game against the Israelite House of David and beat them, 1–0, the club told him they needed good pitching and hired him to fill both starting and relief roles.[199] In his last season, 1948, he was written about as the head of their seven-man pitching staff.[200] After baseball, he bought and operated a small farm.

Eddie Deal, born in 1901 in New Hampton, Iowa, was perhaps the favorite outsider of them all. He was always a fan favorite for his humor and baseball acumen. He had a multiple-year baseball resume before he joined the House of David team in 1929: Fairmont Cardinals, the first semipro team in Minnesota in 1924, Superior in Northern League in 1925–26, player-manager of Jamestown, North Dakota, in 1927, followed by three teams in 1928—the Waterloo Hawks and Cedar Rapids Bunnies in the Mississippi Valley League and the Decatur Commodores in the Three-I League.[201]

Deal had the longest tenure of all non-commune players (1929–1942), when he was known as one of the older and best catchers on the circuit. He always said his style was to "mix pleasure with business," and he quickly became known as a friendly and funny man enjoyed by everyone.²⁰² In addition to doing all the catching duties, he led his squad in home runs for 11 consecutive years, with a batting average close to .400. He was also on the pepper team with Lloyd Dalager and David Harrison. As player-manager of the Home Team, he led them to the championship of the Michiana League in 1940, the only year any squad from the commune played in an organized league.²⁰³

In an interview with the *News Palladium*, Deal recalled a conversation with former scout Cy Slapnicka, then GM of the Cleveland Indians, who signed future Hall of Fame pitcher Bob Feller, among others. "One day Slap and I were sitting in the stands talking before the start of the game and he told me I could be the best catcher there ever was in the major leagues if I'd sign with him." He refused, telling Slapnicka he was happy with the baseball schedule where he was and enjoyed his off-season job managing the commune hotel.²⁰⁴

Eddie Deal was a licensed pilot who owned and operated a successful charter service called Deal's Flying Service that catered to a variety of celebrities after his baseball days. It's reported that when he was on his deathbed at age 98, he was told about the House of David starting a new team for old-timers called the Echoes. In true Deal style, he said, "I'll be there," and turned over and died.²⁰⁵

Norman Blieding—sometimes misspelled "Bleiding"—was born in Indiana in 1904. Little was written about his baseball career. He was a well-liked player who only played the game for four years, two with the Bearded Beauties. In 1931, he

Top and right: **Popular Eddie Deal (courtesy Brian Ziebart, House of David Commune archives).**

was a catcher for the House of David under manager Grover Cleveland Alexander when the team faced the Homestead Grays in the first night game at Island Park.[206] Always a workhorse, Blieding caught 186 of 190 games played in 1932.[207]

In 1936, he caught on the Medford Team in the Central Wisconsin Association,[208] and in 1937 he managed the Marshfield Athletics in the same association.[209] Following his playing days, he umpired in the Northern League, Three-I League, and Wisconsin State League for several years.[210] He remained in Wausau, where he was a member of the Old Timers Baseball Association of Wisconsin-Illinois-Indiana and, according to daily advertisements in the local paper over a period of years, he owned and operated the Chatterbox Beer Garden from 1945 to 1968. He died in 1974 at age 70.[211]

Charles "Moose" Swaney, born circa 1880 in Missouri,[212] was a big southpaw dubbed "Moose" while playing in Moosejaw, Saskatchewan, in the Western Canada League.[213] Before joining Lou Murphy's House of David in 1931 at age 51, he had completed ten minor league seasons which included stops in the International League and Piedmont League.[214] In an article about an upcoming visit of the House of David nine in 1941, the *Asbury Park Press* stated, "Moose Swaney is somewhat of an attraction in his own right, having pitched in nearly every minor league in the country during a long career."[215] Described as "Old Moose," this left-handed troubadour of the mound, finally pitched his final game for the House of David at age 58.[216] Prior to that, one of his stints was with the Hartford Senators in 1923–1924, when Lou Gehrig broke in, and the two were roommates.[217]

Known as a "junk pitcher," he gained national fame during his tenure with the Davids due to his comedic antics and status as the oldest pitcher in the game,[218] a combination that often made his team "baseball's most colorful aggregation." But he was a man who spoke his mind. When asked about playing with the House of David, he surprised many when he replied, "an old ballplayer can't drop any further than the House of David. This is an absolute zero in the profession."[219] He was particu-

Norman Blieding (Brian Ziebart, House of David Commune Files).

larly angry about opponents forcing him to have his bushy beard trimmed, claiming it impaired their ability to see the ball.[220]

Moose Swaney died in a Veterans Hospital in 1961.[221]

Herman "Flip" Fleming, catcher, was born in Iowa in 1898. Information about him is limited. In 1922, he caught for the Maquoketa Merchants, where he was an instant hit, and followed this by a stint in the Mississippi Valley League.[222] He went on to play for both the House of David and the City of David from 1929 to 1935. He was a leader at the plate in the 1932 *Denver Post* Tournament, when the nine made its first appearance in the competition and finished seventh.[223] Fleming is remembered not as a power hitter but as a hustling, athletic player who fought for every hit, as seen in 1934 when he hit .350 in 160 games.[224] In 1935, he was a playing manager with the Lost Nation Indees, where local papers agreed he "still displays much of his ginger and pep."[225]

Lew Hummel, born in 1918, was a three-sport man at Northumberland High School in Pennsylvania. After graduation in 1937, he played minor league baseball in the Class B Interstate League and the Class A Eastern League, interspersed with two seasons of winter ball in the Ismithian League in Panama before being drafted into the army.

While in the service, he met George Anderson, who invited him to play on his City of David team. He accepted the offer and manned second base in 1946–1947. One memory he loved to talk about while with the House of David was a rainy day in Kansas when they were to face the Monarchs in an exhibition game if the field was playable. In an effort to dry the field before game time, they doused the entire field with two tanks of gasoline and set it on fire. That only helped a little bit.[226] After his stint in Benton Harbor, he played minor league baseball in Class B and C leagues through the 1951 season.

After he retired from the game, he was a railroad man for 30 years. Looking back years later, he recalled, "We never had much money but it sure was fun." He died in September 2006 at age 88.[227]

Dick Hummel, older brother of Lew, pitched and played third base in the Michigan State League and Piedmont League, then did a stint in the military before he barnstormed with the City of David in 1946–1947.[228] With the House of David, he logged a 12–7 record as a starter and also made many appearances in relief before he hung it up to coach and umpire high school and college sports for 30 years.[229]

It was relatively commonplace for barnstorming players on different teams to collect newspaper articles in places they played and keep scrapbooks and journals of their adventures. Dick Hummel kept a day-by-day record of every place the Davids played during his tenure and later sent it to his daughter in the form of a journal. (This can be seen in the Appendix.)[230] "It was a lot of fun." he said. "We tried to win all the games, but it was free and easy. We didn't worry about our batting averages."[231]

Lou Vann, shortstop, born Luigi G. Varanese in 1909 in Fall River, Massachusetts, was one of ten children. He quit school after the eighth grade to help support the family. He went to work in the textile mill with his father, a job he found distasteful, and played shortstop on the town team. In the first two years of his professional career, 1932–1933, he appeared with three teams: Class A Eastern League New Haven Bulldogs, beginning 1933 with the Class A Harrisburg Senators of the short-season New York-Penn League, and completed the season with the New Bedford Whales in the Class B New England League.[232]

He moved to Lou Murphy's House of David team from 1935 to 1937, a decision he made because they offered better money. However, still unable to give up his dream of a professional baseball career, he started again, this time with Sydney in the Class D Cape Breton Colliery League in Canada, when it converted from amateur to professional status. Things didn't work out there, and when the league folded in 1939, Vann returned to the House of David from 1940 to 1942, where he was described as one of the fastest men on the club as well as a leading hitter.[233] During those years, he served as team captain, manned third base,[234] and became a popular part of the pepper game team with pitcher Moose Swaney and first baseman Jimmy Woods.[235] In October 1942, he enlisted in the Marine Corps and was killed in an accident at Camp Pendleton in California. He was 34 years old.

Allen "Bullet Ben" Benson was a hard-throwing pitcher born in 1905 in Hurley, South Dakota. He had a pitching career that can best be described as bizarre. From 1927 to 1929, he appeared with four minor league teams: Dallas, Class A, Texas League; Akron, Class B Central League; Charleroi, Class C Mid-Atlantic League; Minneapolis, Class AA American Association.[236] After the 1929 season, with a 24–25 lifetime record, and tried farming until he realized he couldn't make enough money to support his family.

He wanted to return to baseball, this time to try his hand in the barnstorming ranks. Because he already had a beard, he was signed by the House of David for the 1934 season, when there were a handful of House of David teams. Babe Didrikson and Satchel Paige also spent small portions of that year with the Davids, though they never played on the same team.[237]

At the same time, Calvin Griffith, president of the woeful Washington Senators, was busily seeking a means to change the fate of his lackluster team. With that goal, Benson became the first player ever signed by Griffith's longtime friend, famed scout Joe Cambria.[238] However, Benson's major league career was brief: parts of two games in which he pitched 9⅔ innings, logging an 0–1 record with a whopping 12.10 ERA. He was immediately released.[239] One commentary read, "House of David Moundsman Lost First Game," while others described it as "less than a full cup of coffee, a tragedy, a game that will live in infamy."[240] The *Minneapolis Star Tribune* reported that before Benson's second outing was over, Griffith announced he would be sent back to the House of David.[241]

According to baseball-reference.com, he split the 1935 season between two minor league teams: Albany, Class AA, International League, and Harrisburg, Class A, New York-Penn League,

Allen Benson (courtesy Brian Ziebart, House of David Commune archives).

then bounced around with several minor league teams through 1946.[242] Throughout his career, he pitched 110 games and logged an overall 33–36 record.[243]

Benson's son reported that his father, who called Dizzy Dean a close friend, got requests for autographs until he died at age 94 in 1999.[244]

Ardys B. "Art" Keller, was born in Octavia, Nebraska. After high school graduation in 1934, he played amateur baseball for two seasons as a catcher on the Schuyler team when the squad won the Elkhorn Valley League championship,[245] and returned for the 1935 season. After he did a brief stint with the St. Louis Browns' affiliate, the Palestine Pals, in the Class C East Texas League in 1936, he played semipro ball in the Lincoln Baseball League. Keller was on the All-American section in Hap Dumont's National Baseball Congress in Wichita in 1937.

Despite having been well-scouted in the Wichita Tournament, Keller did not have a contract in his hand for 1938. However, on January 24, John Tucker, City of David manager, invited the soft-spoken catcher to join the team, explaining that in addition to $160 per month pay, the team paid all hotel bills and transportation while players took care of their own meals and laundry. Keller accepted and stayed with the team for one year.[246] The instant fan-favorite had a busy year as he caught 176 games, including a tripleheader on Labor Day, and posted a .322 batting average. When it was learned he had signed a contract with the Browns, an article appeared in a St. Louis paper saying Keller's story could be called "From Beards to Browns."[247]

At the time he signed with the St. Louis Browns, he was one of four catchers in camp, knowing the club intended to keep only three. He was odd man out and was sent to their Class B affiliate, Springfield, in the Three-I League, where he played for three years through 1941, then had two successful seasons, 1942–1943, with Toledo in the Class AA American Association. Ardys Keller entered the army on October 6, 1943.[248] He was a corporal in the infantry when he was killed in France on September 29, 1944.[249] He was 28 years old.

Eddie Popowski, born in Sayreville, New Jersey, in 1913, was an "eat-sleep-and-breathe" baseball man. At age 17, when he was operating an ice truck in his hometown, he was seen playing infield on a Sayreville, New Jersey, town team by someone from the House of David and quickly signed. He was conspicuous for his diminutive size (5'4"), his talent at second base, and his inability to grow a beard due to his youth. He played as many as 256 games a season, earning a $175 monthly salary plus an additional $25 for Pepper Team antics.[250] He was still with the Original House of David in 1936 when Red Sox scouts signed him in mid-season. He remained with the Davids until the end of the season, explaining that he felt duty-bound to complete the House of David season before reporting to the Red Sox.[251]

Eddie Popowski then began a 60-year-plus association with the Red Sox organization as a player, coach, instructor, and manager in 15 minor leagues before joining the major league club in 1969.[252] He played baseball while in the military in World War II until a collision at second base severely injured his knee, which ended his playing career and earned him an honorable discharge from the military.[253]

In 1994, Eddie Popowski, "Pops," was inducted into the New Jersey Sports Writers Association Hall of Fame for his positive involvement in the careers of many Boston players over the years, some of whom would later be inducted into the Baseball Hall of Fame at Cooperstown.[254]

After a brief illness, he died in Sayersville in 2001 at age 88.[255]

6. Memorable Players

Albert "Lefty" Tolles, a Michigan native, was born May 22, 1906, in Geneva Township. The team captain and ace pitcher at Michigan State College[256] was later described as one of the best pitchers in Michigan State baseball history.[257] He left college late in the 1928 season when he was "taken over" by the St. Louis Cardinals. However, when they offered him a contract for 1929, he returned it, saying the salary was too low, which earned him a reputation as "one of the first—if not *the* first—major league hold-outs."[258]

He was recruited by the House of David for 1929. In contrast to one report that he played for the House of David from 1929 to 1935, commune records indicate he played for them in 1929, 1931, 1933, and 1934, when he batted over .380 and helped the team win the 1934 *Denver Post* Tournament.[259] Tolles, always considered a great hitter for a pitcher, was kept in the lineup every day, roaming the outfield on days he didn't pitch.[260]

Albert Tolles spent 1936–1940 with five minor league teams: 1936, Sioux Fall Canaries, Class D Nebraska State League, 24 games; 1937, unaffiliated Jonesboro Giants, Class D Northeast Arkansas League, 80 games; 1938, Hot Springs Bathers, Detroit Tigers affiliate, Class C Cotton State League, 125 games; 1939, returned as player/manager, Chicago White Sox affiliate, Jonesboro Giants, Northeast Arkansas League, 100 games; 1940, unaffiliated Ocala Yearlings, Florida State League, 15 games. There are no overall pitching stats listed for his 344 minor league appearances, most likely because as he got older, he was always listed as an outfielder, as he posted a .305 career batting average.[261] He died at age 41 in 1948.[262]

Epilogue

The self-sufficient religious commune called House of David, founded in Foctoria, Ohio, in 1923, is remembered for its variety of contributions to Berrien County and surrounding areas, the most memorable of which was its hirsute semipro baseball teams that thrived for decades before time and circumstances witnessed their decline. The business acumen of founder Benjamin Purnell, continued by his successor, Judge H. T. Dewhirst, who once described the commune as "the biggest industry in the area," and supplemented by the many talents of its membership plus the later addition of the City of David nine, left a variety of diverse footprints that still linger.

Benton Harbor and the site of the commune itself have undergone a multitude of changes since the barnstorming era, when the teams played an average of 175–200 games a season as they covered the United States, southern Canada, and Mexico. They played against all comers from all-white teams, racially mixed teams, numerous representatives of Negro Leagues, and other black squads. In the process, they perhaps unintentionally helped break the color line created by the Gentlemen's Agreement.

The Eden Springs Ballpark, where up to 3,500 enthusiastic baseball fans witnessed their home games, is today a trailer park; Eden Springs Amusement Park, known as a pre–Disneyland amusement park, no longer has its zoo, aviary, or train rides; many of Benton Harbor's businesses no longer exist; the House of David bands, choirs, and orchestras that entertained at the amphitheater and around the country are silent. Several of the centerpiece buildings erected by a proud group of highly skilled architects and craftsmen from the commune are now in a state of neglect and decay, while others have been renovated and restored.

Mary's Israelite City of David was honored by being placed on the National Register of Historic Places as a Historic District. The Whirlpool Corporation—the 1929 merger of the Upton Machine Company of neighboring St. Joseph and the Whirlpool Corporation of Binghamton, New York, to manufacture and market electric washing machines, still retains its world corporate headquarters in Benton Harbor. The restored downtown area and the City of David Museum remain popular attractions for tourists. Walking tours of the commune are conducted periodically by City of David historian/archivist Ronald Taylor.

As a tribute to Original House of David and City of David baseball, the House of David Echoes Base Ball Club under the Vintage Base Ball Association in Columbus, Ohio, appeared on the scene in 2001.

This squad of older men—some with beards, others without—plays a season of up to 14 weekend games against local teams the Davids had faced in years past.

They play by vintage baseball rules established as far back as the Civil War: players do not use mitts; pitches must be underhand tosses; pitchers must throw the ball where the "striker" wants it; runners cannot overrun first base; sliding and bunting are not allowed; umpires do not call balls and strikes except when the striker swings and misses; foul balls are not strikes; the striker is out if he hits a fly ball that is caught in the air or after just one bounce; runs are called aces. Due to the varied ages and abilities of volunteer players, the games are slow-paced and entertaining, played like a gentlemen's sport for exercise and fresh air.

Debbie Boyersmith, granddaughter of early player Earl Boyersmith, who briefly played on the team and then ran the miniature trains in the park, is now a regular volunteer with a local preservationist group at the former amusement park. This group works tirelessly to restore the grounds as well as the baseball park.

The history of the House of David, the commune itself, and remembrances of the unique men who played on their baseball teams are respected and preserved by two men: Brian Ziebart, trustee/historian/archivist of Benjamin Purnell's Israelite House of David, and Ronald Taylor, trustee/historian/archivist of the House of David as Reorganized by Mary Purnell (the City of David).

Appendix

Rosters listed here were found in newspaper articles and box scores from games played by the House of David, the City of David, and the House of David Home Team, initially known the Junior Team of the younger commune players. In addition, Lou Murphy sent out numerous teams whose only connection to the House of David was as franchise teams who paid for the use of the name. They were successful because the public did not understand the difference.

Team rosters were fluid and may seem repetitive, with one or two players changing as players came and went. I attempted to note these frequent changes whenever possible. Unfortunately, many rosters presented in print, especially in the early days, were far from perfect: the records used were incomplete and not totally accurate; players were listed by last names only (often misspelled but corrected by the author whenever possible, with corrections noted); and positions were frequently omitted. In addition, newspapers failed to differentiate among the teams, calling them all House of David, which severely impeded identification of specific squads. I have listed them the way I found them.

The purpose of including them here at this time is twofold: (1) to assist future researchers, thus sources are included when possible; (2) to aid those "looking for grandpa" or other relatives who may have been connected with the baseball teams. More research needs to be done in this area. Author's note: When an article mentioned just one or two players without giving a box score, I omitted it to avoid confusion.

1915

Horace Hannaford 3B, Ezra Cookie Hannaford 1B, Hubert "Hip" Vaughan P, Lesley Bell LF, David Harrison 3B, Dwight Baushke SS. [*The Herald Press* (St. Joseph, MI), June 2, 1969, page 3. Howard Olson's personal photo labeled 1913 HOD team found in an old scrapbook; but the uniforms look more like 1922–1923.]

Francis Thorpe Mgr., Ezra Hannaford, Richard Marcum, Barlow Tally, Swaney Tally, Jesse Lee Tally, Frank Hornbeck, Horace Hannaford, Paul Mooney, Frank Wyland, Monroe Wulff, and Rueben Jeff (listed as Reuben Jaft, not a member of the team). [Brian Ziebart, House of David Commune File—the first known photo of team.]

1916

Francis Thorpe Mgr., Dutch Faust 2B, Doc Tally RF, Art Vieritz CF, Charlie Falkenstein C, Horace Hannaford 3B, Ezra "Cookie" Hannaford 1B, Hubert "Hip" Vaughn P, Leslie Bell LF, David Harrison 3B, William Frye SS, Dwight "Zeke" Baushke SS.

Francis Thorpe Mgr., Glenn Klum, Swaney Tally, Barlow Tally, Horace Hannaford, Frank Hornbeck, Austin "Tex" Williams, Jerry Hansel, Frank Wyland, Paul Mooney, Ezra "Cookie" Hannaford, Jesse Lee, "Doc" Tally. [Hawkins-Bertolino, 1916 Berrien County Champions, *The House of David*, 11.]

1917

This year the team was still establishing itself in the barnstorming world under the leadership of manager Francis Thorpe. They joined the Inner City Baseball Association of Chicago, and their games were mentioned in local newspapers with some regularity, but none included a roster. It's assumed the roster was the same as 1916.

1918

Glenn Klum, Cookie Hannaford, Hip Vaughan, Doc Tally, Horace Hannaford, Frank Hornbeck, Charley Falkenstein, Art Vieritz, Paul Mooney, Austin "Tex" Williams, Frank Wyland, Jerry Hansel. [Hawkins-Bertolino, *The House of David*, 14.]

1919

Paul Mooney, Jerry Hansel, Charley Falkenstein, Jesse Tally, Horace Hannaford, Ezra Hannaford, Frank Wyland, Glenn Klum, Austin "Tex" Williams. [*Chicago Defender*, May 19, 1919.]
Williams 2B, Klum CF, Wyland LF, E. (Hanefoot) Hannaford 1B, H. (Hanefoot) Hannaford SS/3B, Vieritz 3B/SS, Fisher C, Craft P, Vaughan P. [HOD: *Argos Reflector* (Argos, IN), November 6, 1919, 1,4.]
Francis Thorpe Manager, Klum OF, Vieritz utility, Williams 2B, E. Hannaford 1B, Mooney P, Hansel C, Wyland LF, Vaughan P/utility, H. Hannaford SS, Falkenstein 3B, Jesse Tally P/OF. [HOD: *St. Louis Dispatch*, November 25, 1919, 26.]
Francis Thorpe Manager, Glenn Klum CF, Austin Williams 2B, Ezra Hannaford 1B, Jerry Hansel C, Frank Wyland LF, Hip Vaughan C/P, Horace Hannaford SS, Charley Falkenstein 3B, Jesse Tally OF & P, Paul Mooney P. [HOD: *Times Herald* (Port Huron, MI), December 12, 1919, 3.]

1920

Percy Walker and Wesley Schneider Mgrs., Dwight Baushke, Stan Bell, Frank Wyland, Jerry Hansel, Elijah Berkland, Bert Johnson, Cyril "Mickey" McFarland, Manna Woodworth [Woodward], Paul Mooney, Hiram Croft. [HOD Home Team: Hawkins-Bertolino, *House of David*, 17.]
Francis Thorpe, Mgr., Vieritz RF/2B, Klum CF, Williams 2B, E. Hannaford 1B, Falkenstein SS, H. Hannaford LF, McCarthy C, Faust 3B, Doc Tally LF, Eddie Phalon C, (?) LaBate P, Lloyd Miller P. [*Evening Report*, August 6, 1920, 5.]
Falkenstein SS, Williams 2B, Klein CF, (Verity) Vieritz RF, (Pally) Tally LF, Hannaford 2B, McCarthy C, Grumwald P. [*Morning Call* (Allentown, PA), August 4, 1920, 11.]
Falkenstein SS, Williams 2B, Klum CF, Vieritz LF, Tally P-LF, (*Fhelan*) Phalen C, Hannaford 3B, Wagner P, Faust 3B. [HOD: *Chicago Defender*, August 7, 1920, 8.]
Falkenstein SS, Klum CF, Williams 2B, (Nieritz) Vieritz LF, H. Hanaford 3B, Faust 2B, E. Hannaford 1B, McCarthy C, Hughes P. [HOD Home Team: *Washington Herald* (Washington, D.C.), August 10, 1920.]
Williams RF, Klum CF, Tally CF, H. Hannaford 3B, Falkenstein C, Vieritz SS, Faust 2B, E. Hannaford 1B, Mooney P, Cornifrey P. [HOD: *Press and Sun Bulletin* (Binghamton, NY), August 27, 1920, 24.]
Phalen Mgr./C, Williams RF, Klum CF, Tally LF, Lantz P, Falkenstein 3B, Vieritz SS, H, Hannaford 2B, E. Hannaford 1B, Redon P. [HOD: *Scranton Republic* (Scranton, PA), August 28, 1920, 16.]
Francis Thorpe Mgr., Austin "Tex" Williams RF, Glenn Klum CF, Doc Tally LF, Eddie Phalon

C, _ LaBate P, Lloyd Miller P, Charlie Falkenstein SS, Art Vieritz 2B, Horace Hannaford 3B, Ezra "Cookie" Hannaford 1B. [*Brooklyn Daily Eagle* (Brooklyn, NY), August 29, 1920.]

1921

Francis Thorpe, Mgr., Austin Williams 1B, Glenn Klum CF, Charlie Falkenstein C, Doc Tally P, Dutch Faust 2B, Hip Vaughan RF, Artie Vieritz SS, Les Bell, 3B, (?) McFarland, LF. [*Decatur Herald* (Decatur, IL), May 27, 1921, 4.]

Williams, (Veereits) Vieritz, Prince, Tally, Vaughan, (Foust) Faust, Hess, Falk, Mooney. [HOD: *Huntington Herald*, "Much Touted Benton Harbor Team Beaten," June 13, 1921, 2.]

Williams, Klum, E. Hannaford, Tally, H. Hannaford, Mooney, Faust, Ninty, Falk. [*Huntington Post-Gazette*, August 21, 1921, 21.]

Francis Thorpe Mgr., James Moore, Estelle Hornbeck, John Bulley, Joseph Bulley, Edmund Bulley, Benny Hill, Wes Snyder, Tom Adkins. ["Third Team" of younger players later called "Home Team," Christopher Soriano, *The House of David*, Arcadia Publishing, South Carolina, 2007, 97.]

Williams, Klum, E. Hannaford, Tally, Falk, H. Hannaford, Mooney, Faust, Ninty. [*Pittsburgh Post Gazette*, "David Tribe Defeats Local Giants, 2–1," August 21, 1921, 21.]

Williams 1B, Vieritz SS, Tally LF, Prince RF, Hess CF, Faust 2B, Bell 3B, Falk C, Klum P. [*Fort Wayne Sentinel* (Fort Wayne, IN), June 8, 1921, 10.]

Thorpe, Mgr., Williams, Faust, Bell, McFarlane, Klum, Tally, Falkenstein, Mooney, Vaughan, (Dallager) Dalager. [HOD: *Huntington Press*, June 11, 1921, 6.]

Williams 1B, Vieritz, SS, Prince 3B, Tally LF, Vaughan RF, Faust 2B, Hess CF, Falk C, Mooney P. [HOD: *Huntington Herald*, June 13, 1921, 2.]

Klum CF, H. Hannaford 3B, Williams RF, Tally P/LF, E. Hannaford 1B, Varietz SS, Faust 2B, Falk C, Mooney LF/P. [HOD: *Chicago Defender*, August 6, 1921.]

Duryea 1B, Klum CF, E. Hannaford 1B, Tally LF, Falk C, (McGory) McGary P, H. Hannaford 3B, Faust 2B, Vieritz SS. [*Asbury Park Press* (Neptune, NJ), August 13, 1921, 14.]

Falk C, Klum CF, E. Hannaford 1B, Tally RF, Barnes LF, H. Hannaford 3B, Faust 2B, Vieritz SS, Signer P. [HOD: *Courier News* (Somerville, NJ), August 15, 1921, 8.]

Klum CF, Mooney RF, Tally LF, E. Hannaford 1B, H. Hannaford 3B, Faust 2B, Vieritz SS, (Glerbfred?) Gilfred C, McGary P. [HOD: *Star Gazette* (Elmira, NY), September 10, 1921, 9.]

1922

Horace Hannaford 3B, Charles Falk C, Leslie Bell INF, Glen Klum CF, Dwight Baushke OF, Manna Woodworth P, Cookie Hannaford 1B. [HOD: *Ogden Standard-Examiner* (Ogden, UT), January 28, 1922, 6.]

Francis Thorpe, Mgr., George Anderson, Doc Tally, Victor Smith, Horace Hannaford, Artie Veritz, Jerry Hansel, Charles Falkenstein, Paul Mooney, Ezra Hannaford, Percy Walker, Zeke Baushke. [HOD at Muzzy Field, Douglas S. Malan, *Muzzy Field: Tales from a Forgotten Ballpark*, iUniverse Star, New York, 2008, 85.]

Faust 2B, Hannaford 1B, Falk 3B, Andrews C, Tally P, Knapp P, Vaughan LF, Baussie RF, Baushke CF, Vieritz SS. [HOD: *Chicago Defender*, June 22, 1922.]

Faust 2B, E. Hannaford 1B, H. Hannaford 3B, Buysse RF, Andrews C, Vaughan LF, Baushke CF, Tally P. [HOD: *Akron Beacon* (Akron, OH), July 7, 1922, 22.]

Faust 2B, Tally LF, Buyesse (?) RF, (Looney) Mooney P, Wolfe SS, Fish C, Hannaford 1B, Vieritz 3B, Baushke CF. [HOD: *Times Herald* (Port Huron, MI), September 15, 1922, 19.]

1923

Francis Thorpe Mgr., Walter "Dutch" Faust 2B, Jesse "Doc" Tally RF/P, Art Vieritz CF, Charlie Falkenstein C, Horace Hannaford 3B, Ezra "Cookie" Hannaford 1B, Hubert "Hip" Vaughan P, Les Bell LF, David "Egg" Harrison 3B, Dwight Baushke SS. [HOD: Lineup from Howard Olson photo—year determined by uniform word, 1923–1924, *Herald Press* (St. Joseph, MI), June 2, 1969, 3.]

Faust 2B, Vieritz SS, Moon RF, Tally LF, H. Hannaford 3B, E. Hannaford 1B, Baushke CF, Falk C, Hill P, Mullas ??? P (maybe Tolles or Hallas) [HOD: *The Evening News* (Harrisburg, PA) August 1, 1923, 15.]

David Harrison SS, C. (Cookie) Hannaford 1B, W. Faust 2B, H. Hannaford 3B, Baushke LF, Vieritz CF, Milkler RF, Bell C, Moon–Carteaux–Bauman pitchers. [HOD: *Fort Wayne Journal-Gazette* (Fort Wayne, IN), August 18, 1923, 9.]

Faust 2B, Vieritz CF, E. Hannaford 1B, H. Hannaford 3B, Harrison SS, Baushke RF, Moon C, Baufman P, Miller P, Hill P. [HOD: *Pittsburgh Courier*, August 25, 1923, 7.]

1924

Baushke SS, Harrison 3B, Faust 2B, Tally LF, E. Hannaford 1B, Bowerman C, Vaughan RF, Bell RF, Vieritz, L, Miller P, Mullis P, Heckman P. [HOD: *Journal-News* (Middletown, OH), June 11, 1924, 8.]

Baushke SS, Harrison 3B, Faust 2B, Tally LF/P, E. Hannaford 1B, Vaughan RF, Vieritz CF, Miller LF-CF, Bell C/CF, Mullis P, Smith C. [HOD: *Times Recorder* (Zanesville, OH), June 20, 1924, 13.]

Baushke SS, Harrison 3B, Faust 2B, Tally LF, Hannaford 1B, Vaughan RF, Bell (maybe Bruce) C, Miller P, Smith P, Heckman P. [HOD: *Coshocton Tribune* (Coshocton, OH), June 24, 1924, 3.]

(Falke) Falk C, H. Hannaford 3B, Glenn Klum CF, Doc Tally LF, Walter Faust SS, L. Mooney RF, Art Vieritz SS, Paul Mooney P, Falk P, (Wulff), Tally P. [HOD: *Indiana Gazette* (Indiana, PA), August 25, 1924, 1.]

1925

Faust, Tucker, Harrison, Tally, Wulff, Falkenstein, Wyland, Bell, Boone. [HOD: *News-Palladium* (Benton Harbor, MI), May 11, 1925, 10.]

Faust 2B, Harrison 3B, Tally RF, Sherrock 1B-RF, Tucker CF, Davis C, Wulff 3B, Boone SS, Bunvan P, Heckman P. [HOD: *Iowa City Press* (Iowa City, IA), June 17, 1925, 11.]

Baushke SS, H. Hannaford 2B, F. Wyland LF, Falkenstein C, Bell CF, E. Hannaford 1B, Dewhirst 3B, Harold "Pup" Smith RF, Schmiegle P. [*News Palladium* (Benton Harbor, MI), July 16, 1925, 5.]

Frank Wyland LF, Les Bell CF, Tom Dewhirst 3B, Robert Dewhirst 1B, (?) Robinson RF, Oscar Sassman SS, Hip Vaughan 2B, Beans Johnson C, (?) Schmiegle. [HOD Home Team, *News Palladium* (Benton Harbor, MI), October 6, 1925, 5.]

Faust SS, Hipp RF, Champion 2B, Wenz CF, Heckman LF, Tanner 1B, Harrison 3B, Kendall C, Smith P. [HOD: *Sedalia Democrat* (Sedalia, MO), October 7, 1925, 2.]

Boothby 1B, Champion 2B, Faust SS, Harrison 3B, Tally LF, Wenz CF, A. B. Hipp RF, Kendall C, Smith P. [HOD Home Team: *Sedalia Democrat* (Sedalia, MO), October 8, 1925, 8.]

1926

A. B. Hipp 2B, Harrison 3B, Heckman CF, Champion C, Tally LF, Tucker, 1B, Faust SS, Sharrock RF, Curtis, RF, Smith P. [HOD: *Rhinelander Daily News* (Rhinelander, WI), January 26, 1926, 5.]

Faust SS, Hipp CF, Sharrock RF, Champion 2B, Tally LF, Kendall C, Harrison 3B, Tucker 1B, Miller P. [HOD: *Chicago Defender*, May 22, 1926.]

Faust SS, Harrison 3B, Hipp CF, Heckman RF, Champion 2B, Tally LF, Tucker 1B, Kendall C, Curtis P, Miller P. [HOD: *Billings Gazette* (Billings, MT), July 23, 1926, 8.]

Hipp CF, Harrison 3B, Champion 2B, Tally LF, Sharrock RF, Faust SS, Kendall C, Miller P, Curtis P, Smith P. [HOD: *News Palladium* (Benton Harbor, MI), August 7, 1926, 14.]

1927

David Harrison, Manager, Jimmie Crow, Hobie Nelson, Glendon "Red" Wiltbank, Billy Link, Ernie Selby, George Anderson, Lionel Everett, Jack Crow, Earl Boyersmith, Sidney Smith, Leo "Lefty" Wiltbank. [HOD Junior Team, Hawkins, Bertolino, *House of David*, 24.]

McKay LF, Corneglia CF, McCafferty 2B, Newell SS, Tucker 1B, Harrison 3B, Tally RF, Kendell C, Hoffman P, Woodhouse P. [*Chicago Defender*, April 17, 1927.]

Faust SS (Danager) Danaher 2B, A. B. Hipp 3B, Jay Sharrock RF, Bill Heckman CF, Champion C, Simmons LF, Falk 1B, Warren "Lefty" Wierman P, Schaud P. [HOD: *Spokane Daily Chronicle* (Spokane, WA), May 30, 1927, 2.]

Faust SS, Danager (Danaher?) 2B, Hipp 3B, Heckman CF, Champion C, Simmons LF, Falk 1B, Bell RF, Steele P. [HOD: *Independent Record* (Helena, MT), June 5, 1927, 12.]

Atherton SS, Hipp 3B, Sharrock RF, Heckman CF, Champion C, B. Miller LF, Condon 2B, Falk 1B, L. Miller P. [HOD: *Winnipeg Evening Tribune* (Winnipeg, Manitoba, Canada), August 18, 1927, 12.]

1928

Francis Thorpe, Mgr., A. V. "Rip" Atherton, Roy "Old Folks" Blackmore, Joe Gilmore, "Bud" Zediker, Doc Tally, Joe "Windy" Radloff, George "Lefty" Gilbert, A. B. Hipp, John Tucker, B. D. "Red" Smith, Page Neve, Carl "Cyclone" Pederson, Clifford Reed, Ed "Keke" Coykendall. [HOD: Hawkins-Bertolino, *House of David*, 26.]

David Harrison, Mgr., Jimmy Crow, Hobson Nelson, Leo Wiltbank, Glendon (Whitbank) Wiltbank, Ernie Selby, Billy Link, George Anderson, Joe Everett, Jack Crown, Earl Boyersmith, Clay Williams. [Home Team: *News-Palladium* (Benton Harbor, MI), April 11, 1970, 16.]

Percy Walker Mgr., Bert Johnson C, John Tucker 1B, George Anderson 2B, Dave (Eggs) Harrison 3B, Dutch Faust SS, Tom Dewhirst LF, Bob Dewhirst CF, Miles Crow (sometimes incorrectly listed as "Crowe") RF, Mason "Mac" Perry P, Al Stemm LF. [Home Team/Junior Team, Hawkins-Bertolino, *House of David*, 28.]

Hipp 3B, Tally LF, Atherton 2B, Reed RF, Tucker 1B, Pederson CF, Blackmoor SS, Kendell C, Fred "Windy" Radloff P [COD: *Bismarck Tribune* (Bismarck, ND), June 25, 1928, 8.]

Percy Walker, Mgr., Bob Dewhirst CF, Tom Dewhirst LF, John Tucker 1B, Miles Crow RF, Bert Johnson C, Dave Harrison 3B, Frank Wyland P, Mason "Mac" Perry P, Al Stemm LF, George Anderson 2B, Clay Williams SS [HOD: Clare E. Adkin, Jr., *Brother Benjamin: A History of the Israelite House of David*, Andrews University Press, Berrien Springs, Michigan, 1990, 78.]

Dave Harrison, Mgr., Coach Billy Link, Coach George Anderson, Jimmy Crow, Hobson Nelson, Leo Wiltbank, Ernie Selby, Joe Everett, Jack Crown, Earl Boyersmith, Clay Williams, Glendon Wiltbank. [HOD Home Team: *News Palladium* (Benton Harbor, MI), July 28, 1928.]

Hipp 3B, Tally LF, Atherton 2B, Reed RF, Tucker 2B, Blackmore SS, Kendall C, Pederson CF, Jabo (Jebo?) P, Neve P. [*Winnipeg Tribune* (Winnipeg, Manitoba, Canada), "House of David Take Two Games from Giants," August 7, 1928, 16.]

Ernie Selby 1B, Sid Smith SS, Wes Clark C, Barney Dalager 3B, Jimmy Crow 2B, Leo Wiltbank CF, Joe O'Signac RF, Earl Boyersmith LF, Jack Crow P. [HOD Home Team, *News Palladium* (Benton Harbor, MI), July 15, 1928, 8.]

1929

Heller 3B, Savant SS, Kenny 1B, Smith C, Carpenter 2B, Reed CF, Cheedo LF, Mauzy P, Crow, RF. Miles Crow P. [Murphy HOD: *Brooklyn Daily Eagle* (Brooklyn, NY), May 20, 1929, 29.]

Heller 3B, Savant LF, Kenny 1B, Smith C, Carpenter 2B, Reed CF, Chied SS, Kruel RF, Proctor P. [Murphy HOD: *Philadelphia Inquirer*, May 26, 1929, 39.]

Carpenter 2B, Crowe OF, Jenny (famed clown) OF, Heller 3B, Menzie LF, Kenny 1B, Smith C, Reid SS, Janesco P. [Murphy HOD: *Central New Jersey News* (New Brunswick, NJ), June 6, 1929, 18.]

H. V. "Van" Atherton 2B, Hipp CF, Dewhirst LF, Heckman 1B, Bill Siddle RF, Faust SS, Harrison 3B, Eddie Deal C, E. McCall, P. [HOD: *Newspaper of the Home* (Calgary, Alberta, Canada), June 27, 1929, 18.]

Beans Johnson Mgr./ C, Al Stemm 3B, Chief Coughlin 1B, Pinky King LF, (?) O'Signac SS, Cook SS, Clay Williams 2B, Bob Dewhirst CF, (?) Whiting, P [HOD *News Palladium* (Benton Harbor, MI), July 8, 1929, 10.]

Williams 2B, McCafferty 3B, Reed RF, Tucker 1B, Pederson CF, Fleming C, Tally LF, Blackmore SS, Gilbert P. [HOD: *Chicago Defender*, July 14, 1926.]

Ernie Selby 1B, Sid Smith SS, Wes Clark C, Barney Dalager 3B, Jimmy Crowe 2B, Leo "Lefty" Wiltbank CF, Joe O'Signac RF, Earl Boyersmith LF. [HOD Home Team/Junior Team, *News Palladium* (Benton Harbor, MI), July 22, 1929, 8.]

Percy Walker Mgr., H. V. "Van" Atherton 2B, Hipp CF, Dewhirst LF, Heckman1B, Faust SS, Hall, LF, Harrison 3B, Deal C, Tolles P. [HOD: *Montana Standard* (Butte, MT), August 19, 1929, 8.]

O'Signac 2B, Coughlin 3B, Price 1B, King LF, Stemm RF, Johnson C, Black (?), Williams SS, T. Dewhirst CF, Wyland PF, Leffler P, Leyme P. [HOD *News Palladium* (Benton Harbor, MI), September 3, 1929, 11.]

Atherton 2B, Hipp SS, Dewhirst LF, Heckman 1B, Hall RF, Harrison 3B, Tolles RF, Haruska C, McCall P. [*Newspaper of the Home* (Calgary, Alberta, Canada), June 27, 1929, 18.]

Percy Walker Mgr., O'Signac 2B, D. Harrison 3B, Chief Caughlin 1B, Price 1B, King CF, Dewhirst LF, Al Stemm RF, Dutch Faust SS, Bert "Beans" Johnson C, Leyme, P [HOD: *News Palladium* (Benton Harbor, MI), October 14, 1929, 9.]

1930

Buster Kenny 1B, Al Albert P, Mike Janesco P, Shorty Shaudt OF, Bernard Eisenbath LF, Jim Smith C, Carl O'Grady OF/P, Joe Nettles OF, Dick Stubey (or Stubay) P, Ben Segist (or Seguist) P, Carl Ellerbe OF, Pepper Martin LF, (Ed) Johnny Carpenter 2B. [Baseball Hall of Fame Archives, circa early 1930s.]

Atherton 2B, Hipp CF, Pederson RF, Tucker 1B, Fleming C, Faust SS, Tally LF, McCafferty 3B, Heckman P, Crotty P. [COD: *Monroe Morning World* (Monroe, LA), March 27, 1930, 10.]

Atherton 2B, Hipp CF, Pederson RF, Tucker 1B, Fleming C, Faust SS, Tally LF, McCafferty 3B, Neve P, Heckman P, Crotty P. [COD: *Chicago Defender*, March 28, 1930.]

Percy Walker, Mgr., Bert "Beans" Johnson C, Bob Dewhirst 1B, Clay "Mud" Williams 2B, Sidney Smith SS, Dave Harrison 3B, Tom Dewhirst OF, James "Pinky" King OF, Al Stemm OF, Lloyd Miller, P. [HOD: *News Palladium* (Benton Harbor, MI), May 3, 1930, 9.]

Kenny 1B, (Schandt) Shaudt RF, Carpenter 2B, Smith C, Eisenbath SS, Ellerbe 3B, Nettleton LF, Shadowen CF, O'Grady P, Sawyer RF, Quinn P. [Murphy HOD: *Evening News* (Harrisburg, PA), May 5, 1930.]

Stemm RF, Williams 2B, T. Dewhirst LF, Crow LF, King CF, Harrison 3B, Johnson C, B. Dewhirst 1B, Miller P, Smith SS. [HOD: *News Palladium* (Benton Harbor, MI), May 5, 1930, 8.]

Hipp CF, Tucker 1B, Pederson RF, Tally LF, Fleming C, McCafferty 3B, Williams 2B, Rip Atherton SS, Bass, P, Heckman, alternate. [COD: *St. Cloud Times* (St. Cloud, MN), June 9, 1930, 12.]

Stemm RF, Williams 2B, T. Dewhirst LF, King CF, Johnson C, B. Dewhirst 1B, L. Miller P, O'Signac 3B, King CF, Johnson. [HOD: *Springfield Leader* (Springfield, MO), June 16, 1930, 8.]

John Tucker 1B, Bill Knapp 2B, Sid Smith SS, Chief Coughlin 3B, Happy Heppler C, T. Dewhirst LF, Matt Butch CF, Al Stemm RF, Pinky King substitute, Dave Harrison substitute, Lefty Thompson, P. [COD: *News Palladium* (Benton Harbor, MI), September 23, 1930, 8, Berrien County All-Stars.]

Eisenbath 3B, Kenney 1B, Carpenter 2B, Smith C, (Ellibee) Ellerbe SS, Eddie Sawyer RF, Paris CF, Nettleton LF, Stuby P. [HOD: *Chicago Defender*, June 23, 1930.]

1931

Drager, Bowers, Hogers, Joby Couch, Doc Tally, George Anderson, Swift, Joe "Windy" Radloff, Dunden, George "Lefty" Gilbert, John Tucker, Page Neve, Harold "Dutch" Witte, Thomas "Mac" McCafferty, Herman "Flip" Fleming. [COD: Hawkins-Bertolino, *House of David*, 33.]

Schaudt RF, Woods 1B, Eisenbath 3B, Ellerbe, LF, Heller SS, Burrows 2B, Herbst RF, Lewis C, Shadowen CF, Hanley P. [Murphy HOD: *Chicago Defender*, April 8, 1931.]

Tom Dewhirst Mgr./LF, Bob Dewhirst 1B, Clay "Mud" Williams 2B, Sid Smith SS, Al Stemm 3B, Leo Wiltbank CF, Ernie Selby RF, Frank Wyland C, Glenn Wiltbank C, Bert "Beans" Johnson,

Mason "Mac" Perry P, Jack Crowe P. [HOD Central States: *News Palladium* (Benton Harbor, MI), April 18, 1931, 9.]

Tom Dewhirst Mgr./OF, Mason Perry P, Al Stemm OF, Jackie Crow P, Frank Wyland C, Ernie Selby 1B, Hobie Nelson 2B, Williams 3B, Bob Dewhirst OF. [HOD Home Team: *News Palladium* (Benton Harbor, MI), May 2, 1931, 16.]

Dumas SS, Carpenter 2B, Ellerbe 3B, Graves LF, Woods 1B, Herbst RF, Shadowen CF, Lewis C, Segrist P, Weirman P, Janesco, P. [Murphy HOD: *Brooklyn Daily Eagle* (Brooklyn, NY), May 11, 1931, 21.]

Shorty Shaudt RF, Johnny Woods 1B, Eisenbath 3B, Heller SS, Burrows 2B, Keller Herbst C, Lewis , Howard Shadowen CF, Hanley P. [COD Central States: *Schenectady Gazette* (Schenectady, NY), May 14, 1931, 18.]

Tom Dewhirst, Mgr., Earl Boyersmith, Sidney Smith, Jack Crow, J. B. Boone, Oscar Wade, Jack Harron, Bob Dewhirs, Frank Wyland, Ernie Selby, Leo "Lefty" Wiltbank, Miller Wilson, Hobson "Hobie" Nelson, Clay "Mud" Williams, John (?). [HOD Central States Travelers, Hawkins-Bertolino, May 1931, 32–33.]

Alexander Mgr./P, Williams 2B, Hipp CF, LaFleur 1B, Moore LF, Pederson RF, Harrison 3B, Faust SS, Blieding C, Miller P. [HOD: *Daily Tribune*, June 9, 1931, 5.]

Drager, Bowers, Hoger, Joby Couch, Doc Tally, George Anderson, Swift, Fred Radloff, Dunden, George "Lefty" Gilbert, John Tucker, Page Neve, Harold "Dutch" Witte, Thomas "Mac" McCafferty, Herman "Flip" Fleming. [COD: Hawkins-Bertolino, *House of David*, 33.]

Tom Dewhirst, Mgr., Ernie Selby 1B, Hob Nelson 2B, Sid Smith SS, Clay Williams 3B, Mason Perry P, Frank Wyland C, Bob Dewhirst CF, Al Stemm RF. [HOD Central States Team: *News Palladium* (Benton Harbor, MI), June 20, 1931, 9.]

Bower SS, McCafferty 3B, Tucker 1B, Fleming C, Witte RF, Tally LF, Anderson 2B, Gilbert P, Neve P, Radloff P, Dunden P, Drager P. [HOD: *Ogden Standard Examiner* (Ogden, UT), August 7, 1931, 16.]

T. Dewhirst LF, (Faucet) Faust RF, R. Dewhirst CF, Stemm 2B, Williams 3B, Selby 1B, Smith SS, Johnson C, Berndt P, Daisy P, Jimmy Crow P. [HOD: *New York Times*, September 10, 1931, 10.]

Shadowen CF, Woods 1B, Dumas LF, Meyers 3C, Barrett C, Carpenter 2B, Lewis RF, Walker SS, (Wierman P game one), (Janesco P game two). [Murphy HOD: *Brooklyn Daily Eagle* (Brooklyn, NY), September 14, 1931, 24.]

Alexander Mgr./P, LaFleur CF, Williams 2B, Moore LF, Hickman 1B, Tolles RF, Harrison 3B, Faust SS, Harden C, Laufer P. [COD: *Alton Evening Telegraph* (Alton, IL), September 26, 1931, 8.]

Martin 2B, Woods 1B, Dumas CF, Meyers 3B, Barrett C, Brower SS, Carpenter LF, Lewis RF, Wierman P, Janesco P. [Murphy HOD: *Brooklyn Daily Eagle* (Brooklyn, NY), October 5, 1931, 25.]

Thomas Dewhirst, Robert Dewhirst, Earl Boyersmith, Jack Crow, John Herron, Ernie Selby, Jess Tally, Oscar Wade, Sidney Smith, Frank Wyland, Leo "Lefty" Wilbank, Clay Williams, Miller Wilson. [Communal Societies House of David Postcards, Hamilton College Digital Archive Photo Collection.]

1932

Grover Cleveland Alexander, Mgr., Spike Hunter P, John Tucker 1B, Diester, Elmore Ambrose, Hardin, Dick Wykoff, Hutson, Dick Atwell, Lawrence, Doc Tally RF, Dewey Hill. [HOD: 1932 Spring Training Roster, donated to Baseball Hall of Fame.]

Charles "Moose" Swaney P, Jimmy "Wheels" Woods 1B, Lou Vann 1B, Jumbo Barrett C, Carl O'Grady P/OF, Warren "Lefty" Weirman P, Howard Shadowen OF, Martin 3B, Dumas OF, Friedman OF, Bandrimm 2B, Haller, Cronk P. [Murphy HOD: www.timesnewsweeklyonline.com, 2004.]

LaFleur CF, Harrison LF, ("Talles") Tally RF, Heckman 1B, Atherton 3B, (Blakey) Blakney SS, Williams 2B, Bleiding C, Becker P, Alexander P. [COD: *Charleston Daily Mail* (Charleston, WV), April 30, 1932, 16.]

Grover Cleveland Alexander, Mgr., "Lafleur" LaFleur LF, Willis 2B, Tolles RF,

Heckman 1B, Jacobs LF, Blakney SS, Blieding C, Hardin, P. [HOD: *Harrisburg Telegraph* (Harrisburg, PA), June 2, 1932, 12.]

Alexander P, La Fleur CF, Faust 3B, Tolles RF, Heckman 1B, Jacobs LF, Atherton 2B, Blakney, SS, Bleiding C, Miller P. [HOD: *Warren Times Mirror* (Warren, PA), June 20, 1932, 7.]

Alexander Mgr./P., Grant CF, Williams 2B, Tolles RF, Heckman 1B, Jacobs LF, Atherton 3B, Blakney SS, Bleiding C, LaFleur P. [*Nashua Telegraph* (Nashua, NH), July 8, 1932, 10.]

Francis Thorpe Mgr., Red Lawrence, Lefty Gilbert, Ray "Skeeter" Powell, John Tucker, George Anderson, Doc Tally, PeeWee Bass, Emery Savage, Herman "Flip" Fleming, Rolla "Softball" Mapel, Dick Atwell, Tom "Mac" McCafferty, Page Neve, Charles "Chuck" Noel. [COD: *Denver Post* Tournament, July 13, 1932, Hawkins-Bertolino, *House of David*, 35.]

Charles "Moose" Swaney P, Jimmy "Wheels" Woods 1B, Lou Vann 1B, "Jumbo" Barrett C, Mike Janesco P, Carl O'Grady P, Warren Wierman (Weirman ?) P, Harold "Shad" Shadowen OF, Martin 3B, Dumas OF, Friedman OF, Bandrimer 2B, Haller SS, Cronk P. [Murphy HOD: December 2, 2004.]

Ray "Skeeter" Powell, John Tucker, George Anderson, Francis Thorpe, William "Red" Lawrence, PeeWee Bass, Emery Savage, Herman "Flip" Fleming, Dick Atwell, Tom "Mac" McAfferty, Page Neve, George "Lefty" Gilbert, Charles "Chuck" Noel. [COD: July 13, 1932.]

Alexander Mgr./P, LaFleur CF, Williams 2B, Tolles RF, Heckman 1B, Jacobs LF, Blakeney C, Grant P. [COD: *Middletown Times Herald* (Middletown, NY), July 19, 1932.]

Lawrence P, Savage CF, Tucker 1B, Powell RF, Fleming C, Tally LF, Atwell SS, Mack 3B, Gilbert P, Radloff LF. [COD: *Salt Lake Telegram* (Salt Lake City, UT), July 30, 1932, 8.]

Shadowen CF, Dumas SS, Sawyer LF, Barrett C, Martin 3B, Vann 1B, Haller 2B, Ushka RF, Klevenhoven P. [Murphy HOD: *Courier-News* (Somerville, NJ), July 19, 1932, 13.]

Lawrence 2B, Tucker 1B, Savage CF, Powell RF, Tally LF, McCafferty 3B, Atwell SS, Fleming C, Windy Radloff P, Neve P, Noel P, Bass P, Gilbert. [COD: *Oakland Tribune* (Oakland, CA), August 7, 1932.]

Lawrence 2B, Savage CF, Tucker 1B, Powell RF, Fleming C, Tally LF, Atwell DD, McCafferty 3B, Gilbert P, Base P, Neve P, Radloff P, Noel P. [*Oregon Statesman* (Salem, OR), August 12, 1932, 10.]

Alexander's Eastern Travelers: La Fleur LF, Williams 2B, Jacobs LF, Heckman 1B, Blieding RF, Tolles RF, Blakney SS, Faust 3B, Miller P, Alexander P.

T. Dewhirst's Western Travelers: Fawcett RF, Williams 2B, Harrison 3B, T. Dewhirst LF, R. Dewhirst CF, Deal C, Smith SS, Selby 1B, Hagen P, Bernt P. [*News-Palladium* (Benton Harbor, MI), "Colony and Alexander's Teams Will Clash Tonight," August 19, 1932, 8.]

Lawrence 2B, Savage CF, Tucker 1B, Powell RF, Fleming C, Atwekk SS, Mack 3B, Maple P. [HOD: *La Grande Observer* (La Grande, OR), August 30, 1932, 6.]

Alexander Mgr./P, LaFleur LF, Williams 2B, Elmoor RF, Hickman 1B, Woeber LF, Faust 2B, Blakeney SS, Bleiding C. [*Lincoln Star* (Lincoln, NE), September 4, 1932, 5.]

1933

Buster Kenney 1B C (clown), Al Albert P, Mike Janesco P, Shorty Shaudt OF, Bernard Eisenbath LF, Jim Smith C, Carl O'Grady OF?P, Joe Nettles OF, Dick Stubey (Stubay?) Ben Segrist P, Carl Ellerbe OF, Peppy Martin P, Red Carpenter P. [Murphy COD, circa 1933, donated to Baseball Hall of Fame.]

Tolles RF, Smith 2B, Harrison 3B, Heckman 1B, T. Dewhirst LF, Deal C, Faust SS, R. Dewhirst CF, Berndt P. [HOD: *News Palladium* (Benton Harbor, MI), May 22, 1933, 8.]

Alexander Mgr./P, Huxell CF, Lawrence 2B, John Tucker 1B, Dick Wykoff RF, Diesler LF, Summers 3B, Dick Atwell SS, Dewey Hill C, Hunter P. [HOD: *Scranton Republican* (Scranton, PA), April 6, 1933, 15.]

LaFleur OF, Scott SS, Emmer 3B, Holland LF, Joseph 2B, Cross 1B, Anderson RF, Fleming C, Benson P. [COD: *Wilkes-Barre Record* (Wilkes-Barre, PA), July 1, 1933, 18.]

Hutson LF, Lawrence 2B, Tucker 1B, Wykoff 3B, Diester RF, Tally LF, Atwell SS, Hill C, Hardin P. [HOD: *Emporia Gazette* (Emporia, KS), August 22, 1933, 3.]

Charles "Moose" Swaney P, Jimmy "Wheels" Woods 1B, Lou Vann 1B, Jumbo Barrett C, Mike Jansesco P, Carl O'Grady P/OF, David Wierman P, Howard Shadowen OF, Martin 3B, Dumas

OF, Friedman OF, Banrimer 2B, Haller SS, Cronk P. [Murphy HOD: *www.timesnewsweekly.com*, December 2, 2004.]

Alexander Mgr./P, Houston CF, Lawrence 2B, Tucker 1B, Deister RF, Atwell SS, Hill C, Hunter LF, Ambrose P. [COD: *Salt Lake Tribune* (Salt Lake City, UT), September 2, 1933, 31.]

Jacobs LF, Scott SS, Cross 1B, LaFleur CF, Holland RF, Emmer 2B, Anderson 3B, Fleming C, Mitchell P. [COD: *Minneapolis Star*, September 5, 1933, 11.]

1934

Alexander Mgr./P., Lloyd Smith (10-year veteran), Elmer E. "Army" Ambrose, Spike Hunter, Art Stokes, Lefty Weirman, Lefty Tolles, Dutch Faust, Eddie Deal, Bill Heckman, Dewey Hill, Jack Cross, Bill Mullens, Blakeney, Flip Fleming, Egg Harrison, Tom Dewhirst, Bob Dewhirst, Holland Horn, Mud Williams. [HOD Spring Training: *News Palladium* (Benton Harbor, MI), April 19, 1934, 12.]

Shadowen CF, Foreman RF, Catina SS, Beazley LF, Getz 3B, Stravecan 2B, Woods 1B, O'Grady C, Janesco P, Ramsey pinch-hitter, Swaney P. [Murphy HOD: *Times Recorder* (Zanesville, OH), May 4, 1934, 14.]

Jacobs CF, Josephine 3B, Didrikson P, Miller P, Waytula RF, Hunter P, Holland RF, Cross 1B, Tolles LF, Muller 2B, Blakeney, SS, Hill C. [HOD: *Chicago Tribune*, May 7, 1934, 23.]

Deal C, Brannon SS, Heckman 1B, Fenton LF, Harrison 3B, Wright RF, Williams CF, Smith 2B, Gilbert P. [HOD: *Chicago Tribune*, June 11, 1934, 23.]

Hutson CF, Lawrence 2B, Tucker 1B, Wykoff 3B, Deiser RF, Tally LF, Atwell, SS, Hill C, Andros P. [COD: *Daily Tribune*, June 21, 1934, 5.]

Alexander, Mgr., Williams 2B, Cooley RF, Bosse 1B, Waytula LF, Blakeney SS, Smith C, Laufer P, Benson P, Walsh P, Stokes, P. [HOD: *Racine Journal* (Racine, WI), June 25, 1934, 14.]

Olive CF, Mullen 2B, Cross 1B, Holland RF, Tolles LF, Blakeney SS, Faust 3B, Hill C, Didrikson P. [HOD: *Oregon Statesman* (Salem, OR), July 8, 1934, 8.]

Olive CF, Mullen 2B, Cross 1B, Holland RF, Tolles LF, Blakeney SS, Faust 3B, Hill C, Weirman P, Didrikson P. [HOD: *Daily Capital Journal* (Pierre, SD), July 9, 1934, 8.]

Hutson RF, Hansen 2B, Tucker 1B, Wykoff P, Clift CF, Atwell SS, Anderson 3B, Tally LF, Fleming C, [COD: *Eugene Guard* (Eugene, OR), July 11, 1934, 6.]

Shadowen CF, Woods 1B, Getz LF, Forman RF, Catina SS, O'Grady C, Fan'ella (?) 2B, Ramsey 2B, Hoffner 3B, Callahan 3B, Sloan P [Murphy HOD: *Pottstown Mercury* (Pottstown, PA), August 9, 1934, 5.]

Williams 2B, Moulder SS, Conley LF, Traynor 3B, Bosse 1B, Jacobs CF, Lucas RF, Smith C, Didrikson P, Stokes P. [*Pittsburgh Post-Gazette*, August 17, 1934, 17.]

Grover Cleveland Alexander, Mgr./P, Ingram CF, Mullen 2B, Holland RF, Perkins C, Tolles LF, B. Joseph 3B, Cross 1B, Blakeney SS, Paige P, Hill C, L. Miller P., Hunter P, Murphy 3B. [HOD, *Denver Post* Tournament: *Pittsburgh Courier*, August 18, 1934, 14.]

Hansen 2B, Hutson LF, Tucker 1B, Wycott RF, Clift CF, Atwell SS, Anderson 3B, Fleming C, Tally P, Brady P, Speisman P, Nusser P. [COD: *St. Cloud Times* (St. Cloud, MN), August 24, 1934, 10.]

Williams 2B, Moulder SS, Canley LF, Thayer 3B, Bosse 1B, Jacobs CF, Lucas RF, McDougal C, Didrikson P, Whitehill P. [HOD: *Chicago Defender*, August 25, 1934, 13.]

Didrikson P, Williams 2B, Conley 3B, Rosse 1B, Waytula LF, Jacobs CF, Moulder SS, McDougal C, Laufer P, Walsh P, Stokes P. [HOD: *Racine Journal-Times* (Racine, WI), August 29, 1934, 16.]

Ramsey LF, Stankey SS, Forman RF, Ragnow C, Walus 2B, CF, Hoffner 3B, Huggard 3B, Janesco P, O'Grady P. [Murphy HOD: *Brooklyn Daily Eagle* (Brooklyn, NY), September 10, 1934, 11.]

Anderson 3B, Hansen 2B, Tucker 1B, Wykoff RF, Clift CF, Atwell SS, Jutson LF, Nusser P, Speisman P, Fleming C. [COD: *Pampa Daily News* (Pampa, TX), September 20, 1934, 3.]

1935

Bob Dewhirst, Mgr., "Pep" Brannon SS, Dave Harrison 3B, Al Liftin OF, Deal C (captain), Louis Cato 2B, Tom Pearson 1B, Noel Rothburb P. [HOD Central States: *Escanaba Daily Press* (Escanaba, MI), March 23, 1935, 9.]

174   Appendix

Shadowen CF, Woods 1B, Williams LF, Ragnow C, Catina SS, O'Grady RF, Cummings 2B, Carney 3B, Grot P, Knothe P, Ramsey P. [Murphy HOD: *Beckley Post-Herald* (Beckley, WV), April 27, 1935, 8.]

Pitchers, Doc Tally, Wykoff, Bass, Wapp, Tucker; Catcher, Flip Fleming; First base, John Tucker; Second Base, Hub Hansen; Third Base, Andy Anderson; Shortstop, Dick Atwell; Left field, Vernon Deck, Center Field, Frank Clift; Right Field, Roy Hutson. [COD: *Emporia Gazette* (Emporia, KS), May 16, 1935, 5.]

Rathburn CF, Brannan CF, Leftian LF, Eddie Deal C, Cato 2B, Harrison 3B, Pearson 1B, Dewhirst RF, Ray Moore, P. [HOD Central States: *Gary Post-Tribune* (Gary, IN), May 27, 1935, 15.]

Lloyd Miller, Anderson, Eckert, Bosse, Dacus, Ambrose, Mullen, Chozen, Zoellers, Faust, Ingram, Tolles. [COD: *Daily Inter Lake* (Kalispell, MT), May 29, 1935, 6.]

Rathburn RF, Shannon SS, Liftin LF, Deal C, Cato 2B, Harrison 3B, Heckman 1B, Yonavich CF, Curtis P. [HOD Home team: *Newark Advocate* (Newark, OH), June 11, 1935, 8.]

Scott 3B, Uhas SS, LaFleur CF, Dorn 1B, Smith C, Schroeder LF, Mullen 2B, Anderson RF, Dean P, Hunter P. [COD: *Oshkosh Northwestern* (Oshkosh, WI), June 21, 1935, 19.]

Cummings 2B, Woods 1B, Forman CF, Durning LF, Bennett SS, Ragnow C, Catina 3B, Sloan RF, Carney RF, Ramsey P. [Murphy HOD: *Asbury Park Press* (Neptune, NJ), June 22, 1935, 13.]

Dorn 1B, Mullen 2B, Uhas SS, Scott 3B, Conley LF, LaFleur CF, Orwall RF, Joseph C. [COD: *Warren Times-Mirror* (Warren, PA), July 17, 1935, 8.]

Tom Dewhirst Mgr., "Pep" Brannon SS, Dave Harrison 3B, Al Liftin OF, Eddie Deal, C (captain), Louis Cato 2B, Tom Pearson 1B, Noel Rothburb P. [HOD Central States: *Escanaba Daily Press* (Escanaba, MI), July 23, 1935, 6.]

Harry Laufer, Bill Hunter, Lefty Weirman, Hank LaFleur, Bill Joseph, Ham Oliver, Jimmy Doran, Moon Mullen, Ray Schroeder, Bill Scott. [COD: *Ottawa Citizen* (Ottawa, Ontario, Canada), August 6, 1935, 5.]

Vann 3B, Woods 1B, Shadowen CF, Ragnow C, Forman RF, Catina SS, Popowski 2B, Ramsey P, Lavack P. [Murphy HOD: *Gazette and Daily* (York, PA), August 10, 1935, 10.]

Tucker 1B, Hansen 2B, Hutson RF, Clift CF, Deck LF, Atwell SS, Wykoff 3B, Anderson C, Tally P/LF. [COD: *Daily Herald* (Arlington Heights, IL), August 12, 1935, 6.]

Vann 3B, Woods 1B, Shadowen CF, Durning RF, Ragnow C, Forman LF, Catina SS, Popowski 2B, Swaney P. [Murphy HOD: *Brooklyn Daily Eagle* (Brooklyn, NY), August 19, 1935, 21.]

Ingram CF, Williams 2B, Bosse 1B, Zollers LF, Tapson 3B, Tolles RF, Chozen SS, Hill C, Irwin, P. [COD: *Moberly Monitor-Index* (Moberly, MO), August 24, 1935, 5.]

Tom Dewhirst Mgr., Tony Zitta, Pep Brannon, Fred Cato, Eddie Deal, Bob Collenberger, David Harrison, Jim Minogue, Lloyd Dalager, Matt Collins, Vernon "Lefty" Deck, McGraw, Louis Buck. [HOD Central States: *Alton Evening Telegraph* (Alton, IL), August 16, 1937, 8.]

Zollers 3B, Tapson 2B, Bower 1B, Young 1B, Clements CF, Brittwell RF, Tolles LF, Chozen SS, McCue C, Irvin P, Paulson P. [COD: *Denver Post* Tournament, September 16, 1935.]

Shadowen CF, Woods 1B, Fischer RF, Ragnow C, Bennett 2B, Cicero RF, Vann 3B, Caino SS, Ramsey P. [Murphy HOD: *Gazette and Daily* (York, PA), September 21, 1935, 10.]

Robert Dewhirst Mgr., Louis Cato, Eddie Deal, Ernie Selby, Germain "Jerry" Bush, Bill Heckman, Arky Fenton, Clay Williams. [HOD Central States, mid–1930s, Hawkins & Bertolino, *House of David*, 98.]

1936

Chick Genovese CF, Lou Vann 3B, Jimmy Woods 1B, Catina SS, Blair LF, Durning RF, Popowski 2B, Drenberg C, Grancio pinch-hitter, P, Janesco P, Red Durning RF. [Murphy HOD: *Charleston Daily Mail* (Charleston, WV), May 3, 1936, 61.]

Ramsey LF, Woods 1B, Vann 3B, Genovese CF, Caline SS, Popowski 2B, Swaney P, Sloan P, Durning RF, Grancio pinch-hitter. [Murphy HOD: *Asbury Park Press* (Neptune, NJ), July 8, 1936, 14.]

Durning LF, Woods 1B, Vann 3B, Genovese CF, Johnson RF, Catina SS, Popowski 2B, Weismier C, Swaney P, Grancio pinch-hitter. [Murphy HOD: *Brooklyn Daily Eagle* (Brooklyn, NY), August 3, 1936, 8.]

Cato 3B, Miller LF, Dalager C, Brannon SS, Zitta 1B, Ambrose P, Deal C, Harrison RF, Collenberger 2B. [HOD Home Team: *Detroit Free Press*, August 21, 1936, 16.]
Brannon SS, Collenberger 2B, Collins CF, Cato LF, Deal C, Tolles P, Harrison 3B, Minogue P, Elliott P. [HOD Home Team: *Times*, August 31, 1936, 13.]
David Harrison 3B, Eddie Deal C, Pep Brannon SS, Collenberger 2B, Tony Zitta 1B, Lefty Tolles OF/P, Fred Cato LF, Matt Collins CF, ___ P. [HOD: *Alton Evening Telegraph* (Alton, IL), September 5, 1936, 8.]
Al Nusser, Paul "Mickey" Flynn, Roy Hutson, Doc Tally, Cecil Tucker, Don Henry, Fred Cato, George Anderson, John Hubbell, Harold "Dutch" Witte, John Tucker, Bill Marlott, Sam Scaling, Dick Atwell. [COD: Hawkins & Bertolino, *House of David*, 101.]
Al Nusser, Paul "Mickey" Flynn, Roy Hutson, Doc Tally, George Anderson, John Hubbell, Dutch Witte, John Tucker, Bill Marlott, Cecil Tucker, Don Henry, Fred Cato, Dick Atwell, Sam Scaling. [*Honolulu Advertiser* (Honolulu, HI), September 24, 1936, 14.]

1937

George Anderson, John Tucker, Arnie Valcheck, Doc Tally, Willard Pike, Gordon O'Brien, Hub Hansen, Harold Gilbert, Eddie Lick, Gordon O'Saughnessey, Art Keller, Francis Buck. [COD: Photo caption of 1937 game, in a scrapbook kept by John Tucker and George Anderson. Photo featured for sale on eBay.]
George Anderson, Scrappy McCollister, Joe Zantora, Lefty Deck, Dave Cheeves, Ike Bohn, John Tucker, Fred Cato. Pitchers: Doc Tally, Bill Anderson, Randy Williams, Dick Farrell, Herb Anderson, Smokey Lewis. [COD: *Hope Star* (Hope, AR), May 7, 1937, 5.]
George Anderson 3B, Eggleston SS, Ventura CF, Deck LF, Cato RF, McCallister 2B, Tucker 1B, Lasky C, H. Anderson P, Armstrong P, Tally P. [COD: *Pampa Daily News* (Pampa, TX), May 18, 1937, 3.]
George Anderson 2B, Eggleson SS, Cato 3B, Lefty Deck RF, John Tucker 1B, Armstrong LF, Laski C, H. Anderson P, Zentura CF. [COD: *Chicago Daily Tribune*, June 7, 1937, 23.]
Shadowen CF, Pierce SS, Vann 2B, Custaferri 3B, Woods 1B, Miller LF, Pierson RF, Martin C, Sacony P. [Murphy HOD: *Central New Jersey Home News* (New Brunswick, NJ), June 9, 1937, 16]
John Tucker, Lefty Deck, Doc Tally, Anderson, Fred Cato, Dave Cheeves, Joe Zantora, Scrappy McAllister, Ike Bohn, Bill Anderson, Randy Williams, Dick Farrell, Herb Anderson, Smokey Lewis. [COD: *Daily Tribune*, June 16, 1937, 5.]
Anderson C, Eggleston SS, Thenhaus P, Zentura 2B, Deck RF, Tucker 1B, Tally LF, Lewis CF, Armstrong 3B. [COD: *Algona Upper Des Moines* (Algona, IA), June 24, 1937, 10.]
Mitleman RF, Rea RF, Leonard SS, Casaccio 2B, Pierce 3B, Woods 1B, Dietz C, Luckey LF, Janesco P, Ramsey P, Swaney P. [Murphy HOD: *Brooklyn Daily Eagle* (Brooklyn, NY), July 22, 1938, 13.]
Anderson SS, Eggleston LF, Thenhaus 3B, Zentura CF, Tucker 1B, Woodage RF, Snell 2B, Austin C, Clay P. [COD: *Bend Bulletin* (Bend, OR), July 27, 1937, 2.]
Vann 2B, Leonard SS, Shadowen CF, Pierce 3B, Ragnow C, Martin C, Lucchi LF, Woods 1B, Cicconey RF, Lavoc P, Swaney P, Krepps 2B, Quinn P. [Murphy HOD: *Brooklyn Daily Eagle* (Brooklyn, NY), September 7, 1937, 18.]
Vann RF, Leonard 2B, Shadowen CF, Pierce 3B, Keifer SS, Lucchi LF, Woods, 1B, Martin C, Spiro P, Jacobson (?). [Murphy HOD: *Brooklyn Daily Eagle* (Brooklyn, NY), September 9, 1937, 20.]
Shadowen CF, Popowski 2B, Vann RF, Pierce 3B, Lucchi LF, Monendey SS, Woods 1B, Martin C, Janesco, P. [Murphy HOD: *Baltimore Sun*, September 23, 1937, 17.]

1938

Lesnick LF, Baker SS, Shires 2B, Panciera 3B, Rea CF, Woods CF, Mittleman RF, Marchiando RF, Swaney P, Scully P, catcher ?? [Murphy HOD: *Tampa Tribune*, March 18, 1938, 19.]
Anderson 3B, Hansen 2B, Velcheck CF, Pike RF, Munitz LF, Lick SS, Thacker 1B, Keller C, O'Brian P. [COD: *Courier News* (Somerville, NJ), April 25, 1938, 6.]
Lefty Wilson P, Moose Swaney P, Casaccio 3B, Baker SS, Vann LF, Panciera RF, Woods 1B,

Mittleman CF, Brown 2B, Rudisell C. [Murphy HOD: *Daily News Times* (New Brunswick, NJ), April 25, 1938, 6.]

Mittleman CF, Rea RF, Vann 3B, Woods 1B, Casaccio 2B, Saxton C, Sacony LF, Ransey P, Dietz C. [Murphy HOD: *Brooklyn Daily Eagle* (Brooklyn, NY), May 31, 1938, 18.]

Mitleman CF, Piero 3B, Vann LF, Casaccio 2B, Woods 1B, Kohler RF, Menendez SS, Gray C, Ciccone P, Swaney P, Janesco P. [Murphy HOD: *Brooklyn Daily Eagle* (Brooklyn, NY), June 20, 1938, 14.]

Mittleman CF, Rea RF, Leonard DD, Casaccio 2B, Pierce 3B, Woods 1B, Dietz C, Janesco P, Ransey P, Swaney P. [Murphy HOD: *Brooklyn Daily Eagle* (Brooklyn, NY), July 22, 1938, 13.]

Strassione SS, Rea RF, Cassachio 2B, Delore CF, Woods 1B, Dietz C, Lockey LF, Scheffield P, Ramsey C, J. Smith P. [Murphy HOD: *Brooklyn Daily Eagle* (Brooklyn, NY), August 1, 1938, 13.]

Andy Anderson 3B, Hub Hansen 2B, Arnie Velcheck RF, Bill Pike CF, Sam Munitz LF, Eddie Lick SS, John Tucker 1B, Ardys Keller C, Merritt Hubble P, Doc Tally P, Clifford "Count" Clay P, Myron Morriss P, Gordon O'Shaunessy P, Ossie Swinehart P. [COD: *Marshfield News-Herald* (Marshfield, WI), August 30, 1938, 8.]

Lick SS, Tucker 1B, Valcheck CF, Gilbert RF, Anderson 3B, Hansen 2B, Pike LF, Keller C, Gordon P. [COD: *Eau Claire Leader* (Eau Claire, WI), August 31, 1938, 10.]

Lick SS, Tucker 1B, Velchek P, Gilbert RF, Anderson 3B, Hansen 2B, Pike LF, Reinhart C, Clay P. [COD: *Marshfield News-Herald* (Marshfield, WI), September 1, 1938, 14.]

Lick SS, Tucker 1B, Gregory CF, Gilbert RF, Anderson 3B, Marquard 2B, Pike LF, Kelley C, Clay P, Tally P. [COD: *Nebraska State Journal* (Lincoln, NE), September 28, 1938, 11.]

1939

Smoller 3B, Grant LF, Lesnick SS, Thomas CF, Woods 1B, Jones 2B, Butler RF, Chew C, Sheffield P, Martina P, Ciccone alternate. [Murphy HOD: *Brooklyn Daily Eagle* (Brooklyn, NY), May 15, 1939, 16.]

Grant LF, Murphy SS, Copak RF/3B, Woods 1B, Thomas CF, Figle (?) 3B, Flanagan RF, Chew C, Cloonie P. [Murphy HOD: *Asbury Park Press* (Neptune, NJ), June 7, 1939, 11.]

Lick SS, Tucker 1B, Velchek CF, Bilbert RF, Minor C, Anderson 3B, Wilson 2B, Bass LF, Freeman P. [COD: *Green Bay Press* (Green Bay, WI), June 10, 1939, 15.]

Olive Mgr. CF, Butler 2B, Smith 1B, Amata SS, Sass LF, Kunette C, Beck 3B, Straw LF, Lund P, Paabe P. [Murphy HOD: *Escanaba Daily Press* (Escanaba, MI), July 26, 1939, 10.]

Leck, Wilson, Valcheck, Gilbert, Anderson, Miner, Egnatic, Bass, Okeson. [COD: *Eugene Guard* (Eugene, OR), July 28, 1939, 10.]

Jones RF, Leonard 3B, Shadowen LF, Pearl 2B, Pierce SS, Woods 1B, Thomas LF, Comiskey C, Taone P, Lavac P, Spero P, Marion P. [Murphy HOD: *Brooklyn Daily Eagle* (Brooklyn, NY), July 31, 1939, 14.]

Lick SS, Tucker 1B, Velchek CF, Gilbert RF, Okeson LF, Anderson 2B, Minor C, Wilson 3B, Hanson P, Tally P, Chauncy P. [COD: *Reno Gazette-Journal* (Reno, NV), August 2, 1939, 13.]

Jones 2B, Leonard 3B, Shadowen LF, Pierce SS, Woods 1B, Grant RF, Thomas CF, Chew C, Janesco P, Kelly P. [Murphy HOD: *Delaware County Times* (Upper Darby Township, PA), August 11, 1939, 13.]

Lick SS, Tucker 1B, Velchek CF, Gilbert RF, Okeson LF, Anderson 3B, Miner C, Wilson 2B, Bass P, Swinehart P. [COD: *Ogden Standard Examiner* (Ogden, UT), August 15, 1939, 8.]

Grover Cleveland Alexander Mgr., Jones 2B, Pierce SS, T. Thomas CF, Woods 1B, Shadowen LF, Grant RF, Chew 3B, Brady C, Swaney P. [Murphy HOD: *Kingston Daily Freeman* (Kingston, NY), August 16, 1939, 7]

Anderson 3B, (Lich) Lick SS, Tucker 1B, Velchek CF, Gilbert RF, Okeson LF, Miner C, Wilson 2B, Bass, P. [COD: *Ogden Standard Examiner* (Ogden, UT), August 16, 1939, 6.]

Wilson 2B, Tucker 1B, Velchek CF, Summers RF, Okeson LF, Anderson 3B, Miner C, Lick SS, Hensen P. [COD: *Macon Chronicle-Herald* (Macon, MO), September 23, 1939, 6.]

Tony Caliendo SS, Andy Gibson 2B, Nick Raab LF, Pat Patterson 3B, Ed Duke 1B, Bill Luhrs P/CF, Lon Her C, Abe Spiro P, Mike Janesco p, John Scully P, Roland Van Slate P, Dale Bowyer P, Moose Swaney, P. [Murphy HOD: *Morning Herald*, October 30, 1939, 6.]

1940

Farmer 2B, Pugh LF, Ueck CF, Bohn SS, Deal C, Pallas RF, Anderson 3B, Selby 1B, Pavlick P. [HOD Home Team: *News Palladium* (Benton Harbor, MI), May 31, 1940, 10.]

Lou Parently 3B, Ed Hamman SS, Joe Darcy RF/P, Mickey Bell CF, Steve Yargo 1B, John Murphy 2B, Red Handley C, Bill Gelbudal LF, Joe Sovoca P, Ronnie Gains P, Covich P, Bodin P, Jones 2B. [Murphy HOD: *Morning Call* (Allentown, PA), June 8, 1940, 11.]

Gallo 2B, Vann 3B, Battle SS, Alexander CF, Shadowen 1B, Wrongrick RF, Comiskey C, Peden LF, Stryker P. [Murphy HOD: *Asbury Park Press* (Neptune, NJ), July 2, 1941, 14–15.]

Watson CF, Vann 2B, Shadowen LF, Helixon 3B, Pierce 3B, Woods 1B, Battle SS, Comisky C, McGloin P. [Murphy HOD: *Brooklyn Daily Eagle* (Brooklyn, NY), July 25, 1940, 15.]

Adams 2B, Dalager RF, Ueck CF, Pallas P, Bohn SS, Deal C, Selby 1B, Anderson 3B, Richmond LF, Dodd P. [HOD Home Team: *News Palladium* (Benton Harbor, MI), July 29, 1940, 8.]

Farmer 2B, Dalager RF, Ueck CF, Bohn SS, Deal C, Selby 1B, Richmond LF, Anderson 3B, Wagner P, Pallis P. [HOD Home Team: *News Palladium* (Benton Harbor, MI), July 30, 1940, 7.]

McGraw 2B, Gardner CF, Anderson 3B, Miner C, Reichert F, Campbell RF, Smith SS, Tucker 1B, Stelle, P, Schroeder P. [COD: *Nevada State Journal* (Reno, NV), August 3, 1940, 8.]

McGraw 2B, Gardner CF, Anderson 3B, Miner C, Reincelt LF, Campbell RF, Smith SS, Tucker 1B, Stelle P, Schroeder P, Wykoff P, Tally P. [COD: *Nevada State Journal* (Reno, NV), August 6, 1940, 10.]

McGraw 2B, Lee Gardner CF, George Anderson 3B, D. E. "Beans" Miner C, George Reichelt LF, Campbell RF, Smith SS, John Tucker 1B, Dick Wykoff P, Doc Tally P. [COD: *Nevada State Journal* (Reno, NV), August 7, 1940, 9.]

Deal C, Adams 2B, Dalager RF, Ueck CF, Pallas 1B, Bohn SS, Richmond LF, Anderson 3B, Pavlick P. [HOD Home Team: *News Palladium* (Benton Harbor, MI), August 12, 1940, 6.]

George Anderson 3B, Clarence "Fats" Hetherly 2B, Arnie Valcheck CF, Cecil Campbell RF, Chet Smith SS, John Tucker 1B, D. E. "Beans" Miner C, Doc Tally P, Clifford "Count" Clay P, Dick Wykoff P, Gene Hanson P, Mike Schrater P. [COD: *Ogden Standard-Examiner* (Ogden, UT), August 17, 1940, 5.]

McGraw 2B, Gardner CF, Anderson 3B, Miner C, Reichelt LF, Smith SS, Tucker 1B, Wykoff P, (Shroder) Schroeder, P. [COD: *Ogden Standard Examiner* (Ogden, UT), August 20, 1940, 8.]

McGraw 2B, Campbell RF, Tucker 1B, Anderson 3B, Gardner CF, Chet Smith SS, Miner C, "Count" Clay P, Reichelt LF. [COD: *Eugene Guard* (Eugene, OR), July 13, 1940, 6.]

Adams 2B, Farmer 3B, Dalager RF, Pallas P, Deal C, Selby 1B, Richmond LF, Bohn SS, Ueck CF, Pavlick P. [HOD Home Team: *News Palladium* (Benton Harbor, MI), September 9, 1940, 8.]

Leach 2B, Dalager 3B, Deal C, Snyder SS, Sinn CF, Tally RF, Selby 1B, Pallas LF, Schumacher P, Adams 2B, Farmer 3B, Richmond LF, Bohn RF, Ueck CF, Pavlick P. [HOD Home Team: *News Palladium* (Benton Harbor, MI), September 30, 1940, 8.]

1941

Gallo 2B, Lehmuth 3B, Battle SS, Peden CF, Woods 1B, Shadowen LF, Comiskey C, Rhodes RF, McKinney P. [Murphy HOD: *News Leader* (Staunton, VA), April 20, 1941, 8.]

Partial lineup: Jack Rhodes P, Jimmie Woods 1B, Mike Janesco P, Howard "Dusty" Rhodes RF, Charles "Moose" Swaney P, Vince Battle SS. [Murphy HOD: *News Letter*, April 19, 1941, 6.]

Tucker 1B, McGraw 2B, Gardner CF, Deck RF, Olsen RF, Miner C, Fielder 3B, Anderson SS, Clay P. [COD: *Arizona Daily Star* (Tucson, AZ), April 22, 1941, 8.]

Gallo 2B, Vann 3B, Battle SS, Alexander CF, Woods 1B, Shadowen RF, Comisky C, Paden LF, Sarle P, Lester P. [Murphy HOD: *Courier News* (Somerville, NJ), May 31, 1941, 15.]

Atkinson 3B, Osler SS, Anderson 3B, Deck LF, McGraw 2B, Hauser C, Gardner CF, Tucker 1B, Biggers P. [COD: *Eugene Guard* (Eugene, OR), July 23, 1941, 6.]

Atkinson 3B, Oster SS, G. Anderson RF, Lefty Deck LF, John McGraw 2B, Chick Hauser C, Gardner CF, Tucker 1B, Red Biggers P. [COD: *Eugene Guard* (Eugene, OR), July 27, 1941.]

Gardner CF, Oster SS, Anderson 3B, Deck LF, McGraw 2b, Tucker 1B, Smith C, Clay P, Wykoff. [COD: *Reno Journal* (Reno, NV), August 6, 1941, 13.]

1942

"Due to the war, the colony nine will not attempt a schedule this season." [*News Palladium* (Benton Harbor, MI), March 31, 1942, 6] Lou Murphy's squad made scattered appearances throughout the season.

Tarrant RF, Puckett 2B, Vann SS, Alexander CF, Duber 1B, Krol LF, Martin C, Manno C, Dyball 2B, Novak P, Tiant P. [Murphy HOD: *Quad City Times* (Davenport, IA), May 29, 1942, 8.]

Claude (Torrant) Tarrant RF, Jack (Pluckett) Pucket 2B, Lou Vann SS, Roy Alexander RF, Joe Krol LF, Ed Duber 1B, Joe Manno C, Don Dyball 3B, John Novak C, Charles Lester P. [Murphy HOD: *Times*, June 4, 1942, 14.]

Gardner CF, Osler SS, Anderson 3B, Deck LF, Clay RF, McGraw 2B, Tucker 1B, Griffith P, Smith C, Tally P, Wykoff P. [COD: *Salt Lake Tribune* (Salt Lake City, UT), August 26, 1942, 11.]

1943

Bill Leach, Fay Sinn, Ike Bohn, Army Clements, Bob Crossman, Joe Anderson, Bill Dudas, Barney Dalager, Fizz Clupper, Harvey Pallas, Doc Tally, Eddie Deal. [COD Home Team: *News Palladium* (Benton Harbor, MI), June 17, 1943, 14.]

1944

Nothing found due to World War II hiatus.

1945

2B, Vandetta 3B, Hayden LF, Riordan 1B, Schmidt RF, Miller C, Hornicki CF, Fauci SS, McMahan P.[Murphy HOD: *Reno Gazette Journal* (Reno, NV), August 17, 1945, 16.]

Al Osof P, Stan Osonowski C, Bill Hayden C/INF, Jim McMahon P, Harry Riordan 1B, Irv Beckwitt OF, Hayden 3B, Schmidt CF/RF, Haynicki LF, S. Miller C, Blahut 2B, McMahon CFRF, Gamunson P, D. Miller P. [Former minor league players on House of David. COD: *Standard Examiner* (Ogden, UT), August 17, 1945, 8.]

1946

George Anderson, Pop Griffen, George Reichelt, Lee Gardner, Dick Wykoff, Rocky Kallis, Doc Tally, Red Edward, Earl (Crappe) Crapp, Bill Rich, __ Green, Paul Jarvis, L. Hummel. [COD Spring 1946, Hawkins & Bertolino, *House of David*, 111.]

George Reichelt, Lee Gardiner, Dick Wykoff, Rocky Kallis, Doc Tally, Red Edward, Earl Crapp, Bill Rich, (?) Green, Paul "Pete" Jarvis, Lew Hummel, Dick Hummel. [COD: 1946, article from Baseball Hall of Fame Archives.]

Atkinson 2B, Hanover LF, Reichelt OF, Kallis SS, Rich 3B, Monroe CF, Jarvis 1B, Anderson C, Allen P, Minor P, McDougal P, Wykoff P, Gardner CF. [COD: *Paris News* (Paris, TX), April 16, 1946, 3.]

Ken Atkinson 2B, Lee Gardner CF, George Reichelt LF, Lanny Kallis SS, Bill Rich 3B, Bob Monroe RF, Lewis Hummel C, Ted Hanover utility, Paul Jarvis utility, Doc Tally P, Dick Wykoff P, Don Miner P, Glen Miner, P, Dick Hummel P. [COD: *Paris News* (Paris, TX), April 17, 1946, 7.]

Atkinson 2B, Edwards LF, Kallis SS, Reichert CF, Rich 3B, Wykoff RF, Jarvis 1B, Anderson C, Brandy P. [COD: *Amarillo Daily News* (Amarillo, TX), April 25, 1946, 8.]

Kallis 2B, Gardner CF, Anderson 1B, L. Hummel C, Boettcher SS, Reichelt LF, Rich 3B, Edwards RF, D. Hummel P, Tally P. [COD: *Warren Times Mirror* (Warren, PA), June 13, 1946, 14.]

Lanny Kallis 2B, Lee Gardner CF, Bill Rich SS, George Reichelt LF, Ed Brady RF, Paul Jarvis 3B, Lew Hummel C, Doc Tally P, Dick Wykoff P, Pop Griffith P, Red Clard P, Earl Crapp P, George Green P. [COD: *Star Press* (Muncie, IN), June 17, 1946, 6.]

Kallis 2B, Gardiner CF, Anderson 3B, L. Hummel C, Reichelt LF, Boettcher SS, Jarvis 1B, D. Hummel P, Wykoff P. [COD: *Star Press* (Muncie, IN), June 18, 1946, 9.]

George Anderson 1B, Lanny Kallis 2B, Lee Gardner CF, Bill Rich SS, George Reichelt LF, Ed Brady RF, Paul Jarvis 3B, Lewis Hummel C, Doc Tally CF/P, Dick Wykoff P, Pop Griffith P, Red Lark P, Earl Crapp P. [COD: *St. Cloud Times* (St. Cloud, MN), June 27, 1946, 16.]

Kallis 2B, Gardner CF, Anderson 3B, L. Hummel C, Reichelt LF, Boettcher SS, Jarvis 1B, Hanover RF, Crapp P, Reed P. [COD: *St. Cloud Times* (St. Cloud, MN), June 28, 1946, 13.]

DiLuccia LF, Riley 2B, Hines 1B, Clark 3B, O'Dell CF, Duke 1B, Gibson SS, Stauffer C, Ciccone P. [Murphy HOD: *Delaware News-Journal* (New Castle, DE), July 15, 1946, 15.]

Lanny Kallis 2B, Leo (Lee?) Gardner CF, Nike Boettcher SS, George Reichelt LF, Dick Hummel 3B, Lewis Hummel C, Jim Mabry CF, Doc Tally P, Dick Wykoff P, C. Griffith P, C. "Red" Edwards P, Earl Crapp P. [COD: *Bakersfield Californian* (Bakersfield, CA), August 8, 1946, 14.]

Reilly SS, Novosol 3B, Sires RF, Clark LF, O'Dell CF, Guinn P, Gilson 2B, Baker P, Mike Janesco P, Spero alternate. [Murphy HOD: *Philadelphia Inquirer*, August 18, 1946, 30.]

Anderson 3B, Jarvis 1B, Reichelt LF, Hummel C, Gardiner CF, Bryant SS, Costello RF, Thiel 2B, Wykoff P. [COD: *News Palladium* (Benton Harbor, MI), September 13, 1946, 6.]

1947

Jack Scott, Sandy Sanders, Bill Horne, Lee Gardiner, Earl Crapp, Dick Wykoff, Neil Bryant, Paul "Pete" Jarvis, Bill Mansfield, Doc Tally, Al Costello, Dick Bryant. [COD: Hawkins & Bertolino, *House of David*, 112.]

Al Costello 3B, Johnny Theile 2B, George Anderson mgr./C, George Reichelt RF, Lee Gardner CF, Paul Jarvis 1B, George Lanier LF, Neil Bryant SS, Dick Wykoff P, James Tally P, Joe Verve P, Dick Bryant P, Doc Tally P. [COD: May 9, 1947, 2.3.]

Costello 3B, Jarvis 2B, Reichelt RF, Anderson 1B, Gardner CF, Saunders LF, Bryant SS, Horne C, Wykoff P. [COD: *Eugene Guard* (Eugene, OR), July 3, 1947, 7.]

Collendo SS, Gibson 2B, Patterson 3B, Raab LF, Duke 1B, Luhrse RF, O'Dell CF, Beradonna C, Mitleman CF, Spiro P, Swaney P. [Murphy HOD: *Brooklyn Daily Eagle* (Brooklyn, NY), July 21, 1947, 12.]

Sandy CF, Anderson 1B, Gardner RF, N. Bryant SS, Schiesz 2B, Costello 3B, Jarvis LF, Horne C, Scott utility, Mansfield utility, Slater P, D. Bryant P, Barnes P, Wykoff P, Tally P. [COD: *Ogden Standard-Examiner* (Ogden, UT), August 10, 1947, 23.]

Tony Caliendo SS, Andy Gibson 2B, Lloyd Patterson 3B, Bill Luhrs LF*, Ed Duke 1B, Don O'Dell LF*, Al Taffy CF, Louis Beragona C, Spiro P, Slate P, Swaney P. Newspaper listed both players as LF with no RF player listed. [COD: *Evening News* (Harrisburg, PA), August 23, 1947, 8.]

Sand's (?) CF, Horne 3B, Gardner RF, Bryant SS, Wykoff 1B, Jarvis LF, Thiel 2B, Hummel C, Mansfield P. [COD: *Nebraska State Journal* (Lincoln, NE), September 3, 1947, 12.]

1948

Pitchers Earl Crapp, Dick Wykoff, Bob Wegner, Bill Mansfield, Vic Barnes, J. L. Tally; catchers Dick Crapp, Ronald Bucher; infielders (Mike) George Anderson 1B, Merlin Baker; outfielders Everett Clark, Arch Warner, Lee Gardner, Darryl (Wileman) Wierman. [COD: *Corpus Christi Caller-Times* (Corpus Christi, TX), April 8, 1948, 21.]

Doc Tally Asst. Mgr., George Anderson 1B, (?) Bucher C, Ted (Dick?) Crapp C, Walter Dunaway P, Johnny Fine P, Lee Gardiner OF, (?) Hayes 3B, Jimmy Hines 2B, Charley Kafoury CF/C, Gus (Maurer) Mauer P, Bob Wegner P, Dick Wykoff [COD, 1948.]

Kafoury RF, Anderson 1B, Gardner CF, J. Hayes 2B, G. Hayes 3B, (Maurer) Mauer SS, Martineau LF, Crapp P, Wykoff P. [COD: *Lincoln Journal* (Lincoln, NE), June 5, 1948, 5.]

Charles Kafoury 2B, George Anderson 1B, Lee Gardner CF, George Hayes 3B, Gus (Maurer) Mauer SS, Brad Trine LF, Bob Honus RF, (Romey) Ronnie Bucher C, Vic Martineau P. [COD: *Humboldt Republican* (Humboldt, IA), June 11, 1948, 1.]

Hershock Mgr./LF, Davenport 2B, Ellis CF, Mackery 3B, Palladino RF, Watson SS, Cline 1B, Mocrick C, Petrongolo, backup catcher. [Murphy HOD: *Evening Herald* (Syracuse, NY), June 16, 1948.]

Walsh 2B, Curtis SS, Spiro 1B, Dunlap RF, Fraker LF, Harper 3B, Norman C, Janesco P, Marin P, Alexander P. [Murphy HOD: *News Journal* (New Castle, DE), June 28, 1948, 20.]

Kafoury RF, J. Hayes 2B, Martineau LF, Hines SS, Wykoff 1B, Gardner CF, Bucher C, Anderson 3B, Hornes P, Fine P. [COD: *Great Falls Tribune* (Great Falls, MT), July 3, 1948, 9.]

Tom Walsh 3B/2B, Don Curtis SS, Paul Dunlap 1B, Dick Fraker LF, Bob Marren RF, Jim Marvis CF, Nick Mangrieri 2B, Earl Newman C, Eddie Krutillo C, Roy Alexander P, Mike Janesco P, Bill Meyer P, Frank Mares P, Abe Spiro P. [Murphy HOD: *Advance Patchogue* (Brookhaven, NY), July 29, 1948, 6.]

Pitchers Dick Wykoff, Bob Honus, Johnny Fine, Walter Dunaway, Vic Martineau, Earl Crapp, Doc Tally; catchers Ronnie Bucher, Dick Crapp; infielders Mike Anderson, Jimmy Hines, Gus Mauer, George Hayes; outfielders Charles Kafoury, Lee Gardner, Al Fine. [COD: *Bend Bulletin* (Bend, OR), August 4, 1948, 2.]

Ronnie (Baucher) Bucher, Ted Crapp, George Anderson, Jimmy Hines, Gus Maurer, George Hayes, Charles Kafourny, Lee Gardner, Al Fine, Doc Tally, Earl Crapp, Dick Wykoff, Vic Martineau, Walter Dunaway, Brad Trine, Johnny Fine, Bob Honus. [COD: *Nevada State Journal* (Reno, NV), August 8, 1948, 13.]

Kafoury CF, G. Hayes 3B, Ashman 1B, J. Hayes 2B, Gardner RF, Fine LF, Maurer SS, Anderson C, Trine P. [COD: *Journal-Gazette* (Fort Wayne, IN), September 20, 1948, 5.]

1949

George Anderson Mgr./1B, Jim (Hays) Hayes 2B, "Zank" Glossenger SS, George (Hays) Hayes 3B, John Saba C, William Spradlin C, Chet Ashman RF, Charles Kafoury CF, Dick Porter LF, Bob Wegner P, Dick Mulline P, Walter Denaway P, Jerry Sebring P, Hugh Cook P, Doc Tally P. [COD: *Jefferson City Post-Tribune* (Jefferson City, MO), May 26, 1949, 11.]

George Anderson Mgr./1B, Jim (Hays) Hayes 2B, George (Hays) Hayes SS, "Zank" Glossenger 3B, Jim Boatman C, Chet Ashman OF, Charles Kafoury OF, Ray Tomski OF, Bill Spradlin OF, Joe Gillian P, Dan Leach P, Paul Knippen P, Bob Wegner P, Dick Mullins P, Jerry Sebring P, Doc Tally P. [COD: *Independent Record* (Helena, MT), June 30, 1949, 5.]

Kafoury CF, Tomski RF, G. Hayes 3B, C. Ashman 1B, J. Hayes 2B, Cook LF, Berkland SS, Glossenger C Beam P. [COD: *Great Falls Tribune* (Great Falls, MT), July 5, 1949, 11.]

George Anderson Mgr./1B, Jimmy Hayes 2B, George Hayes SS, Roy Berkland 3B, Ray Tomski C, Charles Kafourny CF, Chet Ashman RF, Hugh Cook LF, "Zank" Glossenger utility. [COD: *Bakersfield Californian* (Bakersfield, CA), July 9, 1949, 22.]

1950

George Anderson Mgr./3B, Kafoury SS, Bolen RF, (Chapetta) Capetta 1B, (Maurer) Mauer 2B, Morrow LF, Chew C, Kish P, CF omitted. [COD: *Jefferson City Post-Tribune* (Jefferson City, MO), June 8, 1950, 13.]

George Anderson Mgr./3B, B. Self CF, Frank Cirello 2B, John Bodine RF, Rocky Carlini SS, Ben Owens LF, C, Kimball 1B, Jack Cartleau 2B, Will LaSalle P, Timko P. [COD: 1950, Hall of Fame Archives, no added information.]

1951

Kafoury LF, Irvin RF, Ledwidge CF, Gatta 3B, Carlini SS, Owens C, Cockrell 2B, Kimball 1B, Liska P. [COD: Hall of Fame Archives, no added information.]

George Anderson Mgr./2B, Rudy Kelsch 3B, Jim Mabry CF, Tony Sileo SS, Bob Mitchell 1B, Morley Cato RF, Jack Byrkett LF, Ray Chew C, Homer Garner P, Miles Carroll P, Jack Feldman P, "Zank" Glossenger P, Clare Westphal P. [COD: *Independent Record* (Helena, MT), July 2, 1951, 8.]

Anderson Mgr./2B, Ellis 3B, Byrkett 1B, Lavelli CF, Boettcher SS, Garner LF, Cato RF, Olson C, Hall pinch-hitter, Feldman P, Kish P. [COD: *Medford Mail Tribune* (Medford, OR), August 13, 1951, 6.]

Charles Kafoury LF, Irvin RF, Ledwidge CF, Gatta 3B, Carlini SS, Owens C, Cockrell 2B,

Kimball 1B, Liska P, Blankfeld P. [parts of rosters found in a variety of sources such as www.attheplate.com.]

1952

George Anderson Mgr./2B, Bob Mitchell 1B, Al Sternberg SS, Jack Garrett 3B, Dick Drain C, Charles Capetta LF, Wayne Goodman CF, Morley Cato RF, Charles Liska P, Clare Westphal P, Lefty Floyd P, Manuel Madrigal P, Homer Garner P, Frank "Bobo" Nickerson P. [COD: *Corsicana Daily Sun* (Corsicana, TX), April 25, 1952, 6.]

1953

Anderson Mgr., Halorich 2B, Williams SS, Kafoury 3B, Mitchell 1B, Tomski C, Sanders CF, Boatman LF, Keller RF, Liska P. [COD: *Joplin Globe* (Joplin, MO), June 9, 1953, 10.]

1954

Anderson Mgr., Kafoury LF, Irvin RF, Ledridge CF, Gotta 3B, Carlini SS, Owens C, Cockreil 2B, Kimball 1B, Liska P. [COD: article donated to Baseball Hall of Fame, no additional source listed.]

John "Red" Kennedy LHP, William Kimball RHP, Lee Berkenamp RHP, Ray Wisneski RHP, Charles Liska RHP, Tom Gatews 3B, Ben Owens C, Bob Mitchell 1B, Tom Kyler 2B, Charles Kafoury SS, Bill Duffy CF, Tex Donovan RF, Homer Garner LF. [COD: *Independent Record* (Helena, MT), July 30, 1954, 23.]

1955

B. Self CF, Frank Cerillo 3B, John "Moose" Bodine RF, Rocky Carlini SS, Ben Owens LF, B. Kimball 1B, George Anderson 2B, Russ C, Jack Carlier P, Timko P, Will La Salle SS. [COD: *News Palladium* (Benton Harbor, MI), June 18, 1955, 10.]

1956

George Anderson Mgr., Chet Ploza SS. Chuck Edge OF, Ted Russ C, Bill Swanson OF, __Robinson SS, Levers OF, Carluccio 1B, Sheary 3B, Sam Zelms P, Gary Wykoff OF/P, John Chezik P, Jack Garrett P, John Bodine OF. [COD: *Moberly Monitor-Index* (Moberly, MO), June 13, 1956, 13.]

George Anderson Mgr./ utility, Bill Swanson CF, Mel Sheary 3B, Chester Ploza SS, Hank Robinson 2B, Chuck Edge LF, Ted Russ C, Bill Carluccio 1B, John Bodine RF. [COD: *Independent Record* (Helena, MT), July 15, 1956, 13.]

George Anderson Mgr., Bill Swanson, Mel Sheary, Chester Plaza, Hank Robinson, Chuck Edge, Ted Russ, Bill Carlluccio, John Bodine, Sam Zelms, John Chezik, Jack Garrett. [COD: *Great Falls Tribune* (Great Falls, MT), July 20, 1956, 20.]

Doc Tally, Hubert "Hub" Hansen, Herman "Flip" Fleming, Richard "Dick" Atwell, Roy Hutson, John Tucker, (?) Clift, Brady, George Anderson, Richard "Dick" Wykoff, promoter Walter "Dutch" Witte. (Cecil Tucker, Herman "Flip" Fleming, and Spiesman were not allowed to play as they had only tourist passports) [COD, Mexico, Hawkins & Bertolino, *House of David*, 99.]

Uber Tucker, Amos Edwards, Jimmy Crow, Henry Taft, Melvin Tucker, Louie Buck, Frank Kolesar, Cecil Tucker, Miles Crow, Ben Caudle, Everett Buck. [COD: Hawkins & Bertolino, *House of David*, 91.]

Additional players in 1956, found in various articles: John Chezik, P; John Bodine, RF; Bill Swanson, CF; Chester "Chet" Ploza, 2B; Gary Wykoff, RF, P, one article mentions he is the son of HOD player Nick Wykoff—probably Dick Wykoff; Hank Robinson, SS; Chuck Edge, LF; Ted Russ, C; Bill Carluccio, 1B; Jack Garrett, P; Sam Zelms, P. Players with no first names listed: Leeves, LF; Poiszaj, CF; Barik, RF; Sells, CF; Evers, SS.

* * *

From mid–April through mid–September 1946, second baseman/pitcher Lou Hummel and his brother, catcher Dick Hummel, played their only season with the House of David. They discussed it as their most memorable summer. During their journey, Dick kept a day-to-day travel journal for his daughter. Note: All listings here are just as they appeared in Mr. Hummel's journal.

April

(12) Texarkana, Texas, (13) Tyler, Texas, (14) Lufkin, Texas, (15) Tyler, Texas, (16) Texarkana, Texas, (17–18) Paris, Texas, Sherman, Texas, (20) Quanah, Texas, (21) Clovis, New Mexico, (22–23) Albuquerque, New Mexico, (24–25) Amarillo, Texas, (26–27–28) Waco, Texas, (29) Beaumont, Texas, (30) Austin, Texas.

May

(1) Austin, Texas, (2–3) Bayton, Texas, (4) Tyler, Texas, (5) Sulphur Springs, Texas, (6) Oklahoma City, Okla., (7–8) Enid, Okla., (9) Independence, Kan., (10) Junction City, Kan., (11) Eldorado, Kan., ((12) Wichita, Kan., (13) Dodge City, Kan., (14) Hays, Kan., (15) Russell, Kan., (16) Salina, Kan., (17) Manhattan, Kan., (18) Arkansas City, Kan., (19) McPherson, Kan., (20) Clinton, Mo., (21) Jefferson City, Mo., (22) Pittsburgh, Kan., (23) Tulsa, Okla., (24) Wichita, Kan., (25) Salina, Kan., (26–27) Kansas City, Kan., (28) Belleville, IL, (29) Lafayette, IL, (30) Cincinnati, Ohio, (31) Springfield, Ohio.

June

(1) Newark, Ohio, (2) Columbus, Ohio, (3) Warren, Ohio, (4) travel day, (5) Watertown, NY, (6) Harrisville, NY, (7) Governor, NY, (8) Oswego, NY, (9) Rochester, NY, (10) Batavia, NY, (11) Erie, PA, (12) Irvine, PA, (13) Norwalk, Ohio, (14) E. Liverpool, Ohio, (15) Lima, Ohio, (16) Gas City, Ind., (17) Muncie, Ind., (18) Ft. Wayne, Ind., (19) Holland, Mich., (20) St. Joe, Mich., (21) Muskegon, Mich., (22) Muscatine, Mich., (23) Woodstock, Mich., (24) Madison, Wisc., (25) Black River Falls, Wisc., (26) Eau Claire, Wisc., (27) St. Cloud, Minn., (28) Watertown, SD, (29) Huron, SD, (30), Council Bluff, Iowa.

July

(1) Sioux Falls, SD, (2) Fargo, ND, (3) travel day, (4) Billings, Mont., (5) Great Falls, Mont., (6) Helena, Mont., (7) Missoula, Mont., (8) Kellogg, Idaho, (9) Lewiston, Idaho, (10) Walla Walla, Wash., (11) Yakima, Wash., (12) Everett, Wash., (13–18 omitted) (19) Bremerton, Wash., (20) Ft. Louis, Wash., (21) Bellington, Wash., (22) Tacoma, Wash., (23) Centralia, Wash., (24) Portland, Oregon, (25) Yakima, Wash., (26) Albany, Oregon, (27) Eugene, Oregon, (28) Roseburg, Oregon, (29) Medford, Oregon, (30) Eureka, Cal., (31) Oakland, Cal.

August

(1) San Jose, Cal., (2) Vallejo, Cal., (3–4) Reno, Nev., (5) Visalia, Cal., (6) San Jose, Cal., (7) Salinas, Cal., (8) Bakersfield, Cal., (9) San Bernardino, Cal., (10) Ventura, Cal., (11) Santa Maria, Cal., (12) Stockton, Cal., (13) Medford, Oregon, (14) Portland, Oregon, (15) Seattle, Wash., (16) Spokane, Wash., (17) travel day, (18) Pocatello, Idaho, (19) Salt Lake City, Utah, (20) travel, (21) Denver, Colo., (22) Lexington, Neb., (23) York, Neb., (24) Ft. Dodge, Iowa, (25) Cedar Rapids, Iowa, (26) Bellville, Ill., (27) Jefferson City, Mo. End of month omitted.

September

(1) Muscatine, Iowa, (2) Chicago, Ill., (3) South Bend, Ind., (4) Kenosha, Wisc., (5) Holland, Mich., (6) Muskegon, Mich., (7) travel, (8) Gas City, Ind., (9) Springfield, Ill., (10) Ft. Wayne, Ind., (11) Dayton, Ohio, Benton Harbor, Mich., (13) Canton, Ill., (14) Lost Nation, Iowa, (15) Davenport, Iowa. End of season.

Chapter Notes

Preface

1. Adam Langer, "The Last Days of the House of David," June 30, 1994, www.chicagoreader.com.

Introduction

1. William Donn Rogosin, "Black Baseball: The Life in the Negro Leagues" (PhD diss., University of Texas, 1981), 270.
2. Joel Zoss and John Bowman, *Diamonds in the Rough: The Untold History of Baseball* (Lincoln: University of Nebraska Press, 1989), 419.
3. "The Earliest Known Newspaper Report of a 'Bass-Ball' Challenge," *The Delhi (New York) Gazette*, July 13, 1825, 4.
4. Dean Sullivan, ed., *Early Innings: A Documentary History of Baseball, 1825–1908* (Lincoln: University of Nebraska Press, 1995), 1.
5. John Blassingame, *Slave Testimony: Two Centuries of Letters, Speeches, Interviews and Autobiographies* (Baton Rouge: University of Louisiana Press, 1977), 655–77.
6. Ibid., 657.
7. Lawrence B. Hogan, *Shades of Glory: The Negro Leagues and the Story of African-American Baseball* (Washington, D.C.: National Geographic Society, 2007), 6.
8. Mark Ribowsky, *A Complete History of the Negro Leagues, 1884–1955* (New York: Birch Lane Press, 1995), 11–12.
9. Todd Boyd, *African American and Popular Culture* (Chicago: University of Chicago Press, 2008), 31.
10. "Spirit of the Times, Formation of the National Association of Base Ball Players in New York (1857)," in *Early Innings*, ed. Dean Sullivan (Lincoln: University of Nebraska Press, 1995), 22.
11. Michael E. Lomax, *Black Baseball Entrepreneurs, 1860–1901* (Syracuse, NY: Syracuse University Press, 2003), 21.
12. Charles C. Alexander, *Our Game: An American Baseball History* (New York: Henry Holt Publications, 1997), 14.
13. Leslie A. Heaphy, *The Negro Leagues 1869–1960* (Jefferson, NC: McFarland, 2003), 10.
14. Lomax, *Black Baseball Entrepreneurs, 1860–1901*, 28.
15. Timeline of Events in Professional Black Baseball, www.negroleaguebaseball.com.
16. Negro League Baseball, Historical Timeline, www.cnlb.org.
17. University of Pennsylvania Archives & Records Center, "Penn's First Organized Sport," www.upenn.edu.
18. Ibid.
19. "Long Innings," *Harvard Magazine*, August 2013, https://harvardmagazine.com/2013/07/long-innings.
20. "Baseball," *Brooklyn Daily Eagle*, April 30, 1860, 2.
21. Bert Soloman, *The Baseball Timeline in Association with Major League Baseball* (New York: DK Publishing, 2001), 27.
22. "The Brooklyn Excelsiors: Baseball's First Road Gang," www.nationalpastimemuseum.com./brooklynexcelsiors.
23. "The Grand Excursion of the Brooklyn Excelsiors," *Troy Daily Whig*, July 4, 1860, https://sabr.org/bioproject.
24. "Negro Baseball League Timeline," https://www.thoughtco.com/negro-baseball-league-timeline-45421.
25. Geoffrey C. Ward and Ken Burns, *Baseball, An Illustrated History* (New York: Knopf, 1994), 13–14.
26. Jim Miklich, "Jim Creighton," 2016, www.19cbaseball.com.
27. "The Premature Death of Baseball's First Superstar," *Brooklyn Eagle*, October 20, 1862, in Sullivan, *Early Innings*, 47.
28. William J. Ryczek, *Baseball's First Inning: A History of the National Pastime Through the Civil War* (Jefferson, NC: McFarland, 2009), 194.
29. John Thorn, "Jim Creighton," https://sabr.bioproject.
30. "A Ball Player's Monument," *Brooklyn Daily Eagle*, February 6, 1898, 9.
31. John P. Rossi, *The National Game: Baseball and American Culture* (Chicago: Ivan R. Dee Publishers, 2000), 11.
32. Nafeesa Syeed, "Exhibit charts black baseball history in Washington, D.C.," May 20, 2008, C5.

33. "Reconstructing Negro League & Latin American Baseball History," July 21, 1947, 12, www.agetype.typepad.com.
34. Syeed, "Exhibit Charts," C5.
35. Jerrold Cassaway, "Octavius Catto and the Pythians of Philadelphia," *Pennsylvania Legacies* (Historical Society of Pennsylvania), May 2007, 5–9.
36. Lomax, *Black Baseball Entrepreneurs, 1860–1901*, 15.
37. Ibid., 26.
38. Sullivan, "Exclusion of African-Americans from NAABP (1867)," *Ball Players' Chronicle*, December 19, 1867, in Sullivan, *Early Innings*, 68–9.
39. Heaphy, *Negro Leagues*, 10–11.
40. Harold Seymour, *Baseball: The People's Game* (New York: Oxford University Press, 1990), 537–8.
41. Christopher De Vine, "Harry Wright," https://sabr.org/bioproject.
42. Terry R. Furst, *Early American Baseball and the Sporting Press: Shaping the Image of the Game* (Jefferson, NC: McFarland, 2014), 129, 140.
43. "Pro Baseball Actually Got Its Start 105 Years Ago," *The Morning Call*, April 18, 1976, 13.
44. Michael Haupert, https://sabr.bioproject.
45. Lomax, *Black Baseball Entrepreneurs, 1860–1901*, 29.
46. Soloman, *The Baseball Timeline*, 30.
47. Timothy M. Gay, *Satch, Dizzy & Rapid Robert* (New York: Simon & Schuster, 2010), 21.
48. Hogan, *Shades of Glory*, 19–22.
49. Heaphy, *Negro Leagues*, 50.
50. "Negro Baseball League Timeline," https://www.thoughtco.com/negro-baseball-league-timeline-45421.
51. Ribowsky, *Complete History of the Negro Leagues*, 23.
52. "It's Time for Baseball to Acknowledge Cap Anson's Role in Erecting the Color Barrier," *Washington Post*, December 2, 2015, 1.
53. "Woody's World," *Des Moines Register*, August 13, 1971, 26.
54. David Fleitz, *The Grand Old Man of Baseball* (Jefferson, NC: McFarland, 2005), 5.
55. David Nemec, *The Beer and Whiskey League* (Guilford, CT: Lyons Press, 2004), 15–16.
56. J. Thomas Hetrick, *Chris Von der Ahe and the St. Louis Browns* (Latham, MD: Scarecrow Press, Inc., 1999), 72–73.
57. "World Champion St. Louis Browns Refuse to Play Cuban Giants," *St. Louis Dispatch*, September 13, 1887.
58. Hetrick, *Chris Von der Ahe*, 72–3.
59. Bruce Chadwick, "Barnstorming America: When the Game Was Black and White, An Illustrated History of the Negro Leagues," *Syracuse University Magazine* 9, no. 4 (1933), 3, 8–13.
60. Jonathan Fraser Light, *The Cultural Encyclopedia of Baseball, Second Edition* (Jefferson, NC: McFarland, 2005), 1012.
61. Ibid.
62. William A. Young, *J.L. Wilkinson and the Kansas City Monarchs: Trailblazers in Black Baseball* (Jefferson, NC: McFarland, 2016), 14–15.
63. "All Nations Team," *Duluth News Tribune*, June 12, 1912, 12.
64. "John Donaldson, The Greatest Pitcher You've Never Heard Of," www.thepostgame.com.
65. "Fan Fodder," *The Kansas City Sun*, February 14, 1920, 8.

Chapter 1

1. Judge Orville Coolidge, *A Twentieth Century History of Berrien County, Michigan*, self-published, 1906, 241.
2. Joseph L. Price, *Rounding the Bases: Baseball and Religion in America* (Macon, GA: Mercer University Press, 2006), 50.
3. Linsey Helen Meldrim, "A Case Study of the Israelite House of David" (Master's thesis., Kent State University, 2012), 2.
4. William F. Ast, III, "100 Years Ago This Month the House of David Religious Colony Took Root in Benton Township," *Herald-Palladium*, March 16, 2003, 1, https://www.heraldpalladium.com/localnews.
5. Clare E. Adkin, Jr., *Brother Benjamin: A History of the Israelite House of David* (Berrien Springs, MI: Andrews University Press, 1990), 42.
6. Peter L. Berger, "Charisma and Religious Innovation: The Social Location of Religious Prophesy," *American Sociological Review* 28, no. 6 (December 1963), 940–950.
7. Meldrim, "A Case Study of the Israelite House of David," 9–12.
8. Adkin, Jr., *Brother Benjamin*, 9.
9. Nick Rennison, "Who Were the Jezreelites?" *BBC History Magazine*, April 2011, 95.
10. Crawford Gribbean, *Evangelical Millennialism in the Trans-Atlantic World, 1500–2000* (London: Palgrave Macmillan, 2011), 92–109.
11. Adkin, Jr., *Brother Benjamin*, 49.
12. Ibid., 7.
13. Ibid., 5.
14. Robert S. Fogarty, *The Righteous Remnant: The House of David* (Kent, OH: Kent State University Press, 1981), 43.
15. Wayne Jackson, "Alexander Campbell and Christ's Church," www.christiancourier.com.
16. "First Wife Testifies," *The Buffalo Times*, May 27, 1923, 47.
17. "House of David Leader Admits He Is a Bigamist," *The Tampa Tribune*, August 13, 1927, 1.
18. Adkin., Jr., *Brother Benjamin*, 7.
19. Fogarty, *The Righteous Remnant*, 43.
20. "Purnell Takes Witness Stand on Own Behalf," *The News-Journal*, August 12, 1927, 1.
21. "Ben's First Wife and 'Queen' Mary Meet Face to Face," *News-Palladium*, May 18, 1927, 9.
22. Meldrim, "A Case Study of the Israelite House of David," 15.
23. Adkin, Jr., *Brother Benjamin*, 11.
24. *History Magazine Notes and Queries*, Vol. 23. (Manchester, NH: S.C. Gould Publishers), 905.

25. Fogarty, *The Righteous Remnant*, 45.
26. Adkin, Jr., *Brother Benjamin*, 12–13.
27. Adkin, Jr., *Brother Benjamin*, 13.
28. *Ibid.*
29. Brian Ziebart, Trustee/Historian/Archivist Israelite House of David, multiple emails and conversations with author.
30. "Highlights in Queen Mary's Career," *The Herald Press*, August 21, 1953, 10.
31. "Son in Defense," *The News-Palladium*, September 21, 1907, 1.
32. "Coy Purnell, Son of King Ben, Dies Following Long Illness," *The Arizona Republic*, January 9, 1924, 1.
33. "Queen Mother Keeps Her Faith As Son of 'King' Goes to Resting Place," *The News-Palladium*, January 30, 1924, 4.
34. "Eight Persons Killed," *The Bismarck Tribune*, February 17, 1903, 2.
35. "Let the Dead Bury the Dead," *The News-Palladium*, February 11, 2006, A2.
36. "Purnells Left Fostoria," *The Palladium-Item*, March 16, 2003, 6.
37. Mary's City of David Archives.
38. Meldrim, "A Case Study of the Israelite House of David," 15.
39. Fogarty, *The Righteous Remnant*, 47.
40. "Text of Judge Fead's Opinion Against the House of David," *The News-Palladium*, November 10, 1927, 10.
41. Meldrim, "A Case Study of the Israelite House of David," 15.
42. "North Berrien Museum Has Something for Everyone," *The Herald-Palladium*, December 14, 1940, 1.
43. "Bicentennial Show Opens Tomorrow," *The News-Palladium*, June 8, 1933, 11.
44. The Berrien County Michigan Genealogy Project, transcribed by Brenda Sears, 2003, 2004.
45. Adkin, Jr., *Brother Benjamin*, 16.
46. Robert P. Sutton, *Modern American Communes: A Dictionary* (Santa Barbara, CA: Greenwood Publishing, 2005), 136.
47. Adkin, Jr., *Brother Benjamin*, 18.
48. "Text of Judge Fead's Opinion Against the House of David," *The News-Palladium*, November 10, 1927, 10.
49. Adkin, Jr., *Brother Benjamin*, 23.
50. *Ibid.*, 18.
51. *Ibid.*, 27.
52. The National Register Informational System, National Register of Historic Places, National Park Service, March 13, 2009.
53. Adkin, Jr., *Brother Benjamin*, 35.
54. Meldrim, "A Case Study of the Israelite House of David," 23.
55. Adkin., Jr., *Brother Benjamin*, 22–3.
56. *Ibid.*, 101–2.
57. Price, *Rounding the Bases*, 54.
58. *Ibid.*, 54.
59. *Ibid.*, 54–5.
60. Ast, III, "100 Years Ago," 1–5.
61. www.maryshouseofdavid.org/homepage.
62. Fogarty, *The Righteous Remnant*, 55.
63. Adkin, Jr., *Brother Benjamin*, 23.
64. Fogarty, *The Righteous Remnant*, 44.
65. Adkin, Jr., *Brother Benjamin*, 24.
66. "Health Found at Springs of Michigan Watering Place," *The Inter Ocean*, June 30, 1912, 24.
67. Fogarty, *The Righteous Remnant*, 67–8.
68. "Something Gone Forever Came Back Last Weekend," *The Herald-Palladium*, November 6, 2011, C5.
69. Brian Ziebart, multiple emails and conversations with author.
70. "San Bernardino Judge Dewhirst Seeks Peace at House of David," *The Los Angeles Herald*, September 17, 1920, 137.
71. Adkin, Jr., *Brother Benjamin*, 40.
72. "Photographer for H. of D. Dead at 77," *The News-Palladium*, January 29, 1963, 12.
73. Adkin, Jr., *Brother Benjamin*, 22.
74. Ronald Taylor, Trustee/Historian/Archivist, The Israelite House of David as Reorganized by Mary Purnell (City if David), interview with author, February 2014.
75. *Ibid.*
76. Price, *Rounding the Bases*, 57.
77. Adkin, Jr., *Brother Benjamin*, 26.
78. "Lake Michigan's Island Mystique," *Michigan History Magazine* 73, no. 2 (March/April 1989), 38.
79. "Michigan's Siberia: The House of David on High Island," *The Appleton Post-Crescent*, June 18, 1986, 2–4.
80. Fogarty, *The Righteous Remnant*, 125.
81. "Free Living Is Creed on High Island," *Wisconsin State Journal*, May 30, 1920, 13.
82. "H.C.L. Solved by Cult Living on High Island," *The Bismarck Tribune*, June 14, 1920, 3.
83. "Sailing Vessel Found Floating Bottom Side Up," . *The Brainerd Daily Dispatch*, October 31, 1921, 1.
84. *Ibid.*
85. Ann Woodward, "High Island Childhood, A Boy's Life with the House of David," *Michigan History Magazine* 73, no. 2 (March/April 1989), 33–39.
86. *Ibid.*
87. Brian Ziebart, multiple emails and conversations with author.
88. Meldrim, "A Case Study of the Israelite House of David," 17.
89. Adkin, Jr., *Brother Benjamin*, 94–5.
90. *The News-Palladium*, November 9, 2007, 6.
91. Meldrim, "A Case Study of the Israelite House of David," 17.
92. Fogarty, *The Righteous Remnant*, 110.
93. "Cult Petition Is Dispatched to Washington: Review of Hansels' Case Sought in New York," *Escanaba Press*, November 20, 1924, 1.
94. "Wreckage of Local Boat Comes Ashore," *The News-Palladium*, December 12, 1921, 1.
95. "House of David Colony Quits," *The Charlotte News*, March 11, 1922, 2.
96. "Warrant Issued for Cult Leader," *The Brooklyn Daily Eagle*, May 21, 1923, 2.

97. "King Ben's Disciples, Lured by Free Press Reward, Furnish Tips," *Detroit Free Press*, June 15, 1923, 1.
98. Brian Ziebart, multiple emails and conversations with author.
99. Fogarty, *The Righteous Remnant*, 113.
100. Ibid., 111.
101. "Purnell Has Witness Seat Own Defense," *Clarion-Ledger*, August 13, 1927, 1.
102. "'King' Purnell Released on $120,000 Bond," *Des Moines Register*, November 18, 1926, 1.
103. Adkin, Jr., *Brother Benjamin*, 150.
104. "Cult Lawyer Peeved When Asked Plans," *Herald-Palladium*, November 15, 1927, 1, 3.
105. "Colony Officials and Leaders Silent as They Get News of Opinion," *The News-Palladium*, November 10, 1927, 14.
106. "'King' Purnell of House of David Dead," *Boston Globe*, December 19, 1927, 10.
107. Meldrim, "A Case Study of Israelite House of David," 22.
108. "Founder of David House Passes On," *Moline Daily Dispatch*, December 19, 1927, 1, 21.
109. *The Herald-Palladium*, June 3, 1929, 1.
110. Adkin, Jr., *Brother Benjamin*, 199.
111. Ibid.
112. Price, *Rounding the Bases*, 64–5
113. "State of Michigan Department of Natural Resources, High Island," www.revolvy.com.
114. "All Colony's Holdings Divided; Two Cults Formed," *The News-Palladium*, February 22, 1930, 1.
115. Adkin, Jr., *Brother Benjamin*, 210–11.
116. "King Ben Exiled from Colony of House of David: Michigan Wins 'Nuisance' Case Against Purnell," *The Chicago Tribune*, November 11, 1927, 4.
117. Ron Taylor, Trustee/Historian/Archivist, The Israelite House of David as Reorganized by Mary Purnell (City if David), interview with author, February 2014.
118. Adkin, Jr., *Brother Benjamin*, 212–14.
119. Ibid., 41.
120. www.maryshouseofdavid.org
121. "Do You Remember: 25 Years Ago," *The News-Palladium*, January 15, 1963, 2.
122. Adkin, Jr., *Brother Benjamin*, 41.
123. Adkin, Jr., *Brother Benjamin*, 266.
124. Ibid., 277.
125. Ibid., 276.
126. "H.T. Dewhirst, Colony Head, May Enter Race for Congress," *The News-Palladium*, June 2, 1936, 1.
127. Data compiled from official sources by Le Roy D. Brandon under the direction of South Trimble, Clerk of the Michigan House of Representatives.
128. "Hoffman Winner by 8,000," *The News-Palladium*, September 16, 1936, 1.
129. Gordon Melton, *Encyclopedia of American Religion, Seventh Edition* Farmington Hills, MI: The Gale Group, 2003).
130. D.C. Allen Archival Collection, 1795–1980, Bentley Historical Library, University of Michigan.
131. Adam Langer, June 30, 1994, www.chicagoreader.com.
132. Florence Rachuig, Saugatuck-Douglas Historical Society Slide Presentation, April 18, 1992, Saugatuck, Michigan.

Chapter 2

1. Ronald Taylor, Trustee/Historian/Archivist, The House of David as Reorganized by Mary Purnell (City of David) interview with author, February 2014.
2. George Wilkes, ed., *The Spirit of the Times Collection, 1868–1892*, April 19, 1873.
3. Brian Ziebart, Trustee/Historian/Archivist Israelite House of David Commune, numerous conversations and emails with author.
4. Scott Simkus, *Outsider Baseball: The Weird World of Baseball on the Fringe,1876–1950* (Chicago: Chicago Review Press, 2014), 187.
5. Randy Roberts, *The Menassa Mauler* (Champaign: University of Illinois Press, 2001), 288.
6. Jeremy D. Bonifiglio: "Stirring Echoes," *South Bend Tribune*, August 12, 2007, 1.
7. Joel Hawkins and Terry Bertolino, *The House of David Baseball Team* (Charleston, SC: Arcadia Publishers, 2000), 10.
8. Adkin, Jr., *Brother Benjamin*, 245–6.
9. Baseball Hall of Fame Museum and Archives, donated material. Articles only, no titles or dates.
10. www.houseofdavidmuseum.org/baseball.
11. Hawkins and Bertolino, *The House of David Baseball Team*, 117.
12. "Old Photo Stirs Memories of Early Baseball," *New-Palladium*, June 2, 1969, 3.
13. "House of David Handily Defeated Onward Athletic Club of Chicago," *Herald-Palladium*, June 19, 1914, 5.
14. "Waites Win Out Over House of David," *News-Palladium*, July 20, 1914, 2.
15. "Chicago All Stars Lose to House of David," *News-Palladium*, August 3, 1914, 4.
16. www.baseball-almanac.com./ballplayers/cyyoung.
17. "Hasn't Played a Game of Ball This Summer," *New Philadelphia Daily Times*, August 27, 1914, 5.
18. "Cy Young Dead at 88," *Taylor Daily Press*, November 4, 1955, 1.
19. Hawkins and Bertolino, *The House of David Baseball Team*, 10.
20. Simkus, *Outsider Baseball*, 25.
21. Ward and Burns, *Baseball: An Illustrated History*, 178.
22. Herald Seymour, *Baseball, The People's Game* (New York: Oxford University Press, 1990), 271.
23. Tygel Papers, "Oral Collections from the Baseball Hall of Fame Museum," 13.
24. Jay Sanford, *Denver Post Tournament, A Project of the Rocky Mountain Chapter of the Soci-*

ety for American Baseball Research (Cleveland, OH: SABR, 2003), 49.

25. Seymour, *Baseball*, 280–84.

26. Matthew Kasper Repplinger II, *Baseball in Denver* (Charleston, SC: Arcadia Publishing, 2013), 45.

27. Eric Mark Stoneberg, "The Denver Post Tournament and Pre-Organized Baseball Integration" (Masters thesis, Arizona State University, 2009), 50.

28. Seymour, *Baseball*, 271.

29. "Oilers Need Angel: Invited to Play in Denver Post Tournament This Year," *Iola Register*, August 23, 1921, 6.

30. Sanford, *Denver Post Tournament*, 1–3.

31. *Ibid.*, 51.

32. *Ibid.*, 5.

33. "Local Pickings," *Fort Scott Daily Monitor*, October 2, 1915, 6.

34. Sanford, *Denver Post Tournament*, 85.

35. "Invitation to Athletes for Ball Tourneys," *Sedalia Democrat*, June 14, 1931.

36. "Uncle Sam's Soldiers Here for Two Days," *News-Palladium*, June 22, 1915, 1.

37. Hawkins and Bertolino, *The House of David Baseball Team*, 10, 11.

38. Compilation of varied newspaper articles, title and sources unidentified.

39. "Diamond Doings," *The News-Palladium*, June 12, 1916, 4.

40. "Good Game House of David Sunday," *The News-Palladium*, August 12, 1916, 3.

41. Baseball Hall of Fame Museum and Archives, donated material. Articles only, no sources or titles.

42. "House of David—Galian in Slugfest At Eden Springs Park," *Chicago Defender*, September 25, 1916, 4.

43. "Two Games Are Taken by Ball Teams of House of David," *News-Palladium*, July 31, 1916, 3.

44. Hawkins and Bertolino, The House of David Research Project, www.peppergame.com.

45. www.maryscityofdavid.org./html/baseball.html.

46. "Good Tilt at House of David," *News-Palladium*, June 17, 1916, 3.

47. Adam Langer, *Last Days of the House of David, Adam Langer Collection 1984–2011*, Chicago Public Library Special Collections and Preservation Division, July 1, 1994.

48. "Feeney's Owls on Field," *Indianapolis Star*, April 29, 1915, 14.

49. "Amateur Baseball," *Pittsburgh Post-Gazette*, March 19, 1916, 20.

50. "Independent Baseball Outfits Prepare for Opening Season," *Pittsburgh Post-Gazette*, March 13, 1921, 22.

51. "Citizen Daily," *Brooklyn Daily Eagle*, April 12, 1919, 5.

52. "Inside Stuff," *Oakland Tribune*, January 20, 1917, 7.

53. "Some Whiskers with Baseball," *Chanute Daily Tribune*, September 20, 1917, 6.

54. "Queerest Baseball Team in Existence," *Fort Wayne Journal-Gazette*, September 23, 1917, 10.

55. Richard E. Derby, Jr., and Jim Coleman, "House of David Baseball," *Society for American Baseball Research* 14 (1994), 9.

56. Hawkins and Bertolino, *The House of David Baseball Team*, 11.

57. *Ibid.*

58. Simkus, *Outsider Baseball*, 193.

59. Baseball Hall of Fame Museum and Archives, donated material, articles only without titles and dates.

60. "Austrian Heir and His Wife Shot to Death After Escaping Bomb," *Washington Herald*, June 29, 1914, 1.

61. Woodrow Wilson: Message to Congress, 63rd Congress, 2nd Session, Senate Doc. No. 566 (Washington, 1914), 3–4.

62. Fogarty, *Righteous Remnant*, 101–2.

63. "Fort Custer Training Center, Michigan National Guard," www.minationalguard.com.

64. "Whiskers Arrive at Camp Custer," *New Philadelphia Daily Times*, November 26, 1917, 2.

65. Clare E. Adkin, Jr., "Interview with Colony Member Melvin Tucker in Benton Harbor," June 3, 1989, 96–7.

66. "Custer Peace Pair Get Year," *Escanaba Morning Press*, July 10, 1918, 3.

67. "Conscientious Objectors Will Work on Farms," *Chicago Daily Tribune*, July 3, 1918, 7.

68. "All Around Our Town," *News-Palladium*, March 15, 1947, 1, 3.

69. "House of David in Bad with Village," *News-Palladium*, August 9, 1918, 4.

70. "Says Colony Is Helping Government: Francis Thorpe Defends House of David in Face of Censor," *News-Palladium*, July 31, 1918, 1.

71. "Letters from People," *News-Palladium*, September 18, 1918, 4.

72. "Free Grand Patriotic Display of Distinctive House of David Fireworks," *News-Palladium*, July 27, 1918, 2.

73. "House of David Ball Park: Goshen Grays House of David," *News-Palladium*, July 7, 1918, 2.

74. "Stealing Wall Schang's Stuff," *Washington Herald*, January 14, 1918, 10.

75. "Help in War Effort by Conserving Our Baseballs," *Pittsburgh Daily Post*, February 15, 1918, 9.

76. "Ball Season Opens Sunday," *Herald Press*, April 25, 1918, 5.

77. Adkin, Jr., *Brother Benjamin*, 25.

78. Ronald Taylor interview with author, February 2014.

79. David W. Blight, "Teaching a People's History: The First Decoration Day," 2001, www.zinnedproject.org .

80. "House of David Shut Out 2–0 in First Game," *Chicago Defender*, May 6, 1918, 5.

81. Hawkins and Bertolino, *The House of David Baseball Team*, 14.

82. Heaphy, *Negro Leagues*, 9, 10.

83. "Ring Lardner Column," *Medford Mail Tribune*, September 26, 1933, 4.
84. Ring Lardner, "In the Wake of the News," *Chicago Daily Tribune*, July 9, 1918, 11.
85. Ring Lardner, "In the Wake of the News," *Lincoln Evening Journal*, July 11, 1918, 11.
86. "The Influenza Pandemic of 1918," *Journal of American Medical Association, Final Edition*, https://virus.stanford.edu.
87. Heaphy, *Negro Leagues*, 38.
88. Simkus, *Outsider Baseball*, 134–5.
89. "Official Final Standings of American League Clubs," *Boston Globe*, October 1, 1919 10.
90. "Eight White Sox Players Are Indicted on Charges of Fixing the 1919 World Series; Cicotte Got $10,000 and Jackson $5,000," *New York Times*, September 29, 1920, 1.
91. "Israelites Open Season," *Herald Press*, April 25, 1919, 5.
92. "Mooney and Hansel Scheduled Battery," *Chicago Defender*, April 28, 1919, 5.
93. "House of David More Aggressive on the Diamond," *Chicago Defender*, May 31, 1919, 4.
94. "Chicago Hartford Giants, Fastest Traveling Colored Team in the World, vs. The House of David," *News-Palladium*, 5, 1919, 2.
95. Price, *Rounding the Bases*, 69–70.
96. "Speeds Win; Israelites Lose Game," *News-Palladium*, August 25, 1919, 1.
97. "House of David Loses Fast Tilt," *News-Palladium*, July 15, 1918, 3.
98. "Only Their Foliage Keeps Them in the Busher Parks," *Reading News*, July 29, 1920, 6.
99. "Long-Haired, Bearded Player Sought by Cubs, and His Teammates," *St. Louis Dispatch*, November 25, 1919, 26.
100. "The House of David Is Beaten," *Scranton Republican*, August 28, 1920, 16.
101. Douglas S. Malan, *Muzzy Field, Tales from a Forgotten Ballpark* (Bloomington, IN: iUniverse, 2009), 84–5.
102. "Long-Haired Baseball Wizard Offered Place on Yankees with Babe Ruth," *Boston Post*, July 25, 1920, 72.
103. Malan, *Muzzy Field*, 85.
104. "Baseball at House of David," *News-Palladium*, October 16, 1919, 1.
105. "Susie and Emma Make a Great Battery: House of David Girls as Ball Players Show Speed and Class," *News-Palladium*, June 2, 1919, 4.
106. "Baseball—July 4, Two Games at House of David Park," *News Palladium*, July 1, 1919, 2.
107. "H. of D. Girls Will Meet All-American," *News-Palladium*, June 19, 1919, 5.
108. Hawkins and Bertolino, *The House of David Baseball Team*, 15.
109. Price, *Rounding the Bases*, 55.
110. Hawkins and Bertolino, *The House of David Baseball Team*, 15.
111. Ibid.
112. "Long-Haired, Bearded Player Sought by Cubs, and His Teammates," 26.

Chapter 3

1. "100 Years of Ford," *Lincoln Journal Star*, July 27, 2003, 107.
2. "Birth of Ford Assembly Line Put Manufacturing in New Era," *Courier-Journal*, October 14, 1988, 23.
3. Compilation of several newspaper articles from 1920s era.
4. "Installation of Talkies at Havre Theatre Marks New Era in Moviedom Here," *Havre Daily News*, July 26, 1929, 8.
5. "World Pays Tribute to Daring Young American for Successful Paris Trip," *Times Signal*, May 22, 1927.
6. www.thedeadballera.com.
7. https://amp.mlb.com/44049012-the-evolution-of-baseball.amp.html.
8. "Value of Spitball Clearly Demonstrated," *Pittsburgh Post-Gazette*, December 20, 1914, 20.
9. "Pithy Tips from the Sport Ticker," *Philadelphia Inquirer*, August 15, 1926, 64.
10. "Fatal Pitch: Mays and Chapman Are Forever Linked by the Only Ball That Killed," *St. Louis Post-Dispatch*, August 27, 1995, 36.
11. "Spitball Hurlers Losing Out but Few Mound Veterans Remain," *El Paso Herald*, November 30, 1920, 10.
12. https://www.baseball-reference.com/bullpen/Spitball.
13. "Baseball Hall of Famer Burleigh Grimes Is Dead," *Santa Fe New Mexican*, December 10, 1895, 14.
14. "Babe Ruth Is Sold to New York Yankees," *Scranton Republican*, January 6, 1920, 14.
15. https://baseballhall.org/hall-of-famers/landis-kenesaw.
16. "Landis Threatens to Quit but Later Accepts Ball Dictatorship," *Pittsburgh Daily Post*, January 12, 1921, 9.
17. "Segregation Timeline," *Philadelphia Daily News*, July 2, 1996, 64.
18. Heaphy, *The Negro Leagues*, 5.
19. Timothy Odzer, "Rube Foster," https://sabr.org/bioproject.
20. African-American Registry, www.aaregistry.org.
21. "Rube Foster, Negro Diamond Mogul, Dead," *Cumberland Evening Times*, December 11, 1930, 16.
22. "Sport Scribe," *Kansas City Sun*, December 25, 1920, 4.
23. Odzer, "Rube Foster."
24. Mark Ribowsky, *Complete History of the Negro Leagues, 1884–1955* (New York: Carol Publishing Group, 1995), 137.
25. Heaphy, *Negro Leagues*, 56–71.
26. "Ed Bolden Dies at Darby; Czar of Negro League Baseball," *Delaware County Daily Times*, September 29, 1950, 1.
27. Heaphy, *Negro Leagues*, 56.
28. "Tom Wilson," https://nlbemuseum.com/nlbemuseum/history/players/wilsont.html.
29. William J. Plott, "Food for Thought Lec-

ture Presentation," July 12, 2016, www.archives.alabama.gov.
30. Brian McKenna, "Gus Greenlee," https://sabr.org/bioproject.
31. https://history.com/topics/sports/negroleague-baseball.
32. "Paige Defeats Monarchs in 2–1 Thriller: Satch Wins Three in Five Days in Big Denver Tourney," *Pittsburgh Courier*, August 18, 1934, 14.
33. https://www.britannica.com/sports/Negro-league.
34. Paul DeBono, *The Chicago American Giants* (Jefferson, NC: McFarland, 2007), 90.
35. Justice B. Hill, "Negro League Legacy: Traveling Show," http://mlb.mlb.com/mlb/history/mlb_negro_leagues_story.jsp?story=barnstormin.
36. Janet Bruce, *The Kansas City Monarchs, Champions of Black Baseball* (Lawrence: University Press of Kansas, 1985), 61.
37. *Ibid.*
38. "House of David Sued by Former Cult Members," *Arkansas Democrat*, November 4, 1921, 14.
39. "From Farm Boy to Itinerant Preacher Purnell Lived to Head Wealthy Cult," *Battle Creek Enquirer*, December 19, 1927, 11.
40. Malan, *Muzzy Field*, 86.
41. Derby, Jr. and Coleman, "House of David Baseball," 7–10.
42. Hawkins and Bertolino, *The House of David Baseball Team*, 20.
43. *Brooklyn Daily Eagle*, August 21, 1996, B1–2.
44. Jerry Kirshenbaum, "The Hairiest Team of All," *Sports Illustrated*, April 13, 1970, 104–06.
45. Derby, Jr. and Coleman, "House of David Baseball," 8–10.
46. "Hyatsville Beats House of David," *Washington Herald*, April 26, 1920, 11.
47. "House of David Odd, but Oh My How Those Whiskered and Long Haired Persons Can Play Ball!" *Brooklyn Daily Eagle*, July 18, 1920, 55.
48. "Long Haired Baseball Wizard Offered Place on Yankees with Babe Ruth," 72.
49. "Mid-Week Pictorial," *New York Times*, July 29, 1920, 17.
50. Alan M. Klein, *Baseball on the Border* (Princeton, NJ: Princeton University Press, 1997), 57.
51. "Long-Haired Baseball Wizard Offered Place On Yankees with Babe Ruth," 72.
52. "Ballplayer Spurns Offer," *Ogden Standard Examiner*, January 28, 1922, 6.
53. www.baseball-almanac.com/BabeRuth.
54. "Their Foliage Keeps Them in the Busher Ranks," *New Castle Herald*, July 26, 1920, 8.
55. "Baseball Team Is Ready for the Big Season," *News-Herald*, May 2, 1922, 3.
56. "Mooney Rejects Yankees Offer," *Reading News Times*, July 19, 1920, 6.
57. Malan, *Muzzy Field*, 85.
58. "The Sporting World from All Angles," *The New York Age*, July 21, 1920, 6.
59. "House of David Team Tomorrow," *Brooklyn Daily Eagle*, August 20, 1920, 6.
60. "The House of David Cannot Prevail Against Old J.P.," *Brooklyn Daily Eagle*, August 22, 1920, 54.
61. "Whiskerless Joe Makes No Hit with House of David," *Brooklyn Daily Eagle*, August 29, 1920, 55.
62. "Foliage No Handicap for Those Players," *Decatur Daily News*, August 1, 1920, 6.
63. "House of David to Play Here: Famous Long Hair Stars Will Battle Bethlehem," *Harrisburg Telegraph*, August 5, 1920, 15.
64. "House of David Badly Shaken: Lose Game to Bethlehem Steel Leaguers," *Harrisburg Telegraph*, August 7, 1920, 1.
65. "House of David Prove Fiasco in Thursday's Game: Three Thousand Fans Out to See Much Heralded Aggregation," *Evening Post*, August 6, 1920, 5.
66. "Tall Cedars of Lebanon Cut Hair and Whiskers of House of David Men," *Lebanon Daily News*, August 6, 1920, 12.
67. "Washington Giants Defeat House of David," *Washington Herald*, August 10, 1920, 6.
68. "House of David Odd," *Brooklyn Daily Eagle*, July 18, 1920, 55.
69. "House of David Team Is Beaten: Scranton Nine Trims Wihskers [sic: Whiskers] of Unique Ballplayers," *Scranton Republican*, August 28, 1920, 16.
70. "House of David Team Wants Date with Kane," *The Kane Republican*, August 31, 1920, 3
71. "Titusville Game to Attract Local Fans," *News-Herald*, September 8, 1920, 11.
72. "Peace Descends on Ball World After Meeting," *Journal and Courier*, January 13, 1921, 10.
73. "Landis Scores Ruth and Others in Baseball Row," *Buffalo Enquirer*, October 17, 1921, 1.
74. "Play Three Innings in Sea of Mud," *Logansport Pharos-Tribune*, April 23, 1921, 10.
75. *Ibid.*
76. Malan, *Muzzy Field*, 85.
77. Price, *Rounding the Bases*, 78.
78. "Bearded Baseball Team Ready for Season, Develops Stars," *Times-Herald*, May 2, 1922, 10.
79. Malan, *Muzzy Field*, back cover.
80. Malan, *Muzzy Field*, 86.
81. "Evansville Wins," *Courier-Journal*, May 1, 1922, 3.
82. "Riot Ends Ball Game," *News-Palladium*, July 5, 1922, 5.
83. "Riot Ends Ballgame," *News-Palladium*, July 15, 1922, 8; "Israelite First Team, Flushed with Victory, Returns from Big Tour," *News-Palladium*, September 29, 1922, 5.
84. *News-Palladium*.
85. "Israelite First Team, Flushed with Victory, Returns from Tour," *News-Palladium*, September 8, 1922, 4.
86. Adkin, Jr., *Brother Benjamin*, 244–62.
87. Jonathan Fraser Light, *The Cultural Encyclo-

pedia of Baseball, Second Edition (Jefferson, NC: McFarland, 1997), 694.

88. "Two Games Won by Palmyra," *Harrisburg Evening News*, July 7, 1936, 13.

89. "Bearded Boys Have Won 33 of 37 Games," *Pampa Daily News*, May 7, 1935, 3.

90. "Deal Recalls Glory Days of House of David Team," *News-Palladium*, July 18, 1962, 20.

91. Hawkins and Bertolino, The House of David Research Project, www.peppergame.com.

92. "Fans to Follow Chairs," *Sheboygan Press Telegraph*, September 30, 1923, 5.

93. Malan, *Muzzy Field*, 89.

94. Hawkins and Bertolino, *The House of David Baseball Team*, 68.

95. Adkin, Jr., *Brother Benjamin*, 241.

96. Seymour, *Baseball*, 271.

97. "Israelites to Open 123 Ball Season Sunday," *Herald-Press*, May 11, 1923, 2.

98. "House of David to Open Baseball Season Sunday," *News-Palladium*, May 10, 1923, 1.

99. "Season's First Game Victory for Israelites," *News-Palladium*, May 14, 1923, 5.

100. "Fort Wayne Defeated by Israel 3–2," *News-Palladium*, May 30, 1923, 7.

101. "From Farm Boy to Itinerant Preacher Purnell Lived to Head a Wealthy Cult," *Battle Creek Enquirer*, December 19, 1927, 11.

102. "The House of David Is Now Falling Down," *Macon Republican*, December 7, 1926, 2.

103. Fogarty, *The Righteous Remnant*, 112.

104. "Buckeye Brevities," *Coshocton Tribune*, June 18, 1923, 2.

105. Mears Monthly Auctions, "Maggie Riley $10,000 Wonder Girl," Lot 684, www.mearsonlineauctions.com.

106. "Norwoods Book Riley's Devil Dogs," *Asbury Park Press*, June 27, 1924, 13.

107. "House of David Baseball Team Plays Maggie Riley Girl Nine at Polo Grounds," *Springfield Republican*, July 21, 1923, 11.

108. "Davidites Swamped by Hoosier Sluggers," *Pittsburgh Courier*, August 25, 1923, 7.

109. "Eden's Lads Defeated in 12 Hot Frames," *News-Palladium*, September 24, 1923, 5.

110. "Darkness at Fitz's Arena Halts Battle: Local Fans See Baseball in Closing of Season," *News-Palladium*, October 8, 1922, 5.

111. "Esther Hansel Again Branded 'Liar' in Court," *Herald Press*, August 3, 1927, 1.

112. "Be-whiskered Ball Players May Play Here," *Oakland Tribune*, September 5, 1923, 24.

113. "Israelite Ball Team Prepares for Season: Long-Haired Semi-Pros to Hit Trail Early This Year," *News-Palladium*, April 18, 1924, 5.

114. "Racism One Obstacle Owens Couldn't Hurdle," *Journal News*, April 25, 1999, 39.

115. www.baseball-reference.com/jesseowens.

116. "Thorpe's Daughter Relieved," *Rocky Mount Telegram*, October 14, 1982, 12.

117. "Jim Thorpe Medals Returned," *Indianapolis Star*, October 14, 1982, 1.

118. "Thorpe, Indian Wonder, Here Tomorrow," *News-Palladium*, April 26, 1924, 5.

119. "Record Crowd to See Clash on Local Lot: Local Team in Best of Shape with Bearded Batters," *Davenport Democrat and Leader*, August 1, 1924, 5.

120. "They're Knocking 'Em Down," *News-Palladium*, July 17, 1924, 5.

121. "House of David Nine Strong Combination," *Journal News*, June 11, 1924, 8.

122. "Grays Humble Famous House of David Team 7–3 Yesterday; Vierit's [sic: Vieritz] Arm Paralyzed by a Hot One from Griffith," *Times Recorder*, June 20, 1924, 14.

123. "Bewhiskered Men Play Here Wednesday," *Daily Times*, June 26, 1924, 3.

124. Francis Thorpe Photo Caption, *Coshocton Tribune*, June 26, 1924, 11.

125. "Seats for Game Here Saturday to Be Reserved," *Davenport Democrat and Leader*, July 30, 1924, 7.

126. "House of David Team Attracts Much Attention," *Indiana Gazette*, August 20, 1924, 6.

127. *Indiana Gazette*, August 25, 1924, 1.

128. "House of David Bowed to Indiana by Score of 21–6," *Indiana Gazette*, August 26, 1924, 3.

129. "Israelite Barnstormers Home After Another Winning Trip," *News-Palladium*, September 13, 1924, 5.

130. *Ibid.*

131. "Israelite Nine Scores Only One Run in 19-Inning Battle," *News-Palladium*, September 15, 1924, 5.

132. "House of David Pitcher Signs with Fort Smith," *Argus-Leader*, February 20, 1925, 7.

133. "Long Haired Hurler of House of David Signed by Harper Lloyd; Miller Expected to Prove a Big Drawing Card," *Springfield Leader*, February 23, 1925, 8.

134. "House of David Slabman Signs with Fort Smith," *Daily News*, February 24, 1925, 9.

135. "Fort Smith Twins Start Tonight on Lengthy Road Tour: House of David Stars to Appear This Season with Harper's Team," *Springfield Leader*, April 1, 1925, 8.

136. https://www.baseball-reference.com/register/player/fog2?+miller00211.

137. "Weber Blues Halt Colony, 6–2; Daisy Stops HD Nine, 6–0," *News-Palladium*, June 16, 1930, 6.

138. "Home Runs Aid House of David Defeat Joe Green's Giants," *News-Palladium*, July 14, 1930, 10.

139. Hawkins and Bertolino, *The House of David Baseball Team*, 61.

140. "Smelterites Grab Break and Win Close Contest from Bearded Men," *Independent Record*, June 5, 1927, 12.

141. https://www.baseball-reference.com/register/player.fog?=faust-001wal.

142. The House of David Baseball Team Research Project, www.peppergame.com.

143. "Both Outfits Are Beaten in Double Tilts," *News-Palladium*, July 6, 1925, 10.

144. "House of David to Show a Strong Team

on Sunday," *Davenport Democrat and Leader*, June 11, 1925, 7.
145. "House of David First Team Is Going Good," *News-Palladium*, September 5, 1925, 5.
146. "House of David Defeated Ottawa, 10–4," *Iola Register*, September 19, 1925, 3.
147. "First Game Arranged for This Weekend," *News-Palladium*, October 6, 1925, 5.
148. Simkus, *Outsider Baseball*, 192.
149. "Iowa Man Will Plan Tour for House of David," *Davenport Democrat and Leader*, March 29, 1925, 26.
150. "Riverside Loses 3–1; Famous House of David Wins Eleven Inning Thriller," *Iowa City Press*, June 17, 1925, 11.
151. "House of David Ball Team Again to Hit Trail," *News-Palladium*, March 10, 1925, 5.
152. *Greene Recorder*, August 19, 1925, 4.
153. "House of David Band 25 Weeks on Road," *News-Palladium*, May 16, 1925, 8.
154. "House of David Nine Drops Game to K-B's," *Suburbanite Economist*, August 5, 1925, 7.
155. "Sport Chatter," *Emporia Daily Gazette*, September 18, 1925, 1.
156. "House of David Ball Club Probably Wins Lots of Games by a Whisker," *Joplin Globe*, October 4, 1925, 16.
157. "House of David Club Plays Here," *Sedalia Democrat*, October 7, 1925, 2.
158. *News-Palladium*, February 25, 1926, 1, 9.
159. *Quad City Times*, February 16, 1926, 4.
160. "Bewhiskered Aggregation Long on Beards and Flowing Locks Will Clash with Rexmen in Twilight Contest," *Billings Gazette*, July 11, 1926, 10.
161. "The Beard Growers Play Two Games with Havre," *Havre Daily News*, July 19, 1926, 3.
162. "Brief Bits of Sports Gossip," *Manitowoc Herald Times*, June 7, 1926, 11.
163. Tom Dunkel, *Color Blind* (New York: Atlantic Monthly Press, 2011), 314–5.
164. "House of David Team to Appear at Miller Park," *Lancaster Eagle-Gazette*, July 27, 1949, 11.
165. "Ball Players to Wear Long Hair," *Winnipeg Tribune*, August 5, 1926, 11.
166. "House of David Ball Team Ties with Stars," *Winnipeg Tribune*, August 7, 1926, 14.
167. " Long Haired Ball Team Defeats All Stars 4–0," *Winnipeg Tribune*, August 9, 1926, 11.
168. "Benjamin Purnell Under Arrest; Seized at Midnight at Colony," *News-Palladium*, November 17, 1926, 1.
169. "House of David Is Now Falling Down," 2.
170. Adkin, Jr., *Brother Benjamin*, 145–6.
171. "Baseball Series Here Wednesday: House of David and Colored Giants Play First Game at Wesley Park," *Winnipeg Tribune*, August 16, 1927, 13.
172. "Bearded Ball Players Take Opener from Colored Giants: House of David Team Noses Out Close Win," *Winnipeg Tribune*, August 18, 1927, 12.
173. "House of David and Giants Stage Thrilling Finish," *Winnipeg Tribune*, August 9, 1927, 14.
174. "Bearded Ball Players Take Opener from Colored Giants," 12.
175. "King Benjamin in Admission of Being Bigamist," *Sedalia Democrat*, August 19, 1927, 8.
176. "'King' Benjamin Is Released on Bonds," *The Pantagraph*, November 18, 1926, 1.
177. "King Ben Is in Law's Toils," *Richmond Item*, November 18, 1926, 1–2.
178. "King Benjamin, Famous Cult Leader, Dead," *Escanaba Daily Press*, December 20, 1927, 1.
179. "The Eagle," *Sporting News*, November 29, 1927, 3.
180. "Connell to Hurl Against David Nine," *Modesto News-Herald*, April 16, 1927, 4.
181. "House of David Nine to Play Woodland Club Here Thursday at 3:30 O'clock," *Woodland Daily Democrat*, April 19, 1927, 4.
182. "Fans Hopped Up Over Game with House of David Nine Wednesday Afternoon," *Klamath Falls Evening Journal*, April 25, 1927, 13.
183. "Pelican Nine Is Victorious: Pulls Upset and Defeats House of David," *Klamath Falls Evening Journal*, April 28, 1927, 8.
184. "Bend Elks Beat House of David in Best Ball Game of Season," *The Bend Bulletin,* May 11, 1927, 2.
185. *Ibid.*
186. *Manitowoc Herald-Times,* May 17, 1927, 8.
187. Seymour, *Baseball*, 206.
188. Bill Heward and Dimitri V. Gat, *Some Are Called Clowns* (New York: Thomas Crowell, 1974), 73.
189. *Ibid.*
190. "Sports Stew," *Odessa American*, June 29, 1952, 12.
191. Seymour, *Baseball*, 275.
192. Simkus, *Outsider Baseball*, 193–4.
193. "Herald Mail Bag," *Decatur Herald*, May 2, 1928, 6.
194. Kirshenbaum, "The Hairiest Team of All," 104–06.
195. *The Dugout, Vol. 3, No. 1* (Bisbee, AZ: Friends of Warren Ball Park, 2011), page unlisted.
196. "Along the Line," *Decatur Evening Herald* (date not legible), 1928, 20.
197. "Four Bismarck Errors Donate Game to Daves," *Bismarck Tribune*, June 25, 1928, 8.
198. Hawkins and Bertolino, *The House of David Baseball Team*, 28.
199. "House of David Takes Two Games from Giants," *The Winnipeg Tribune*, August 7, 1928, 16.
200. "Cult Team Is Hard-Pressed by Imposters," *Chillicothe Tribune*, October 13, 1928, 6.
201. Hawkins and Bertolino, *The House of David Baseball Team*, 28.
202. "Clash Between State, Colony," *Escanaba Daily Press*, January 4, 1928, 2.
203. Brian Ziebart, Trustee,/Historian/Archivist Israelite House of David, multiple emails and conversations with author.
204. Price, *Rounding the Bases*, 60.

205. "Two Teams to Hit Road for Israelites," *News-Palladium*, February 20, 1929, 12.
206. "Walker Leaves Israel's 'Official' Traveling Outfit," *News-Palladium*, March 27, 1929, 12.
207. Adkin, Jr., *Brother Benjamin*, 203–4.
208. "Three Oaks Plays Here Tomorrow," *News Palladium*, May 29, 1929, 10.
209. "Walker to Take Israel's Squad to Hot Springs Soon," *News-Palladium*, March 14, 1929, 12.
210. *News-Palladium*, July 3, 1929, 12.
211. "Coaches Call First Workout on Diamonds: Israel's Team Plays First Game Here on April 28," *News-Palladium*, April 12, 1929, 16.
212. "Two Teams to Hit the Road for Israelites," *News-Palladium*, February 20, 1929, 12.
213. "House of David Board Acts to Halt Thorpe Team," *News-Palladium*, March 27, 1929, 15.
214. "Thorpe Steals March on Baseball Rivals, Takes Team South to Train," *News-Palladium*, March 16, 1929, 9.
215. "Thorpe Makes Warm Reply to Dewhirst," *News-Palladium*, February 25, 1929, 9.
216. Chriss Lyon, "Fred 'Killer' Burke, Charles Skelly: A Fateful Meeting in Berrien County," https://www.berriencounty.org/419/FredBurke---CharlesSkelly.
217. Don Gittersonke, "Baseball's Bearded Boys," Self Published Booklet, University of Michigan, 1996, 71.
218. "Walker Leaves with Israel's 'Official' Traveling Outfit," 12.
219. "House of David Club Will Furnish Opposition for Joplin Here Today," *News-Palladium*, March 24, 1929, 10.
220. "Ex-Catcher's Still Flying High: Deal Recalls Glory Days of House of David Team," *News-Palladium*, July 18, 1962, 20.
221. "The House of David Team Plays Here Thursday," *Angola Herald*, May 17, 1929, 1.
222. "House of David Team Plays Here Next Week: Local Fans Will Have a Chance to See Snake Siddle in Detective Disguise," *Winnipeg Tribune*, June 1, 1929, 23.
223. "What's What In Sports Circles," *Winnipeg Tribune*, June 5, 1929, 17.
224. "Arnison Pitches Great Ball to Beat Bearded Players," *Winnipeg Tribune*, June 7, 1929, 14.
225. "Local All-Stars Beat House of David Team: Winnipeg Boys Once More Too Much for Bearded Ball Players at Wesley Park," *Winnipeg Tribune*, June 8, 1929, 9.
226. "House of David Ball Club to Play in Town," *Mount Carmel Item*, June 26, 1929, 6.
227. "Novelty Side Show and Good Baseball for Cricket Field," *Altoona Mirror*, June 27, 1929, 22.
228. "Porta Hit in Eighth Defeats House of David Team," *Altoona Mirror*, June 29, 1929, 16.
229. "Bearded Boys Lose Two," *Berkshire Eagle*, August 28, 1952, 23.
230. "Greenberg Helps Bay Parkway Win," *Brooklyn Daily Eagle*, June 3, 1929, 17.
231. "Colony Nine Plays Poorly in Field but Wins 10–5," *News-Palladium*, July 8, 1929, 10.
232. "Bend Takes Holiday to Attend Ballgame," *Bend Bulletin*, July 29, 1929, 1.
233. "Long Hairs to Play Senators Wednesday Eve," *Daily Capital Journal*, July 23, 1929, 3.
234. "La Crosse Star Named Dubuque U. Coach," *La Crosse Tribune*, April 15, 1937, 12.
235. "Senators Win 9–3 Over Michigan Team," *Daily Capital Journal*, July 25, 1929, 8.
236. "Robert J. Acerra Inducted Into Baseball Hall of Fame," *Asbury Park Press*, July 31, 1999, 1.
237. "It Was a Different Time Then," *Fredericksburg Standard*, May 4, 1977, 16.
238. Chad Millman, "Oh, Brother, What a Team: The Barnstorming Frederickson Boys Were a Sensation of the 1920s." *Sports Illustrated*, July 11, 1994, 4.
239. "Bewhiskered Third Sacker," *Montana Standard*, August 17, 1929, 9.
240. "House of David Beats Giants Before 5,000 Crowd," *Montana Standard*, August 19, 1929, 8.
241. "House of David and Cuban Giants Clash On Local Diamond," *Bismarck Tribune*, September 5, 1929, 10.
242. "Second Major League Team to Play Here," *News-Palladium*, August 16, 1929, 11.
243. *Ibid.*
244. *Ibid.*
245. "Former State Hurler Returns Major Offer," *Creek Enquirer*, October 15, 1929, 18.

Chapter 4

1. "'Star Spangled Banner's Officially Named Our National Anthem." *Statesville Records and Landmark*, March 9, 1931, 4.
2. Library of Congress: Crime of the Century Timeline, Hopewell, New Jersey.
3. "Pointed Facts on Prohibition and Its Death," *Greenville News*, December 6, 1933, 1.
4. "Al Capone Is Removed to New Alcatraz Prison," *North Adams Transcript*, August 20, 1934, 1.
5. Tim Nash, "Great Innovation Despite Tough Times," www.thefinertimes.com/automobiles.
6. "Roosevelt's 'Alphabet Soup' Helped State Back to Health," *The Daily Oklahoman*, April 18, 1999, 153.
7. "Boulder Dam Completed Two Years Ahead of Schedule," *Daily Herald*, September 18, 1936, 5.
8. "Mrs. F.D.R. Urges Congress to Take Steps to Help Migrant Workers," *Mexia Weekly Herald*, December 13, 1940, 2.
9. "Not So Costly After All," *Akron Beacon*, April 18, 1964, 6.
10. "Amelia Putnam Lands in Ireland," *Philadelphia Inquirer*, May 22, 1932, 1.
11. "Schoolboy Was Given Name of Clyde in Waco," *Waco News Tribune*, May 24, 1934, 1.

12. "Radio Broadcast Causes Nationwide Panic," *Times-Herald*, October 31, 1938, 1.
13. "Will Rogers and Wylie Post Killed When Their Airplane Crashes in Alaskan Wastes," *Decatur Herald*, August 17, 1935, 1.
14. "What Others Say: Glorifying the County Fair," *Reno Gazette-Journal*, October 30, 1936, 4.
15. "Hitler Became Chancellor of Germany 50 Years Ago Today," *London Observer*, January 30, 1983, 9.
16. Hilda Wilcox, *Leatherstocking Journal*, Issue 3 (Spring 1980), 13–15.
17. Ibid.
18. Francis X. Scully, "Do You Remember the House of David?" *Leatherstocking Journal*, Feature 13 (Summer 1980), 3.
19. Ward and Burns, *Baseball, An Illustrated History*, 198.
20. David J. Wisehart, ed., *The Encyclopedia of the Great Plains* (Lincoln: University of Nebraska Press, 2011), www.plainshumanities.unl.edu .
21. "House of David Will Play Here," *Reno Gazette-Journal*, *Winnipeg Evening Tribune*, August 4, 1926, 10.
22. "House of David Ball Team Ties with Stars," *Winnipeg Evening Tribune*, August 7, 1926, 14.
23. "House of David and Giants Stage a Thrilling Finish," *Reno Gazette-Journal*, *Winnipeg Tribune*, August 19, 1927, 14.
24. "House of David Team Bumped Off by Arenas," *Winnipeg Tribune*, July 3, 1928, 13.
25. "House of David Here Monday," *Winnipeg Tribune*, June 30, 1928, 17.
26. Alan M. Klein, *Baseball on the Border: A Tale of Two Laredos* (Princeton, NJ: Princeton University Press, 1997), 51–53.
27. Ibid., 61.
28. "Sport Slant," *Miami Daily News Record*, February 10, 1931, 5.
29. "Reds Win Majors' First Night Game," *Montana Butte Standard*, May 25, 1935, 8.
30. "2000 Fans See Alex and House of David Defeat Standard Oil, 6–0," *Alton Evening Telegraph*, September 26, 1931, 8.
31. "Louisvillian Ted Witte Recalls First Night Baseball Game Here," *Courier-Journal*, May 24, 1975. Article donated by Baseball Hall of Fame.
32. "Beards Heavy Favorites to Cop Arc Tilt," *Middleton Times-Herald*, July 18, 1932, 9.
33. Sullivan, *Early Innings*, 115.
34. Eric Miklich, "Night Baseball in the 19th Century," www.19cbaseball.com/field-10.html.
35. "House of David Team Carries Own Lighting System," *Hartford Courant*, July 2, 1932, 14.
36. *Boston Post*, September 3, 1880, 1, http://research.sabr.org.
37. Ibid., 11.
38. Adkin, Jr., *Brother Benjamin*.
39. "Split in House of David Not Prompted by Bitter Differences," *San Bernardino County Sun*, April 6, 1930, 13.
40. Wilcox, *Leatherstocking Journal*, 13–15.
41. "When Dodgers Hit Skids Fans Yell 'Bring On the Bushwicks,' Their Owner in His 41st Year," *Chillicothe Gazette*, May 12, 1944.
42. "Blomberg's Perseverance Inspired Teammates," *St. Louis Jewish Light*, April 4, 1979, 20, 33.
43. Simkus, *Outsider Baseball*, 125.
44. "Rosner Quits as Pilot," *Brooklyn Daily Eagle*, January 29, 1935, 18.
45. "When Dodgers Hit Skids, Fans Yell 'Bring On The Bushwicks!'" 9.
46. "Don't Miss the Most Unique Baseball Team in the Whole World," *Middletown Times Herald*, June 16, 1930, 9.
47. "The House of David, the Most Novel Baseball Exhibition in the History of Bridgewater, New Jersey," *Courier News*, Sept. 17, 1930, 21.
48. "Indians Prepare for Exhibition in Spite of Rain," *Oshkosh Northwestern*, June 19, 1935, 12.
49. "Loyal Fans Shun Politics, Brave Cold to Attend," *Oshkosh Northwestern*, June 21, 1935, 11.
50. "Parmalee Stops Colony Nine on One Hit, Giants Win, 6–1," *News Palladium*, August 26, 1930, 8.
51. "St. Louis All-Star Troupe to Play at H. of D. Park," *News Palladium*, September 23, 1930, 8.
52. www.baseball-almanac.com/ballplayers/Alexander.
53. "Two Bits a Day for a Shave," *Journal News*, August 26, 1931, 13.
54. "Singles, Doubles, Triples," *Sedalia Democrat*, August 2, 1931, 4.
55. "Southpaws Win 2 for Bushwick Nine," *Brooklyn Daily Eagle*, October 5, 1931, 25.
56. "House of David Beards Serve as Atmosphere," *Brooklyn Daily Eagle*, May 11, 1931, 21.
57. "House of David to Face Ogden All-Stars," *Ogden Standard Examiner*, August 7, 1931, 16.
58. Wayne McElreavy, "Eddie Popowski," https://sabr.org/bioproject/person.
59. Dennis Pajot, "Famous House of David Plays Nightball at Borchert Field," Milwaukee Brewers Online Museum, 1902–1952, www.borchertfield.com.
60. "Bearded Beauties Play Here Saturday," *Ogden Standard Examiner*, August 7, 1931, 16.
61. "Otto Floto Dead," *Santa Ana Register*, August 5, 1929, 4.
62. Jay Sanford, *Denver Post Tournament: A Project of the Rocky Mountain Chapter of the Society for American Baseball Research* (Cleveland, OH: SABR Publishers, 2003), 37.
63. "Poss Parsons, Sports Writer, Dies," *Alton Evening Telegraph*, August 27, 1942, 1.
64. Eric Mark Stoneberg, "The Denver Post Tournament and Pre-Organized Baseball Integration" (Master's thesis, Arizona State University, 2009), 6.
65. "Rosters of Clubs in Post Tourney," *Denver Post*, August 1, 1930, 25.
66. Stoneberg, "The Denver Post Tournament," 57.
67. Sanford, *Denver Post Tournament*, 40.
68. Stoneberg, "The Denver Post Tournament," 57–8.
69. Sanford, *The Denver Post Tournament*, 43.

70. "Alex to Join Colony for Second Year," *News-Palladium*, February 23, 1932, 8.
71. "Grover Cleveland Alexander, One of All-Time Greats to Start Game Here Against All-Star Nine This Evening," *Independent Record*, August 2, 1933, 7.
72. "House of David Ball Club Stronger Than Ever," *Winnipeg Tribune*, June 14, 1933, 17.
73. "'Pete' and Chief in Mound Duel," *Brooklyn Daily Eagle*, June 26, 1932, 41.
74. "Big Celebration at House of David July 2nd, 3rd, 4th," *Chicago Tribune*, June 29, 1932, 14.
75. "Busy Season for Local Ballclubs," *News-Palladium*, January 1, 1933, 93.
76. Hawkins and Bertolino, *House of David Baseball Team*, 34–5.
77. Sanford, *The Denver Post Tournament*, 43.
78. "John Tucker Voted Most Valuable Player," *Denver Post*, Sept. 4, 1932, 8.
79. "Colony and Alexander's Teams Will Clash Tonight," *News-Palladium*, August 19, 1933, 8.
80. "Bender Manager of Bearded Ball Nine," *Modesto News Herald*, July 6, 1933, 6.
81. "Chief Bender Manages House of David Team," *Star Press*, July 9, 1933, 22.
82. Price, *Rounding the Bases*, 61.
83. "Historical Marker Honors A's Pitcher," *The Sentinel*, October 18, 2003, 19.
84. "Bender Sues House of David for $700," *Shamokin News-Dispatch*, August 3, 1934, 10.
85. "In the Realm of Sports," *Ottawa Journal*, June 4, 1934, 16.
86. "House of David Gets a Girl Pitcher," *New York Times*, July 15, 1933, 13.
87. "Girl Pitcher Fans Babe Ruth and Gehrig, Too," *Reno Gazette-Journal*, April 13, 1931, 13.
88. Stephen Martini, *The Chattanooga Lookouts* (Cleveland, OH: Dry Ice Publishing, 2005), 57.
89. Harold Seymour, *Baseball*, 101.
90. Timothy M. Gay, *Satch, Dizzy & Rapid Robert: The Wild Saga of Interracial Baseball Before Jackie Robinson* (New York: Simon & Schuster, 2010), 278.
91. "Visiting Scribe Compliments City," *Clarion-Ledger*, March 30, 1939, 11.
92. "'Professor' Is the Old Sultan of Swat's New Title," *Mount Carmel Item*, March 5, 1940, 7.
93. "Hurly City Nine Books Two Games," *Ironwood Daily Globe*, August 19, 1933, 7.
94. "Girl Hurls Scoreless Inning Against Cards as House of David Club Wins," *St. Louis Star and Times*, September 13, 1933, 20.
95. Jeremy Bonifiglio, "Exhibition Celebrates House of David Teams," *South Bend Tribune*, August 12, 2007, SouthBendTribune.com.
96. Stoneberg, "The Denver Post Tournament," 59.
97. Sanford, *The Denver Post Tournament*, 45–48.
98. "In 1933 Democratic Party Sponsored Kansas City Rabbits Team in the Denver Post Tournament," *Denver Post*, August 4, 1933, 28.
99. Stoneberg, "The Denver Post Tournament," 63.
100. *Ibid.*, 59–62.
101. *Denver Post*, August 4, 1933, 28.
102. Stoneberg, "The Denver Post Tournament," 59.
103. "House of David Traveling Teams to Open Training at Eden Springs Park May 4," *News Palladium*, April 19, 1934, 12.
104. Susan E. Cayleff, *Babe: The Life and Legend of Babe Didrikson Zaharias* (Chicago: University of Illinois Press, 1995), a compilation of several pages.
105. "Babe Didrikson Hurls as House of David Wins," *Chicago Tribune*, May 7, 1934, 23.
106. "House of David Teams to Open Training at Eden Springs Park May 4," 12.
107. "House of David Sues Promoter; Seeks $2,500," *News-Palladium*, January 20, 1934, 8.
108. "Bearded Nine Wins Game by 32–21 Score," *Pampa Daily News*, July 3, 1934, 6.
109. "'Donkey' Baseball' to Make Debut Here at Cult Park," *News-Palladium*, June 30, 1934, 1.
110. Gay, *Satch, Dizzy & Rapid Robert*, 78–9.
111. "The Fans Await 'Donkey Baseball' to Be Played by the House of David Tuesday Night," *The Battle Creek Enquirer*, July 1, 1934, 11.
112. "House of David Beats Postum but Donkeys Steal Night Show," *Battle Creek Enquirer*, July 5, 1934, 10.
113. "'Old Pete' and His Donkey," *Battle Creek Enquirer*, July 3, 1934, 9.
114. "1996 Hall of Fame Inductees," *The Town Talk*, February 4, 1996, B3.
115. "This Ghost Story Can Now Be Told," *The Town Talk*, June 16, 1996, 17.
116. David L. Porter, *The Biographical Dictionary of American Sports* (Westport, CT: Greenwood Publishing Group, 2000), 1002.
117. Sanford, *The Denver Post Tournament*, 51.
118. Bruce, *The Kansas City Monarchs*, 75–6.
119. "Sez Ches," *Pittsburgh Courier*, April 21, 1934, 5.
120. Bruce, *The Kansas City Monarchs*, 77.
121. Ribowsky, *A Complete History of the Negro Leagues*, 169.
122. Leslie A. Heaphy, *Satchel Paige and Company* (Jefferson, NC: McFarland, 2007), 104.
123. Phil S. Dixon, *John 'Buck' O'Neil: The Rookie, The Man, The Legacy* (Bloomington, IN: Author House, 2009), 175.
124. Stoneberg, "The Denver Post Tournament," 7.
125. Heaphy, *Satchel Paige*, 103.
126. Stoneberg, "The Denver Post Tournament," 64.
127. "Sez Ches," *Pittsburgh Courier*, April 21, 1934, 5.
128. Sanford, *The Denver Post Tournament*, 89.
129. "Denver Ball Tourney Will Begin Aug. 1," *Pampa Daily News*, July 27, 1934, 10.
130. "Kansas City Monarchs Set for Season; to Vie in Denver Tourney," *Pittsburgh Courier*, April 21, 1934, 14.

131. Sanford, *The Denver Post Tournament*, 49.
132. "3500 Watch Monarchs Beat House of David," *Winnipeg Tribune*, July 26, 1934, 12.
133. "House of David Squad Meets Kansas City Monarchs Today in Feature of Doubleheader," *Great Falls Tribune*, July 15, 1934, 12.
134. Sanford, *The Denver Post Tournament*, 52–3.
135. "Sparky Going to Cooperstown, Joined by 'Turkey' Stearns and Bid McPhee," *Standard Speaker*, March 1, 2000, 19.
136. P.J. Dragseth, *A Biographical Dictionary of Major League Scouts* (Jefferson, NC: McFarland, 2011), 202–3.
137. Mark Wyatt, *The Jesus Boys: The House of David*, www.thenationalpastimemuseum.org, November 19, 2014, 3.
138. Hawkins and Bertolino, *The House of David Baseball Team*, 4–6.
139. Heaphy, *Satchel Paige*, 57.
140. Ron Taylor, Trustee/Historian/Archivist Israelite House of David as Reorganized by Mary Purnell, interview with author, February 2014.
141. "Greely Advertisers Downed by Colorado Club, Score 12–1," *Denver Post*, August 2, 1934, 21.
142. Stoneberg, "The Denver Post Tournament," 72.
143. Larry Tye, *Satchel: The Life and Times of an American Legend* (New York: Random House Trademark Paperbacks, 2009), 89.
144. Stoneberg, "The Denver Post Tournament," 71.
145. Derby, Jr., and Coleman, "House of David," 7–10.
146. Ibid.
147. "10 Things You May Not Know About Satchel Paige," https://www.history.com/news/10-things-you-may-not-know-about-satchel-paige.
148. Heaphy, *Satchel Paige*, 59.
149. Stoneberg, "The Denver Post Tournament," 72.
150. Heaphy, *The Negro Leagues*, 148.
151. Darby, Jr. & Coleman, "House of David," 7–11.
152. Gay, *Satch, Dizzy & Rapid Robert*, 75.
153. "House of David to Play Negro Monarchs Tonight for Denver Post Title," *Pampa Daily News*, August 13, 1934, 3.
154. "House of David Nine Feature in Tourney," *Independent Record*, August 12, 1934, 9.
155. "House of David Annexes Denver Post Tourney," *Salt Lake Tribune*, August 14, 1934, 22.
156. "Kansas City Monarchs Lose Championship Game, 2–0," *Independent Record*, August 14, 1934, 10.
157. *Pittsburgh Courier*, August 17, 1934, 9.
158. Hawkins and Bertolino, *The House of David Baseball Team*, 46.
159. "House of David Defeats Monarchs, 2–1," *The Denver Post*, August 11, 1934, 5.
160. "Sez Ches," *Pittsburg Courier*, August 18, 1934, 15.
161. "1934 Tourney Greatest in History," *Colorado Statesman*, August 18, 1934, 2.
162. "Brass Tacks," *Lincoln Star*, August 21, 1934, 8.
163. Stoneberg, "The Denver Post Tournament," 73.
164. "House of David Wins Denver Post Tourney: Colony $5,800 Richer Today," *News-Palladium*, August 14, 1934, 8.
165. Charles E. Coulter, *Take Up the Black Man's Burden: Kansas City's African-American Communities, 1865–1939* (Columbia: University of Missouri Press, 2006), 234.
166. "Patrolling the Sport Highway," *Ogden Standard Examiner*, September 2, 1934, 8.
167. Tye, *Satchel*, 90.
168. "House of David Wins Tournament," *Evening Herald*, August 14, 1934, 2.
169. "Colony $5800 Richer Today; Unsigned Letter Case," *News-Palladium*, August 14, 1934, 8.
170. Tom Dunkel, *Color Blind* (New York: Atlantic Monthly Press, 2013), 124.
171. "Colony $5,800 Richer Today; Probe Unsigned Letter Case," *Ogden Standard Examiner*, *News-Palladium*, August 24, 1934, 8.
172. www.baseball-almanac.com/players/player.php?p=benson101.
173. "Road Runners Lose First of Two Game Set," *Pampa Daily News*, September 20, 1934, 3.
174. "House of David and Road Runners to Play Tonight at 8:15 O'clock," *Pampa Daily News*, September 19, 1934, 5.
175. "Road Runners Lose First of Two Games to House of David, 14–9," *Pampa Daily News*, September 20, 1934, 3.
176. "House of David and Monarchs Break Even," *Winnipeg Tribune*, August 14, 1933, 13.
177. "'Gypsy Baseball Is a Tramp's Life' Says Alexander," *Star Press*, October 21, 1934, 3.
178. "Didrikson Signs with House of David," *Reading Times*, March 1, 1934, 13.
179. "Babe Didrikson One of Fastest Players in Game," *News Palladium*, August 24, 1934, 8.
180. Klein, *Baseball on the Border*, 51.
181. Price, *Rounding the Bases*, 69.
182. "Colony Answers to Beer Tilt," *News-Palladium*, September 28, 1934, 8.
183. Bob Broeg, *Baseball's Barnum: Ray Hap Dumont and the National Baseball Congress* (Wichita, KS: The Center for Entrepreneurship at Wichita State University, 1998), 34.
184. "Wichita Bids for Diamond Tourney," *Montana Butte Standard*, August 11, 1935, 48.
185. "Ray Dumont, Wichita Baseball Promoter, Dies," *Wichita Beacon*, July 4, 1971, 1.
186. Dunkel, *Color Blind*, 182.
187. "National Baseball Congress: Future of a Baseball Tradition," https://nbcbaseball.com.
188. "Highclimber Looks 'Em Over," *Eugene Guard*, July 11, 1934, 6.
189. "Old Timers Will Return Here Sunday with House of David Ballclub," *St. Cloud Times*, June 5, 1935, 10.
190. "Tucker Leads Squad to Texas Training Grounds," *News-Palladium*, March 23, 1935, 7.

191. "Jack Quinn to Pilot House of David Team," *Decatur Herald*, April 12, 1935, 26.
192. Untitled, *The Spokane Daily Chronicle*, June 12, 1935, 54.
193. "Bearded Boys Have Won 33 of 37 Games," *Pampa Daily News*, May 7, 1935, 3.
194. "Dutch Faust Joins Doan's Squad," *News-Palladium*, May 4, 1935, 7.
195. "Just Sports," *News-Palladium*, May 17, 1935, 11.
196. "Latest Events in the Sport World: House of David Plays Kalispell Here on June 14," *Daily Inter-Lake*, May 29, 1935, 6.
197. "Bismarck's Semi-pro Team of 1935 'Greatest,' Says Satchel Paige," *Bismarck Tribune*, June 16, 1943, 8.
198. "Babe Ruth Offered House of David Place," *Bend Bulletin*, June 5, 1935, 2.
199. "Babe Ruth May Join House of David," *Evening News*, June 6, 1935, 1.
200. "Four Runs in First Inning Clinched Win," *Gary Post-Tribune*, May 27, 1935, 15.
201. Dunkel, *Color Blind*, 144.
202. Klein, *Baseball on the Border*, 61–65.
203. Sanford, *The Denver Post Tournament*, 56, 60.
204. "'Pete' Alexander Joins Baseball's Immortals," *Big Springs Daily Herald*, January 19, 1938, 8.
205. "'60 Feet Too Far for Old Pete to Throw' He Says," *St. Louis Star and Times*, August 15, 1938, 18.
206. "Alexander Nine Will Play Here," *Winnipeg Tribune*, June 23, 1938, 14.
207. "Sports Roundup," *Massillon Evening Independent*, June 7, 1938, 3.
208. "Pitcher Remembered Generosity of House of David," *Milwaukee Journal*, August 28, 1944, 16.
209. "Relay Race to Bring Olympic Fire to Berlin," *Evening News*, May 28, 1936, 17.
210. "The Political Games," *The Los Angeles Times*, July 14, 1992, 86.
211. Stoneberg, "The Denver Post Tournament," 84.
212. Kelly E. Rusinak, "Baseball on the Radical Agenda: The Daily and Sunday Worker on Desegregating Major League Baseball, 1933–1947," (Master's thesis, Clemson University, 1955).
213. "The House That David Built," *Tri-County Newspapers*, August 5, 2011, www.appeal-democrat.
214. "House of David and Emporia Baseball Teams Clash Friday," *Emporia Gazette*, May 14, 1936, 12.
215. "Colony Team to Return Home," *Honolulu Star-Bulletin*, November 2, 1936, 12.
216. "Unfair to Barbers," *Pittsburgh Press*, April 3, 1937, 9.
217. "Journal Classified Advertising," *Muscatine Journal and News Tribune*, December 19, 1936, 11.
218. "Little 'Chick' with Color Gives Colonels Early Easter Present," *Courier Journal*, March 30, 1918, 18.
219. George Genovese, letter to author, May 14, 2007.
220. George Genovese, telephone interview with author, February 18, 1993.
221. "Even Whiskers Have Training Camp," *Cincinnati Enquirer*, March 12, 1938, 13.
222. "House of David Baseball Club Cuts Up in a Big Way at Spring Training Base," *Daily Capital News*, March 12, 1938, 9.
223. "Swaney to Pitch Again for Davids," *Hartford Courant*, March 12, 1938, 11.
224. "House of David's Famous Ball Club on the Way Out," *Lincoln Evening Journal*, March 19, 1938, 5.
225. "Brunette with Weakness for Cops Captured," *Jefferson City Post-Tribune*, April 23, 1941, 2.
226. Ibid.
227. Title not included, *Washington Post*, May 12, 1939, 25. Article donated by Baseball Hall of Fame.
228. "House of David to Play City Team Here Tonight: Girl Runner Will Appear," *Escanaba Daily Press*, July 25, 1939, 10.
229. "The Old Pepper Game," *Chilliwack Progress*, July 12, 1939, 7.
230. Francis X. Scully, "House of David Revisited," *Sunday Rutland Herald*, July 10, 1977, 2.
231. Ibid.

Chapter 5

1. "Allies Getting Vast Supplies," *The Los Angeles Times*, June 12, 1941, 6.
2. "Benton Harbor Day Draws Big Crowd to Colony Park," *The News-Palladium*, July 29, 1940, 8.
3. "H. of D. Joins Michiana Ball League," *The News-Palladium*, May 22, 1940, 8.
4. "H. of D. Plays Conns Tonight," *The News-Palladium*, June 25, 1940, 7.
5. "H. of D. Beats Niles Sunday, 10–1," *The News-Palladium*, July 29, 1940, 8.
6. "Holland Licks Colony 10–0," *The News-Palladium*, July 30, 1940, 8.
7. "H. of D. Acclaimed Official Champs of Michiana League," *The News-Palladium*, October 29, 1940, 8.
8. "House of David Blanks Kritts Grocers, 9–0 and 3–0: Pavlick Gives 1 Hit, Pallis 6 in Twin Win," *The News-Palladium*, September 30, 1940, 8.
9. "Johnny Pavlick Hurls No-Hitter vs. Conns," *The News-Palladium*, August 12, 1940, 6.
10. "Johnny Pavlick Will Pitch for Locals Sunday," *News-Palladium*, September 22, 1945, 5.
11. "Colony Nine Joins Loop," *Herald-Press*, May 22, 1940, 6.
12. "Satchel Page's [sic] (Paige's) Colored All-Stars Play House of David Here Friday Night," *The Leader-Telegram*, June 19, 1940, 6.
13. "Colored Monarchs, House of David to Tangle at Elgin," *The La Grande Observer*, August 8, 1940, 8.
14. "Satchel Paige Featured as Main Attraction," *The Bismarck Tribune*, June 22, 1940, 6.

15. "Outsiders to Play Bend: Monarchs and House of David to Meet," *Bend Bulletin*, August 3, 1940, 2.
16. "Bewhiskered House of David Sluggers Blast Monarchs," *The Nevada State Journal*, August 7, 1940, 9.
17. "Touching All Bases," *The Ogden State Examiner*, August 21, 1940, 7.
18. "House of David to Clash with All Stars of La Grande, Elgin," *La Grande Observer*, July 5, 1940, 6.
19. Price, *Rounding the Bases*, 60.
20. "Highclimber," *Eugene Guard*, July 11, 1940, 10.
21. "Locals Blast 12 Hits Off Wykoff in Notching Win," *News-Palladium*, September 13, 1946, 6.
22. "Mgr. Anderson, 'Doc' Tally End Summer's Tour," *News-Palladium*, September 12, 1946, 12.
23. "Bushwicks Play House of David in Two Games," *Brooklyn Daily Eagle*, May 12, 1940, 9.
24. "House of David Athletes Shave: There's a Reason," *Belvidere Daily Republican*, July 26, 1940, 6.
25. "House of David Baseball Team Has Financial Troubles," *Dunkirk Evening Observer*, July 26, 1940, 14.
26. "House of David Now in Distress," *Mount Carmel Item*, July 26, 1940, 5.
27. "Bewhiskered Ball Players to Disband," *Bradford Evening Star* and *The Bradford Daily Record*, July 26, 1940, 12.
28. "Bewhiskered Players to Disband," *Vidette Messenger*, July 26, 1940, 8.
29. "House of David Players Will Lose Beards, Salaries," *The News Herald*, July 26, 1940, 12.
30. "News Flashes," *The Lincoln Star*, July 30, 1940, 1.
31. "House of David May Have Baseball Team," *Escanaba Daily Press*, March 13, 1941, 16.
32. "Billies, A's Slate Games," *Eugene Register Guard*, July 20, 1941, 12.
33. *Presidents' and America's Pastime: A Selection of Baseball Documents from the Nation's Presidential Libraries*, Collections of the National Archives and Records Administration, Presidential Libraries.
34. "St. Joe Autos Sponsor Semi-Pro Baseball Nine," *News Palladium*, March 31, 1942, 6, photo caption.
35. "Her Best Friends Were Diamonds," *Los Angeles Times*, April 25, 1983, 48.
36. "Big League Impact," *News Press*, March 25, 2006, 52.
37. "League of Women Ballplayers," National Baseball Hall of Fame Inside Pitch Series, https://baseballhall.org.
38. "Baseball Games, Track Events in Store for Fans," *The Post Register*, August 17, 1945, 8.
39. "Fans Awaiting Jesse Owens' Appearance Here," *Nevada State Journal*, August 15, 1945, 21.
40. "Double Feature Field Program Offers Fans a Rare Sports Dish," *Ogden-Standard Examiner*, August 27, 1945, 8.
41. Basketball Wonders Turn to Baseball for More Success," *Independent Record*, July 15, 1944, 8.
42. "Cool Papa Bell Is Named to Baseball Hall of Fame," *Galveston Daily News*, Feb. 14, 1974, 7.
43. "David Nine, Globetrotters Play at Derks Thursday," *The Salt Lake Tribune*, July 3, 1949, 55.
44. "Semi-Pro Baseball Tournament Off," *Santa Ana Register*, June 3, 1942, 6.
45. "War Is Producing Significant Changes in Semi-Pro Baseball," *Green Bay Press-Gazette*, July 14, 1942, 13.
46. "Sports Changes: Hometown Lineups Replaced by Teams in Service Camps," *The Raleigh Register*, July 14, 1942, 9.
47. "St. Joe Autos Sponsor Semi-Pro Baseball Nine," *News-Palladium*, March 31, 1942, 6.
48. "Fate of Beards and Long Hair Is in Army's Hands," *Daily Telegram*, May 8, 1942, 2.
49. "Autos Display Much Promise in Autos Drill," *Herald Press*, May 18, 1942, 7.
50. "Autos Roster Begins to Take Shape," *News-Palladium*, April 13, 1942, 8.
51. "On the Sportsline," *New-Palladium*, April 28, 1943, 8.
52. "Local Sports Flourish Despite Wartime Restrictions," *News-Palladium*, December 31, 1943, 7.
53. "Bewhiskered First Baseman to Lead St. Joseph Autos," *Battle Creek Enquirer*, July 21, 1946, 19.
54. "Around Town," *News-Palladium*, March 15, 1947, 3.
55.
56. "Jesse Owens, Great Track Star, Will Appear in Reno Aug. 16, 17: Accompanies Harlem 'Trotters, House of David," *Nevada State Journal*, August 5, 1945, 9.
57. "Globe Trotters Win First from Davids," *Reno-Gazette Journal*, August 17, 1945, 16.
58. "Horse Defeats Owens in Contest at Moana," *Nevada State Journal*, August 18, 1945, 6.
59. John Rossi, *The National Game: Baseball and American Culture* (Chicago: Ivan R. Dee, 2000), 154–6.
60. "Heywood Broun Flays Color Ban in Big Leagues," *Pittsburgh Courier*, February 18, 1933, 1, 5.
61. Robert Peterson, *Only the Ball Was White: A History of Legendary Black Players and All-Black Professional Teams* (New York: Oxford University Press, 1970), 176.
62. William A. Young, *J.J. Wilkinson and the Kansas City Monarchs: Trailblazers in Black Baseball* (Jefferson, NC: McFarland, 2016), 139.
63. Peterson, *Only the Ball Was White*, 174–5.
64. John G. Zinn and Paul G. Zinn, *Ebbets Field: Essays and Memoirs of Brooklyn's Historic Ballpark, 1913–1960* (Jefferson, NC: McFarland, 2012), 98.
65. Mark Ribowsky, *A Complete History of the Negro Leagues, 1884–1955* (New York: Carol Publishing, 1995), 260.
66. "Ed Schumacher Named to Face Negro Batsmen," *News Palladium*, May 12, 1945, 5.

67. "Former U.C.L.A. Ace Object of Long Search," *Moines Register*, October 24, 1945, 9.
68. Lee Lowenfish, *Branch Rickey, Baseball's Ferocious Gentleman* (Lincoln: University of Nebraska Press, 2007), 364.
69. "Dodgers Signing of Negro Player New Headaches for Commissioner Chandler," *News-Journal*, October 24, 1945, 19.
70. Janet Bruce, *The Kansas City Monarchs, Champions of Black Baseball* (Lawrence: University Press of Kansas, 1985), 112.
71. "Brooklyn Negro Ball Player for Farm Club: Monarchs Say, 'We Won't Take It Lying Down,'" *Daily Press*, October 1945, 10.
72. Young, *J.J. Wilkinson and the Kansas City Monarchs*, 149.
73. "Monarchs Blend Baseball with Jazz Gimmicks," *St. Cloud Times*, July 23, 1952, 17.
74. Bruce, *The Kansas City Monarchs*, 143.
75. Young, *J.J. Wilkinson and the Kansas City Monarchs*, 180.
76. "Monarchs Purchased by Michigan Man," *Journal and Courier*, February 18, 1956, 7.
77. "Bearded Beauts Here for Tilt with Crater Tonight," *Medford Mail Tribune*, July 29, 1946, 2.
78. "House of David Will Invade de Paris Wednesday Night," *The Paris News*, April 16, 1946, 3.
79. "Fans Set New Attendance Mark in 23-Hit Romp," *Amarillo Daily News*, April 25, 1946, 6.
80. "Famous Baseball Aggregation Here Saturday," *The Independent Record*, July 5, 1946, 9.
81. "Hollidaysburg, House of David in Night Game," *Altoona Tribune*, June 7, 1946, 12.
82. "House of David Brings Pre-War Club to Bluffs," *Council Bluffs Nonpareil*, June 30, 1936, 15.
83. "David Team Has Classy Players," *The San Bernardino County Sun*, August 8, 1946, 21.
84. "Mgr. Anderson, 'Doc' Tally End Summer's Tour," *News-Palladium*, September 12, 1946, 12.
85. "Jackie Robinson: Former Royals GM looks back 50 years later," *The Gazette*, April 15, 1997, 15.
86. John McMurray, "Larry Doby," https://sabr.org/bioproject, no date given.
87. "Negro League Star Praises Robinson," *Indiana Gazette*, March 30, 1995, 11.
88. Tye, *Satchel*, 208.
89. "O'Neil: One special player who few saw in action," *Manhattan Mercury*, August 31, 1994, 20.
90. "Indians Sign on Satch," *Reno Gazette-Journal*, July 8, 1948, 17.
91. "On Second Thought," *Oakland Tribune*, August 10, 1948, 17.
92. "House of David Coach Cries for Good Players," *Press and Sun Bulletin*, June 23, 1948, 32.
93. "Opening Day 2010," *Memories and Dreams: The Official Magazine of the Hall of Fame*, volume 32, number 2, 2010, 19.
94. Joe Palladino and Joe "Reds" Petrongolo, excerpts from telephone interviews with author, September 2013.
95. "Opening Day 2010," *Memories and Dreams*, 17–19.
96. "Trotters, David Here for Game," *Oakland Tribune*, July 16, 1949, 12.
97. "Bait for Bugs," *Decatur Daily Review*, June 6, 1949, 6.
98. "House of David Shades AC 6–4, but Jim Mull Steals the Show," *Pottstown Mercury*, August 18, 1949, 8.
99. Sanford, *The Denver Post Tournament*, 37.
100. "Bearded 9 Will Meet Wasco Team," *Bakersfield Californian*, July 9, 1949, 22.
101. "Cult Chief Expires in Hospital Sunday," *News-Palladium*, October 6, 1947, 1.
102. "Bearded 'Doc' Tally Is Dead," *News-Palladium*, January 25, 1950, 1.
103. "Bearded Baseball Star Dies at 53," *The Ludington Daily News*, January 26, 1950, 1.
104. "Crowd Expected for Sparkling Exhibition," *Independent Record*, July 2, 1951, 8.
105. *Tri-City Herald*, July 29, 1951, 7.
106. "Alcos Tromp Cuban Monarchs 12–3, Slate House of David Tomorrow," *Albany Democrat-Herald*, August 3, 1953, 7.
107. "Queen Mary Purnell Dies," *News-Palladium*, August 21, 1953, 1.
108. "House of David Unique Team," *The Independent Record*, July 1, 1951, 8.
109. "Davids Are Coming to City Friday," *Sedalia Democrat*, May 24, 1950, 12.
110. "Israelite House of David Baseball Team Plays at East Helena Thursday," *The Independent Record*, July 20, 1952, 5.
111. "36th Tour of Nation," *Moberly-Monitor Index*, June 6, 1956, 11.
112. "Wasco Will Meet House of David Club August 15," *The Bakersfield Californian*, August 4, 1953, 21.
113. "Baseball's Dying Clowns," *Cincinnati Enquirer*, July 16, 1974, 28.
114. "House of David to Play Cuban Giants July 15," *The Daily Inter Lake*, July 8, 1953, 5.
115. "BoBo [sic] Nickerson Catches Baseball from Plane 650 Feet in Air," *Kansas City Times*, October 18, 1954, 22.
116. "House of David Coming to Meet Plywood Group," *The Daily Chronicle*, July 26, 1955, 6.
117. "House of David Nine Plays Bend Loggers Here Tonight," *Bend Bulletin*, August 1, 1955, 2.
118. Young, *J.J. Wilkinson and the Kansas City Monarchs*, 178.
119. Neil Lanctot, *Negro League Baseball: The Rise and Ruin of a Black Institution*, I (Philadelphia: University of Pennsylvania Press, 2004), 382–84.
120. "Top Stars to Play in East-West Game," *Pittsburgh Courier*, July 9, 1955, 12.
121. "House of David Baseball Team Plays Here Friday," *Great Falls Tribune*, July 16, 1956, 8.
122. "Collins Corner," *Pampa Daily News*, January 13, 1957, 7.
123. "Frank 'Bobo' Nickerson Catches Baseball from Plane 650 Feet in Air," *Kansas City Times*, October 18, 1954, 22.

124. "House of David Nine to Play Here June 3," *Joplin Globe*, May 18, 1952, 24.
125. "Satchel Paige to Pitch in Benefit," *Arizona Daily Star*, August 1, 1954, 27.
126. "Visitors Play 135 Games," *The Daily Times*, June 27, 1956, 9.
127. "A's Win Over St. Louis Negro Stars with Score of 20–5," *Sedalia Democrat*, June 11, 1956, 6.
128. Ronald Taylor, Trustee/Historian/Archivist, The Israelite House of David as Reorganized by Mary Purnell, interview with author February 2014.
129. Simkus, *Outsider Baseball*, 274.
130. Ibid., 274–5.
131. Gay, *Satch, Dizzy, Rapid Robert*, 278.
132. "Memories of Past Echo in Brooklyn," *Asbury Park Press*, August 12, 1985, 32.

Chapter 6

1. "Rites Thursday for Francis Thorpe: City of David Cult Leader Dies at 81," *News-Palladium*, September 23, 1957, 1.
2. D.C. Allen House of David Collection 1795–1980, Vol. FA25, T518, C, 93, Bentley Historical Library, University of Michigan.
3. "City of David Cult Leader Dies at 81," *News-Palladium*, September 23, 1957, 1.
4. "Bearded 'Doc' Tally is Dead," *News-Palladium*, September 23, 1957, 1, 14.
5. 1920 House of David Federal Census, Berrien County Michigan Genealogy Project, Transcribed by Brenda R. Sears, April 2003.
6. Malan, *Muzzy Field*, 89.
7. Ibid., 84–89.
8. "Ball Players Wear Long Hair," *Winnipeg Tribune*, August 5, 1926, 10.
9. "Around Town," *News-Palladium*, March 15, 1947, 3.
10. *Funk & Wagnalls, The Literary Digest*, Vol. 65, May 1920, 120.
11. "The Sport Highway with Al Warden," *The Ogden Standard-Examiner*, August 1, 1947, 9.
12. Brian Ziebart, Trustee/Historian/Archivist Israelite House of David, multiple emails and conversations with author.
13. Malan, *Muzzy Field*, 89.
14. "Famed 'Doc' Tally of Davids Dies," *The Argus-Leader*, January 26, 1950, 13.
15. "Around Town," *News-Palladium*, March 15, 1947, 3.
16. Ibid.
17. "Jesse Tally Dies from Heart Attack," *The Times*, January 26, 1950, 13.
18. Brian Ziebart, House of David Commune Records.
19. "Last Days of the House of David," Chicago Public Library, Adam Langer Collection, 1984–2011, July 1, 1994.
20. Society for American Baseball Research, *The National Pastime: A Review of Baseball History*, No. 19, 51.
21. "House of David Squad Tough to Beat," *Big Spring Daily News*, March 11, 1935, 2.
22. "Western Stars, Colony Cagers Will Clash Here," *News-Palladium*, February 26, 1946, 5.
23. "House of David at East Helena Tonight," *The Independent Record*, July 24, 1952, 12.
24. "Famed House of David Faces Cubans Tuesday Evening at Pocatello," *Idaho State Journal*, June 25, 1952, 7.
25. Anderson's memory was off in at least one respect: Paige was a right-hander, not a southpaw. Hawkins and Bertolini, *The House of David Baseball Team*, 53.
26. Adam Langer Collection, "The Last Days of the House of David," www.chicagoreader.com./chicago/search?cx=partner-pub.
27. "Anderson Has Really Traveled," *Beatrice Daily Sun*, May 30, 1950, 3.
28. "House of David Team Recalled," *News-Palladium*, April 11, 1970, 16.
29. Ibid.
30. George Anderson Day at Mary's City of David Museum, 1998, www.maryscityofdavid.org/html/centennial_4html.
31. "Theo. Baushke, Pioneer Cult Member, Dies," *News Palladium*, December 14, 1940, 1.
32. Malan, *Muzzy Field*, 88.
33. Ibid., 85.
34. Hawkins and Bertolino, *The House of David Baseball Team*, 15.
35. "Long Hairs to Play Senators Wednesday Evening," *Daily Capital Journal*, July 23, 1929, 3.
36. "Alexander to Hurl Initial 1933 Game At H. of D. in May," *News Palladium*, April 27, 1933, 10.
37. Joel Hawkins and Terry Bertolino, The House of David Baseball Team Research Project, www.peppergame.com.
38. "House of David to Start Stellar Lineup," *Alton Evening Telegraph*, September 5, 1936, 8.
39. "Bearded Babe Ruth Could Belt Them," *Detroit Free Press*, August 23, 1978, 18.
40. "House of David Club Will Furnish Opposition for Joplin Here Today," *Joplin Globe*, April 12, 1929, 8.
41. "But Age Taking Toll of Benton Harbor Sect," *Lansing State Journal*, August 27, 1967, 47.
42. House of David 1920 Federal Census, Berrien County Michigan Genealogy Project, transcribed by Brenda R. Sears, April 2003.
43. "Former Cult Diamond Star Is Signed with Minors," *News Palladium*, April 23, 1924, 5.
44. Howard Olson Photo, *The Herald Press*, June 23, 1969, 3.
45. Hawkins and Bertolino, *The House of David Baseball Team*, 21.
46. Malan, *Muzzy Field*, 21.
47. "Do You Remember? 50 Years Ago Today," *News Palladium*, June 11, 1975, 2.
48. "Former Cult Diamond Star Is Signed with Minors," *News Palladium*, April 23, 1924, 5.
49. "House of David Band Which Tops Yost Vaudeville Bill," *Santa Ana Register*, January 10, 1922, 6.

50. "House of David Plays Decatur Here Sunday," *News Palladium*, July 31, 1925, 6.
51. Jerry Kirshenbaum, "The Hairiest Team of All," *The Sporting News*, April 13, 1970, 104–106.
52. House of David 1920 Federal Census, Berrien County Michigan Genealogy Project, April 2003.
53. Hawkins and Bertolino, *The House of David Baseball Team*, 61.
54. Malan, *Muzzy Field*, 86–89.
55. Ibid.
56. "Ball Players to Wear Long Hair," *The Winnipeg Tribune*, August 5, 1926.
57. "House of David Second Baseman Will Play with Fort Smith Club," *Springfield Republican*, March 31, 1925.
58. "House of David Star Signs with Fort Smith," *Altoona Tribune*, April 1, 1925, 10.
59. "1929 Akron Tyrites Statistics," https://statscrew.com/minorbaseball/stats/t-at10047/y-1928.
60. "Banner Year Expected by Team Pilots," *News-Palladium*, April 20, 1935, 7.
61. "Alexander to Be Here with Davids," *Eugene Guard*, June 20, 1935, 10.
62. "Jazzy Whiskers: Cookie Hannaford's House of David Band," *Indiana Gazette*, April 25, 1925, 10.
63. "Gossip for the Fans," *Bismarck Daily Tribune*, July 26, 1920, 8.
64. "Ball Player Spurns Offer," *Ogden Standard Examiner*, January 28, 1922, 6.
65. "Only Their Foliage Keeps Them in Bushes," *Ogden Standard-Examiner*, July 29, 1920, 10.
66. "Hannaford, Classy First Sackers," *Davenport Democrat & Leader*, August 1, 1924, 23.
67. "House of David Band," *Indiana Gazette*, April 25, 1925, 2.
68. "Local Exchange Club Helps in Baroda's First Party," *News Palladium*, March 14, 1924, 4.
69. Jeremy Bonafiglio, "Stirring the Echoes," *South Bend Tribune*, August 12, 2007, D7, www.SouthBendTribune.com.
70. "Novarro Is Starred; House of David Band and Denny at State," *Minneapolis Star*, October 17, 1925, 23.
71. "Deserts Band to Get a Haircut," *The Evening Review*, February 8, 1928, 11.
72. "House of David to Meet St. Mary's at Sportsman's," *Alton Evening Telegraph*, September 2, 1936, 8.
73. "Lloyd Miller Hurls One Hit Game, Colony Wins, 9–1," *News-Palladium*, May 5, 1930, 8.
74. "Baseball Has Bumper Year in Berrien," *News-Palladium*, January 1, 1929, 85.
75. Hawkins and Bertolino, The House of David Baseball Team Research Project, www.peppergame.com.
76. "Pick Teams to Oppose Cubs in Local Tilt," *News-Palladium*, October 3, 1934, 8.
77. "House of David Team Recalled," *News - Palladium*, April 11, 1970, 16.
78. Hawkins and Bertolino, *The House of David Baseball Team*, 64.
79. "Deal Recalls Glory Days for House of David Team," *News-Palladium*, July 18, 1962, 20.
80. House of David 1920 Federal Census, Berrien County Michigan Genealogy Project.
81. Hawkins and Bertolino, House of David Baseball Team Research Project, www.peppergame.com.
82. "Long Haired Bearded Player Sought by Cubs," *St. Louis Post Dispatch*, November 25, 1919, 26.
83. Jeremy Bonafiglio, "Stirring the Echoes," *South Bend Tribune*, August 12, 2007, www.SouthBendTribune.com.
84. Funk and Wagnalls, *Literary Digest* for May 29, 1920, Vol. 65, 120.
85. "This Odd Looking Team May Furnish the Cubs with Hurler," *Times Herald*, December 12, 1919, 3.
86. "Long-Haired, Bearded Player Sought by Cubs, and His Teammates," *St. Louis Post Dispatch*, November 25, 1919, 26.
87. "Would Keep His Long Hair," *Santa Cruz Evening News*, April 26, 1920, 1.
88. *Historic Oregon Newspapers*: "The Gazette Times, 1912–1925," March 11, 1925, Image 6, 6.
89. "Bewhiskered First Baseman to Lead St. Joseph Autos," *Battle Creek Enquirer*, July 21, 1946, 19.
90. Ron Taylor, Trustee/Historian/Archivist, City of David, interview with author, February 4, 2013.
91. Adkin, Jr., *Brother Benjamin*, 244.
92. "John Tucker Ends Baseball Career," *News-Palladium*, August 23, 1969, 29.
93. "Broken Leg Ends Season for Tucker," *News-Palladium*, September 12, 1935, 12.
94. Hawkins and Bertolino, *The House of David Baseball Team*, 125.
95. Brian Ziebart, Trustee/Historian/Archivist/House of David recalled conversations he had with Lloyd Dalager about John Tucker.
96. "The 1928 Akron Tyrites Statistics," https://statscrew.com/minorbaseball/stats/t-at10047/y-1928.
97. *News-Palladium*, August 13, 1967, 29.
98. Adkin, Jr., *Brother Benjamin*, 40.
99. Hawkins and Bertolino, The House of David Baseball Team Research Project, www.peppergame.com.
100. "Ball Player Spurns Offer," *Ogden Standard-Examiner*, January 28, 1922, 6.
101. *Escanaba Daily Press*, March 31, 1941, 16.
102. Brian Ziebart, House of David Commune Records.
103. House of David 1920 Federal Census, Berrien County Michigan Genealogy Project.
104. "Bearded Beauties from House of David to Play Frick's Nine at College," *Daily Times*, August 1, 1924, 19.
105. Malan, *Muzzy Field*, 89.
106. Hawkins and Bertolino, The House of

David Baseball Team Research Project, www.peppergame.com.

107. "Vierits' [sic: Vieritz] Arm Is Paralyzed by a Hot One from Griffith," *Times Recorder*, June 20, 1924, 13.

108. "Record Crowd to See Clash on Local Lot," *Quad City Times*, August 1, 1924, 8.

109. "Arthur Vieritz, Baseball Star, Farner, Dies," *News-Palladium*, July 16, 1970, 15.

110. "K.O. Circles Form Israel Foe Sunday," *News-Palladium*, June 21, 1928, 6.

111. "Esther Hansel Again Branded 'Liar' In Court," *Herald Press*, August 3, 1927, 1.

112. "Joseph Hannaford Dies; Co-Founder of H. of D.," *Herald Press*, April 25, 1947, 1, 10.

113. Fogarty, *The Righteous Remnant*, 166.

114. "Young Man Member House of David Demented: Hit by Train Near Riverside," *News-Palladium*, April 14, 1916, 1.

115. Hawkins and Bertolino, The House of David Baseball Team Research Project, www.peppergame.com.

116. Brian Ziebart, House of David Commune Records.

117. "2 Israelites Get Term at Federal Pen," *Herald Palladium*, July 2, 1918, 1.

118. "House of David Nine to Play Mishawaka Club Sunday," *News-Palladium*, June 27, 1930, 10.

119. House of David 1920 Federal Census, Berrien County Michigan Genealogy Project.

120. "Bewhiskered Sons of House of David Play First Game on Diamond," *Topeka Daily Capital*, April 20, 1920, 9.

121. D.C. Allen House of David Collection, 1795–1980, Box 19.

122. Adkin, Jr., 48.

123. "Bryant Takes Stars from Cult Deputies," *News-Palladium*, July 24, 1929, 1.

124. "Two Players Hold Key To Colony Team," *News-Palladium*, June 2, 1931, 8.

125. "Colony Sunflower is a 'Four Bloom Special,'" *News- Palladium*, September 13, 1943, 8.

126. "Services Are Held For Frank Wyland," *News-Palladium*, April 25, 1946, 17.

127. Brian Ziebart, multiple emails and conversations with author.

128. Adkin, Jr., *Brother Benjamin*, 114.

129. "State Witness Says 'King' Was at Home When Wanted On Writ," *News-Palladium*, June 3, 1927, 1, 5.

130. "Robert Dewhirst Is Dead at 58," *News-Palladium*, April 30, 1966, 1.

131. "Bob Dewhirst on Program for Lions' Music Festival," *News-Palladium*, November 24, 1933, 2.

132. "Robert Dewhirst Is Dead at 58," *News-Palladium*, April 30, 1966, 1.

133. "A Man of Great Gentleness," *News-Palladium*, May 2, 1966, 2.

134. Hawkins and Bertolino, *The House of David Baseball Team*, 11.

135. House of David 1920 Federal Census, Berrien County Michigan Genealogy Project.

136. Hawkins and Bertolino, The House of David Baseball Team Research Project, www.peppergame.com.

137. "The Sport Whirl," *The Kane Republican*, January 10, 1931, 9.

138. "Three Games on Bill for Second Round," *News-Palladium*, January 12, 1933, 9.

139. "Whys May Find Tough Opposition Against Girl Basketballers Sunday," *Star Press*, December 17, 1931, 10.

140. "The House of David Fell," *Chillicothe Constitution-Tribune*, January 8, 1931, 15.

141. House of David 1920 Federal Census, Berrien County Michigan Genealogy Project.

142. "Short Whiskers Lose Ball Club Directorship," *Reading Times*, February 26, 1929, 13.

143. "Walker Leaves with Israel's 'Official' Traveling Outfit," *News-Palladium*, March 27, 1929, 12.

144. "Players in West, Playing Winning Ball," *News-Palladium*, August 12, 1929, 11.

145. "House of David Team Will Play Here Saturday," *St. Cloud Times*, June 3, 1930, 14.

146. "Two Teams Hit Road for Israelites?" *News-Palladium*, February 20, 1929, 12.

147. "Never Too Old for Baseball," *South Bend Tribune*, April 9, 2004, D2.

148. Hawkins and Bertolino, *The House of David Baseball Team*, 59.

149. "Jackie Crow May Hurl in Sunday Game," *News-Palladium*, August 1, 1930, 11.

150. "Sports Hash as Served by Snorter," *News-Palladium*, July 15, 1947, 8.

151. "Harold Daisy, Jackie Crow Star on Hill," *News-Palladium*, August 24, 1931, 8.

152. "Colony Nine to Play So. Bend Champs," *News-Palladium*, April 30, 1932, 6.

153. Brian Ziebart, multiple emails and conversations with author.

154. Jeremy Bonafiglio, "Stirring the Echoes," *South Bend Tribune*, August 12, 2007, D7.

155. "The House That David Built," *Appeal-Democrat Sports*, August 5, 2011, 2.

156. Brian Ziebart, multiple emails and conversations with author.

157. www.articles.southernbendtribune.com

158. Brian Ziebart, multiple emails and conversations with author.

159. "House of David's 'History Line' is Gone," *News-Palladium*, August 3, 2012.

160. "Mrs. Amelia Klum, 86 Today, in Good Health," *News-Palladium*, July 12, 1939, 4.

161. Hawkins and Bertolino, The House of David Baseball Team Research Project, www.peppergame.com.

162. "House of David Team Is Beaten," *Scranton Republican*, August 28, 1920, 16.

163. "House of David Blanks Columbia City Outfit," *Fort Wayne Sentinel*, June 8, 1921, 10.

164. "House of David Band Which Tops Yost Vaudeville Bill," *Santa Ana Register*, January 10, 1922, 6.

165. Hawkins and Bertolino, The House of David Baseball Team Research Project, www.peppergame.com .

166. "Pavlick Gives 1 Hit, Pallas 6 in Twin Win," *News-Palladium*, September 30, 1940, 8.
167. "Daisy to Oppose Veller on Mound," *News-Palladium*, June 22, 1935, 7.
168. "Pure Oils vs. Colored Giants at Colony Park Tomorrow," *News-Palladium*, June 26, 1937, 6.
169. "Ernie Selby Day Celebrated at Local Ball Park," *News-Palladium*, June 24, 1935, 6.
170. Herald Palladium, "Soldiers Put Up Battle In Speedy Game," July 10, 1944, 9.
171. "House of David Team Recalled," *News Palladium*, April 11, 1970, 16.
172. "B.H., St. Joe Little Leagues Vie Sunday," *News Palladium*, August 15, 1959, 11.
173. United States Census conducted by U.S. Census Bureau, April 15, 1910.
174. "Errors Cost Thorpe Team Sunday Game," *News-Palladium*, May 6, 1929, 10.
175. "King Sport Rules in Berrien County," *News-Palladium*, July 3, 1929. 12."
176. "Wesley Schneider Obituary," *News-Palladium*, June 17, 1958, 13.
177. "Four More Old Driver Tags Turn Up," *News-Palladium*, June 4, 1953, 21.
178. Brian Ziebart, House of David Commune Records.
179. Hawkins and Bertolino, *The House of David Baseball Team*, 15.
180. "Grover Alexander," https://www.baseball-almanac.com/players/player.php?p=alexape0.1
181. Stephen Martini, *The Chattanooga Lookouts: 100 Seasons of Scenic City Baseball* (Cleveland, TN: Dry Ice Publishing, 2005), 57–59.
182. "Cancer Claims Life of Babe Didrikson," *Pittsburgh Press*, September 27, 1956, 1, 2.
183. "Babe Didrikson Joins House of David," *St. Louis Star*, February 28, 1934, 18.
184. "Barnstorming Days," *Pasadena Star News*, February 26, 1985, D-4.
185. Hawkins and Bertolino, *The House of David Baseball Team*, 76.
186. https://www.baseball-reference.com/playerjog?=atwell001.
187. "Atwell Joins Seals," *Press Democrat*, January 18, 1934, 4.
188. "Raimondi Working Hard, but Hitting on Poor Luck," *Oakland Tribune*, March 27, 1934, 21.
189. "Seals Release Former House of David Star," *Fresno Bee-The Republican*, April 25, 1934, 16.
190. "Sport Lines," *Spring Daily Herald*, March 11, 1935, 2.
191. Kevin Nelson, *The Golden Game: The Story of California Baseball* (San Francisco: California Historical Society Press, 2004), 203–4.
192. "House of David Arrives Here Tomorrow," *The Honolulu Star Bulletin*, September 23, 1936, 12.
193. P.J. Dragseth, *A Biographical Dictionary of Major League Baseball Scouts* (Jefferson, NC: McFarland, 2011), 101.
194. "The Sports Parade," *Los Angeles Times*, April 3, 1937, 29.
195. "Atwell Resting After Third Operation," *Pasadena Post*, May 13, 1937, 1.
196. *Pasadena Star News*, May 5, 2008, 18.
197. "Richard Haybes 'Dick' Wykoff, 1966 Inductee," The Osborne County Hall of Fame, https://wordpress.com/2012/11/04/richard-haynes-dick-wykoff-1996-inductee.
198. *Ibid.*
199. "Dick Wykoff Recalls Pitching for Salina Millers in 1925–26," *Salina Journal*, May 1, 1977, 24.
200. "House of David, Monarchs Cavort," *San Bernardino County Sun*, August 18, 1948, 18.
201. "Eddie Deal to Pilot Nine at Colony," *News-Palladium*, May 1, 1940, 6.
202. "Deal to Catch for Colony Club Here," *News-Palladium*, August 27, 1936, 8.
203. "House of David's Deal Dies," *News-Palladium*, July 13, 2000, 1.
204. "Deal Recalls Glory Days for House of David," *News-Palladium*, July 18, 1962, 1.
205. "House of David's Deal Dies," *News Palladium*, July 13, 2000, 1.
206. "Night Game on Island," *The Evening News*, September 2, 1931, 11.
207. "Former Pro Baseballers to Play Legion '9' Monday," *Wausau Daily Herald*, July 1, 1967, 12.
208. "Henry Brunschmidt of Medford to Peg for Local Ball Unit," *Wausau Daily Herald*, June 25, 1935, 10.
209. "Rapids, Medford to Oppose Locals," *Marshfield News-Herald*, May 28, 1937, 12.
210. "Record Herald Sports," *Wausau Daily Herald*, July 1, 1967, 12.
211. "Norman Blieding Obituary," *Wausau Daily Herald*, December 2, 1974, 8.
212. "Charles Swaney, Obituary," *Wausau Daily Herald*, November 23, 1953, 6.
213. "Sports Sputterings and Sparks," *The Daily News*, April 25, 1938, 6.
214. "'Moose' Swaney, Ex-Eastern Hurler, Winning for Bearded House of Davids at Age 51," *Star Gazette*, July 2, 1941, 20.
215. "House of David Pitcher Still Going Strong at 51," *Poughkeepsie Journal*, July 9, 1941, 12.
216. "Late 'Moose' Swaney Was a Legendary Character," *The Tribune*, December 24, 1961, 31.
217. "Moose Swaney, at 51, Can Still Make the Batter A Sucker," *Asbury Park Press*, July 7, 1941, 10.
218. "Legendary Pitcher Passes," *Pittsburgh Post-Gazette*, April 10, 1962, 58.
219. The National Baseball Hall of Fame Archives, House of David Files, April 3, 1937, M.
220. "Gehrig's Old Roomie, Now 51, Is Still Pitching: Moose Swaney, House of David, Gets Second Wind," *Mount Carmel Item*, June 28, 1941, 6.
221. "Swaney, Sandlot Pitcher, Dies," *Pittsburgh Press*, November 7, 1961, 36.
222. "Maquoketa Nine, House of David to Play Thursday," *Daily Times*, May 22, 1934, 12.
223. Sanford, *The Denver Post Tournament*, 88.
224. "Backseat Driving," *Salt Lake Telegram*, July 31, 1935, 12.

225. "Buck's Tavern Is Davenport Nine in Action," *Quad City Democrat*, August 6, 1937, 20.

226. The National Baseball Hall of Fame Archives, House of David Files, "Recall Baseball's Barnstorming Days," October 1988.

227. "Lewis E. Hummel, 88, Northumberland," *Daily Item*, August 21, 1906, A6.

228. "David Team Has Classy Players," *San Bernardino County Sun*, August 8, 1946, 21.

229. Hawkins and Bertolino, *The House of David Baseball Team*, 89.

230. The National Baseball Hall of Fame Archives, House of David Files, "Recall Baseball's Barnstorming Days," October 1988.

231. *Ibid.*

232. Gary Bedingfield, *Baseball's Dead of World War II, A Roster of Players Who Died in Service* (Jefferson, NC: McFarland, 2009), 640.

233. "Statesville Owls, House of David Clash Tonight," *Statesville Daily Record*, April 17, 1942, 4.

234. "Clowns, House of David to Clash Here Thursday Eve," *The Times*, May 24, 1942, 17.

235. "House of David in Fort Lee," *The Record*, June 20, 1940, 5.

236. https://www.baseball-reference.com/players/b/bensonal01.html.

237. Simkus, *Outsider Baseball*, 216.

238. Tom Deveaux, *The Washington Senators 1901–2001* (Jefferson, NC: McFarland, 2001), 127.

239. www.baseball-almanac.com./ballplayers/AllenBenson.

240. "Sox Rout House of David Moundsman," *Decatur Herald*, August 20, 1934, 5.

241. "Indians Rally in 8th to Nose Out Red Sox," *Star Tribune*, August 28, 1934, 15.

242. www.baseball-almanac.com/player.php?=bensonal01.

243. *Ibid.*

244. "Stuffy Benson, Who Played Major League Baseball, Dies," *Argus-Leader*, November 18, 1999, 12.

245. "Ardy Keller Killed; Ex-Browns' Catcher," *Morning News*, October 26, 1944, 14.

246. "Lincoln Youth Signs with House of David," *Lincoln Star*, January 28, 12. October 22, 1934, 8.

247. "From Beards to Browns," *St. Louis Star and Times*, March 18, 1943, 22.

248. Jonathan Fraser Light, *The Cultural Encyclopedia of Baseball*, Second Edition (Jefferson, NC: McFarland, 1957), 1026.

249. "Ardys Keller, Browns Catcher, Killed in France," *St. Louis Post Dispatch*, October 25, 1944, 16.

250. "Popowski: Baseball Has Been My Life," *The Central New Jersey Home News*, August 20, 1998, A1-A2, 2.

251. Wayne McElreavy, "Popowski," https://sabr.org/bioproject, No date given.

252. "Eddie Popowski, 88, Pro-Baseball Legend," *Central New Jersey Home News*, December 5, 2001, 21.

253. "Edward 'Buddy' Popowski Still Active in Baseball," *The Central New Jersey Home News*, December 19, 1943, 13.

254. "Sayresville's Popowski to Be Inducted Into Hall," *The Central New Jersey Home News*, December 18, 1994, 27.

255. "Veteran Boston Coach Dies at 88," *Asbury Park Press*, December 5, 2001, 39.

256. "State's Star Pitcher Quits This Season," *Herald Press*, June 7, 1928, 10.

257. "High Lights," *Lansing State Journal*, May 8, 1938, 8.

258. "State's Big League Rookies Back Home," *Lansing State Journal*, October 15, 1929, 23.

259. Brian Ziebart, House of David Commune Records.

260. "House of David to Start Stellar Lineup," *Alton Evening Telegraph*, September 5, 1936, 8.

261. "Lefty Tolles Dies in Grayling," *News Palladium*, April 9, 1948, 13.

262. *Ibid.*

Bibliography

Interviews

Mel Atwell, brother of shortstop Dick Atwell, House of David and City of David teams.
Debbie Boyersmith, granddaughter of player Earl Boyersmith.
Joe Palledino, outfielder on 1948 House of David squad.
Joe "Red" Petrongolo, catcher on 1948 House of David squad.
Ronald Taylor, Trustee/Historian/Archivist, Mary's City of David.
Brian Ziebert, Trustee/Historian/Archivist, the House of David.

Books and Articles

Ackman, Martha. *Curveball: The Remarkable Story of Toni Stone, the First Woman to Play Professional Baseball in the Negro Leagues.* Chicago: Chicago Review Press, 2012.
Adkin, Clare, Jr. *Brother Benjamin: A History of the Israelite House of David.* Berrien Springs, MI: Andrews University Press, 1990.
African American Registry, online database of African American Heritage. www.aaregistry.org.
Alabama Department of Archives History. July 12, 2016. www.archives.alabama.gov.
Alexander, Charles C. *Breaking the Slump: Baseball in the Depression Era.* New York: Columbia University Press, 2004.
_____. *Our Game: An American Baseball History.* New York: Henry Holt, 1997.
Allen, D.C. *House of David Collection, 1795–1980. Repository.* Ann Arbor: Bentley Historical Library, Michigan Historical Collections, University of Michigan, year not listed.
_____. *House of David Collection, 2005–2006.* Ann Arbor: Bentley Historical Library, Michigan Historical Collections, University of Michigan, 2008.
Alpert, Rebecca. *Out of Left Field: Jews and Black Baseball.* New York: University of Oxford Press, 2011.
Altherr, Thomas L. *Above the Fruited Plain.* Denver: SABR National Convention, 2002.
Anonymous. "Reconstructing Negro League and Latin American Baseball History." July 21, 1947. www.agetype.typepad.com.
Arent-Cauley, Sherry. *Berrien County.* Charleston, SC: Arcadia, 2000.
Barthel, Thomas. *Baseball Barnstorming and Exhibition Games, 1901–1962.* Jefferson, NC: McFarland, 2007.
Baseball Hall of Fame Museum and Archives, donated material, undated clippings and partial clippings without titles.
Bedingfield, Gary. *Baseball's Dead of World War II: A Roster of Professional Baseball Players Who Died in Service.* Jefferson, NC: McFarland, 2009.
Berrien County Genealogy Project. *House of David 1920 Federal Census.* Transcribed by Brenda Sears, April 2003.
Blassingame, John, PhD. *The Slave Community: Plantation Life in the Antebellum South.* Oxford, UK: Oxford University Press, 1979.
_____. *Slave Testimony: Two Centuries of Letters, Speeches, Interviews and Autobiographies.* Baton Rogue: Louisiana State University Press, 1977.
Blight, David W. "The First Decoration Day." April 27, 2015. http://www.davidwblight.com/public-history/2015/4/27/the-first-decoration-day-newark-star-ledger.
Bonifiglio, Jeremy D. "Stirring Echoes." *South Bend Tribune*, August 12, 2007. articles.southbendtribune.com/2007-08-12/news.
Bowerbank, Sylvia. "Joanna Southcott, Prophet and Writer." 2004. www.oxforddnb.com.
Boyd, Todd. *African American and Popular Culture.* Chicago: University of Chicago Press, 2008.

Brandon, Le Roy D., Clerk, Michigan House of Representatives compiled data under direction of South Tremble, Clerk of Michigan House of Representatives, 1936.
Bruce, Janet. *The Kansas City Monarchs: Champions of Black Baseball*. Lawrence: Kansas University Press, 1985.
Cassaway, Jarrold. "Octavius Cato and the Pythians of Philadelphia." *Pennsylvania Legacies* (Historical Society of Pennsylvania), May 20, 2007, 5–9.
Cayleff, Susan E. *Babe: The Life and Legend of Babe Didrikson Zaharias*. Chicago: University of Illinois Press, 1995.
Chadwick, Bruce. "Barnstorming America: When the Game Was Black and White: An Illustrated History of the Negro Leagues." *Syracuse University Magazine* 9, Issue 4 (1933): Art. 3.
Chadwick, Henry, ed. *Spalding's Official Baseball Guide, Spalding's Athletic Library, Group 1, No. 1*. New York: American Sports Publishing, 1907.
Charlton, James, ed. *The National Pastime: A Review of Baseball History, Vol. 24*. Cleveland: Society for American Baseball Research, 2004.
Coolidge, Judge Orville, A. *A Twentieth Century History of Berrien County*. Chicago: Lewis, 1906.
Dann, Martin. *The Black Press. 1927–1890: The Quest for National Identity*. New York: G.P. Putnam's Sons, 1971.
David, Donald. *Charles Sumner and the Rights of Man*. New York: Alfred K. Knopf, 1970.
DeArment, Robert K. *Bat Masterson: The Man and the Legend*. Norman: University of Oklahoma Press, 1989.
Debono, Paul. *The Chicago American Giants*. Jefferson, NC: McFarland, 2007.
Derby, Richard E., Jr., and Jim Coleman. "House of David Baseball." *National Pastime, a Review of Baseball History* 14 (1994): 7–10.
Deveaux, Tom. *The Washington Senators, 1901–1971*. Jefferson, NC: McFarland, 2001.
Devine, Christopher. "Harry Wright." https://sabr.org/bioproj/person/eb17c14e.
Dixon, Phil, and Patrick J. Hannigan. *The Negro Baseball Leagues, 1867–1955*. Mattuck, NY: Amereon, 1992.
Dixon, Phil S. *John "Buck" O'Neil, the Rookie, the Man, the Legend*. Bloomington, IN: Author House, 2009.
Dragseth, PJ. *A Biographical Dictionary of Major League Baseball Scouts*. Jefferson, NC: McFarland, 2011.
Driefort, John E. *Baseball History from Outside the Lines: A Reader*. Lincoln: University of Nebraska Press, 2001.
Dunkel, Tom. *Color Blind*. New York: Atlantic Monthly Press, 2013.
"Earliest Baseball Clubs." http://mlb.mlb.com/memorylab/spread_of_baseball/earliest_clubs.jsp.
Fleitz, David. "Cap Anson." https://sabr.org/bioproj/person/9b42f875.
Flima, John. "John Donaldson, the Greatest Pitcher You've Never Heard Of." March 27, 2011. www.thepostgame.com.
Fogarty, Robert S. *The Righteous Remnant: The House of David*. Kent, OH: Kent University Press, 1981.
Freedman, Lew. *African American Pioneers of Baseball: A Biographical Encyclopedia*. Westport, CN: Greenwood, 2007.
Furst, Terry R. *Early American Baseball and the Sporting Press: Shaping the Image of the Game*. Jefferson, NC: McFarland, 2014.
Gallagher, Mark. *The Yankee Encyclopedia, Sixth Edition*. New York: Sports Publishing, 2003.
Gates, Jim. *Memories and Dreams: The Official Magazine of the Hall of Fame, Vol. 32, Number 2*. Cooperstown, NY: Opening Day, 2010.
Gay, Timothy M. *Satch, Dizzy & Rapid Robert: The Wild Saga of Interracial Baseball Before Jackie Robinson*. New York: Simon & Schuster, 2010.
Gitersnoke, Don. *Baseball's Bearded Boys*. Los Angeles: Self-published by author, 1996.
Glasrud, Bruce A. *African Americans on the Great Plains: An Anthology*. Lincoln: University of Nebraska Press, 2009.
Godfrey, Linda S. *Weird Michigan: Your Travel Guide to Michigan's Last and Best Kept Secrets*. New York: Sterling, 2006.
Goldberg, Robert Alan. *Hooded Empire: The Ku Klux Klan in Colorado*. Chicago: University of Illinois Press, 1982.
Green, Stanley. Laredo, 1755–1920: An Overview. Laredo, TX: Border Studies, 1990.
Gregovich, Barbara. *Women at Play: The Story of Women in Baseball*. San Diego: Harcourt Brace, 1993.
Hall, Alvin, and Thomas Atherr, eds. *Cooperstown Symposium on Baseball and American Culture, 1998*. Jefferson, NC: McFarland, 2002.
Haupert, Michael. "Ed Bolden." https://sabr.org/bioproj/person/84ab3bca.
Hawkins, Joel, and Terry Bertolino. *The House of David Baseball Team*. Charleston, SC: Arcadia, 2000.
Heaphy, Leslie A. *The Negro Leagues, 1869–1960*. Jefferson, NC: McFarland, 2003.
____, ed. *Satchel Paige and Company: Essays on the Kansas City Monarchs, Their Greatest Star and the Negro Leagues*. Jefferson, NC: McFarland, 2006.
Hetrick, J. Thomas. *Chris Von Der Ahe and the St. Louis Browns*. Lanham, MD: Scarecrow, 1999.
Heward, Bill, with Dimitri V. Gay. *Some Are Called Clowns: A Season with the Last of the Great Barnstorming Baseball Teams*. New York: Thomas Y. Crowell, 1974.

Hickok, Ralph. *Negro National League, the Encyclopedia of North American Sports History, Second Edition.* New York: Facts on File, 2002.
Hinds, William Alfred. *American Communities and Societies.* Chicago: C. H. Kerr, 1908.
Hogan, Lawrence D. *Shades of Glory: The Negro Leagues and the Story of African- American Baseball.* Washington, D.C.: National Geographic, 2006.
Horvitz, Peter, and Joachim Horvitz. *The Big Book of Jewish Baseball: An Illustrated Encyclopedia and Anecdotal History.* New York: SPI, 2001.
Houser, Christopher. *The Negro Leagues Chronology: Events in Organized Black Baseball, 1920–1948.* Jefferson, NC: McFarland, 2006.
Hughson, Callum. "The House of David." February 15, 2010. http://mopupduty.com/the-house-of-david/.
"The Influenza Pandemic of 1918." *Journal of American Medical Association, Final Edition. 1918.* https://virus.sanford.edu.
Jackson, Wayne. "Alexander Campbell and Christ's Church." *Christian Courier.* www.christiancourier.com/articles/822.
Jacobs, Jane, and Douglas Jacobs. "Dexter Park." *The Baseball Research Journal* 29 (2000): 41-45.
Jensen, Chris. Baseball State by State: Major and Negro League Players, Ballparks, Museums and Historical Sites. Jefferson, NC: McFarland, 2012.
Kephart, William M., and William W. Zelner. *Extraordinary Groups: An Examination of Unconventional Lifestyles, 5th Edition.* New York: St. Martin's, 1994.
Klein, Alan M. *Baseball on the Border: A Tale of Two Laredos.* Princeton, NJ: Princeton University Press, 1997.
Lanctot, Neil. *Negro League Baseball: The Rise and Ruin of a Black Institution.* Philadelphia: University of Pennsylvania Press, 2004.
Langer, Adam. "The Last Days of the House of David," June 30, 1994. www.chicagoreader.com.
Lester, Larry. *Black Baseball in Kansas City.* Charleston, SC: Arcadia, 2000.
_____. *Rube Foster in His Time: On the Field and in the Papers with Black Baseball's Greatest Visionary.* Jefferson, NC: McFarland, 2012.
Lewis, James R. *The Encyclopedia of Cults, Sects, and New Religion.* Amherst, NY: Prometheus, 2002.
Light, Jonathan Fraser. *The Cultural Encyclopedia of Baseball.* Jefferson, NC: McFarland, 1997.
_____. *The Cultural Encyclopedia of Baseball, Second Edition.* Jefferson, NC: McFarland, 2016.
Lipmann, David, and Satchel Paige. *Maybe I'll Pitch Forever.* New York: Doubleday, 1993.
Lomax, Michael E. *Black Baseball Entrepreneurs, 1860–1901.* Syracuse, NY: Syracuse University Press, 2003.
Madden, W.C., and Patrick J. Stewart. *The Western League: A Baseball History, 1885 through 1999.* Jefferson, NC: McFarland, 2001.
Malan, Douglas M. *Muzzy Field: Tales of a Forgotten Ballpark.* Bloomington, IN: iUniverse Imprint, 2008.
Mann, Arthur. *Branch Rickey: An American in Action.* Boston: Houghton-Mifflin, 1957.
Martini, Stephen. *The Chattanooga Lookouts and 100 Seasons of Scenic City Baseball.* Cleveland, TN: Dry Ice, 2005.
McCarthy, Sarah O. *Denver's Washington Park.* Charleston, SC: Arcadia, 2014.
McKenna, Brian. "Gus Greenlee." https://sabr.org/bioproj/person/fabd8400.
McNeil, William F. *Black Baseball Out of Season: Pay for Play Outside of the Negro Leagues.* Jefferson, NC: McFarland, 2007.
Meldrim, Linsey Helen. "A Case Study of the Israelite House of David." Master's Thesis, Kent State University, 2012.
Melton, Gordon. *Encyclopedia of American Religion, Seventh Edition.* Farmington Hills, MI: National Council of Churches Historic Archive, 2003.
Miklich, Eric. "Jim Creighton." 2016. http://www.19cbaseball.com/players-jim-creighton.html.
Myers, Robert C. *Millennial Visions and Earthly Pursuits: The Israelite House of David.* Berrien County, MI: Berrien County Historical Society, 1999.
National Register of Historic Places "Shiloh House—Benton Harbor, Michigan." National Park Service Register Information System, March 13, 2009.
"Negro League Baseball: Timeline of Events in Black Baseball." www.negroleaguebaseball.com.
Nemec, David. *The Beer & Whiskey League.* Guilford, CT: Lyons Press, 2004.
Noverr, Douglas A., and Lawrence E. Ziewacz. *The Games They Played: Sports in American History, 1865–1980.* Washington, D.C.: Rowman & Littlefield, 1983.
Nowlin, Bill. "The Boston Pilgrims Never Existed." https://www.baseball-almanac.com/articles/boston_pilgrims_story.shtml.
Odzer, Timothy. "Rube Foster." https://sabr.org/bioproj/person/fcf322f7.
O'Neil, John "Buck," with Steve Wulf and David Conrads. *I Was Right on Time.* New York: Simon & Schuster, 1996.
Pajot, Dennis. *Baseball's Heartland War, 1902–1903: The Western League and American Association Vie for Turf, Players and Profits.* Jefferson, NC: McFarland, 2011.

Palmer, Pete, Gary Gillette, Stuart Shea, Matthew Silverman, and Gregg Spira, eds. *The ESPN Baseball Encyclopedia*. New York: Sterling, 2006.
Parr, Royse. "Semipro Baseball's Golden Era (1933–1941): A Tale of Two Cities." *Nine: A Journal of Baseball History and Culture* 15, no. 1 (Fall 2006): 54–67.
Patrick, Jean S. *The Girl Who Struck Out Babe Ruth*. Minneapolis, MN: Millbrook Press, 2000.
Pender, James. *History of Benton Harbor and Tales of Village Days*. Chicago: Braun Printing, 1915.
_____. *Reynolds Historical Genealogy Collection: History of Benton Harbor and Tales of Village Days*. Chicago: Braun Printing, 1925.
Peterson, Richard, F. *The St. Louis Baseball Reader*. Columbia: University of Missouri Press, 2006.
Peterson, Todd. *Early Black Baseball in Minnesota: The St. Paul Gophers, Minneapolis Keystoners and Other Barnstorming Teams of the Deadball Era*. Jefferson, NC: McFarland, 2010.
_____. "May the Best Man Win: The Black Ball Championship 1866–1923." *Baseball Research Journal* 42, no. 1 (Spring 2013): 7–24.
Peyton, Robert. *The Federal League of Baseball Clubs: History of an Outlaw Major League, 1914–1915*. Jefferson, NC: McFarland, 2009.
Pollock, Allan J., and James A. Riley, eds. *Barnstorming to Heaven: Syd Pollack and His Great Black Teams*. Tuscaloosa: University of Alabama Press, 2006.
Price, Joseph. *Rounding the Bases: Baseball and Religion in America*. Macon, GA: Mercer University Press, 2006.
Rachuig, Florence. "The House of David: a History in Pictures." Saugatuck-Douglas Historical Society Slide Presentation. April 18, 1992.
Repplinger, Matthew Kasper, III. *Baseball in Denver*. Charleston, SC: Arcadia, 2013.
Ribowsky, Mark. *A Complete History of the Negro Leagues, 1884–1956*. New York: Birch Line Press, 1995.
Riley, James A. *The Biographical Encyclopedia of the Negro Baseball Leagues*. New York: Carroll & Graf, 1994.
Ritter, Lawrence S. *The Glory of Their Times: The Story of the Early Days of Baseball Told by the Men Who Played It*. New York: Macmillan, 1966.
Robbins, Michael W., ed. *Brooklyn: A State of Mind*. New York: Workman, 2001.
Roberts, Randy. *Jack Dempsey. The Manassa Mauler*. Champaign: University of Illinois Press, 1979.
Rogosin, William Donn. "Black Baseball: the Life in the Negro Leagues." PhD diss., University of Texas, 1981.
Rosengren, John. *Hank Greenberg, the Hero of Heroes*. New York: New American Library, 2013.
Rossi, John P. *The National Game: Baseball and American Culture*. Chicago: Ivan R. Dee, 2000.
Ryczek, William J. *When Johnny Came Sliding Home: The Post-Civil War Baseball Boom 1865–1870*. Jefferson, NC: McFarland, 1998.
Sanford, Jay. "African American Baseballists and the Denver Post Tournament." Denver Colorado Historical Society, Spring, 1995.
_____. *The Denver Post Tournament: A Chronicle of America's First Integrated Professional Baseball Event*. Cleveland: Society for American Baseball Research, 2003.
_____. *The Denver Post Tournament: A Project of the Rocky Mountain Chapter* of the Society for American Baseball Research. Cleveland: SABR Publishers, 2003.
Schaaf, Phil. *Sports Inc., 100 Years of Sports Business*. New York: Prometheus, 2004.
Schulander, Georg. *The High Island Long Hairs House of Virgins: The House of David Cult*. Traverse City, MI: White Pine Press (Northwestern Michigan College), 1914.
Seymour, Harold, PhD. *Baseball: The People's Game*. New York: Oxford University Press, 1990.
Seymour, Harold, PhD, and Dorothy Seymour Mills. *Baseball, the Golden Age*. New York: Oxford University Press, 1971.
Simkus, Scott. *Outsider Baseball: The Weird World of Baseball on the Fringe, 1876–1950*. Chicago: Chicago Review Press, 2014.
Skipper, John C. *Wicked Curve: The Life and Troubled Times of Grover Cleveland Alexander*. Jefferson, NC: McFarland, 2006.
Solomon, Burt. *The Baseball Timeline in Association with Major League Baseball*. New York: Dorling Kindersley, 2000.
Southwest Michigan Business and Tourism Directory. www.swmidirectory.org.
Spatz, Lyle. *Historical Dictionary of Baseball*. Lanham, MD: Scarecrow, 2012.
Spink, Alfred Henry. *The National Game*. Carbondale: Southern Illinois University Press, 1910.
Stentiford, Barry M., and L.M. Nikki, eds. *The Jim Crow Encyclopedia. Vol. 1*. Westport, CT: Greenwood, 2008.
Stoneberg, Eric Mark. "The Denver Post Tournament and Pre-Organized Baseball Integration." Master's thesis, Arizona State University, 2009.
Sullivan, Dean A., editor. *Early Innings: A Documented History of Baseball, 1825–1908*. Lincoln: University of Nebraska Press, 1995.
_____, ed. *Middle Innings: A Documentary History of Baseball 1900–1948*. Lincoln: University of Nebraska Press, 1998.

Surdam, David George. *Wins, Losses, and Empty Seats: How Baseball Outlasted the Great Depression.* Lincoln: University of Nebraska Press, 2011.
Sutton, Robert. *Modern American Communes: A Dictionary.* Santa Barbara, CA: Greenwood, 2005.
Swift, Tom. *Chief Bender's Burden: The Silent Struggle of a Baseball Star.* Lincoln: University of Nebraska Press, 2010.
Terry, James L. *Long Before the Dodgers: Baseball in Brooklyn, 1855–1884.* Jefferson, NC: McFarland, Jefferson, 2002.
Thomas, Keith. *Religion and the Decline of Magic: Studies in Popular Beliefs in Sixteenth and Seventeenth Century England.* New York: Charles Scribner's Sons, 1971.
Thorn, John. *Baseball in the Garden of Eden: The Secret History of the Early Game.* New York: Simon & Schuster, 2011.
_____. "Jim Creighton." https://sabr.org/bioproj/person/2d2e5d16.
Thorn, John, and Pete Palmer. *Total Baseball.* New York: Warner, 1989.
Thorpe, Francis. *Crown of Thorns: House of David Victory and Legal Troubles Revived.* Benton Harbor, MI: Benton Harbor Publishers, 1929.
Tye, Larry. *Satchel: The Life and Times of an American Legend.* New York: Random House, 2009.
Ward, Geoffrey C., and Ken Burns. *Baseball: An Illustrated History.* New York: Alfred A. Knopf, 1994.
Wilkerson, Isabel. *The Warmth of Other Suns: The Epic Story of America's Greatest Migration.* New York: Random House, 2010.
Wilkes, George, ed. *The Spirit of the Times Collection, 1868–1892.* April 19, 1973.
Wishart, David J., ed. Encyclopedia of the Great Plains. Lincoln: University of Nebraska Press 2004.
"Woodrow Wilson: Message to Congress, 63rd Congress, 2nd Session." Senate Doc. No. 566, Washington, 1914.
Woods, Bob, ed. *The Baseball Timeline.* New York: DK, 1997.
Woodward, Ann. "High Island Childhood, a Boy's Life with the House of David." *Michigan History Magazine* 73, no. 2 (March/April 1989).
Worth, Richard. *Baseball Team Names.* Jefferson, NC, McFarland, 2013.
Wyatt, Daniel. The 'Jesus Boys': The House of David. The National Pastime Museum, November 19, 2014. https://sabr.org/latest/wyatt-jesus-boys-baseball-and-house-david.
Young, William A. *J. L. Wilkinson and the Kansas City Monarchs: Trailblazers in Black Baseball.* Jefferson, NC: McFarland, 2016.
Zinn, John G., and Paul G. Zinn, eds. *Ebbets Field: Essays and Memories of Brooklyn's Historic Ballpark, 1913–1968.* Jefferson, NC: McFarland, 2012.
Zoss, Joel, and John Bowman. *Diamonds in the Rough: The Untold History of Baseball.* Lincoln: University of Nebraska Press, 2004.

Archival Sources

House of David 1920 Federal Census, Berrien County Michigan Genealogy Project, transcribed by Brenda R. Sears, April 2003.

Newspapers and Periodicals

(Reporters and article titles found in Endnotes)
Akron Beacon (OH)
Alton Evening Telegraph (IL)
Altoona Mirror (PA)
Altoona Tribune (PA)
Amarillo Daily News (TX)
American Sociological Review
Angola Herald (IN)
Appleton Post-Crescent (WI)
Argus-Leader (SD)
Arizona Daily Star
Arizona Republic
Arkansas Democrat
Asbury Park Press (NJ)
Bakersfield Californian
Battle Creek Enquirer (MI)
Beatrice Daily Sun (NE)
Belvidere Daily Republican (IL)
Bend Bulletin (OR)
Berkshire Eagle (MA)

Big Spring Daily News (TX)
Big Springs Daily Herald (TX)
The Billings Gazette (MT)
Bismarck Tribune
Boston Daily Globe
Boston Post
Bradford Evening Star (PA)
Brainerd Daily Dispatch (MN)
Brooklyn Daily Eagle
The Buffalo Inquirer
The Buffalo Times
Central New Jersey Home News
Chanute Daily Tribune (KS)
Charlotte News
Chicago Daily Tribune
Chicago Defender
Chicago Tribune
Chillicothe Gazette (OH)
Chillicothe Tribune (MO)
Chilliwack Progress (BC)

Clarion-Ledger (MO)
Colorado Statesman
Coshocton Tribune (OH)
Council Bluffs Nonpareil (IA)
The Courier (IA)
Courier-Journal (KY)
Courier News (NJ)
Cumberland Evening Times (MD)
Daily Capital Journal (SD)
Daily Capital News (MO)
Daily Chronicle (IL)
Daily Inter-Lake (MT)
Daily Plainsman (SD)
Daily Press (VA)
Daily Telegram (MI)
Daily Times News (SC)
Davenport Democrat and Leader (IA)
Decatur Daily News (AL)
Decatur Daily Review (IL)
Decatur Evening Herald (IL)
Decatur Herald (IL)
Delaware County Daily (PA)
Delaware County Daily Times (PA)
Delhi Gazette (New Delhi, India)
Democrat & Chronicle (NY)
Denver Post
Des Moines Register
Detroit Free Press
Duluth News Tribune (MN)
Dunkirk Evening Observer (NY)
El Paso Herald (TX)
Emporia Gazette (KS)
Escanaba Daily Press (MI)
Escanaba Evening Post (MI)
Escanaba Morning News (MI)
The Eugene Guard (OR)
Eugene Register Guard (OR)
The Evening Herald (NY)
The Evening News (PA)
The Evening Review (OH)
The Fort Scott Daily Monitor (KS)
The Fort Wayne Journal-Gazette (IN)
The Fredericksburg Standard (TX)
Fresno Bee—The Republican
Funk & Wagnall: The Literary Digest, Vol. 65, May 1920.
Gary Post-Tribune (IN)
Gazette (Montreal, Quebec)
Grand Rapids Press (MI)
Great Falls Tribune (MT)
Green Bay Press-Gazette (WI)
Greenville News (SC)
Harrisburg Evening News (PA)
Harrisburg Telegraph (PA)
Havre Daily News (MT)
Helena Independent Record
Herald-Journal (AL)
Herald-Palladium (MI)
Herald Press (MI)
Honolulu Star-Bulletin
Idaho State Journal
Independent Record (MT)
Indiana Gazette (PA)
Indianapolis Star (IN)
Inter-Ocean (Chicago)
Iola Register (KS)
Iowa City Press
Ironwood Daily Globe (MI)
Jefferson City Post-Tribune (MO)
Joplin Globe (MO)
Journal and Courier (IN)
Journal-Gazette (IN)
Journal News (OH)
Kane (PA) *Republican*
Kansas City Sun
Kansas City Times
Klamath Falls Evening Journal (OR)
The La Grande Observer (OR)
The Lancaster Eagle-Gazette (OH)
Lansing State Journal (MI)
The Leader-Telegram (WI)
The Lebanon Daily News (PA)
The Lincoln Evening Journal (NE)
Lincoln Journal Star (NE)
Lincoln Star (NE)
The Logansport Pharos-Tribune (IN)
Los Angeles Times
Lubbock Avalanche-Journal (TX)
Ludington Daily News (MI)
Macon Republican (GA)
Manhattan Mercury (KS)
The Manitowoc Herald Times (WI)
The Marshfield News-Herald (WI)
The Massillon Evening Independent (OH)
Medford Daily News (OR)
Medford Daily Tribune (OR)
Medford Mail Tribune (OR)
Memories and Dreams: The Official Magazine of the Hall of Fame
Mexia Weekly Herald (TX)
Miami Daily News Record
Middletown Times Herald (NY)
Milwaukee Journal
Moberly Monitor Index (MO)
Modesto News-Herald (CA)
Montana Butte Standard
Montana Standard
Morning Call (PA)
Morning New Bernian (NC)
Morning News (DE)
Morning Register (OR)
Mount Carmel Item (PA)
Muscatine Journal and News Tribune (IA)
Nevada State Journal
The New Castle Herald (New South Whales, Australia)
New Philadelphia Daily Times (OH)
New York Age
New York Times
News-Herald (OH)
News Herald (PA)
News-Journal (DE)
News-Palladium (MI)
The North Adams Transcript (MA)
Oakland Tribune (CA)
Odessa American (TX)
Ogden Standard Examiner (UT)
Ogden State Examiner (UT)

Oshkosh Northwestern (WI)
Ottawa Journal (Ontario)
Pampa Daily News (TX)
Paris News (TX)
Pasadena Star News (CA)
Philadelphia Daily News (PA)
Philadelphia Inquirer (PA)
Pittsburgh Courier (PA)
Pittsburgh Daily Post (PA)
Pittsburgh Post-Gazette (PA)
Pittsburgh Press (PA)
Post Register (ID)
Pottstown Mercury (PA)
Press and Sun Bulletin (NY)
Press Democrat (CA)
Quad City Democrat (IA)
Quad City Times (IA)
Raleigh Register (WV)
Reading Eagle (PA)
Reading News (PA)
Reading News-Times (PA)
Redding Times (PA)
Reno Gazette-Journal
Richmond Item (IN)
The St. Cloud Times (MN)
St. Louis Jewish Light
St. Louis Post-Dispatch
St. Louis Star
St. Louis Star and Times
Salina Journal (KS)
Salt Lake Telegram
Salt Lake Tribune
San Bernardino County Sun (CA)
Santa Ana Register (CA)
Santa Cruz Evening News (CA)

Scranton Republic (PA)
Scranton Republican (PA)
Sedalia Democrat (MO)
Shamokin News-Dispatch (PA)
Sheboygan Press Telegraph (WI)
Spokane Daily Chronicle (WA)
Sporting News (NC)
Sports Illustrated (NY)
Springfield Republican (MA)
Springfield Leader (MO)
Star Press (IN)
Star Tribune (MN)
Statesville Record (NC)
Statesville Records and Landmark (NC)
Suburbanite Economist (IL)
Sunday Rutland Herald
The Tampa Tribune
Taylor Daily Press (TX)
Times-Herald (MI)
Times Recorder (OH)
Times-Signal (OH)
Topeka Daily Capital
Tri-City Herald (KS)
Tri-County Newspapers (KS)
USA Today
Vidette Messenger (IN)
Waco News Tribune
Washington Herald
Washington Post
The Wausau Daily Herald (WI)
Wichita Beacon (KS)
The Winnipeg Evening Tribune (Manitoba)
The Winnipeg Tribune
The Wisconsin State Journal
The Woodland Daily Democrat (CA)

Online Sources

www.aaregistry.org
http://americancollegecricket.com
www.appeal-democrat.com
www.articles.southbendtribune.com
www.attheplate.com
www.barnstormerbaseball.com
www.baseball-almanac.com
www.baseball-reference.com
www.baseballlibrary.com
www.baseballsgreatestsacrifice.com
www.baseballthinkfactory.org
www.borchertfield.com
www.BrooklynBallParks.com
www.chicagohistory.com
www.chicagoreader.com
www.deadballera.com
http://deadspin.com
www.exploritoriam.edu
www.findagrave.com
www.gameuseduniverse.com
www.historicbaseball.com
www.history.com
www.houseofdavid.org.
www.houseofdavidmuseum.org
www.https.com//ochf.wordpress.com
http://johndonaldson.bravehost.com

liberty.i2i.org
www.maryscityofdavid.com
www.minationalguard.com
https://www.mlb.com
www.nbcbaseball.com
www.19cbaseball.com
www.peppergame.com
www.purplerow.com
www.redirectify.com
www.revolvy.com
www.ruf.rice.edu
www.sabr.org
https://sabr.org/bioproject
www.sanfordmariners.com
www.si.com
www.smithsonian.com
www.SouthBendTribune.com
www.sportsreference.com
swmidirectory.org
www.theclassical.org
www.thefinetimes.com
www.thenationalpastimemuseum.com
http://timesnewsweekly.com
www.washingtonpost.com
www.zinnedproject.org

Index

Numbers is ***bold italics*** indicate pages with illustrations.

Abbott, Robert S. 52
Acerra Brothers 87
Adkin, Clare E. 54
Adkin, Clare, Jr. 5
Akron Tyrites 139
Albany Bachelors 7
Albany Champion 7
Albright, Tom "Pistol Pete" 106
alcoholism 17
Alexander, Grover Cleveland 64, 95, 99, ***99***, 100, 101, 102, 103, ***103***, 105, 107, 110, 112, ***112***, 113, 153, 157
Allen, Newt ***104***, 105
Alou brothers 115
Altoona Works 86
Altrock, Nick 74, 145
Ambrose, Elmore E. 106
American Association 11
Anderson, George "Andy" 36, 46, 82, ***98***, 109, 111, 114, ***116***, 119, 122, 125, 130, 132, 134–136, ***135***, 141, 150, 158
Anson, Cap 10–11
Arbaugh, Mae 11
Argyle Athletics 10
Atherton, H.V. "Van" 84
Atlantic Bacharach Giants 63
Atwell, Richard "Dick" ***98***, 103, 109, 114, 153–154, ***154***
Auto Specialties Club 70

Baird, Thomas 4
Baird, Tom 112, 124, 125
Baltimore Hannibals 7
Baltimore Lord Baltimores 10
Bankhead, Sam ***104***, 105
Barber Colts 48
Baroda Independents 74
Baseball Hall of Fame Museum 5
Bass, Pee Wee ***98***, 114
Battle, Vincent ***120***
Baushke, Albert 17
Baushke, Dwight "Zeke" 50, 54, 55, 61, 65, ***66***, ***69***, 75, 136–137, ***136***, 153
Baushke, Frank 115
Baushke, Louis 18
Beatrice Blues 154
Bell, James Thomas "Cool Papa" 121
Bell, Leslie ***69***
Bender, Charles Albert "Chief" 99, 100, 153
Benson, Allen "Bullet Ben" 108, ***108***, 159–160, ***159***
Benton Harbors Pure-Oils 152
Berg, Moe 88
Berrien County Championship 3
Bertolino, Terry 54
Bethany House ***36***
Beverly, Charley ***104***
Big Horn Loop 131
Birmingham Barons 131
Birmingham Black Barons 59, 121
Bisbee Miners 81
Bismarck Grays 81
Black Sox Scandal 52, 58
Blakeney, Buster 106
Blatz, Ralph 96
Blieding, Norman 156–157, ***157***
Bloomer, Amelia Jenks 11
Bloomer Girls 11
Bodine, John 131
Boettcher, Mike 125
Bolden, Ed 59
Bonfils, Fredrick Gilmer 43
Bonnie and Clyde 89
Boone, Jewel 50, ***149***
Bosse, Joseph 111
Boston Red Sox 160
Boston Resolutes 10
Bow, Clara 57
Boyersmith, Debbie 163
Boyersmith, Earl ***34***, 84, ***85***, ***141***, 150, 163
Brewer, Chet ***104***, 105, 106
Bristol New Departures 65
Bronx Giants 62
Brooklyn Brown Dodgers 124
Brooklyn Bushwicks 94, 131
Brooklyn Dodgers 6, 123, 129
Brooklyn Excelsiors 2, 7, 8, ***8***
Brooklyn Meadowbrooks 70
Brooklyn Uniques 59
Brother Benjamin: A History of the House of David 5
Brothers, Richard 14
Broun, Heywood 123
Brown, Angeline 15
Brown, Norman E. 65
Brubaker, Ray 144
Bruce, Janet 124
Buck, Louis 122
Buffalo Niagara (Falls of Niagara) 8
Buford Bona-Allens 122
Burland, Elijah 54, 153
Bus, Ted 131
Buyesse, Chick 68

Calahan, Dick 49
Caldwell, Miss 54
Cambria, Joe 159
Camden Blue Skies 7
Campbell, Alexander 15
Campbellites 15
Capone, Al 84, 89
Carberry, Jack 122
Carlini, Rocky 131
Carnations 48
Cassidy, Jabe 43, 97
Cather, Willa 57
Catto, Octavius Valentine 9
Cedar Rapids Bunnies 155
Central Traveling team 4
Cepeda, Orlando 115
Cerillo, Frank 131
Chace, Edward B. 6
Chamberlain, Neville 116
Chandler, Happy 124
Chaplin, Charlie 40, 57
Chapman, Ray 58

215

216 Index

Charles City Collegians 75
Chase, Hal 79, 143
Chattanooga Lookouts 101, 107
Cheznok, John 131
Chicago All-Stars 48
Chicago American Giants 48, 59, 121
Chicago Ashlands 45
Chicago Barber Colts 51
Chicago Carlisle Athletic Club 51
Chicago Colonels Colored Ladies' team 54
Chicago Cubs 53, 71, 141, 151
Chicago Galligans 74
Chicago Garnet Social and Athletic Club 51
Chicago Giants 59, 70, 71, 100
Chicago Hartford Giants 53, 142
Chicago Holy Name Athletic Club 51
Chicago Ivanhoe Club 51
Chicago Leland Giants 48
Chicago Mont-Clares 70
Chicago Mutes 66
Chicago Onward Athletics 41, 42, 45
Chicago Passenger Club 70
Chicago Raphaels 74
Chicago Union Giants 48, 51
Chicago Uniques 7
Chicago Whales 87
Chicago White Sox 52, 54, 71, 87, 130, 161
Chicago White Stockings 10
Chozen 111
Christenson, Walter 96
Churchill, Neil 111
Churchills 112
Cicotte, Eddie 53, 142
Cincinnati Browns 10
Cincinnati Clowns 121
Cincinnati Red Stockings Base Ball Club 9
Cincinnati Reds 52, 109, 125
Clark, Wes 150
Clarke, Fred 110
Clay, Clifford "Count" *94*, *114*
Cleveland Buckeyes 121
Cleveland Indians 126
Clift, Frank 109
Cobb, Ty 53, 63, 110
Coleman, Red 127
Collins, Jake "Congo" 98
Collins, Jocko 126
Colored Giants of Chicago 77, 81, 90, 150
Colored Union Club 7
Columbus Senators 155
Comiskey, Charles 11, 52, 87
Connell, Freddie 78
Connors, Buster 113
Cooper, Andy *104*

Costner, Paul 71
Couch, Job 115
Coughlin, Chief 87, 95
Coveleski, Stanley 93
Crappe, Earl 125
Crawford, Sam *104*, 105
Creighton, Jim 2, 8, *8*, 9
cricket 7–8
Crosetti, Frank 131
Cross, John 106
Crow, Jack *83*, *118*, *141*, 149–150, *150*
Crow, Jimmie *141*, *152*
Crow, Miles 82
Crown of Thorns: House of David Victory and Legal Troubles Reviewed, Benton Harbor, MI, 1929 133
Cuban Giants 87
Cuban Monarchs 129
Cuban Stars 59

Daisy, Harold 150
Dalager, Hans "Barney" *58*, 75, 84, 113, 150
Dalager, Lloyd 1, 4, 39, 68, 70, 113, 117, *122*, 149, 150–151, *151*, 156
Dallas Steers 74, 82, 139
Day, Joe 81
Dayton Marcos 59
D.C. Capital Citys 10
Deal, Eddie 67, 84, 85, *86*, 87, 117, *118*, 142, 151, 155–156, *156*
Deal, Paul 111
Dean, Dizzy 101, 111, 132, 160
Decatur Commodores 155
Deike Brothers 87
Dempsey, Jack 39
Denver Bears 44, 98, 101
Denver Italian Bakery 106
Denver M&O Cigars 105
Denver White Elephants 106
Des Moines Demons 154
Detroit Rialtos 7
Detroit Stars 59, 125, 131
Detroit Tigers 53, 161
Dewhirst, Bob 82, *83*, 109, 147, *147*, *148*, 149
Dewhirst, Judge H.T. 21, 27, 28, 76, 77, 80, 82, 83, *83*, 84, 87, 88, 93, 102, 117, 120, 128, 137, 147, 149, 162
Dewhirst, Tom *58*, 61, *61*, 78, *78*, 82, *83*, 84, 85, 87, 95, 100, 102, 112, 137, *137*, 147, 149, 150
Diamond Cutters 137
Didrikson, Babe 96, 102, 109, 153, 159
DiMaggio, Joe 144, 154, 155
Disney, Walt 21
Doan, Ray 4, 46, 75, 76, 83, 95,
100, 101, 102, 103, 106, 110, 111, *111*, 112
Doby, Larry 126, 131
Dolan's Athletics of Chicago 45
Donaldson, John 2, 87, 105
Donaldson, Johnson *104*
Douglass, Charles R. 9
Douglass, Frederick 9
Dowagiac Independents 45
Drager, Merle 84
Dumont, Raymond "Hap" 109, 110, 160
Duncan, Frank, Jr. *104*
Duncan, Frank III *104*
Durocher, Leo 101
Dwight, Eddie *104*, 105
Dyer, Braven 155

Earhart, Amelia 89
Eason, Oaklahoma, Oilers 106, 107
Eastern Travelers 4, 99, 100, 102, 110
Echoes, David 162
Eden Springs Amusement Park 21, *21*, 29, 162
Eden Springs Syncopaters 140
Ederle, Gertrude 76
Edgell, Taylor 119
Edison, Thomas 92
Edwards, Red 125
Egan, George 115
Egan, Jack 115
1895 Benton Harbor Motorcycle 18
Eliot, T.S. 57
Elkhart All-Stars 142
Elkhart Conna 117–118
Essik, Bill 155
Ethiopian Clowns 65, 122
Eugene Athletics 119
Everett, Lionel *141*

Faber, Red 101
Fairmont Cardinals 155
Falcon Independents 93
Falkenstein, Charlie 50, 51, 56, 61, *66*, 68, *138*, 138–139
Fall, Charlie 68
Faulkner, William 57
Faust, Walter "Dutch" *22*, 50, 61, 65, *66*, 67, *69*, 72, 74, 77, 78, 82, 84, 85, 87, 111, 134, 136, 139, 143
Feller, Bob 132, 156
Ferber, Edna 57
Fish, Burnett 68
Fitzgerald, F. Scott 57, 60
Fitzke, Bob 87
Fitzsimmons, Floyd 23, 39, 87
Fitzsimmons Speed Boys *24*, 39, 40, 53
Fleming, Herman "Flip" *98*, 109, 158

Index

Floto, Otto 97
Flying Dutchmen *119*
The Flying Roll 14
Fogarty, Robert 4
Fort Smith Twins 74
Fort Wayne Daisies 121
Fort Wayne Giants 69, 74
Fort Wayne Kips 69
Foster, Andrew "Rube" 48, 59
Foster, Willie *104*, 105, 107
Fostoria, Iowa 16
Fostoria, Ohio 3
Fowler, Joseph 17
Foxx, Jimmie 131
Franz Ferdinand, Archduke 48
Frazee, Harry 58
Fredrickson Brothers 87
Fresno Tigers 81
Frisch, Frankie 123

Gaines, Gladys 123
Galien Grays 45, 70
Gardner, Lee 125
Garner, Homer 131
Gary White Eagles 51, 53
Gas House Gang 101
Gates, Jim 127
Gehrig, Lou 87, 101, 116, 123, 153, 157
Genovese, Frank "Chick" 115
Genovese, George 2
Gentlemen's Agreement 3, 6, 9
Gibson, Bob 131
Gibson, Josh 2
Gilbert, George "Lefty" 68, 81, *98*
Giles, George *104*, 105
Gilkerson Union Giants 81
Gillespie, Lucille 25
Gilmore, Q.J. 59
Gilstrap, Harry 125
Gish, Lillian 57
Gleason, Kid 52
Glendora Grays 45
Gomez, Lefty 155
Gordon, Joe 155
Goshen Grays 51, 52
Graham, Charles 154
Grand Excursion *8*
Grand Rapids Chicks 121
Grand Rapids Colored Athletics 69
Green, Joe 71, 100, 150
Green Line Letter 121
Greenlee, Gus 3, 4, 59, 60, 106, 108, 124
Greenlee Advertisers 106
Greenwade, Tom 124
Griffin, C. "Pop" 125
Griffith, Calvin 108, 159
Griffith, Clark 131
Grimes, Burleigh 58, 101, 102
Gulley, "Lefty" 121

Gunthers 48
Gursuch, Don 131

Hall, Frank 88
Hamman, Ed 79
Hammond Morris Athletic Club 74
Hannaford, Ezra "Cookie" 18, 42, *43*, 44, *46*, 50, 51, 52, 55, 61, 62, *63*, 65, *69*, 70, 75, 140, 144–145
Hannaford, Horace *43*, 44, 50, 51, 56, 61, 65, *66*, 68, 75, 145, *145*
Hannaford, Violet *46*
Hansel, Jerry 44, 45, 51, 53, 55, 147
Hanson, "Hub" 109, 114
Harlem Globetrotters 79, 121, 123, 127, 130, 132
Harper, Blake 74
Harrisburg Senators 158
Harrison, David "Eggs *22*, 54, 55, *58*, *66*, 68, *69*, *72*, 77, 82, *83*, 84, 85, 95, 140–142, *141*, 149, 153, 156
Hartford Senators 157
Hawaiian Cubans 131
Hawkins, Joel 54
Heatherly, Clarence "Fats" 119
Heckman, Bill 68, 141
Heilman, Harry *119*
Helena Boosters 125
Hemingway, Ernest 57
Hendricks, P. *24*
Hendrickson, Don 113
Henson, Hub 155
Henson Base Ball Club 7
Hershock, Andy 126
Hewins, Jack 129
Heydler, John 123
Hill, Dewey 106
Hilldale Daisies 59
Hipp, A.B. 84, 87
Hitler, Adolf 57, 89, 113, 116, 117
Hoffman, Clare E. 28
Holland, Carl 106
Holland Flying Dutchmen 117
Holliday, Allen 49
Homestead Grays 131, 157
Hoosier Giants 65
Hornbeck, Frank 41, *43*, 44, 51
Hornsby, Rogers 101
Hot Springs Bathers 161
House of David Amusement Park *31*, *32*, *33*, *34*
House of David Band 49, *50*, 75, 162
The House of David Baseball Team 54
House of David Girls Baseball Team 54–55
House of David Ice Cream Parlor *32*

House of David Ladies Band 54
House of David Machine Shop *34*
House of David Orchestra 18, 140
House of David Park *40*, *42*
House of David Restaurant *31*
House of David Singing Band 140
House of David Traveling Band 137, 140, 146, 151, 152
House of David Zoo *30*
Hoyt, Waite 94
Hulbert, Charles 10
Humber Oilers 106
Humboldt Crabs 130
Hummel, Dick 125, 131, 158
Hummel, Lew 125, 158
Hunter, Spike 106, 107, 108
Huston, Colonel 62
Hutson, Roy 109, 114

Illinois Boosters 70
Indiana All-Stars 51
Indianapolis ABCs 59, 70
Indianapolis Clowns 79
Ingathering 20
Ingram, Mel 106
Institute for the Study of American Religion 29

Jackson, Arthur 54, 153
Jackson, Luther 54, 153
Jacobs, Bill *96*
Jaft, Ruben *43*
Jamestown Tigers 70
Jebo 81
Jesus Boys 105
Jezreel, James 14, 16
Johnson, Bert "Beans" 76, 82, 83, 87, 147, 149, 152
Johnson, Judy 2
Johnson, Roy "Bubba" 60
Jones, Collins 121
Jonesboro Giants 161
Jonnard, Claude "Bubber" *96*
Joplin Miners 127, 154
Joseph, Billy 106
Joseph, Newt "Pep" *104*, 105, 118

Kalamazoo Stationery Independents 53
Kamm, Willie 88
Kansas City Monarchs 3, 4, 11, 43, 59, 60, 103–110, *104*, 116, 118, 119, 121, 122, 124–126, 130–132, 151, 158
The Kansas City Monarchs, Champions of Black Baseball 124
Kansas City Rabbits 102
Keaton, Buster 57
Keenan, James 131
Keller, Ardys B. "Art" 160

Kenosha Comets 121
Keokuk Indians 154
Kerr, Johnny 88
Killefer, Bill 95
Kimball, Bill 131
King, Pinky 87
Kirkham, Henry 22
Klamath Falls Pelicans 79
Klum, Glenn 44, 50, 51, 61, 65, *66*, 68, 151
Knoxville Giants 59
Krichell, Paul 86, 116
K.V.P. of Kalamazoo 70

Lamar, Jean 115
Landis, Kenesaw Mountain 52, 58, 59, 65, 82, 121
Langer, Adam 4
La Porte Boosters 117
La Porte Islemen-Dairys 117
Lardner, Ring 52
Laufer, Harry 96
Lawrence, William *98*
Lazzeri, Tony 155
A League of Their Own 121
Lemon, Bob 126
Lewis, Sinclair 57
Lindbergh, Charles 57, 77, 89
Link, Billy *141*
Liska, Chuck 131
Logan, Edward 131
Logan Squares 84, 102
Los Angeles Dodgers 129
Louis Baushke and Bro. Wagon Shop 18
Louisville Falls City 10
Lovello, Bill 131
Lyons, Ted 88

Mack, Connie 139
Maggie Riley's Devil Dogs 70
S.S. *Malolo* **154**
Malstrom Air Force Base Flyers 132
Mansfield Independents 10
Mantle, Mickey 127
Mapel, Rolla "Lefty" 44, *98*, 100
Marcelle, Oliver "The Ghost" 103
Marcum, Richard 41, *43*, 145
Marichal, Juan 115
Marlott, Bill *110*
Marquettes Roseland Eclipse 48
Marshfield Athletics 157
Mary's City of David Bakery *38*
Mary's City of David Vegetarian Café *38*
Matthews, Wid 124
Mattick, Bobby 155
Mays, Willie 115
McAfferty, Tom *98*
McCall, E. 88

McCall, Henry 121
McCarthy 61
McConkeys of Wheeling 70
McGraw, John 74, 123
McPhee, John "Bid" 105
Meacham, Lewis 10
Medwick, Ducky 101
Mein Kampf 57
Mele, Ernie 96
Melton, Dr. J. Gordon 29
Memories and Dreams 127
Memphis Red Sox 131
Menasha, Wisconsin, Badgers 138
Michigan City Dolls 53
Miller, Lloyd 73, 74, 78, 84, 87, 106, 139
Mills, Michael Keyfor ("Prince Michael") 14, 16
Milwaukee Red Sox 96
Mishawaka Ball Bands 117
Mishawaka Boosters 45
Mishawaka Dodgers 117
Mishawaka Indestructors 53
Mitchell, Fred 53, 142
Mitchell, Virnett "Jackie" 101, 153
Modesto Reds 78
Moline Plowboys 75
Montgomery Grey Sox 59
Montreal Royals 126
Mooney, Cora 16, 17
Mooney, Paul 42, *43*, 44, 45, 51–53, 56, 61–67, *66*, 68, 77, 140, 142–144, *142*, *143*
Mooney, Silas 16, 17
Moran, Pat 52
Mothell, Dink 60, *104*
Mulet, Joe 116
Mullen, Moon 111, 206
Muller, Peter 20
Murphy, Art 106
Murphy, Lou 81, 95, 96, 97, 102, 114–115, 120, 126, 127, 157
Muskegon Lassies 121
Muskogee Reds 127

Nashville Elite Giants 59
Nashville White Sox 59
National Association of Base Ball Players (NABBP) 7, 9–10
National Association of Professional Base Ball Players (NAPBBP) 7
National Registry of Historic Places 19
Nelson, Elisha 24
Nelson, Hattie 24
Nelson, Hobson *141*
Nelson, Mary Ellen 24
Nelson, Otto 24
Nelson, Ramon 24

Neve, Page 81, *98*
New Bedford Whales 158
New Buffalo Buchanans 70
New Haven Bulldogs 158
New Orleans Ads 59
New Philadelphia (Ohio) Noakers 72
The New Shiloh Messenger 133
New York Black Yankees 112
New York Giants 74, 129
New York Gothams 10
New York Knickerbockers 9
New York Metropolitans 10
New York National Advocate 6
New York Yankees 58, 63, 140, 143, 153, 155
Newark Little Giants 10
Newberg Hudson River 8
Newhouse, Frank 43, 97
Newkirk, Joe 71
Nickerson, Frank Bobo 130, *130*
Nickleson, Paul 115
Niles Standards 117
Noel, Chuck *98*
Norris, Charles E. 17
Nusser, Al 109

Oakland Oaks 144
Ocala Yearlings 161
Oldfield, Barney 75, 150
Olive, Ham 120
Olson, Howard 40
O'Neil, Buck *104*, 126
O'Neill, Eugene 57
Original Cuban Giants *see* Argyle Athletics
Ortiz, Bill 121
Oshkosh Indians 94
O'Signac, Bobby 87
O'Signac, Joe 150
Owens, Ben 131
Owens, Jesse 113, 123

Pagan, Jose 115
Paige, Satchel 2, 4, 60, 105–108, 111–113, 118, 125, 126, 130, 132, 159
Palestine Pals 160
Palladino, Joe 5, 126–127, *128*
Pallas, Big Harvey 118
Pampa Road Runners 102
Parsons, Charles Lyman "Poss" 97, *98*, 101, 103, 105
Pavlick, Johnny 118
Peebles, Harry 60
Pelton, Clara 16
Pelton, Dan 16
Pennock, Herb 123
Pennsylvania Association of Amateur Base Ball Players (PAABBP) 9
Peoria Red Wings 121
Perkins, Bill "Cy" 4, 60, 106

Index

Perry, Mason "Mac" 82
Peter & Fox Magazine Cane Factory 17
Petrongolo, Joe "Red" 5, 126
Phalen, Eddie 46
Philadelphia Athletics 10
Philadelphia Excelsiors 59
Philadelphia Phillies 142
Philadelphia Pythians 10
Pickett, John 68
Pickford, Mary 57
Pierce, Whitey **120**
Pittsburgh Crawfords 3, 4, 59
Pittsburgh Keystones 10
Plazaj, Chet 131
P.M.C. of South Bend 74
Pollack, Syd 79
Popowski, Eddie 96, 160
Povich, Shirley 123, 124
Powell, Ray **98**
Powers, Jimmy 113, 123
Price, Sol 87
Pueblo Braves 155
Purnell, Benjamin 3, 4, 13–27, **15**, 29, **32**, 37, 39, **43**, 48, 50, 51, 60, 69, 70, 76–78, 80, 82, 128, 129, 133, 136, 137, 139–140, 143, 147, 162–163
Purnell, Elizabeth 14
Purnell, Heather "Hettie" 16, 17
Purnell, Madison 14
Purnell, Mary 3, 4, 13–28, **15**, **32**, 37, 48, 77, 82, 83, **93**, 115, 129, 134–136, 139–140, 143, 163
Purnell, Samuel Coy 16, 17

Quinn, Jack 110–111

Rachuig, Florence 29
Racine Belles 121
Radcliffe, Theodore Roosevelt "Double Duty" 112, 121
Radloff, Joe "Windy" 81
Rasberry, Ted 125
Ray, Johnny 121
Reichelt, George 125
Rickey, Branch 6, 45, 83, 121, 123, 124
The Righteous Remnant: The House of David 4
Robinson, Jackie 2, 6, 115, 124, 126, 128, 131, 155
Rochester Flour City 8
Rochester Live Oak 8
Rockford Peaches 121
Rocky Farm Orchard **23**
Rocky Mountain Railroaders 71
Rogan, Wilbur "Bullet" **104**, 105
Rogosin, William Donn 6
Romney, Bob 138
Romney, Gov. George 138
Roosevelt, Pres. Theodore 92, 121
Rosa Belle 24–26
Rosner, Max 94
Rossiter, Bill 71
Rotblatt, Marv 129–130
Rowe, Schoolboy 101
Rupert, Colonel 62
Ruth, Babe 58, 62, 78, 101, 112, 137, 149, 153
Ryan, Jack 88

Saginaw Ducks 40
St. Joseph Auto Specialties 122, 123, 143
St. Joseph Locals 40
St. Louis Browns 10, 11, 74, 107, 126, 160
St. Louis Cardinals 101, 123, 126, 131, 161
St. Louis Giants 59
Salem Senators 87
Salina Millers 155
San Bernardino Outlaws 125
San Francisco Giants 129
San Francisco Seals 109, 144
Sandburg, Carl 133
Santo, Ron 151
Saperstein, Abe 121, 123
Sassman, Oscar 54, 55, 153
Savage, Emery **98**
Schaudt, Shorty 115
Schneider, Johnnie 17, 152
Schneider, Wesley 75, 83, 152–153, **153**
Schneider Jewelry 106
Schroeder, Mike 119
Sclaing, Sam 114
Sedalia Athletics 44
Selby, Ernie **83**, *141*, 150, 151–152, **152**
Self, Bob 131
Shadowen, Howard 96, **120**
Sharrock, Jay 78
Shaw, William 14
Shiloh House **30**
Shiloh Mansion 19
"The Shiloh Messenger of Wisdom" 16
Shiloh's Messenger of Wisdom 19
Shires, Art 88, 96
Siddle, Bill "Snake" 84, 85
Sidway, Franklin 8
Silver, John 131
Sioux Falls Canaries 161
Sisler, George 110, 124
Slapnicka, Cy 156
Smith, Chet 119
Smith, Hilton 112
Smith, Sidney 77, **83**, 95, *141*, 150
Sousa, John Philip 19
South Bend Athletics 150
South Bend Blue Cox 121
South Bend Colored Giants 84
South Bend Colored Royal Giants 142
South Bend Conservative Lifes 117
South Bend Grays 70
South Bend Hoosier Creams 51
South Bend Independents *see* South Bend Singers
South Bend Overlands 53
South Bend Overlords 142
South Bend Silver Edge 51
South Bend Singers 71
South Bend Studebaker 74
South Havana La Palomas 119
Southcott, Joanna 14
Southern Michigan Association 40
Spalding, Albert 10
Speaker, Tris 101, 110
Spencer, Joe 121
Spencer Cubs 81
Spokane Indians 119
Springfield Hampdens 155
Stampf, Eddie 96, 97
The Star of Bethlehem: The Living Roll of Life 16
Stearns, Norman "Turkey" **104**, 105
Stegall, Edwin **120**
Steinecke, Bill 114
Stemm, Al 82, 87, 95, 149
Stevens, Helen 116
Stoey, Bill 131
Stovey, George 11
The Strange Effects of Faith 14
Sukeforth, Clyde 124
Swaney, Charles "Moose" 115, 157–158, 159

Tally, Barlow 39, **43**, 44, 134
Tally, Doc 36, 77, 81, 82, **98**, 99, 101, 109, **116**, 119, 122, 123, 126–128, 133–135, **134**, **138**, 139, 152
Tally, Jesse Lee 39, 41, 42, **43**, 44, 45, 49, 51, 53, 61, 65, **66**, 67, 72, 130, 134, 145
Tally, Swaney 39, 42, **43**, 44, 134
Tammen, Harry Heye 43
Tatum, Goose 130
Taylor, Ronald 22, 29, 162, 163
Taylor Trunk Girls 92, **92**, 149
Texas and Southern Association 125
Thompson, Frank P. 10
Thorn, John 9
Thorpe, Francis 3, **22**, 23, 39, 40, 41, **43**, 46, 48, 49, 51, 65, 66, **66**, 67, 70–75, 77, 79, 81–84, 86, 89, **93**, 95, **98**, 99–101, 110, 115, 128, 133–135, 139, 142

Index

Timko, Bill 131
Titusville Independents 65
Tolles, Albert "Lefty" 82, 88, 106, 139, 161
Topeka Jayhawks 154
Treherne, Budd "Lefty" 121
Troy Victory 7
Tucker, Cecil 143–144
Tucker, John 36, 50, *51*, 67, *68*, 82, 86, 92, *92*, 95, *98*, 100, 101, 109, 110, 114, *116*, *118*, 119, 122, 123, 134, 143–144, *144*, 149, 154, *154*, *155*, 160
Tucker, Melvin 54, 144
Turner, George 14
"A Twentieth Century History of Berrien County, Michigan" 13
Twin Cities Merchants 152
Tye, Larry 107
Tyre, Lon 71

Uncle Sam's Bowling Machine 21, *35*
United Fuel of Denver 107

Valentino, Rudolph 57
Vance, Dazzy 94
Vandercook, Roy C. 70
Vangilder, Elam 107
Vann, Lou 158–159
Varietz, Art *66*
Vaughan, Hubert "Hip" 46, 51, 55–56, 62, 65, *66*, 67, 78, 84, 144
Vaughan, James "Hippo" 46
Veeck, Bill 75, 94

Vicksburg Nine 45
Vieritz, Art 51, 61, 65, 71, 72, 74, 144–145
Von der Ahe, Chris 11

Walker, Moses Fleetwood 11
Walker, Percy *58*, 82, 83, *83*, 84, 93, *93*, 149, *149*, 153
Walsh, Ed 88
Warden, Al 107
Washington, Chester 105, 107
Washington Alert 9
Washington Giants 64
Washington Mutuals 7, 9
Washington Senators 84, 108
Waterloo Hawks 155
Watervliet 44–45
Weeksville Unknowns 7
Weirman, Warren "Lefty" 106, 107
Welles, Orson 89
Western Travelers 4, 101, 110
Wharton, Edith 57
Wheeler, George 20
Wheeling Stogies 79
White, James Roland *see* Jezreel, James
Whiting, Frank 87
Wilkinson, J.L. 3, 4, 11, 60, 124
Williams, Austin "Tex" 44, 51, 55, *66*, 68, 148
Williams, Clay "Mud" *83*, 87, *148*, 148–150
Williams, Joe 114
Wilson, Thomas K. 59
Wilson, Pres. Woodrow 48
Wiltbank, Glendon "Red" *141*

Wiltbank, Leo "Lefty" *141*, 150
Winnipeg Maroons 118
Witte, Harold "Dutch" 4, 90, 129
Wolfe, Max 68
Woods, Jimmy 96, 132, 159
Woodworth, Bessie Daniels 26
Woodworth, Manna 48
Woolsey, Judge John M. 80, 102
World War I 134–135
World War II 132, 143
Worth, William 18
Wright, Bruce 121
Wright, Harry 9–10
Wright, William "Billy" 18, 19
Wrigley, Phillip K. 121
Wroe, John 14, 18
Wulff, Elena *146*
Wulff, Monroe *43*, 48, 145–146, *146*
Wykoff, Dick 103, 109, 119, 125, 155
Wyland, Frank 42, *43*, 44, 51, 55, 82, *83*, 146–147, *146*, *147*, 149
Wyse, Matt B. 119

Young, Cy 42, 101
Young, T.J. *104*

Ziebart, Brian 1, 70, 133, 151, 163
Zimmerman, Heinie 62
Zitta, Tony 141

www.ingramcontent.com/pod-product-compliance
Lightning Source LLC
Chambersburg PA
CBHW060342010526
44117CB00017B/2928